Spatial Analysis of Gender Based Workforce In India Using QGIS

Spatial Analysis of Gender Based Workforce In India Using QGIS

A COMPARATIVE STUDY OF VILLAGE LEVEL CENSUS DATA FOR THREE DISTRICTS OF CACHAR, KARIMGANJ, HAILAKANDI IN ASSAM STATE, NORTH EAST INDIA, FOR THE YEARS 1991, 2001, AND 2011

PULAK DAS

AND

PINKI PURKAYASTHA

KALPAZ

Published by

Kalpaz Publications
C-30, Satyawati Nagar,
Delhi – 110052
Ph.: 011-47034999, 9811692060
www.kalpazpublications.com
E-mail: kalpaz@hotmail.com

Distribution Network
gyanbooks.com
India, USA, Canada, UK, Australia, France

ISBN: 978-93-5722-630-1 (PB)
First Published, 2024

Printed at: Gyan Press, Delhi.

Spatial Analysis of Gender Based Workforce In India Using QGIS

Author: Pulak Das — pulakdas.ecology@gmail.com
Pinki Purkayastha — pinki.ecologyevs@gmail.com

Contents

List of Maps

SPATIAL ANALYSIS OF CENSUS VARIABLES, 1991

SPATIAL ANALYSIS OF SOCIO-ECONOMIC INDICATORS, 1991

SPATIAL ANALYSIS OF CENSUS VARIABLES, 2001

SPATIAL ANALYSIS OF SOCIO-ECONOMIC INDICATORS, 2001

SPATIAL ANALYSIS OF CENSUS VARIABLES, 2011

SPATIAL ANALYSIS OF SOCIO-ECONOMIC INDICATORS, 2011

Introduction

Gender equality is a development goal in its own right, as well as a precondition for the achievement of many other developmental goals including sustainable development goal (SDG) (MoSPI 2024). Gender statistics in particular is in focus worldwide after United Nations (UN) declared UN decade for women. MOL&E (2023) mentions that one third of women have now joined the labour force in India and female participation rate in labour force is increasing, although it is below the global average. The reasons for low participation are unpaid work, social norms, rising household income, wage disparity, and unrecognised work (MOL&E 2023). Srija (2023), while arguing about potential of India's future workforce mentions that women participation rate in labour force is much lower than men, both in rural and urban areas. As acknowledged by MoSPI (2024) '*Gender statistics play a crucial role in promoting and measuring gender equality. They provide benchmarks for progress, making visible the similarities and differences between men and women. Gender statistics are instrumental in challenging stereotypes, informing policy-making, and monitoring progress toward equality. Investing in gender statistics enhances the quality of data available for decision-making across various development fields.*'

Chand and Singh (2022) agrees that employment has remained one of the top challenges of policy makers in India owing to improvement in education and skills, increasing aspirations of labour class, uneven growth of industries across regions, divergence between structural changes in the composition of output and employment, and preferring government jobs. They have addressed issues such as decline in worker to population ratio, unemployment, women in workforce, overall employment scenario, gender and youth in agriculture etc. MOL&E (2022) considered 'employment by sector' as one of the key indicators of labour market in India. The indicator is disaggregated into agriculture (agriculture, forestry and fishing), industry (mining and quarrying, manufacturing, and construction and public utilities), and services (wholesale and retail trade, restaurants and hotels, transport, storage and communications, finance, insurance, real estate, and business services, and community, social and personal services). The study argues that agriculture sector is the biggest employer (more than 46%) and largest source of livelihoods in India. Indicating towards a gender disparity, the study further argues that between 1993 and 2005, the percentage of workers in agriculture has declined more rapidly for men as compared to women.

Spatial analysis of census data has been comparatively newer field, and it is advancing. Wong (1990) argued for spatial modelling of census data using an old technique known as cross-Fratar method or biproportional fitting, to recreate the original census information. Blum and Calvo (2001) has mentioned that GIS is a data integrator for census data for spatial analysis. Weeks (2001) argued that earlier either spatial scientist were not inclined towards population research or people practicing demography science had limitations in thinking spatially. This has led to limited work in integration of spatial analysis in population data. But things are changing now owing to improvement in geospatial technology and availability of good quality data. The author further argued that demography is not only spatial but also interdisciplinary in nature. Events such as demographic transition is interlinked with epidemiological transition, fertility transitions, migration transitions, urban transition, age structure transition, family and household transition, population size transition, which ultimately leads to changes in resource utilization and allocation. Cromley et al. (2009) in China used GIS and aerial interpolation for census data analysis and to rectify boundary changes that occur from one census to the next. Palma (2011) discussed about use of GIS in disseminating census data in Mexico. Banerjee (2016) has used spatial analysis for disease mapping and argued that it can be used to detect hot spots or spatial clusters which may arise due to common environmental, demographic, and cultural effects. Moreno et al. (2020) in a study in Columbia used census data to examine family characteristics and industrial farming using spatial and statistical analysis. In a study in Germany, Moos et al. (2021) observed spatial relationship between population density and annual income using choropleth maps. Jain and Kaur (2021) discusses about using GIS based technologies for mapping in upcoming Census in India such as standardisation of GIS spatial database design, geo-referencing of administrative units for built-up area digitisation etc. Fisher (2022) emphasised use of GIS in census data particularly on its benefit in sustainable development goals (SDG) analysis by linking datasets through location. de Silva et al. (2022) analysed association of socio-economic conditions with spatial distribution of pandemic. Ravichandran et al. (2023) used census data of 2011 with geospatial technology in India to develop household quality of living index by integrating four indices; housing facility index, basic facility index, financial asset index, and human capital index. These four indices were developed using twenty-three census indicators. For calculating human capital index, indicators such as literacy rate, male and female literate, and working population are used. Redding (2024) has discussed on benefits of new sources of GIS data in spatial economics, which according to the author, concern with the determinants and effects of the location of economic activity in geographic space.

Open source software such as QGIS is particularly being encouraged worldwide to use for spatial analysis of census data. Hanson (2016a) mentioned steps for downloading and preparing for US census bureau data, focussing on joining files such as excel file (or CSV) with shape file (shp) on QGIS. Hanson (2016b) provided steps for joining census data to a shape file, making a join permanent, and symbolizing data, in QGIS. ESRC (2017) discussed stepwise about obtaining census data, formatting and downloading boundary data, matching data in QGIS, and visualising data in QGIS. la Rúa and Bright (2020) elaborated steps on application of QGIS in census and surveys. Detailed steps are mentioned for QGIS software installation, house locations, enumeration areas, topology cleaning, table join, field calculator, expressions, working with attribute tables, etc. FCC (2021) discussed about the utility of QGIS with elaborated steps on downloading QGIS, downloading census block boundaries from US census, and loading block map etc. Eichelberger et al. (2022) discussed in detail about QGIS and its application in census and survey mapping. Noth (2022) discussed how Canadian census data be downloaded and used in QGIS. The document mentioned about preparing geographic data in QGIS, joining data, calculating percentage population, map symbology, map layout etc. Details on QGIS manual and steps are elaborated in QGIS Desktop 3.22 User Guide (QGIS Project 2023).

Censuses in India are happening since 1872. Since then, eight censuses have taken place before independence in years 1872, 1881, 1891, 1901, 1911, 1921, 1931, 1941, and seven censuses have taken place after independence in years 1951, 1961, 1971, 1981, 1991, 2001, 2011. The primary tool for census operations is census questionnaire. The questionnaire has been updated gradually since beginning to improve the accuracy and quality of the data without losing comparability of data. Twenty-nine questions were asked in the last census in year 2011 (https://censusindia.gov.in/census.website/). These were; Name of person, Relationship to head, Sex, Date of Birth and Age, Current Marital Status, Age at marriage, Religion, Scheduled caste (SC)/Scheduled Tribe (ST), Disability, Mother Tongue, Other Language known, Literacy Status: Literate -1/ Illiterate -2, Status of attendance, Highest educational level attained, Worked any time during last year, Category of the economic activity, Occupation, Nature of the industry, trade or services, Class of workers, Non-economic activity, Seeking or available for work, Travel to place of work (i) one way distance (ii) mode of travel, Fill for person born outside this village/town, Birth Place, If within India, write the present name of village/town, district and State. if outside India, write the present name of the country, Migration characteristics- Fill for person who has come to this village/town from elsewhere-Place of last residence (a) if within India (b) at the time of migration, Reason for migration, Duration of stay in this village/town since migration, Fertility Particulars - Children surviving-Daughters(s) Son(s), Children ever born alive-Daughters(s)-Son(s), and Number of children born alive during last one year-Daughters(s)-Son(s). Censuses are treasure trove of data required for socio-economic planning, but it is now delayed in India (Mallapaty 2024).

The present work is a guide for those who want to learn application of geographic information system (GIS) in census studies with particular reference to workforce and social indicators. The book would be helpful for gender specialists, social scientists, and economists who are interested in village level spatial analysis of census data. They may further their work on socio-economic variables comparing their trend in different census years, and also by studying their inter-relationships in solving complex socio-economic problems. Ecologists and environmental scientists will also find this book interesting for carefully looking into inter-relationship between natural processes and spatio-temporal human processes at village level. The book will also help entrepreneurs to establish businesses, and planners for long term planning for sustainable development of the region. Government agencies and political parties may find this work useful for preparing development goals. Spatial analysis is performed for census variables, and socio-economic indicators derived from census variables, for last three census surveys held in India – 1991, 2001, and 2011. More than two thousand villages within three representative districts; Cachar, Karimganj, and Hailakandi, in southern Assam state of India, is involved for the village level analysis. The work demonstrates detailed stepwise methodology for performing spatial analysis using open source QGIS software (https://www.qgis.org/).

The study involves spatial analysis of thirty-eight (38) census variables for the year 1991, fifty-five (55) census variables for the year 2001 and 2011 each, and thirty (30) census variables which are used for the first time in 2011 census survey in India. For these variables, respective codes are used for the spatial analysis which are mentioned against each variable. Census variables used in 1991 data are number of households, total population, male-female population, population below 7 years of age, scheduled caste

(SC) and scheduled tribe (ST) population, female and male literacy, male and female main workers, male and female marginal workers etc. Census variables used in 2001 and 2011 are number of households; male, female, and total population; male, female and total literates and illiterates; male, female, and total main and marginal workers; male, female, and total cultivators, agricultural laborers, household industry workers, etc. in both main and marginal categories. Census variables introduced in 2011 census survey are male, female, and total marginal workers in different categories such as cultivator, agricultural laborers, household industry etc., who are in work for zero (0) to three (3) months, and three (3) to six (6) months in a year.

The study also involves spatial analysis of socio-economic indicators derived from the census variables. There are sixty-two (62) indicators for the year 1991, fifty-five (55) indicators for the year 2001, and eighty-five (85) indicators for the year 2011. Expression (mathematical formula) are used for all these indicators which are mentioned in separate table against each indicator. Socio-economic indicators for the year 1991, 2001, and 2011 are household size, population density, population sex ratio, child sex ratio, percentage of SC and ST population, and literacy rate. Apart from this, workforce sex ratio in different categories, and work participation rate in different work categories for male, female, and total population is presented. This also involves detailed four-fold occupation categories in 2001 and 2011, and nine-fold occupation categories in 1991, for different genders.

The spatial analysis precedes with a comparative graphical analysis across three study years; 1991, 2001, and 2011, with census variables and socio-economic indicators. Total sixteen variables are covered such as total population, child population, SC and ST population, literate and illiterate persons, total workers, main workers, marginal workers, non workers, main cultivators, main agricultural laborers, marginal cultivators, marginal agricultural laborers, main and marginal non-agricultural workers. Similarly there are graphical comparative analysis between study years for forty-three socio-economic indicators such as household size, population density, population sex ratio, child sex ratio, percentage of SC and ST population, literacy rates, workforce sex ratio for total, main, and marginal categories and among the four fold occupational categories such as cultivators, agricultural laborers, and non agricultural workers (household industries and other workers), non workers, and work participation rate for the total, male, and female categories, main and marginal male and female categories, and among the four fold occupational categories within the main, marginal, male and female categories.

Methodology

Preparing data sets

The attributes and spatial data on village level socio-economy for the years 1991 and 2001 were collected from Data Center in NASA's Earth Observing System Data and Information System (EOSDIS) (https://sedac.ciesin.columbia.edu/). More details on methodology is provided by Meiyappan et al. (2017). The original data has more that 200 variables (Meiyappan et al. 2018) from which only selected variables are used for the current work. The downloaded data was for the Indian state of Assam. From this, the data of three districts of Cachar, Hailakandi, and Karimganj were extracted using following steps.

1. Open QGIS
2. Open the downloaded file of Assam State for the year 1991.

(a) Use 'Layer – Add Layer – Add Vector Layer…'

(b) Click 'Browse' (the three dots) under 'Vector Dataset(s)', under 'Vector' under 'Data Source Manager'

(c) Select the file ‘india-village-census-1991-AS_FINAL.shp’, and click ‘Add’

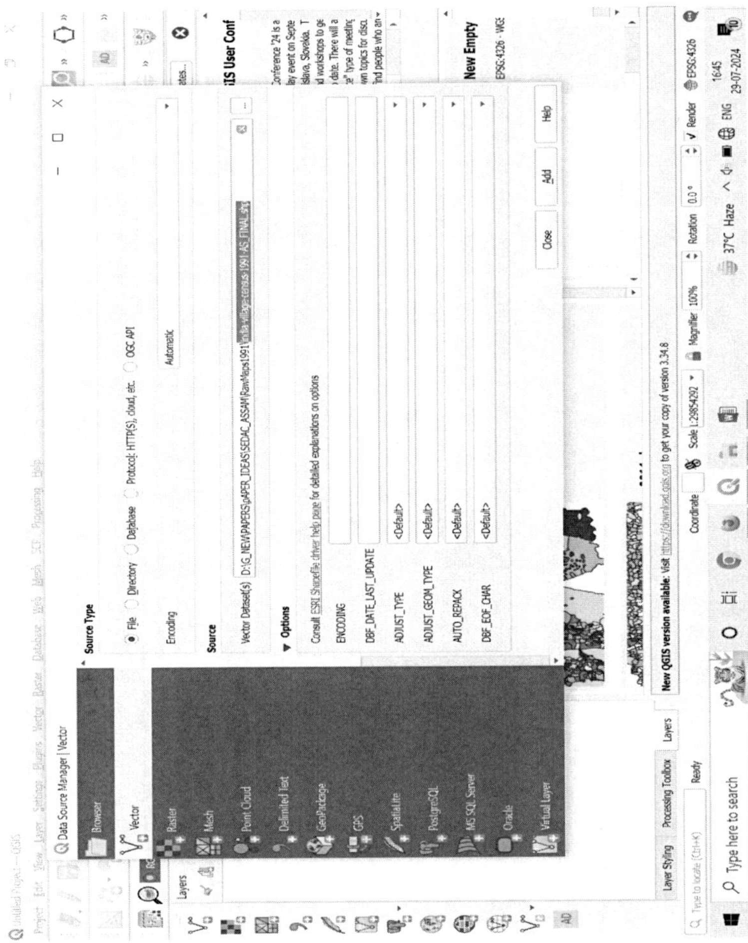

(d) The file will be added under 'Layers'

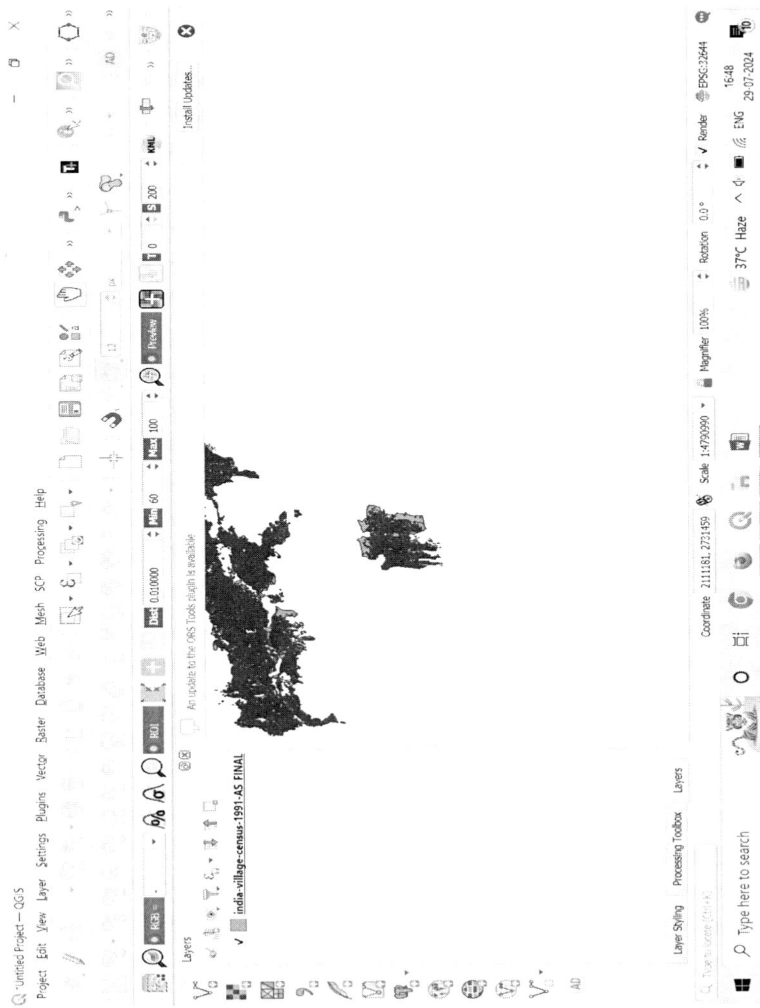

3. Open the attribute table of the downloaded file of Assam state for the year 1991 ('india-village-census-1991-AS_FINAL') by right-clicking the layer, and clicking 'Open Attribute Table.

4. An attribute table will be opened with same name.
5. Now we will extract the three study districts; Cachar, Karimganj, and Hailakandi using a feature in the attribute table called 'Select features using an expression'. We will use the three unique district identifier (for each district), provided in the attribute table named 'DID' (or District ID)
6. Click 'Select features using an expression' in the Attribute table.

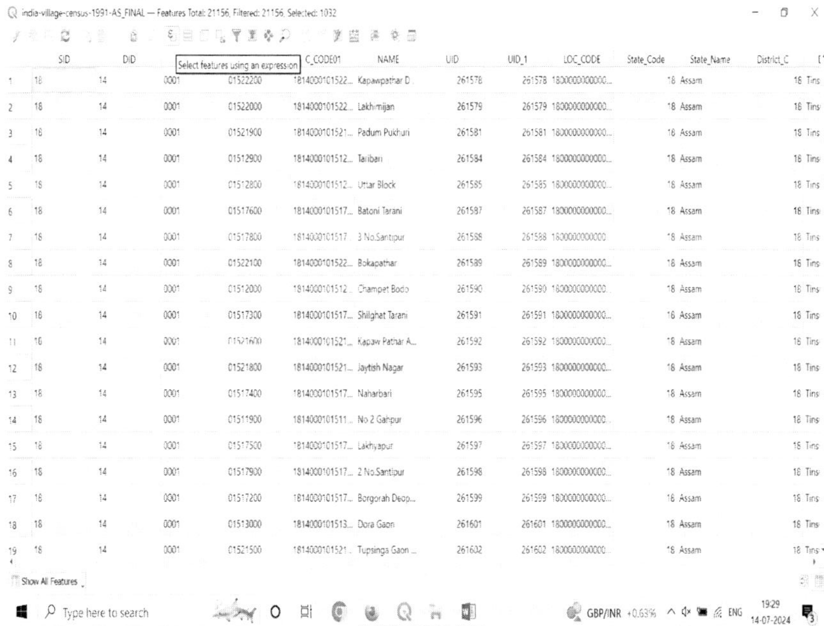

7. Use the expression "DID" = 21, and click 'Select Features'.

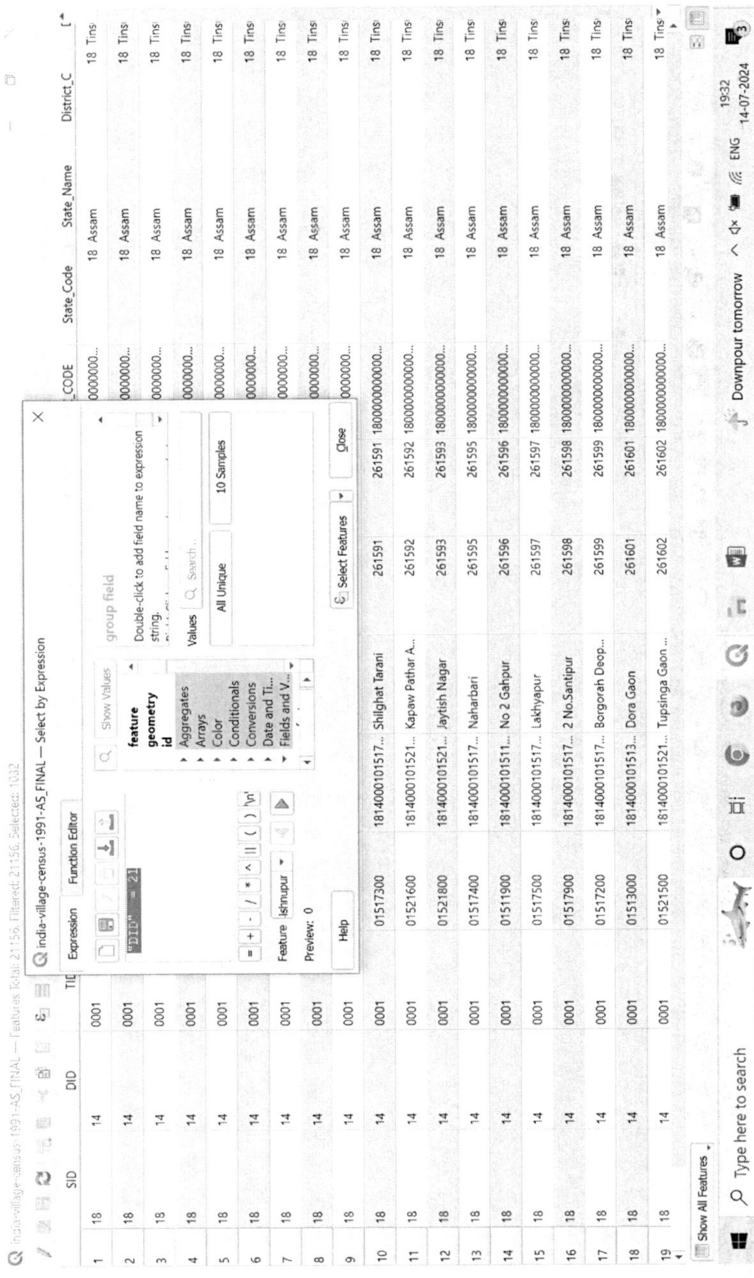

8. District Cachar will be selected, as the Cachar's district code is 21

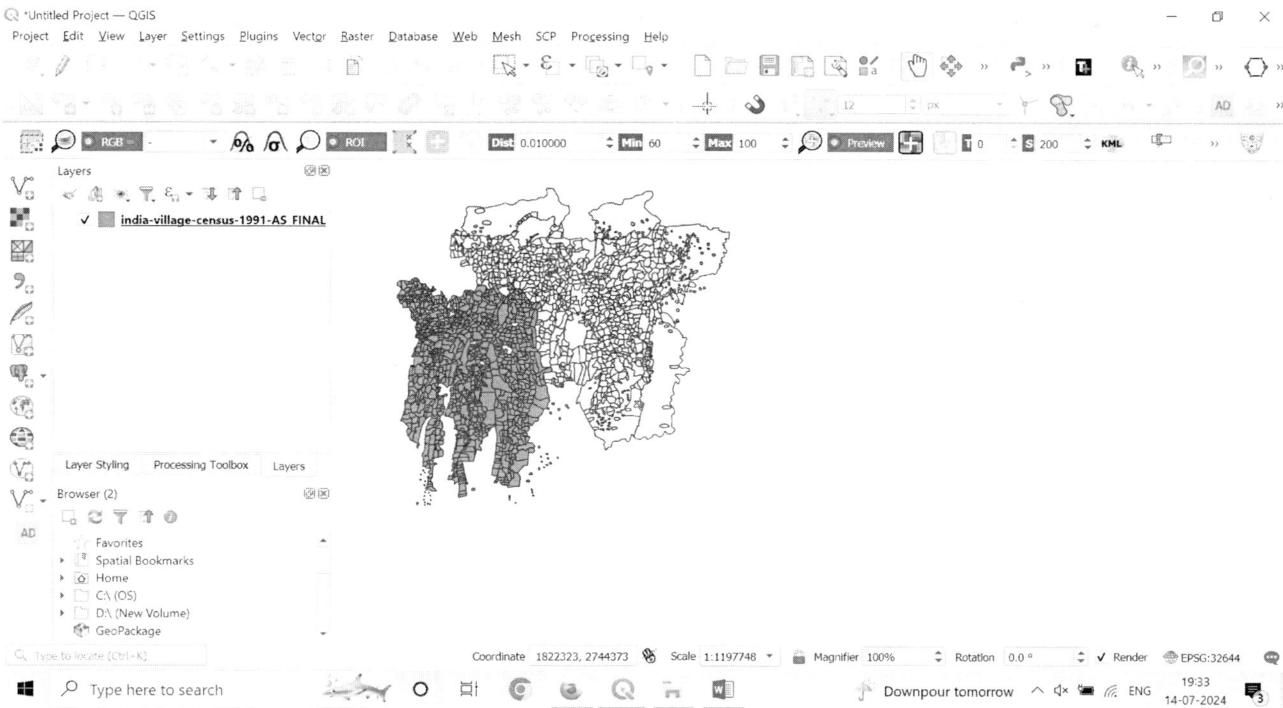

9. Now save the selected district using 'QGIS – Layer (Right Click) – Export – Save Selected Features As...'

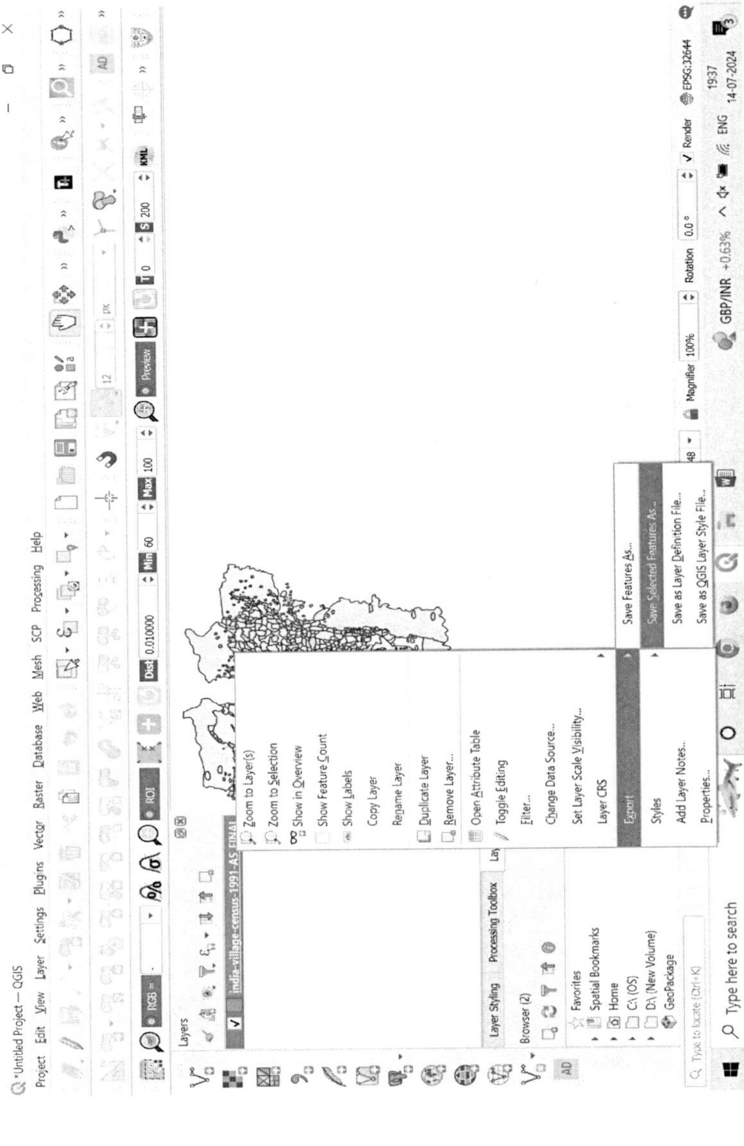

10. Similarly use code 22 and 23 for extracting the Karimganj and Hailakandi districts respectively.
11. Now open all the three districts and merge them using 'Vector – Data Management Tools – Merge Vector Layers…'

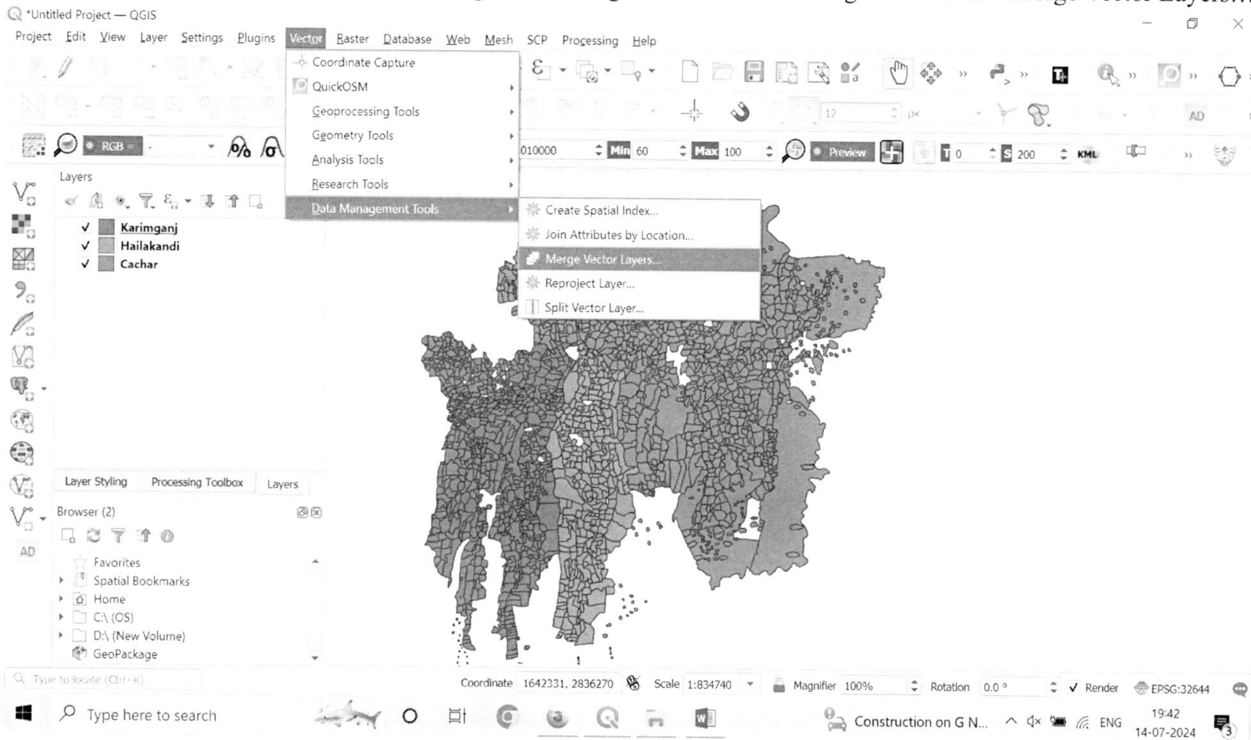

12. Under the 'Input layers' within 'Merge Vector Layers', Click 'Select All', and Click 'OK'

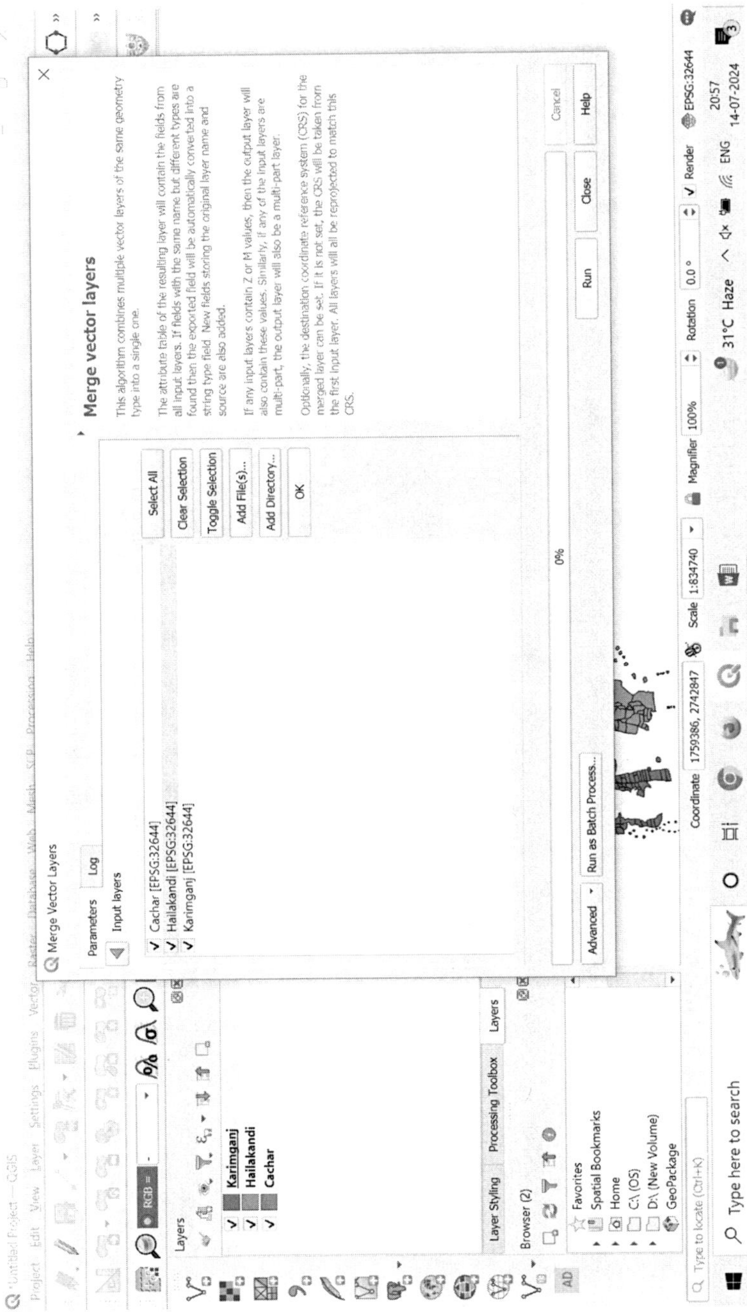

13. Under the 'Merged' section, within 'Merge Vector Layers', Click 'Save to File' and save the merged file as 'BarakValley' in appropriate location.

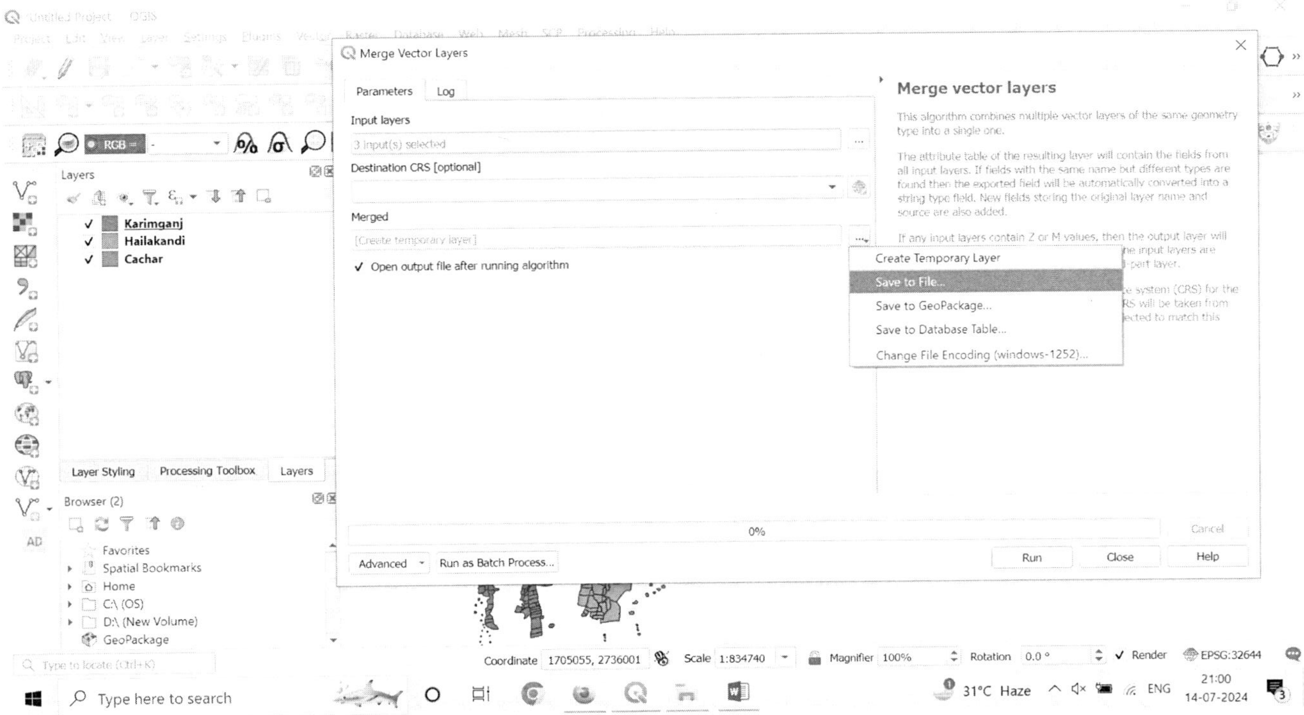

14. The 'BarakValley' file will be added into the layer. Remove the three individual districts from the Layers. This layer has shape file and all the census variables for the year 1991.

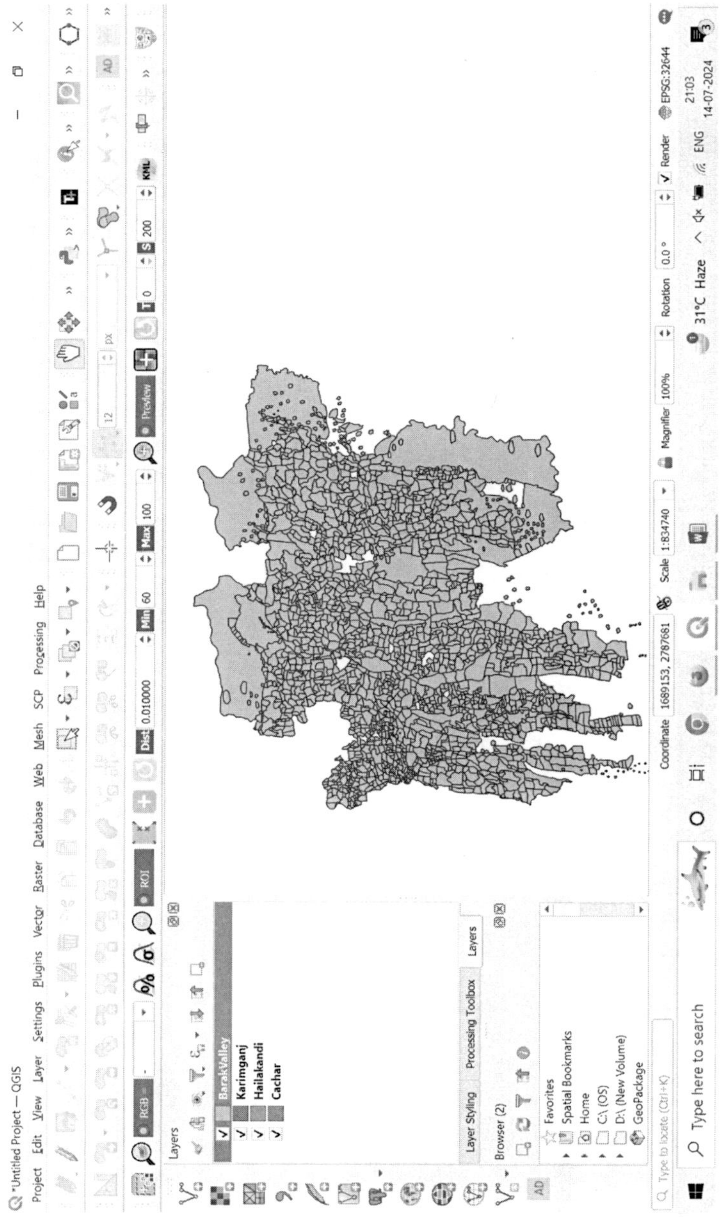

15. Repeat above steps for extracting shape file and socio-economic data of Barak Valley for the year 2001.

The shape file with attributes for the year 2011 is not readily available. We need to join two separate data using the spatial join method. The first data is socio-economic attributes in MS Excel form for the year 2011, which is collected from the census data (Primary Census Abstract C.D. Block wise, Assam) (https://censusindia.gov.in) for the three districts of Cachar, Karimganj, and Hailakandi for the year 2011.

16. Save these excel files as CSV file (CSV (Comma delimited)).

    (a) Open an individual excel file, Click 'File' on the top left

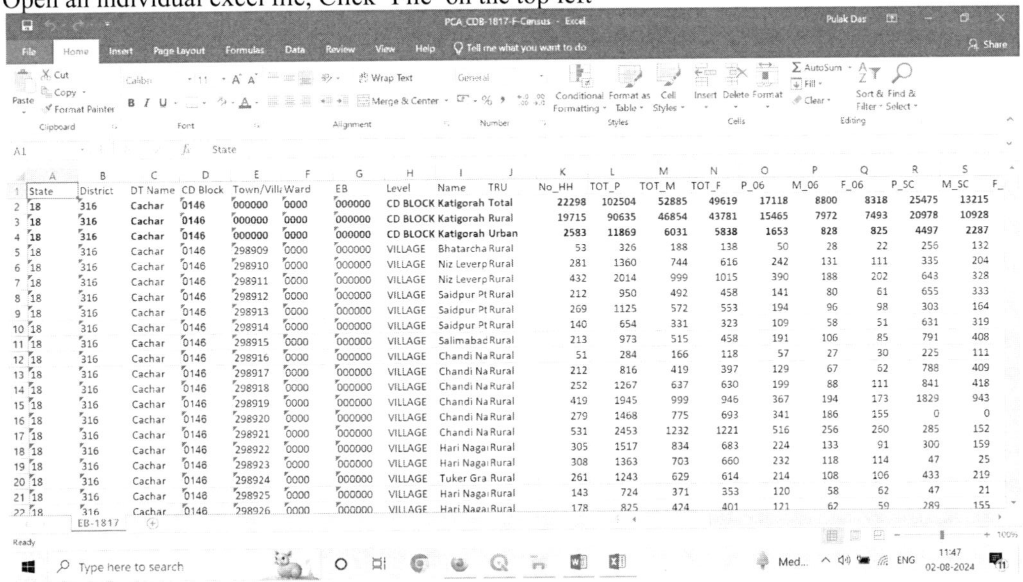

State	District	DT Name	CD Block	Town/Vill	Ward	EB	Level	Name	TRU	No_HH	TOT_P	TOT_M	TOT_F	P_06	M_06	F_06	P_SC	M_SC
18	316	Cachar	0146	000000	0000	000000	CD BLOCK	Katigorah	Total	22298	102504	52885	49619	17118	8800	8318	25475	13215
18	316	Cachar	0146	000000	0000	000000	CD BLOCK	Katigorah	Rural	19715	90635	46854	43781	15465	7972	7493	20978	10928
18	316	Cachar	0146	000000	0000	000000	CD BLOCK	Katigorah	Urban	2583	11869	6031	5838	1653	828	825	4497	2287
18	316	Cachar	0146	298909	0000	000000	VILLAGE	Bhatarcha	Rural	53	326	188	138	50	28	22	256	132
18	316	Cachar	0146	298910	0000	000000	VILLAGE	Niz Leverp	Rural	281	1360	744	616	242	131	111	335	204
18	316	Cachar	0146	298911	0000	000000	VILLAGE	Niz Leverp	Rural	432	2014	999	1015	390	188	202	643	328
18	316	Cachar	0146	298912	0000	000000	VILLAGE	Saidpur Pt	Rural	212	950	492	458	141	80	61	655	333
18	316	Cachar	0146	298913	0000	000000	VILLAGE	Saidpur Pt	Rural	269	1125	572	553	194	96	98	303	164
18	316	Cachar	0146	298914	0000	000000	VILLAGE	Saidpur Pt	Rural	140	654	331	323	109	58	51	631	319
18	316	Cachar	0146	298915	0000	000000	VILLAGE	Salimabad	Rural	213	973	515	458	191	106	85	791	408
18	316	Cachar	0146	298916	0000	000000	VILLAGE	Chandi Na	Rural	51	284	166	118	57	27	30	225	111
18	316	Cachar	0146	298917	0000	000000	VILLAGE	Chandi Na	Rural	212	816	419	397	129	67	62	788	409
18	316	Cachar	0146	298918	0000	000000	VILLAGE	Chandi Na	Rural	252	1267	637	630	199	88	111	841	418
18	316	Cachar	0146	298919	0000	000000	VILLAGE	Chandi Na	Rural	419	1945	999	946	367	194	173	1829	943
18	316	Cachar	0146	298920	0000	000000	VILLAGE	Chandi Na	Rural	279	1468	775	693	341	186	155	0	0
18	316	Cachar	0146	298921	0000	000000	VILLAGE	Chandi Na	Rural	531	2453	1232	1221	516	256	260	285	152
18	316	Cachar	0146	298922	0000	000000	VILLAGE	Hari Nagai	Rural	305	1517	834	683	224	133	91	300	159
18	316	Cachar	0146	298923	0000	000000	VILLAGE	Hari Nagai	Rural	308	1363	703	660	232	118	114	47	25
18	316	Cachar	0146	298924	0000	000000	VILLAGE	Tuker Gra	Rural	261	1243	629	614	214	108	106	433	219
18	316	Cachar	0146	298925	0000	000000	VILLAGE	Hari Nagai	Rural	143	724	371	353	120	58	62	47	21
18	316	Cachar	0146	298926	0000	000000	VILLAGE	Hari Nagai	Rural	178	825	424	401	121	62	59	289	155

(b) Click ‘Save As’ and select an appropriate folder.

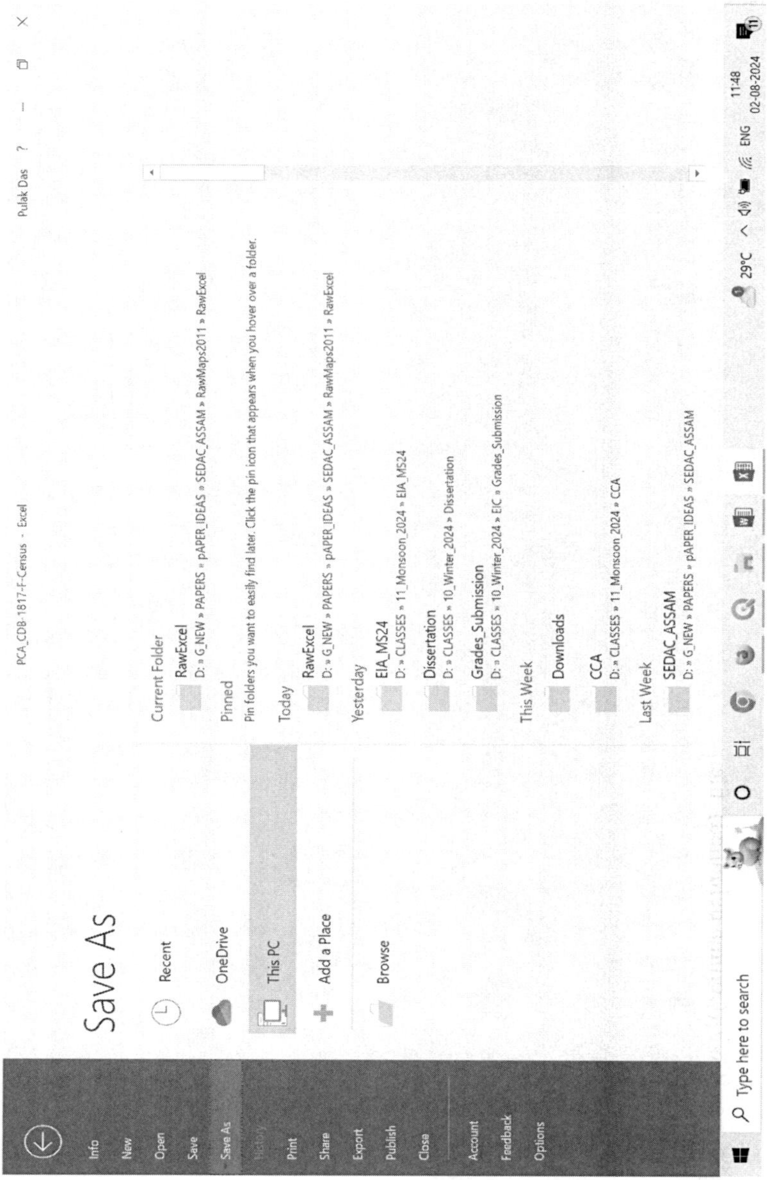

(c) Save as 'CSV (Comma delimited)' file.

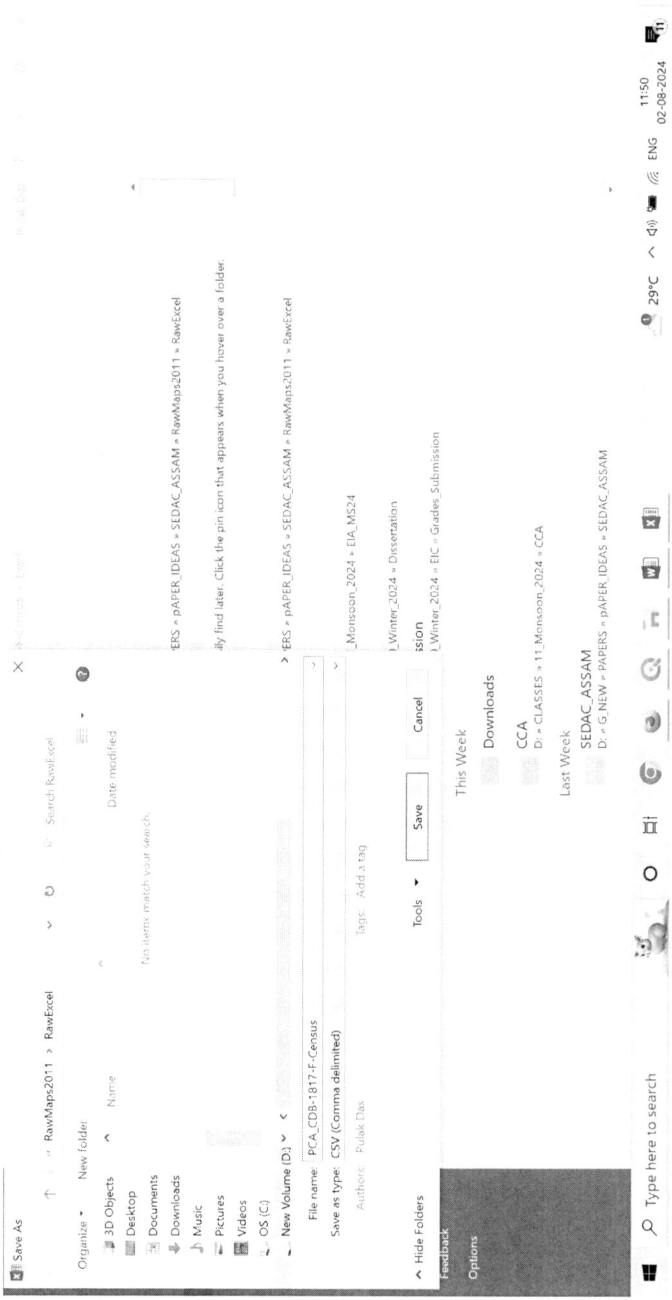

(d) Repeat this for all the three excel files.

The second data is a spatial data of individual districts from the year 2001, extracted earlier. The attribute used for joining these two sets of data is the unique village level code (UID). The UID is available in 2001 data but for 2011 data, it is meticulously inserted against village names since names are common for both the data.

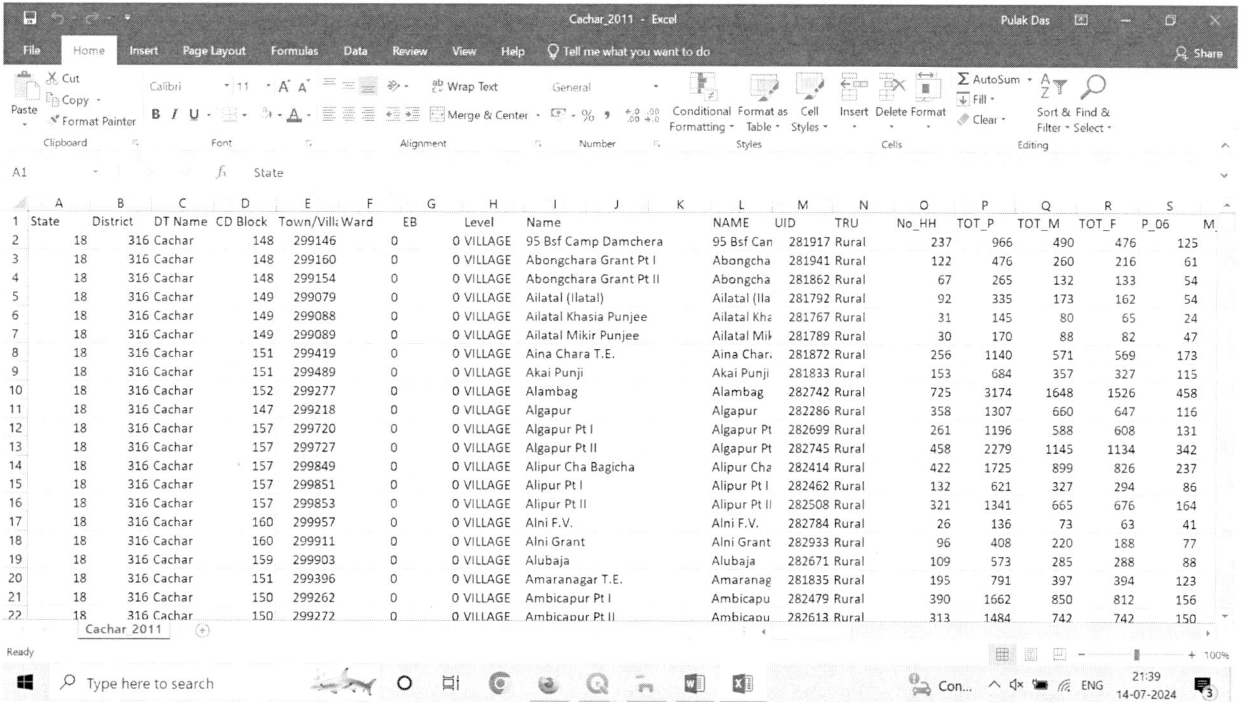

	State	District	DT Name	CD Block	Town/Vill	Ward	EB	Level	Name	NAME	UID	TRU	No_HH	TOT_P	TOT_M	TOT_F	P_06
2	18	316	Cachar	148	299146	0	0	VILLAGE	95 Bsf Camp Damchera	95 Bsf Can	281917	Rural	237	966	490	476	125
3	18	316	Cachar	148	299160	0	0	VILLAGE	Abongchara Grant Pt I	Abongcha	281941	Rural	122	476	260	216	61
4	18	316	Cachar	148	299154	0	0	VILLAGE	Abongchara Grant Pt II	Abongcha	281862	Rural	67	265	132	133	54
5	18	316	Cachar	149	299079	0	0	VILLAGE	Ailatal (Ilatal)	Ailatal (Ila	281792	Rural	92	335	173	162	54
6	18	316	Cachar	149	299088	0	0	VILLAGE	Ailatal Khasia Punjee	Ailatal Khe	281767	Rural	31	145	80	65	24
7	18	316	Cachar	149	299089	0	0	VILLAGE	Ailatal Mikir Punjee	Ailatal Mik	281789	Rural	30	170	88	82	47
8	18	316	Cachar	151	299419	0	0	VILLAGE	Aina Chara T.E.	Aina Char.	281872	Rural	256	1140	571	569	173
9	18	316	Cachar	151	299489	0	0	VILLAGE	Akai Punji	Akai Punji	281833	Rural	153	684	357	327	115
10	18	316	Cachar	152	299277	0	0	VILLAGE	Alambag	Alambag	282742	Rural	725	3174	1648	1526	458
11	18	316	Cachar	147	299218	0	0	VILLAGE	Algapur	Algapur	282286	Rural	358	1307	660	647	116
12	18	316	Cachar	157	299720	0	0	VILLAGE	Algapur Pt I	Algapur Pt	282699	Rural	261	1196	588	608	131
13	18	316	Cachar	157	299727	0	0	VILLAGE	Algapur Pt II	Algapur Pt	282745	Rural	458	2279	1145	1134	342
14	18	316	Cachar	157	299849	0	0	VILLAGE	Alipur Cha Bagicha	Alipur Cha	282414	Rural	422	1725	899	826	237
15	18	316	Cachar	157	299851	0	0	VILLAGE	Alipur Pt I	Alipur Pt I	282462	Rural	132	621	327	294	86
16	18	316	Cachar	157	299853	0	0	VILLAGE	Alipur Pt II	Alipur Pt II	282508	Rural	321	1341	665	676	164
17	18	316	Cachar	160	299957	0	0	VILLAGE	Alni F.V.	Alni F.V.	282784	Rural	26	136	73	63	41
18	18	316	Cachar	160	299911	0	0	VILLAGE	Alni Grant	Alni Grant	282933	Rural	96	408	220	188	77
19	18	316	Cachar	159	299903	0	0	VILLAGE	Alubaja	Alubaja	282671	Rural	109	573	285	288	88
20	18	316	Cachar	151	299396	0	0	VILLAGE	Amaranagar T.E.	Amaranag	281835	Rural	195	791	397	394	123
21	18	316	Cachar	150	299262	0	0	VILLAGE	Ambicapur Pt I	Ambicapu	282479	Rural	390	1662	850	812	156
22	18	316	Cachar	150	299272	0	0	VILLAGE	Ambicapur Pt II	Ambicapu	282613	Rural	313	1484	742	742	150

17. The attribute data for 2001 is cleaned by removing all other attributes except the 'UID' and Village 'Name'. For that, use following steps.

    (a) Open attribute table and click 'Toggle editing mode (Ctrl+E)'

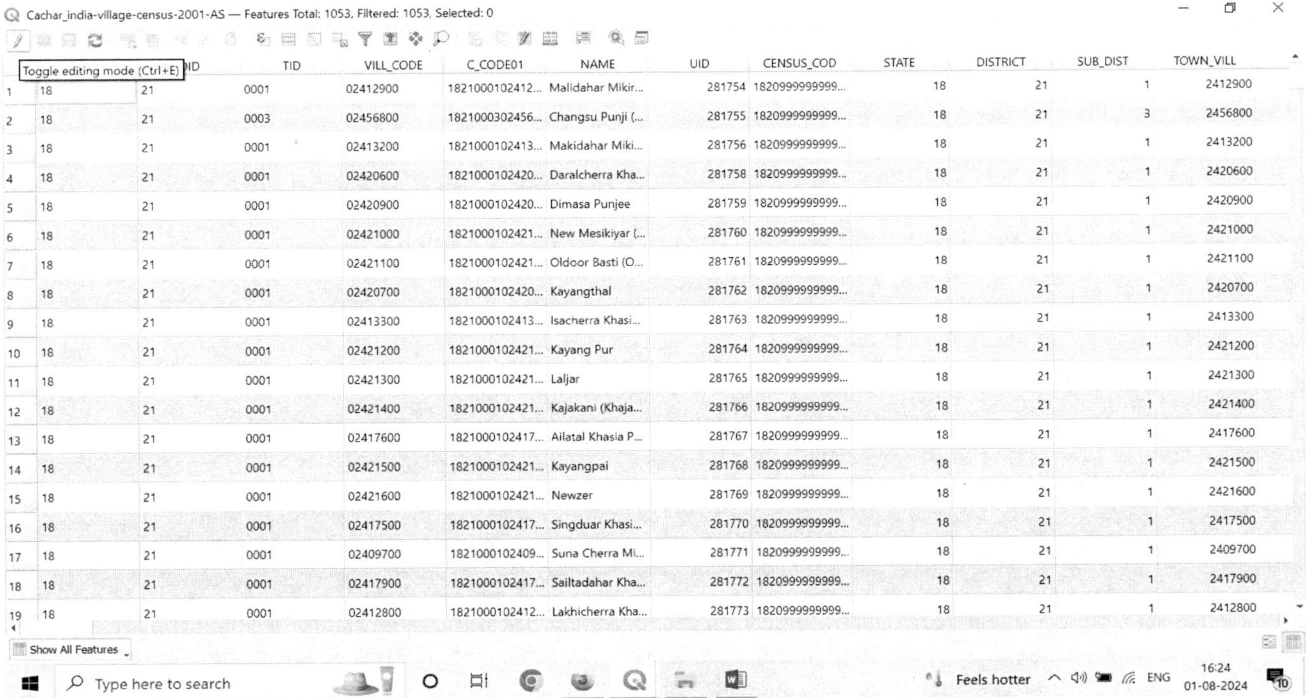

		ID	TID	VILL_CODE	C_CODE01	NAME	UID	CENSUS_COD	STATE	DISTRICT	SUB_DIST	TOWN_VILL
1	18	21	0001	02412900	1821000102412...	Malidahar Mikir...	281754	1820999999999...	18	21	1	2412900
2	18	21	0003	02456800	1821000302456...	Changsu Punji (...	281755	1820999999999...	18	21	3	2456800
3	18	21	0001	02413200	1821000102413...	Makidahar Miki...	281756	1820999999999...	18	21	1	2413200
4	18	21	0001	02420600	1821000102420...	Daralcherra Kha...	281758	1820999999999...	18	21	1	2420600
5	18	21	0001	02420900	1821000102420...	Dimasa Punjee	281759	1820999999999...	18	21	1	2420900
6	18	21	0001	02421000	1821000102421...	New Mesikiyar (...	281760	1820999999999...	18	21	1	2421000
7	18	21	0001	02421100	1821000102421...	Oldoor Basti (O...	281761	1820999999999...	18	21	1	2421100
8	18	21	0001	02420700	1821000102420...	Kayangthal	281762	1820999999999...	18	21	1	2420700
9	18	21	0001	02413300	1821000102413...	Isacherra Khasi...	281763	1820999999999...	18	21	1	2413300
10	18	21	0001	02421200	1821000102421...	Kayang Pur	281764	1820999999999...	18	21	1	2421200
11	18	21	0001	02421300	1821000102421...	Laljar	281765	1820999999999...	18	21	1	2421300
12	18	21	0001	02421400	1821000102421...	Kajakani (Khaja...	281766	1820999999999...	18	21	1	2421400
13	18	21	0001	02417600	1821000102417...	Ailatal Khasia P...	281767	1820999999999...	18	21	1	2417600
14	18	21	0001	02421500	1821000102421...	Kayangpai	281768	1820999999999...	18	21	1	2421500
15	18	21	0001	02421600	1821000102421...	Newzer	281769	1820999999999...	18	21	1	2421600
16	18	21	0001	02417500	1821000102417...	Singduar Khasi...	281770	1820999999999...	18	21	1	2417500
17	18	21	0001	02409700	1821000102409...	Suna Cherra Mi...	281771	1820999999999...	18	21	1	2409700
18	18	21	0001	02417900	1821000102417...	Sailtadahar Kha...	281772	1820999999999...	18	21	1	2417900
19	18	21	0001	02412800	1821000102412...	Lakhicherra Kha...	281773	1820999999999...	18	21	1	2412800

(b) Click 'Delete field (Ctrl+L)'

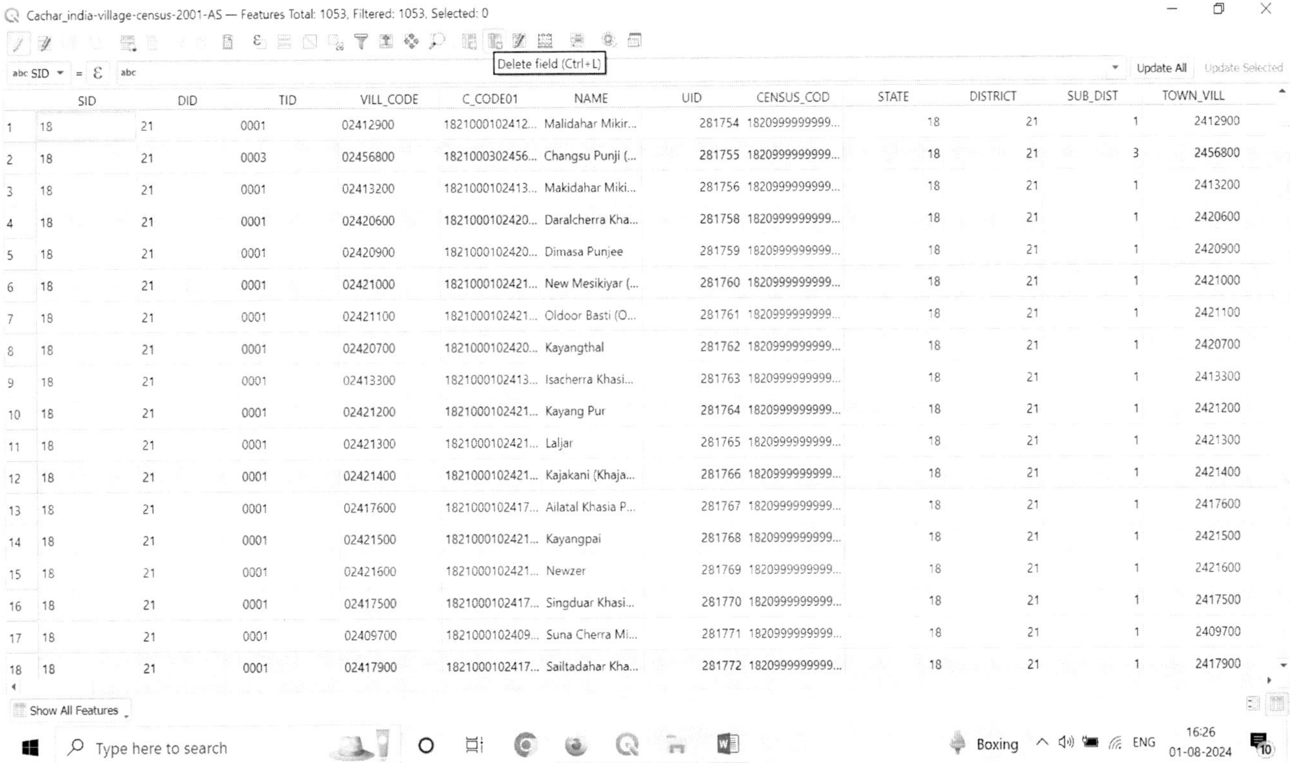

(c) Under 'Delete Fields', select all the fields except 'Name' and 'UID' (Ctrl+L)', and click 'OK'

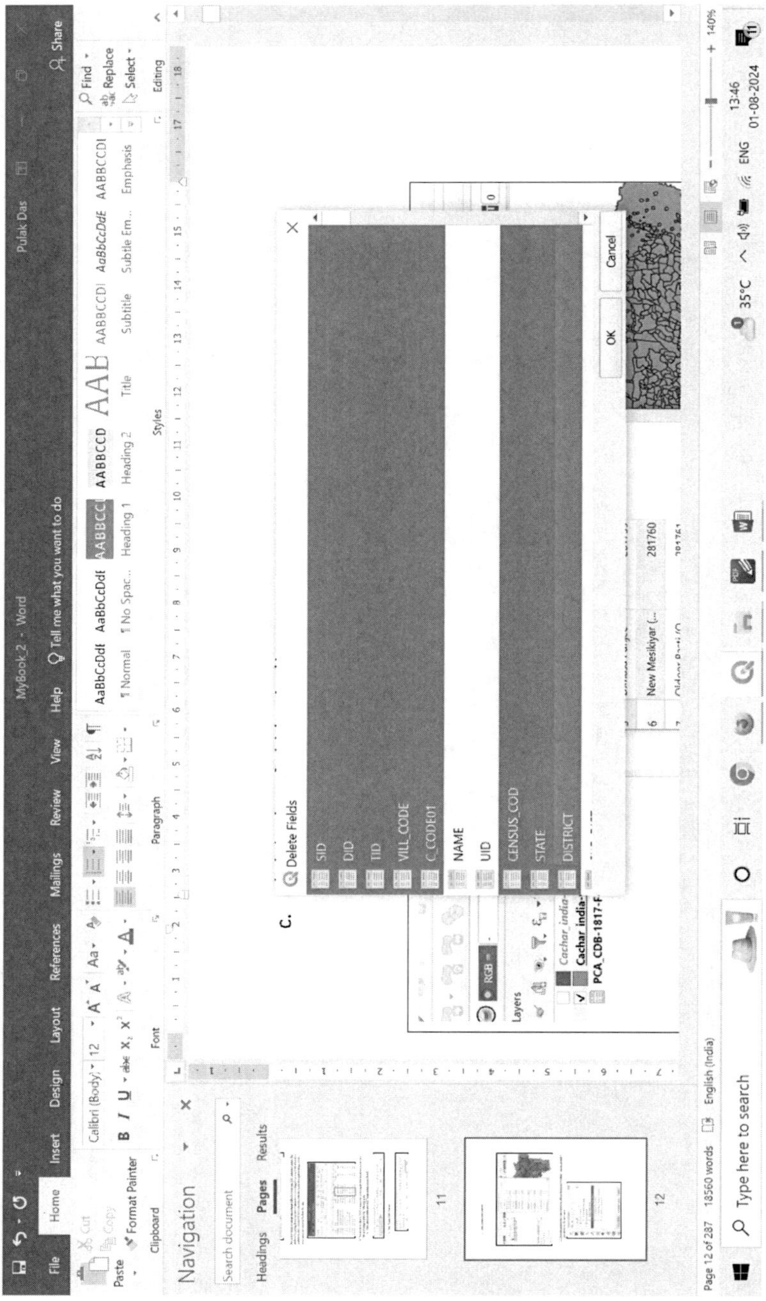

(d) Click ‘Toggle editing mode (Ctrl+E)’ again and save the attributes. Now your attribute table will show only two fields, ‘NAME’ and ‘UID’.

18. For spatial joining, use 'Processing Toolbox – Vector general – Join attributes by field value'

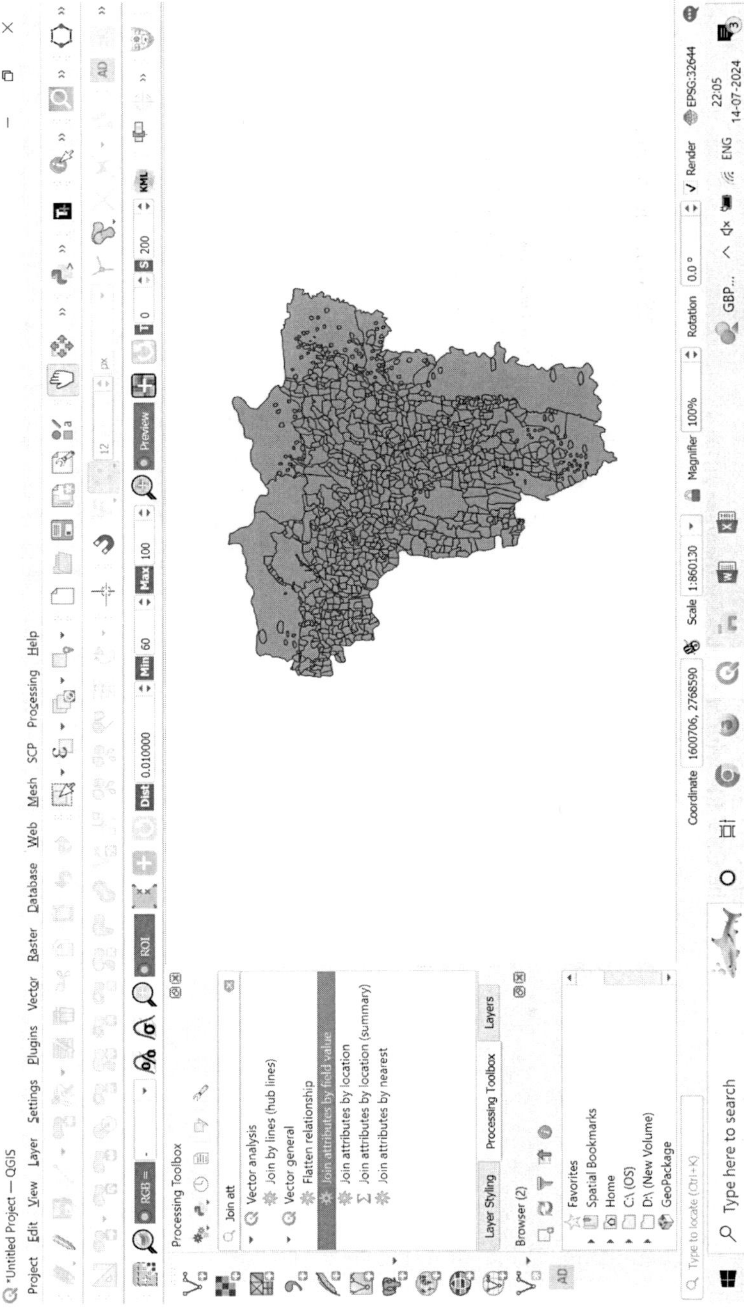

19. The sub-window 'Join Attributes by Field Value' will open
    (a) Under 'Input layer', select the shape file of 2001 (mentioned above);
    (b) Under 'Table field', select 'UID';
    (c) Under 'Input layer 2', select the CSV file with attributes for the year 2011;
    (d) Under 'Table field 2', select 'UID'.
    (e) Now save the shape file with appropriate name (Cachar_india-village-census-2011-AS.shp) and within appropriate folder, and click 'Run'.

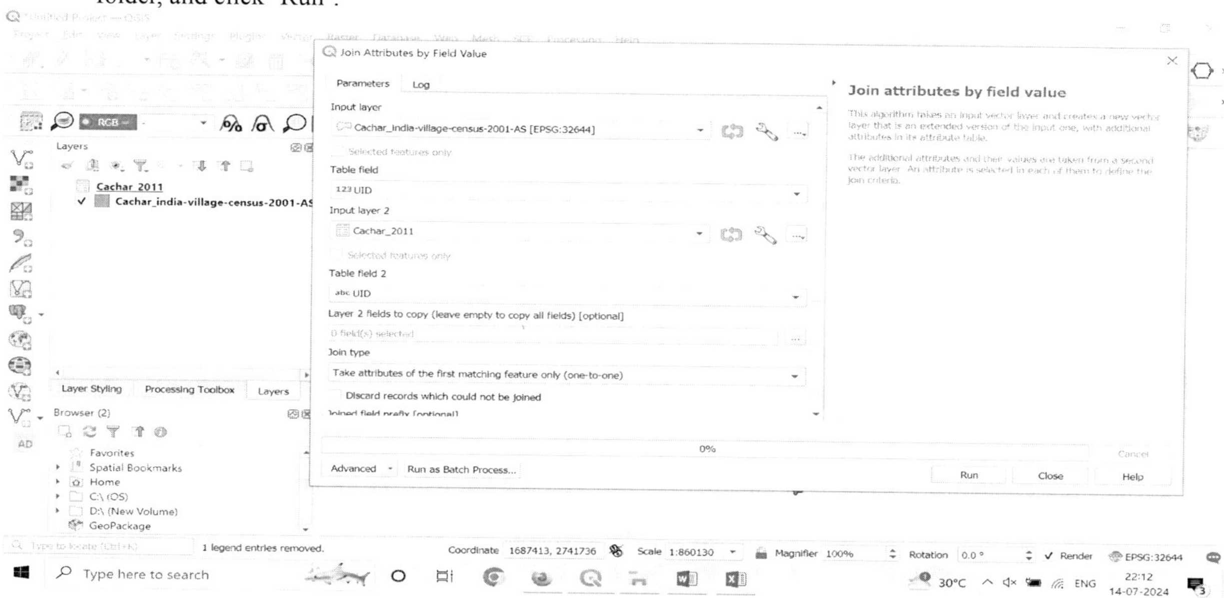

20. Repeat the above processes for other two districts also.
21. Now before merging the three new shape files check whether the attribute tables match
    (a) For that, open attribute table of the final shape file just created above (which has both Name and UID) of the first district.
    (b) Click 'Select all'

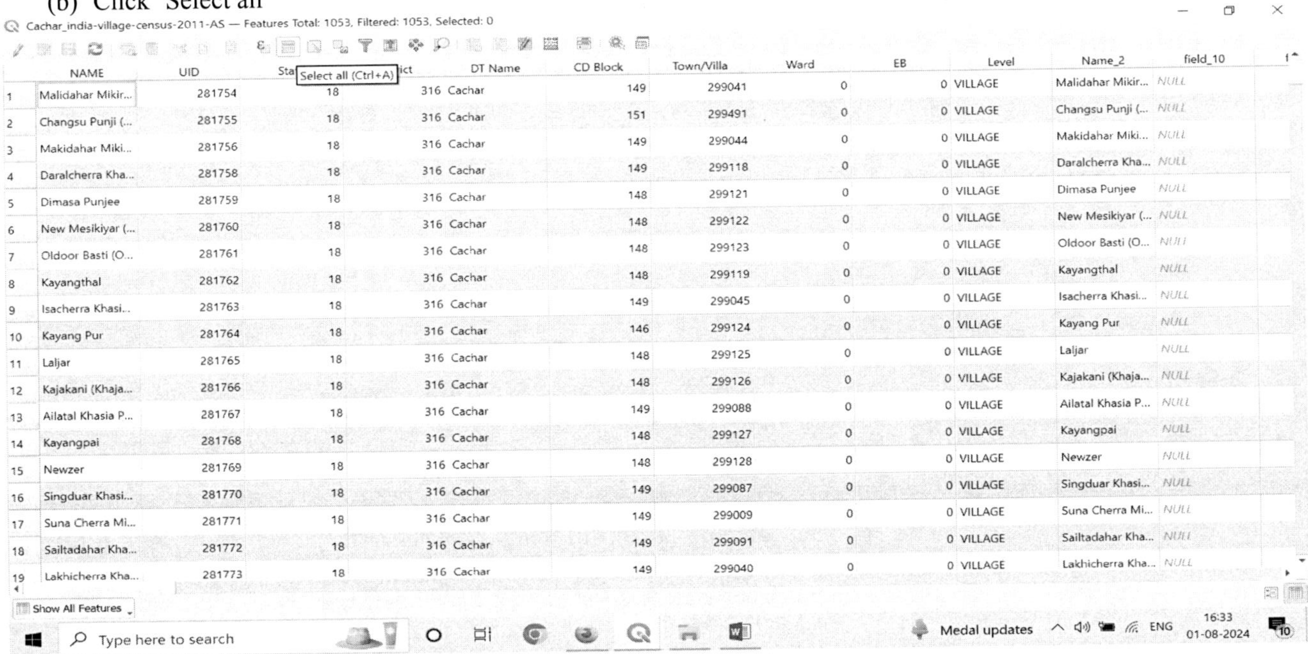

(c) Click 'Copy selected rows to clipboard (Ctrl+C)'

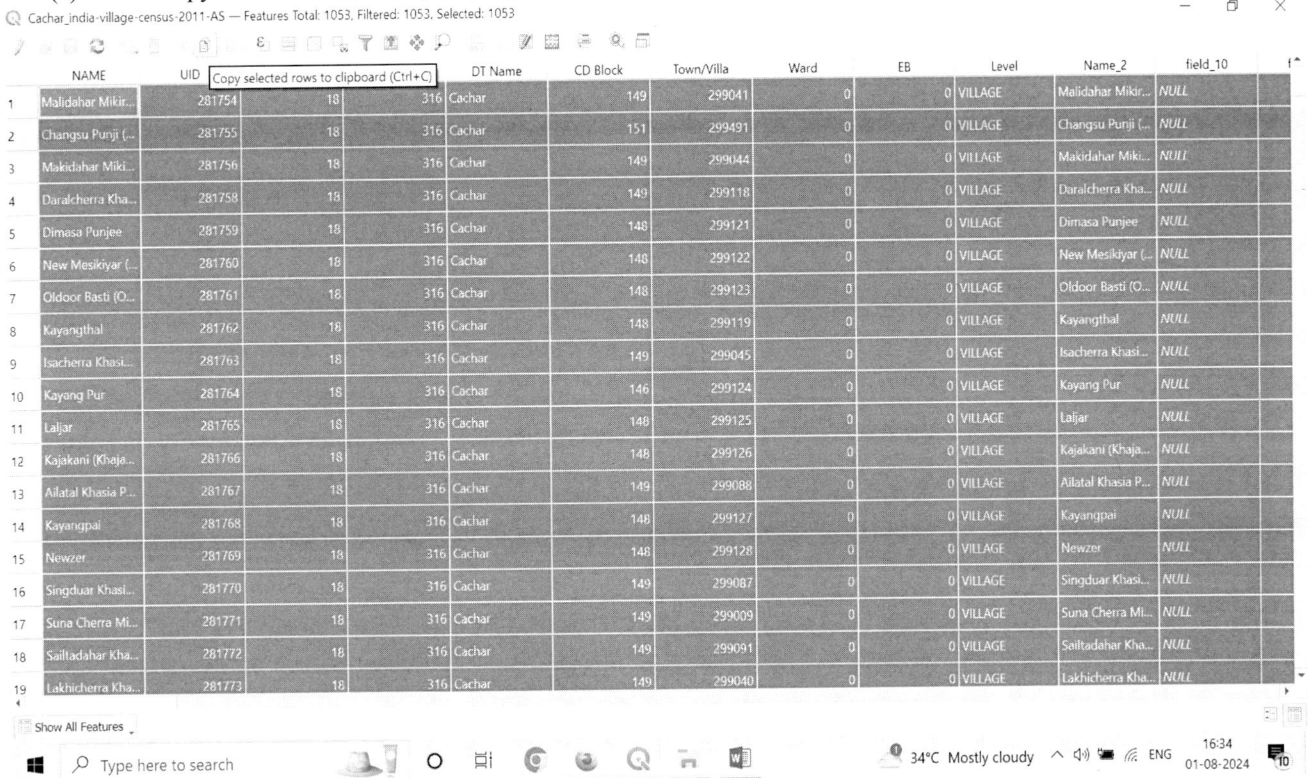

	NAME	UID			DT Name	CD Block	Town/Villa	Ward	EB	Level	Name_2	field_10
1	Malidahar Mikir...	281754	18	316	Cachar	149	299041	0	0	VILLAGE	Malidahar Mikir...	NULL
2	Changsu Punji (...	281755	18	316	Cachar	151	299491	0	0	VILLAGE	Changsu Punji (...	NULL
3	Makidahar Miki...	281756	18	316	Cachar	149	299044	0	0	VILLAGE	Makidahar Miki...	NULL
4	Daralcherra Kha...	281758	18	316	Cachar	149	299118	0	0	VILLAGE	Daralcherra Kha...	NULL
5	Dimasa Punjee	281759	18	316	Cachar	148	299121	0	0	VILLAGE	Dimasa Punjee	NULL
6	New Mesikiyar (...	281760	18	316	Cachar	148	299122	0	0	VILLAGE	New Mesikiyar (...	NULL
7	Oldoor Basti (O...	281761	18	316	Cachar	148	299123	0	0	VILLAGE	Oldoor Basti (O...	NULL
8	Kayangthal	281762	18	316	Cachar	148	299119	0	0	VILLAGE	Kayangthal	NULL
9	Isacherra Khasi...	281763	18	316	Cachar	149	299045	0	0	VILLAGE	Isacherra Khasi...	NULL
10	Kayang Pur	281764	18	316	Cachar	146	299124	0	0	VILLAGE	Kayang Pur	NULL
11	Laljar	281765	18	316	Cachar	148	299125	0	0	VILLAGE	Laljar	NULL
12	Kajakani (Khaja...	281766	18	316	Cachar	148	299126	0	0	VILLAGE	Kajakani (Khaja...	NULL
13	Ailatal Khasia P...	281767	18	316	Cachar	149	299088	0	0	VILLAGE	Ailatal Khasia P...	NULL
14	Kayangpai	281768	18	316	Cachar	148	299127	0	0	VILLAGE	Kayangpai	NULL
15	Newzer	281769	18	316	Cachar	148	299128	0	0	VILLAGE	Newzer	NULL
16	Singduar Khasi...	281770	18	316	Cachar	149	299087	0	0	VILLAGE	Singduar Khasi...	NULL
17	Suna Cherra Mi...	281771	18	316	Cachar	149	299009	0	0	VILLAGE	Suna Cherra Mi...	NULL
18	Sailtadahar Kha...	281772	18	316	Cachar	149	299091	0	0	VILLAGE	Sailtadahar Kha...	NULL
19	Lakhicherra Kha...	281773	18	316	Cachar	149	299040	0	0	VILLAGE	Lakhicherra Kha...	NULL

(d) Paste the data in an excel file

22. Once convinced that attribute tables match, merge all the three districts as shown previously with name as BarakValley for the year 2011.
23. Now all the three maps of Barak Valley for all the three years are ready for further spatial analysis. We will call these the Master files – 1991, 2001, 2011.

Spatial analysis

1. Open the Master file – 1991 in QGIS.
2. For spatial analysis of census variable use the following-
   (a) Under 'Layer Styling', select 'Graduated' as renderer;
   (b) Under 'Value' select appropriate census variable (for example number of household or 'No_HH');
   (c) Under 'Color ramp', select 'YelloGreenBlue' (YlGnBu);
   (d) Under 'Mode', select appropriate spatial analysis mode (for example Natural Breaks (Jenks)), and click 'Classify'.

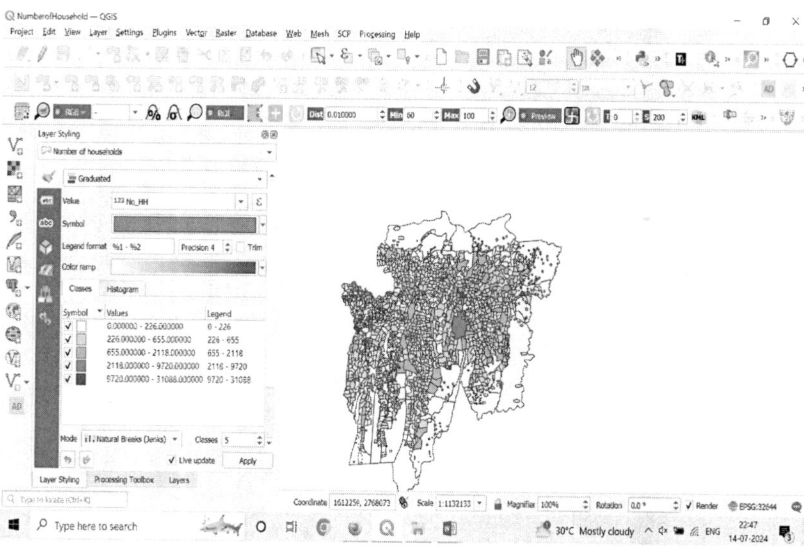

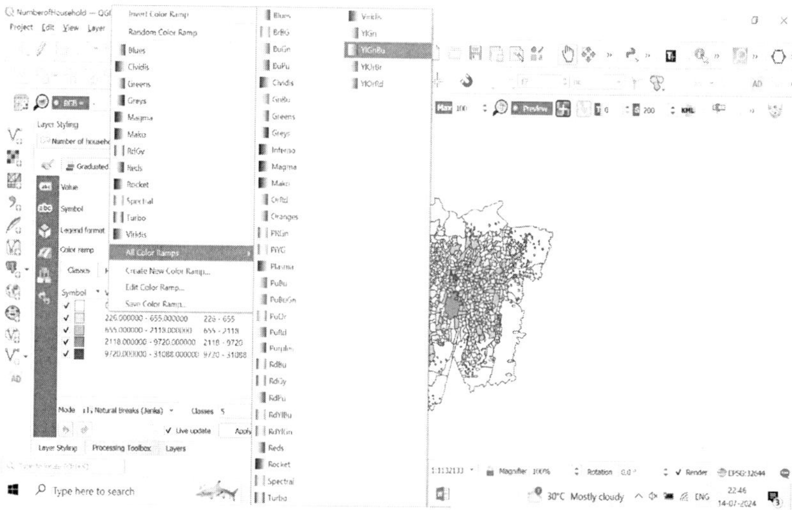

(e) A classified map will be generated as shown above.

(f) Repeat the process for all census variables mentioned in table 4.

3. For spatial analysis of socio-economic indicators, same Master file – 1991 will be used as follows-

(a) Under 'Layer Styling', select 'Graduated' as renderer;

(b) Under 'Value' select appropriate expression. For example to calculate child sex ratio, use the following expression (("POPLN_F6" / "POPLN_M6") * 1000) (See Table 7 for further details)

(c) Under 'Color ramp', select 'Blues';

(d) Under 'Mode', select appropriate spatial analysis mode, and click 'Classify'

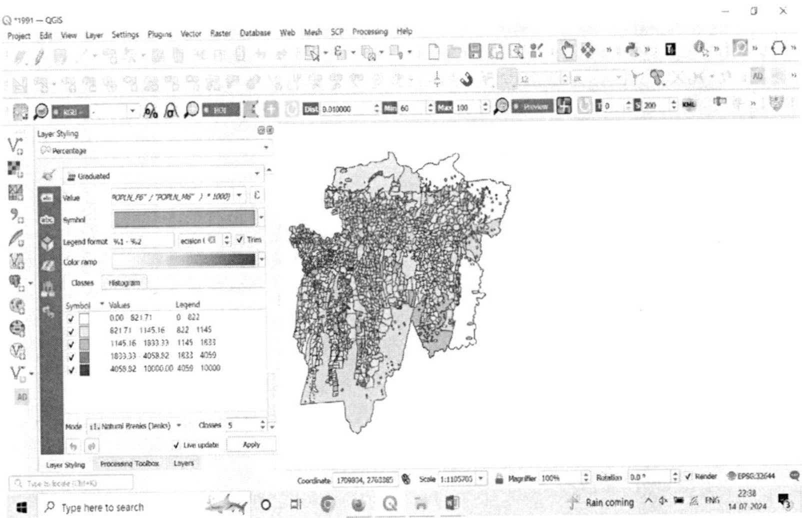

4. For inserting map elements and for a presentable form of the map, use the following
   (a) Click 'Project – New Print layout…'
   (b) Under 'Create Print Layout', write an appropriate name (e.g. Child sex ratio 1991)
   (c) Click 'OK'

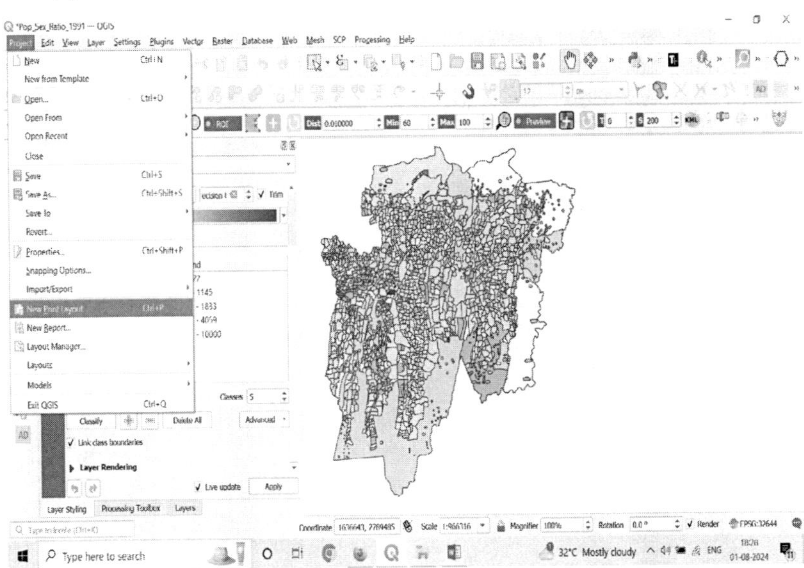

Create Print Layout
Enter a unique print layout title
(a title will be automatically generated if left empty)
Child sex ratio 1991
OK
Cancel
Help
Layer Styling
Percentage
Legend format %1 - %2
Trim
Color ramp
Classes
Histogram
Symbol
Values
Legend
0.00 - 821.71
0 - 822
821.71 - 1145.16
822 - 1145
1145.16 - 1833.33
1145 - 1833
1833.33 - 4058.82
1833 - 4059
4058.82 - 10000.00
4059 - 10000
Mode
Natural Breaks (Jenks)
Classes 5
Classify
Delete All
Advanced
Link class boundaries
Layer Rendering
Live update
Apply
Layer Styling
Processing Toolbox
Layers
Coordinate 1643547, 2783604
Scale 1:966316
Magnifier 100%
Rotation 0.0 °
Render
EPSG:32644
Type here to search
Athletics
ENG
18:30
01-08-2024

(d) A new Print Layout page will open named ‘Child sex ratio 1991’

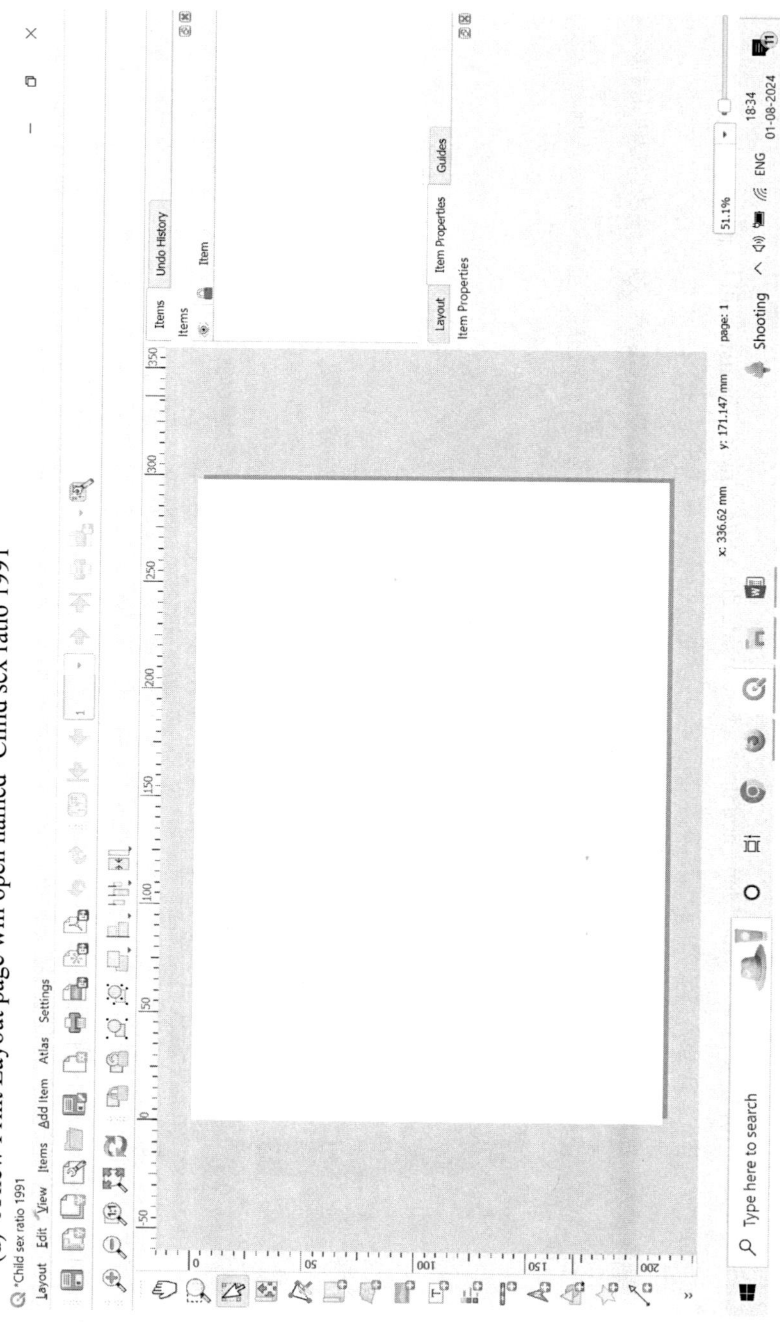

(e) Under 'Toolbox', Click 'Add Map', and draw a box inside the white canvas. The map will be inserted

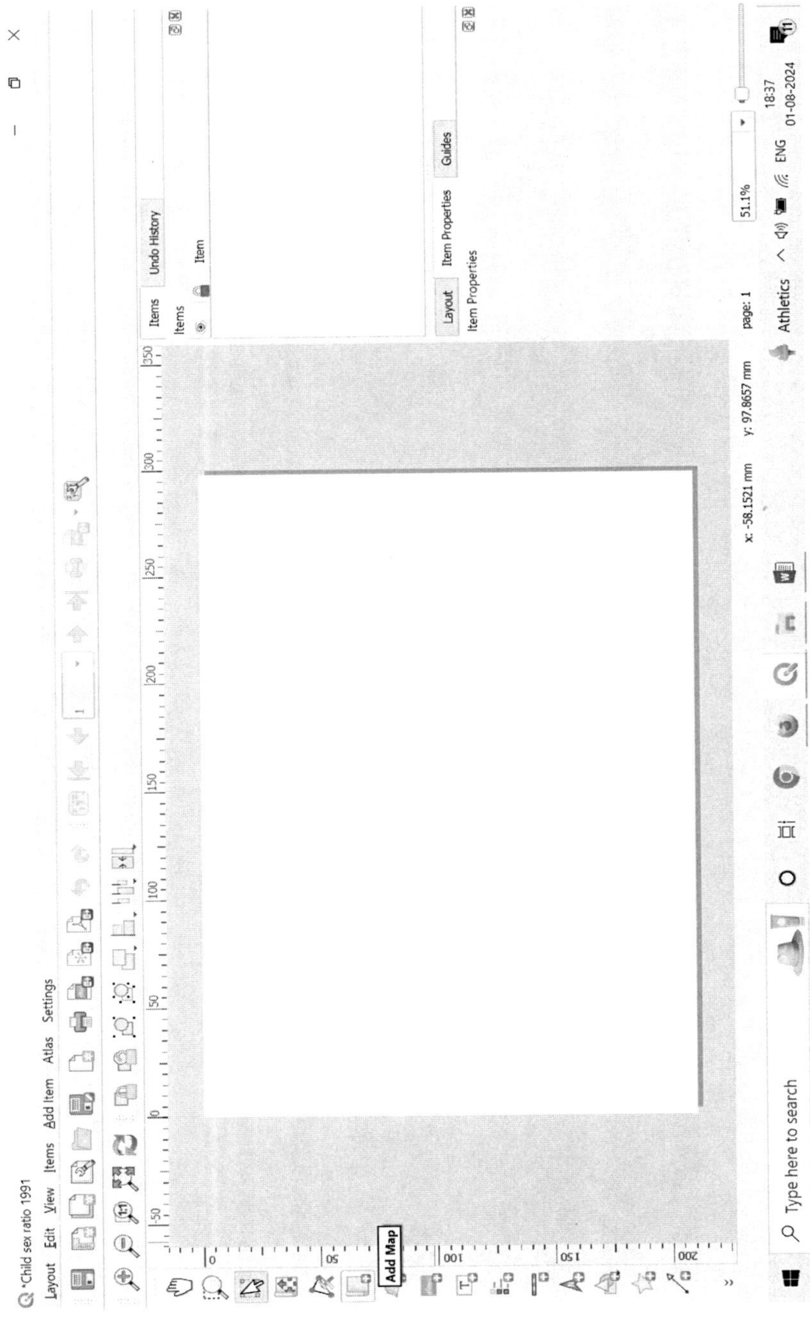
*Child sex ratio 1991
Layout Edit View Items Add Item Atlas Settings
Items
Undo History
Item
Layout
Item Properties
Guides
Item Properties
Add Map
x: -58.1521 mm
y: 97.8657 mm
page: 1
51.1%
Type here to search
Athletics
ENG
18:37
01-08-2024

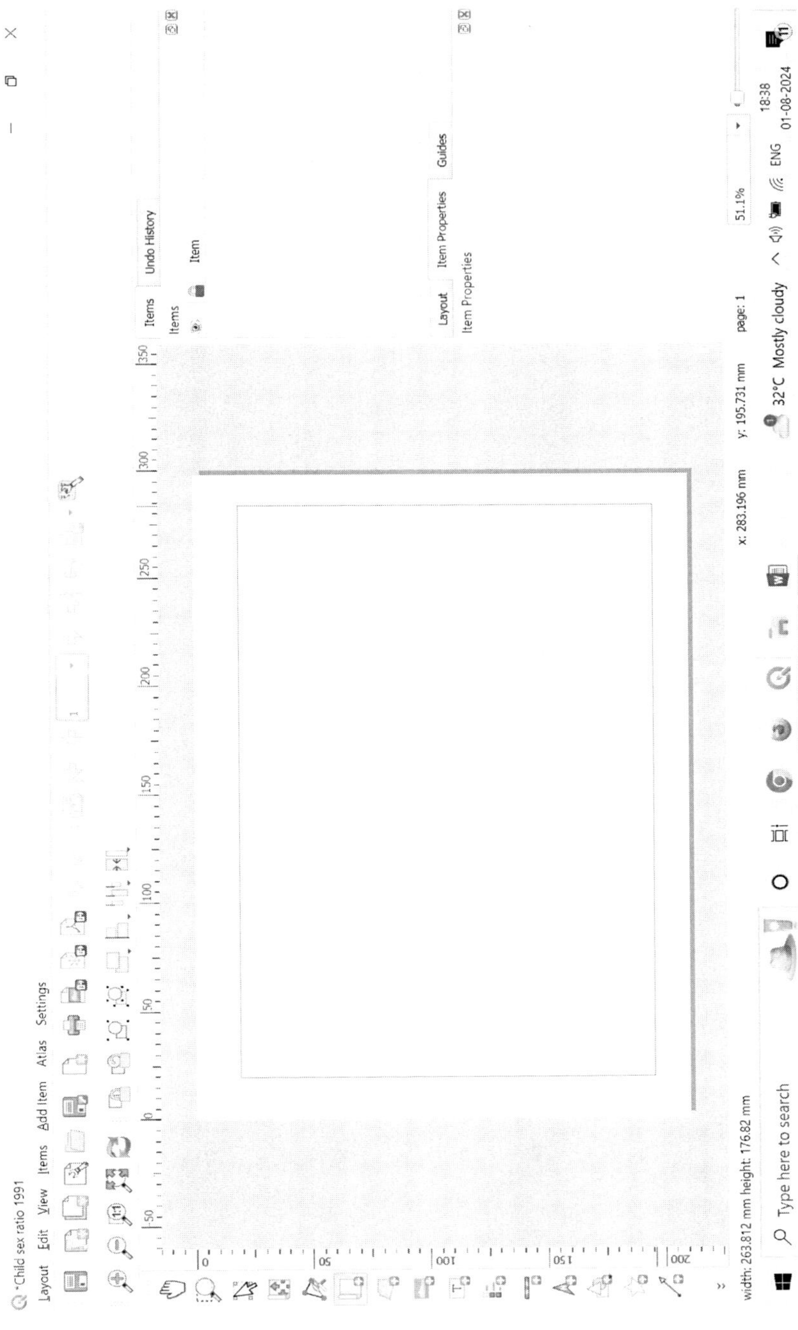
*Child sex ratio 1991
Layout Edit View Items Add Item Atlas Settings
Items
Undo History
Item
Layout
Item Properties
Guides
width: 263.812 mm height: 176.82 mm
x: 283.196 mm
y: 195.731 mm
page: 1
51.1%
Type here to search
32°C Mostly cloudy
ENG
18:38
01-08-2024

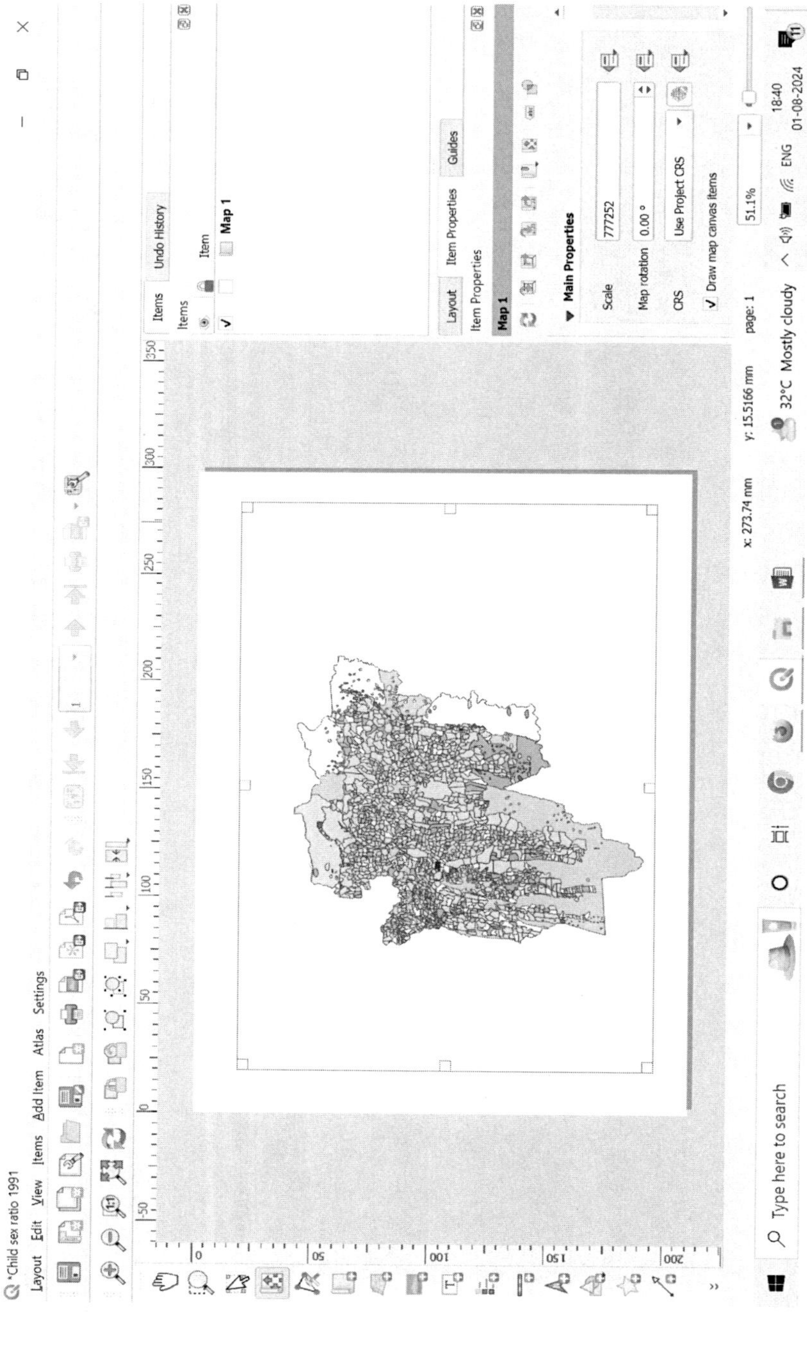
*Child sex ratio 1991
Layout
Edit
View
Items
Add Item
Atlas
Settings
Items
Undo History
Item
Map 1
Layout
Item Properties
Guides
Map 1
Main Properties
Scale
777252
Map rotation
0.00 °
CRS
Use Project CRS
Draw map canvas items
51.1%
x: 273.74 mm
y: 15.5166 mm
page: 1
Type here to search
32°C Mostly cloudy
ENG
18:40
01-08-2024

(f) Now from the 'Toolbox', insert map elements such as Title using 'Add Label', Legend using 'Add Legend', Scale using 'Add Scale Bar', and North arrow using 'Add North Arrow'.

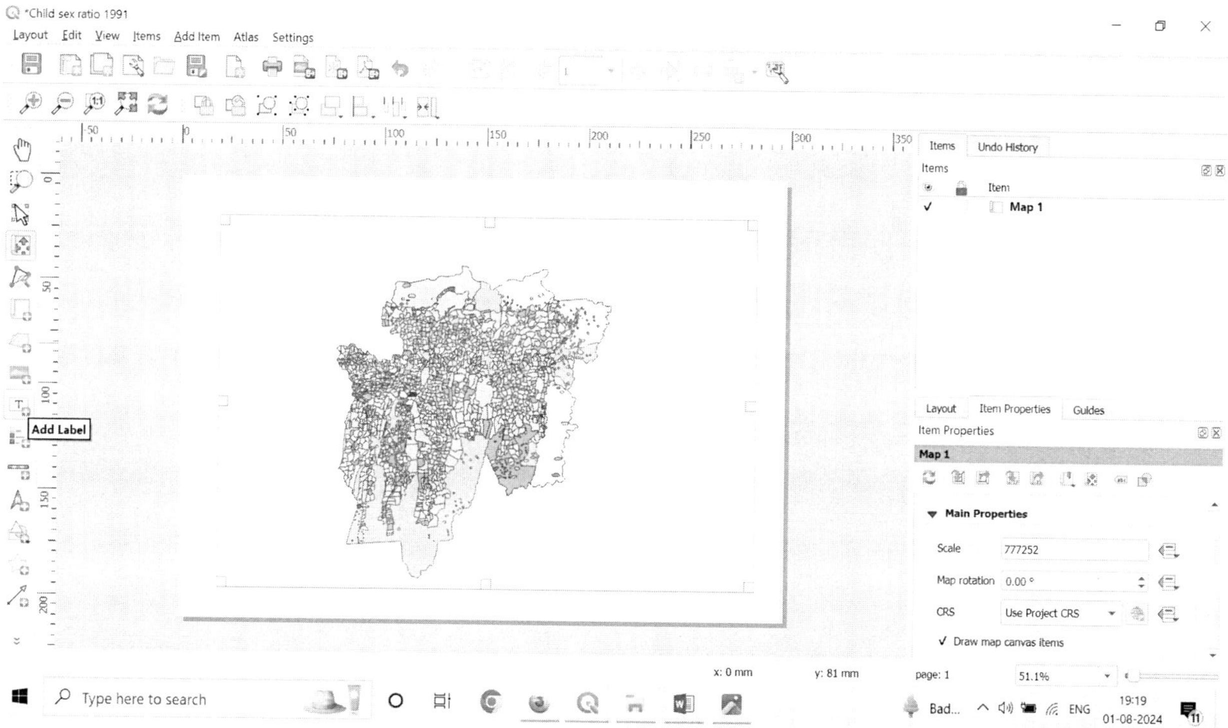

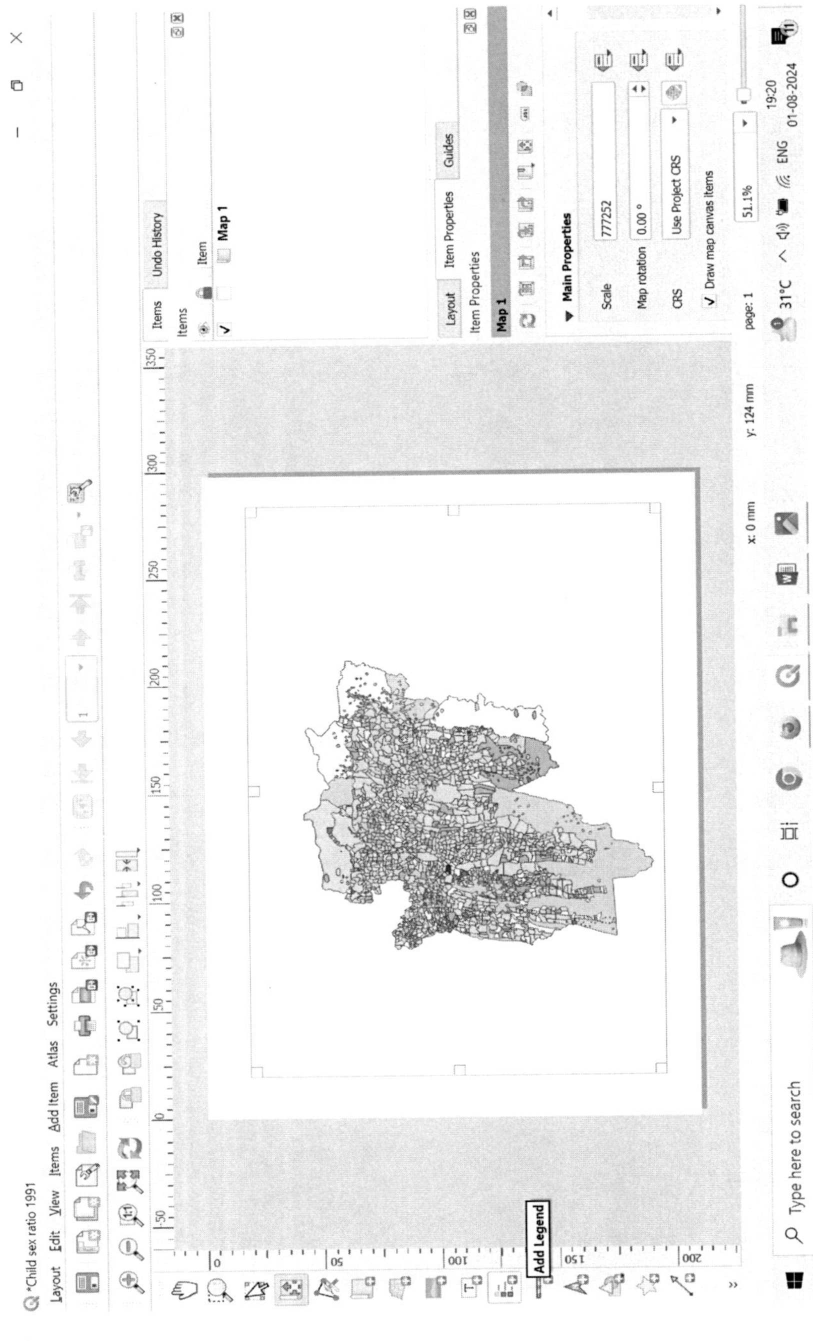
*Child sex ratio 1991
Layout Edit View Items Add Item Atlas Settings
Add Legend
Items
Undo History
Item
Map 1
Layout
Item Properties
Guides
Main Properties
Scale
777252
Map rotation
0.00 °
CRS
Use Project CRS
Draw map canvas items
x: 0 mm
y: 124 mm
page: 1
51.1%
Type here to search
31°C
ENG
19:20
01-08-2024

*Child sex ratio 1991
Layout Edit View Items Add Item Atlas Settings
Add Scale Bar
Items
Undo History
Item
Map 1
Layout
Item Properties
Guides
Main Properties
Scale
777252
Map rotation
0.00 °
CRS
Use Project CRS
Draw map canvas items
x: 0 mm
y: 140 mm
page: 1
51.1%
Type here to search
ENG
19:21
01-08-2024

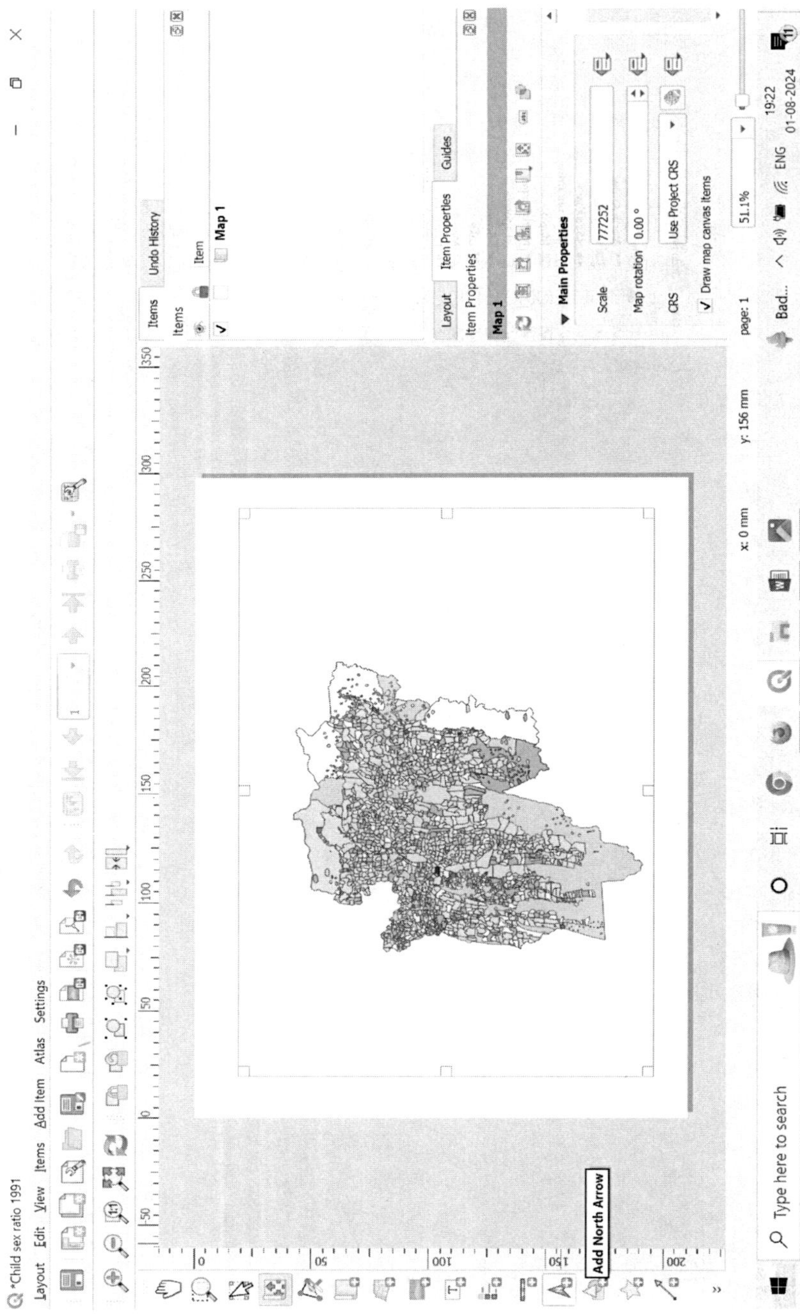
*Child sex ratio 1991
Layout Edit View Items Add Item Atlas Settings
Add North Arrow
Items Undo History
Map 1
Layout Item Properties Guides
Main Properties
Scale 777252
Map rotation 0.00 °
CRS Use Project CRS
Draw map canvas items
page: 1
51.1%
Type here to search
19:22
01-08-2024

(g) Now save the above map as image using 'Layout – Export as Image…', with an appropriate name and folder

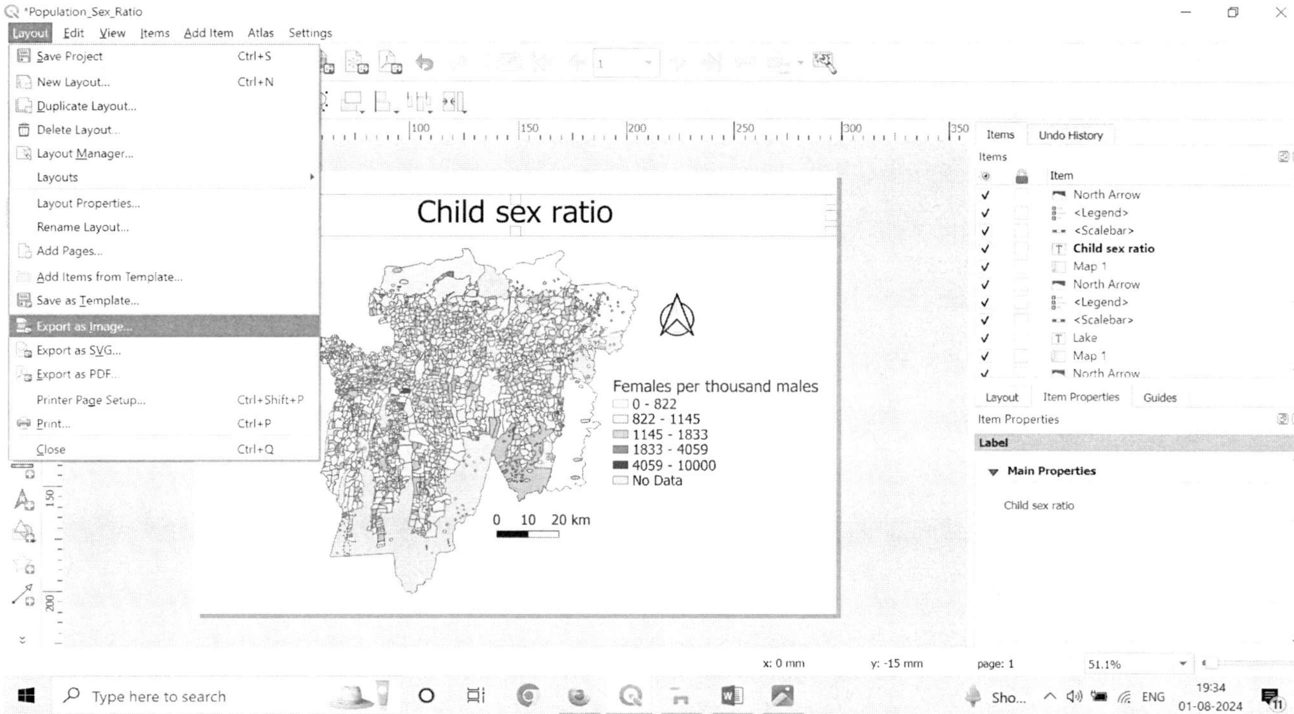

5. Repeat the same process for all the census variables and socio-economic indicators and save them as image.

The Study area

India is a union of states, with a total number of 28 states and 8 Union territories in the country (https://knowindia.india.gov.in/states-uts/). Assam is one of these twenty-eight states, which is constituted of thirty-five admininstrative districts within five divisions (https://assam.gov.in/about-us/396). Barak Valley is one of these five divisions made up of three districts namely Cachar, Hailakandi, and Karimganj (Fig. 1).

The Cachar district in southern Assam is geographically bounded by Barail and Jaintia hills on the north, Mizoram state towards south, Manipur state towards east, and Karimganj and Hailakandi districts towards west. The geographical area of the district is around 3800 km^2 (https://cachar.gov.in/portlets/district-profile). The central part of the district is more or less plain which is surrounded by hills. As per the district census handbook of Cachar (DCHB Cachar, 2011), the total population is over 17 lakhs with male population of over 8 lakhs 86 thousand, and female population of over 8 lakhs 50 thousand. Percentage of urban population is over 18 and remaining are rural population. The population growth rate during 2001 and 2011 is over twenty percent. The district has a sex ratio of 959 females per 1000 males and has a literacy of over 79%, with female literacy of 73.7% and male literacy of 84.8%. As per 2001 census, the scheduled caste population (SC) is over 15% and scheduled tribe (ST) population is over 1 %. Population density of the district is around 459 persons per km^2. As per the government portal there are 2 subdivisions, 5 revenue circles, 895 revenue villages, 15 development blocks, 15 community information center, 2 towns, 163 Gaon Panchayat, 7 legislative assembly constituencies (LAC), 1 house of parliament constituencies (HPC). The district Cachar is one of the two-hundred fifty most backward districts in India and has received fund from Backward Regions Grant Fund Programme (BRGF). The total working population in the district is 35% in which male and female constitute over 50% and 27% respectively. Remaining 65% of the population is non-worker. The four major categories of workers are cultivators, agricultural laborers, household industry worker, and other workers. There share in the population is around twenty percent, eleven percent, four percent, and sixty-five percent respectively

Hailakandi is another district in Barak Valley division. The district has 2 sub divisions, 4 revenue circles, 5 developmental blocks, 1 municipality board, 62 Gaon Panchayats, 289 revenue villages, 15 forest villages, 6 police stations, 3 legislative assembly constituencies (LAC), 1 house of parliament constituencies (HPC), 2 fire stations, and 35 bank branches (https://hailakandi.assam.gov.in/about-district/district-glance). The total geographical area of the district is over 1300 km^2. The total population is over 6 lakhs 59 thousand with the male population over 3 lakhs 37 thousand, and female population over 3 lakhs 21 thousand. The sex ratio in the district is around 951. The decadal growth rate in the population during 2001 and 2011 is over 21%. The literacy rate is over 74% with male and female literacy around 81% and 68% respectively. The population density is around 497 persons per km^2. Where as the rural population is over 92% and the urban population is over 7%, the percentage of SC and ST population is around 10% and 0.1% respectively (DCHB Hailakandi, 2011). Over thirty-two percent of the population is working and remaing over sixty-seven percent is non-workers. Within the working-class male percentage is over fifty and female percentage is over thirteen. The percentage of cultivators, agricultural laborers, household industry workers, and other workers comprise of around thirty, forteen, three, and fifty-one respectively.

The third district in the Barak Valley division is Karimganj. The district has 3 sub-divisions, 5 revenue circles, 7 developmental blocks, 1 municipality board, 96 Gaon panchayats, 1147 revenue villages, 15 forest villages 7 police stations, and 24 tea estates (https://karimganj.assam.gov.in/about-district/district-glance). The total geographical area of the district is over 1800 km^2. The total population is over 12 lakhs where male and female population is over 6 lakhs 25 thousand and over 6 lakhs 2 thousand respectively. Population density is around 679 persons per km^2. Sex ratio in the district is 963 which ranges from 961 to 982 for rural and urban areas respectively. Rural and urban population constitute around 91% and 9% respectively. The district has witnessed over 21 percent of decadal population growth during 2001 and 2011. Where as the average literacy rate is over 78%, male and female percentages are over 84 and over 72 respectively. Ramkrishna Nagar is the most populous and Badarpur is the least populous revenue circle in the district. There are 179 inhabited villages in south Karimganj community development (CD) block which is the highest, and 80 inhabited villages in Badarpur CD block which is the lowest in the district. Mirjapur Pt-I is the largest village and Barbari is the smallest village in the district, population wise. There are over

2 lakhs 47 thousand houses in the district. Where as main and marginal workers together contribute to over 32% of total population, males dominate with over 51% and female contribution is around 13%. Main workers individually constitute of around 24% of the population with male and female share of around 41 and 6 percentage respectively. Marginal

Fig. 1: Study area showing the three districts (Karimganj, Hailakandi, Cachar) of Assam state in India

worker constitutes over 8% with share of males is over 10% and that of females is 7%. Over 67% of the population is non-worker, and the male & female share is around 48% and 86% respectively. As per the census 2011, there are four major categories of workers, cultivators, agricultural laborers, household industry workers, and other workers. The percentage of main and marginal cultivators in the population is around 23 with male & female components of around 26% and 12%. The agricultural laborers in the main and marginal categories comprise over 16% with male and female percentage of over 16 and 18 respectively. Workers in household industry constitutes over 4% with male share of over 2% and female share around 13%. Other workers in main and marginal categories constitute roughly around 55% in total, male, and female each (DCHB Karimganj, 2011).

Total number of villages observed in Barak Valley in the present study is 2345. The highest number of villages are in Cachar district (1053), followed by Karimganj district (952), and Hailakandi district (340). The location of villages is given below (Fig. 2). For convenience the villages are numbered in the map and names are provided according to same numbers in the table which follows- (Table 1 to Table 3).

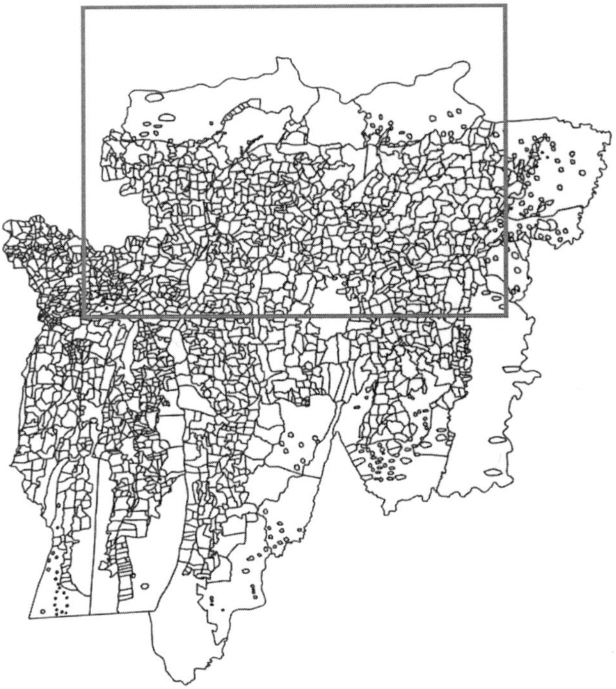

(a)

Fig. 2 (a-e). Villages in three districts in Barak valley with their serial numbers

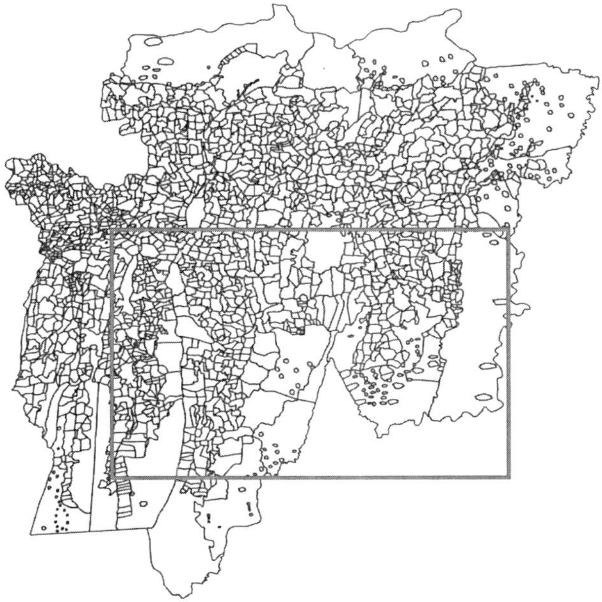

(b)

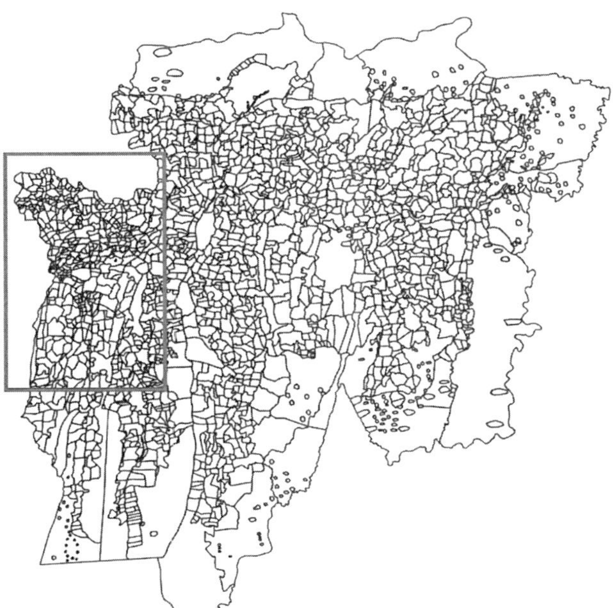

(c)

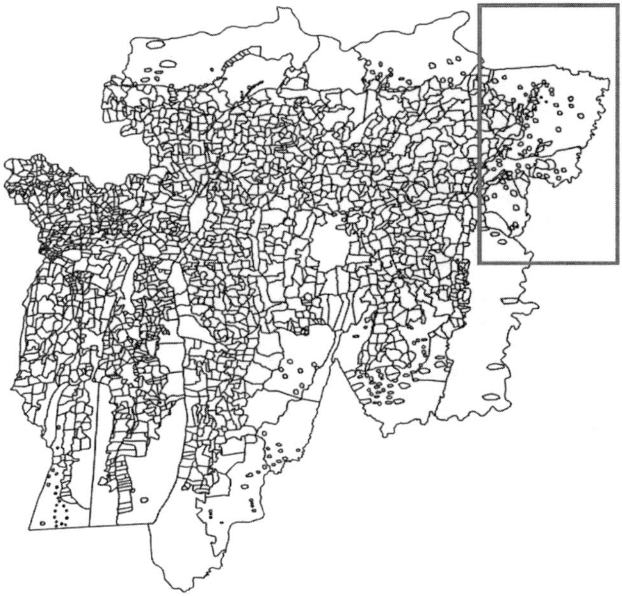

(d)

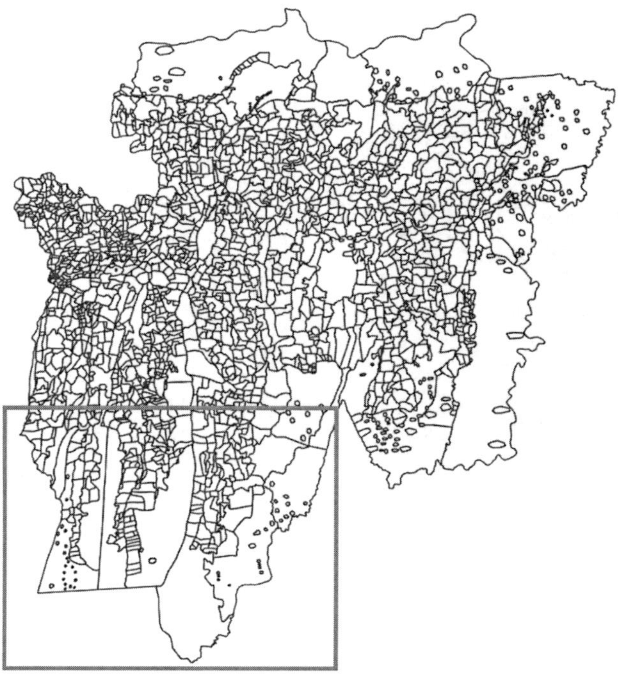

(e)

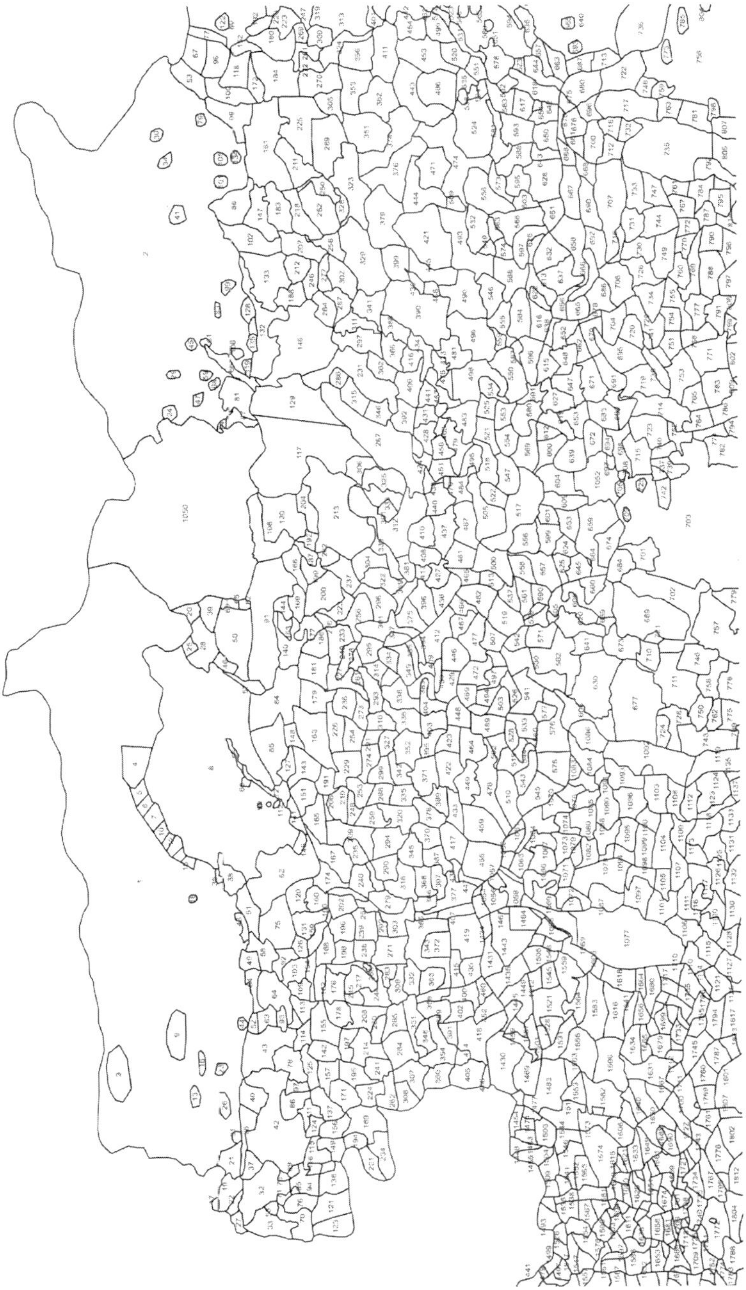

(a)

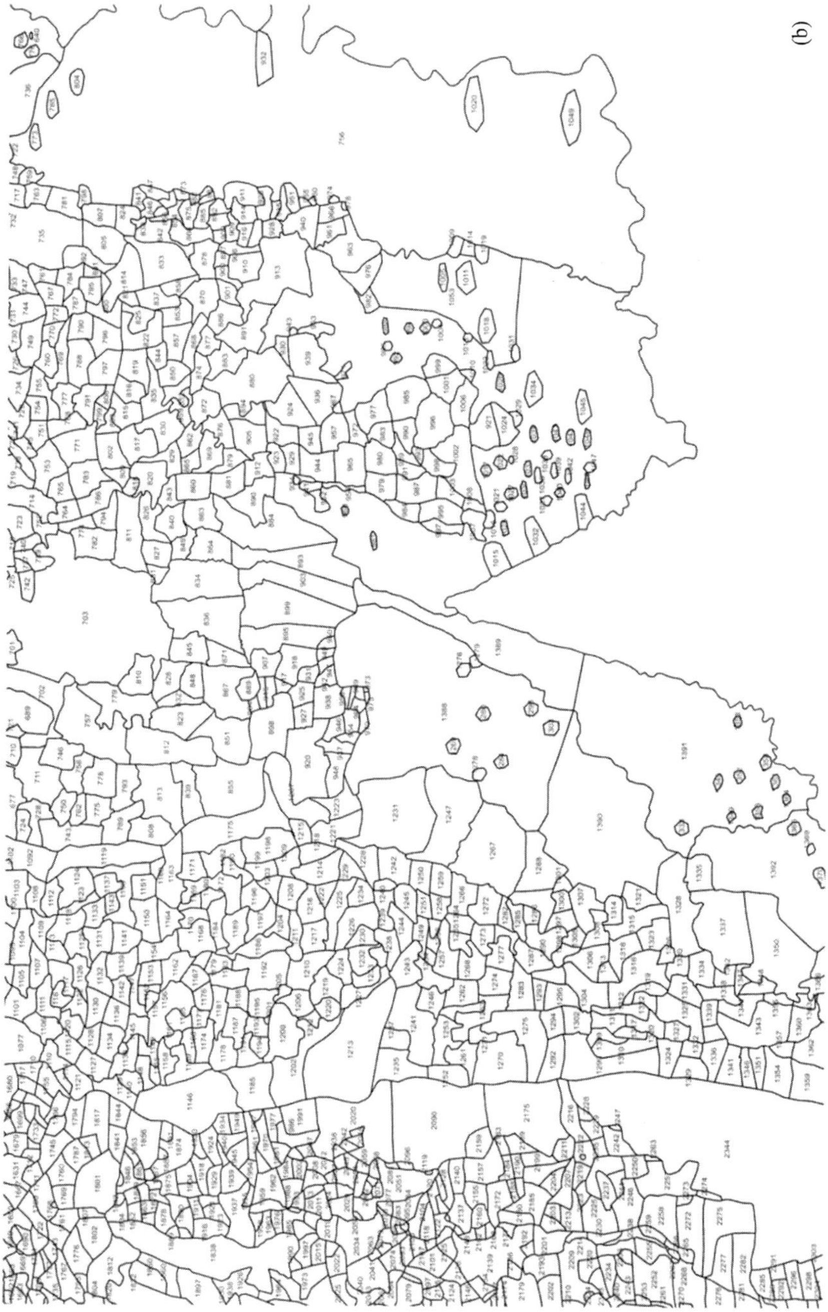

(b)

(c)

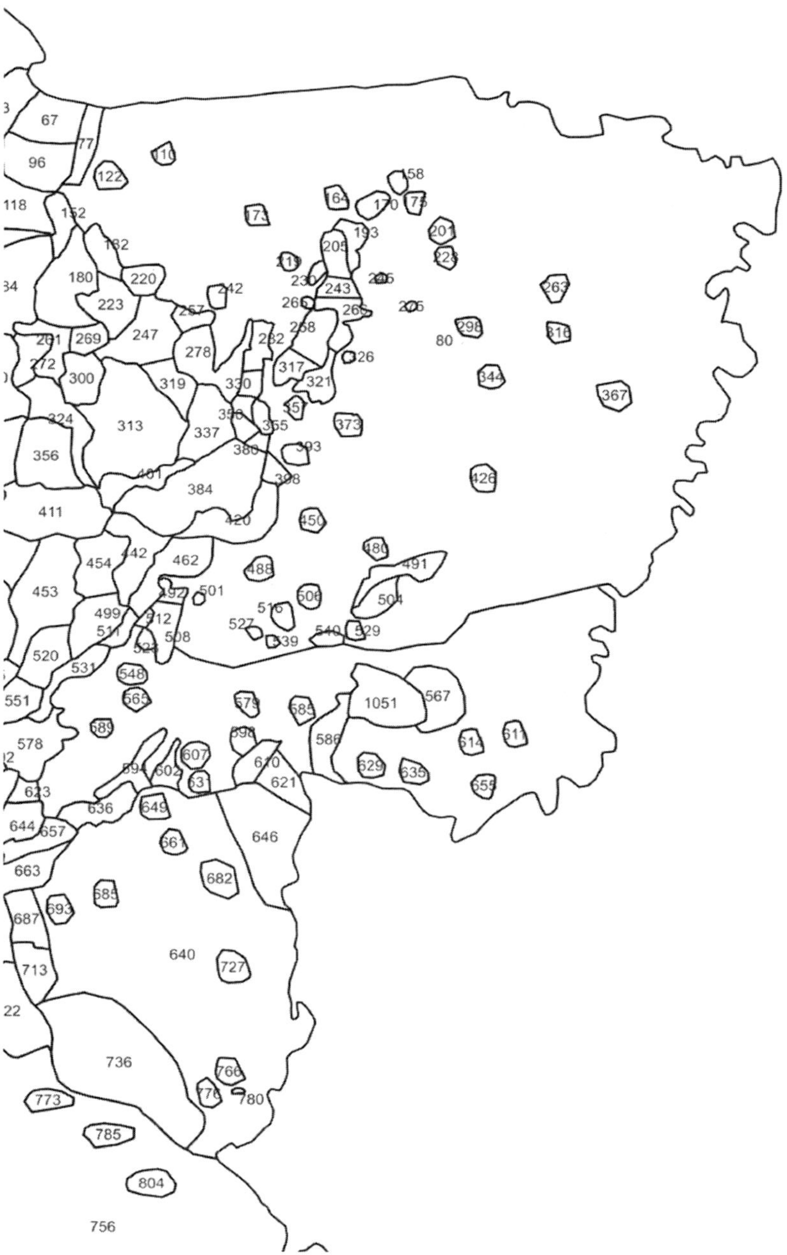
67
96
118
122
152
180
220
223
247
269
278
300
313
319
337
356
384
411
454
453
462
499
520
551
578
567
1051
586
621
646
640
682
713
736
773
785
804
756
80
367
501
491
243
205
193
170
158
321
317
373

(d)

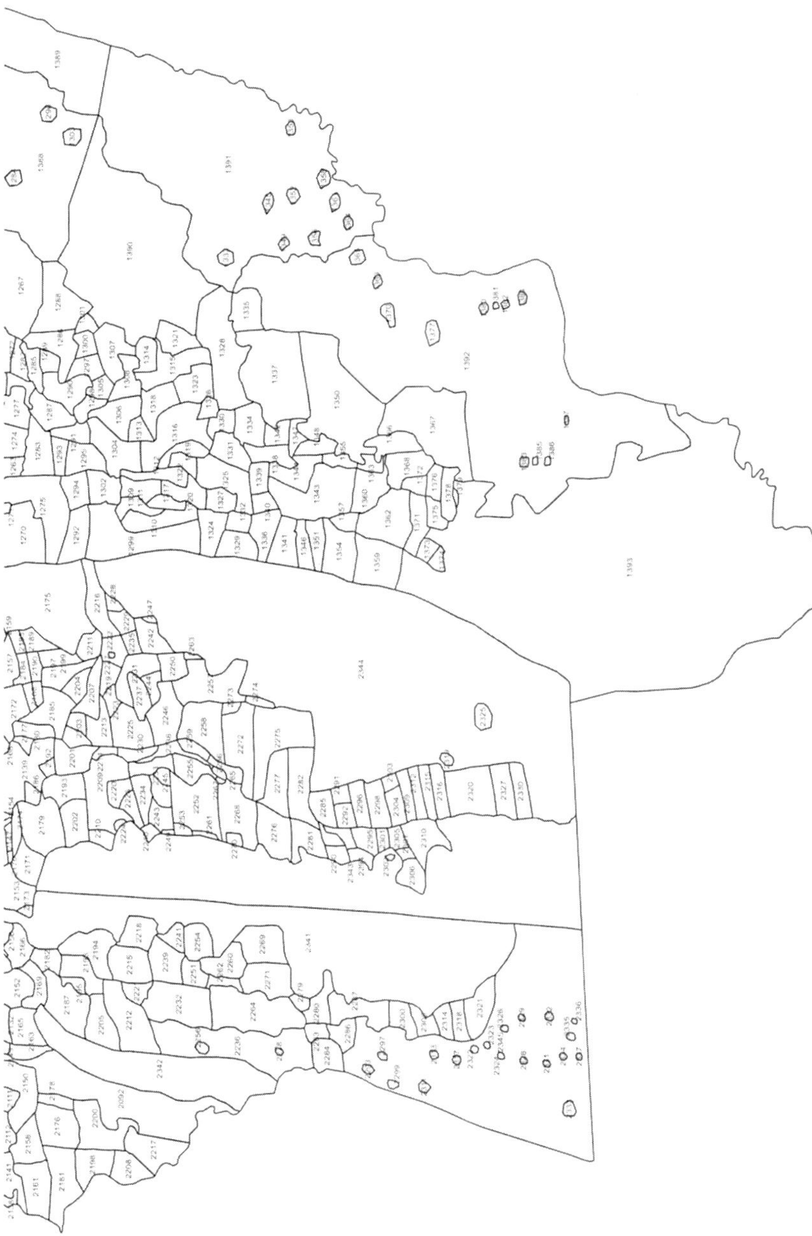

(e)

Table 1. Villages in Cachar District

S No	NAME	S No	NAME	S No	NAME	S No	NAME
1	Malidahar Mikir Punjee	265	Paschim Kumachara	529	U.S.Diglichur Punji	793	Chibitabichia Pt XI
2	Changsu Punji (Chanshu Punji)	266	Kumachara	530	Srikona Grant	794	Menipur Pt II
3	Makidahar Mikir Punjee	267	Borodudhpatil Grant	531	Tritya Dikchamukh	795	Nutan Ramnagar Pt IV
4	Daralcherra Khasia Punjee	268	Paschim Mutrachara	532	Alipur Cha Bagicha	796	Dakshin Mohanpur Pt VIII
5	Dimasa Punjee	269	Sonpur	533	Ghagrapar Pt II	797	Dakshin Mohanpur Pt IV
6	New Mesikiyar (New Machangjai)	270	Langlachera Pt II	534	Nutan Dayapur	798	Machkhal Pan Tangia Village
7	Oldoor Basti (Oldjuhar Basti)	271	Baraitoli Pt IV	535	Rangmaijeng Rengmai F.V.	799	Dakshin Mohanpur Pt I
8	Kayangthal	272	Joypur Pt IV	536	Tarapur Grant	800	Dakshin Mohanpur Pt VII
9	Isacherra Khasia Punjee	273	Heirbond Pt I	537	Tarapur Pt III	801	Nutan Ramnagar Pt V
10	Kayang Pur	274	Rangar Pt I	538	Mahalthal	802	Berabak Pt II
11	Laljar	275	Purba Kumachara	539	U.S. Chiru Punji (Us Charepunji)	803	Berabak Pt III
12	Kajakani (Khajakhan)	276	Ujan Gram	540	U.S. Lakhichera Pt VI	804	Naraindhar T.E.
13	Ailatal Khasia Punjee	277	Nayagram	541	Srikona Pt II	805	Chengsur Grant (Chenjur Grant)
14	Kayangpai	278	Thipunagar	542	David Sonapur	806	Dakshin Mohanpur Pt III
15	Newzer	279	Katirail T.E.	543	Sripur Pt II	807	Machkhal Pt II
16	Singduar Khasia Punjee	280	Burunga Pt IV	544	Ghagrapar Pt I	808	Chibitabichia Pt I
17	Suna Cherra Mikir Punji	281	Jarailtala	545	Salchapra Pt III	809	Berabak Pt I
18	Sailtadahar Khasia Punjee	282	Dharamnagar	546	Chandrapur Pt II	810	Irongmara
19	Lakhicherra Khasia Punjee	283	Baraitoli Pt III	547	Rongpur Pt IV	811	Clever House T.E.
20	Karbiland	284	Chandi Nagar Pt IV	548	U.S. Chur Punji Pt III	812	Rosekandi Grant Pt I
21	Dam Cherra Khasie Punjee	285	Chandi Nagar Pt V	549	Alipur Pt I	813	Salchapra T.E. (Shahpur T.E.)

22	Ratha Cherre Khasia Punjee	286	Larsingpar Basti	550	Kasipur Grant	814	Boaligrant
23	Isacherra Mikir Punjee	287	Chandi Ghat Pt II	551	Lalangkitta Labocpar Pt III	815	Nagdirgram Pt I
24	Katlir Punji	288	Bhangerpar Pt II	552	Digliriang Punji	816	Nutan Kanchanpur
25	Durgacherra Grant	289	Indragram T.E.	553	Berenga Pt V	817	Nagdirgram Pt II
26	Craigpark Mikir Punjee	290	Behara Pt VI	554	Berenga Pt IV	818	Narsingpur Pt I
27	Rathacherra Mikir Punjee	291	Rangar Pt II	555	Niz-Banskandi Pt IV	819	Bhaurikandi Pt I (Bhanri)
28	Sabajpur Bagicha	292	Baraitoli Pt V	556	Ambikapur Part-X	820	Clever House Pt IV
29	Atik Punji	293	Durgapur	557	Ambicapur Pt I	821	Kachudaram Pt I
30	Sungjang Punji (Sunjan)	294	Behara Pt V	558	Tarapur Pt V	822	Dakshin Mohanpur Pt V
31	Menam Mikir Punjee	295	Ujangram	559	Nutan Doyapore Chak	823	Rosekandi Grant Pt II
32	Baleswarpur Gnt (Baleswargrant)	296	Kalinagar Pt I	560	Salchapra Pt I	824	Machkhal Pt I
33	Natanpur Grant	297	Pangram Pt I	561	Tarapur Pt IV	825	Dakshin Mohanpur Pt VI
34	Euback Punjee	298	Kalinagar Pt I	562	Banadurpur Cha Bagicha	826	Clever House Pt III
35	Ailatal Mikir Punjee	299	Bhangerpar Pt IV	563	Monipur Kitta Dakshin Sonapur	827	Clever House Pt II
36	Kalain Cherra Grant	300	Kanakpur Pt IV	564	Lakhichera F.V Pt.II	828	Choto Jalenga Pt I
37	Rajagarh Khasia Punjee	301	Chesri	565	Kalam Naga Punji	829	Narsingpur Pt II
38	Ailatal (Ilatal)	302	Kaspur Bagerkona	566	Monipur Pt II	830	Nagdirgram Pt III
39	Damcherra East Tomas Punjee	303	Niz Katigorah Pt I	567	Santipur	831	Clever House Pt I
40	Kalain Cherra Bagicha	304	Boro Rampur Garden	568	Chandrapur Pt II	832	Choto Jalenga Pt II
41	Lutatal Punji	305	Langlachera Pt I	569	Berenga Pt III	833	Didarkosh Pt I
42	Talkar Grant	306	Leburbond	570	Bangala Ghat Grant	834	Derby T.E.
43	Craigpark Bagicha	307	Chandi Nagar Pt II	571	Indragarhgrant	835	Nagdirgram Pt IV
44	Boalcherra Khasia Punjee	308	Chandi Nagar Pt I	572	Banglaghat Pt I (Baglaghat)	836	Elanpur T.E.
45	Chalita Chara	309	Jagadishpur Pt I	573	Sibpur Pt III	837	Kachudaram Pt II

46	Elyas Khasia Punjee	310	Heirbond Pt II	574	Alipur Pt II	838	Bhubannagar Pt.VI
47	Fatik Punji	311	Chandi Ghat Pt III	575	Salchapra Pt II	839	Ratanpur Pt II
48	Bumbaital Mikir Punjee	312	Dudhpatil Pt I	576	Srikona Pt III	840	Bor Jalenga Pt XI
49	Bool Cherra	313	Kanakpur Pt III	577	Salchapra Grant	841	Unsurvey Bhubannagar
50	Tibong Chera Khasia Punjee	314	Chutra Sangan	578	Lalangkitta Labocpar Pt II	842	Didarkush Grant
51	Singduar T.E.	315	Jhapirbond Pt I	579	Makhan Nagar	843	Bor Jalenga Pt V
52	Boalcherra Mikir Punjee	316	Kalinagar Pt II	580	Kachipur Pt I	844	Bhaurikandi Pt II
53	Tatai Chara T.E.	317	Molong Pt II	581	Sibpur Pt I	845	Barjalenga Pt I
54	Kunapara Khasia Punjee	318	Mohanpur Pt I	582	Indragarh Block	846	Mohanpur
55	Bhauripara Pt II	319	Doloichera	583	Lalangkitta Labocpar Pt I	847	Bhubannagar Pt VIII (Pt VI)
56	Baikam Khasia Punjee	320	Sewti Pt IV	584	Niz-Banskandi Pt III	848	Bor Jalenga Grant
57	Katlichara Grant (Bagicha)	321	Harinagar	585	Kharjan Punji	849	Bor Jalenga Pt X
58	Mejenta T.E.	322	Kalinagar Garden	586	Digligaon	850	Bidrohipar
59	Baroidisha Punji	323	Kumbhirgram T.E.	587	Badripar	851	Choto Jalenga Grant
60	Bandar Khal Punjee	324	Salamatpur Pt II	588	Lalang Pt III	852	Sundari Pt I
61	Daya Disha Punji	325	Gorer Bond Pt II	589	Cherenga Punji	853	Kachudaram Pt III
62	Karkari T.E.	326	Purba Dakhin Mutrachara	590	Bajantipur Pt I	854	Bhubannagar Pt IV
63	Gilatail (Ghilatail)	327	Rangar Pt III(Rangghar Pt III)	591	Kachipur Pt II	855	Ratanpur Pt I
64	Kunapara Grant	328	Digar Khaspur	592	Lalang Kitta Labocpar Pt V	856	Bhubannagar Pt V
65	Durbin Tilla Punji	329	Kaspur Grant	593	Lalang Pt II	857	Kachudaram Pt IV
66	Madhupur (Madhvpur)	330	U.S. Dharamnagar	594	U.S. Labongkhal Pt IV	858	Didarkosh Pt II
67	Digun Chara Grant	331	Chandi Nagar Pt VI	595	Lalang Pt IV	859	Rukni Pt I (Rukhi Pt I)
68	Daya Punji	332	Jagadishpur Pt II	596	Niz-Banskandi Pt I	860	Bor Jalenga Pt VI
69	Deswali Basti	333	Mulidahar Grant	597	Chirirpar Pt I	861	Nayagram

70	Natanpur	334	Bhairab Nagar	598	U.S. Umednagar Pt II	862	Narsingpur Pt III
71	Karaballe Grant	335	Bhangerpar Pt III	599	Ambicapur Pt VIII	863	Barjalenga Pt III
72	Bhauripara Pt I	336	Chandpur Pt IV	600	Berenga Pt II	864	Barjalenga Pt IX (Pt XI)
73	Digor Mahadevpur	337	Chatridoyal (Charatdagal)	601	Uttar Krishnapur Part-I	865	Narsingpur Pt IV
74	Indragram Pt II	338	Barjatrapur	602	Uttar Lalpani	866	Thankimnagar Pt I
75	Baikuntapur T.E.	339	Kharil Bagicha	603	Uzan Tarapur	867	Choto Jalenga Pt III
76	Biswambarpur	340	Raninagar	604	Uttar Krishnapur Pt II	868	Boalihaor
77	Lailchara (Langlachera)	341	Arunabond T.E.	605	Bangalaghat Pt II (Bagaighat)	869	Narsingpur Pt V
78	Gobindakupa	342	Bhangerpar Pt V	606	Digorsrikona Pt I	870	Didarkosh Pt IV
79	Akai Punji	343	Jagadishpur Pt III	607	U.S. Uttar Lalpani Pt V	871	Bar Jalenga Pt II
80	Harinagar Khasia Punji	344	Naithang Punji	608	Chenglorie Grant	872	Rukni Pt II
81	Amaranagar T.E.	345	Gobindapur Pt I	609	Kanakpur Part-II	873	Panichowki
82	Durgacharra Punjee	346	Jhapirbond Pt II	610	Umed Nagar	874	Sundari Pt II
83	Boronagadum Punji	347	Purandarpur	611	Lakhinagar F.V.	875	Bhubannagar Pt III
84	Sonachera Grant	348	Chandi Nagar Pt III	612	Berenga Pt I	876	Punirmukh
85	Kalibari Grant	349	Krishna Pur	613	Chandrapur Pt III	877	Sundari Pt III
86	Rajyeswarpur Pt I	350	Pahelpur	614	Lakhichera F.V. Pt I	878	Didarkosh Pt III
87	Indragram Pt I	351	Thailu Cha Bagicha	615	Badripar Pt I	879	Narsingpur Pt VI
88	Nastsul	352	Chandpur Pt III	616	Niz-Banskandi Pt II	880	Rukni T.E.
89	Kushierkul (Kushiyarkul)	353	Jaipur Grant Pt II	617	Lalang Pt I	881	Bor Jalenga Pt VII
90	Un-Survey Kaminipur	354	Hari Nagar Pt IV	618	Digor Fulertol Pt I	882	Kusumpur
91	Panichar Grant	355	Paschim Dikcha	619	Dadripar Pt V (Badrapar V)	883	Rukni Pt III
92	Kalibari T.E.	356	Jaipur Pt III	620	Natun Kanchanpur	884	Paloipunji T.E.
93	Iltargul	357	Molong Pt I	621	Jirighat Cha Bagicha Pt II	885	Bhubannagar Pt I

94	Tarapur	358	Karai Kandi Pt I	622	Ratanpur	886	Sundari Pt IV
95	Gumra Grant	359	Teli Tikar Pt I	623	Lalang Kitta Labocpar Pt IV	887	Bhubannagar Pt II
96	Gunti Bari Grant	360	Hari Nagar Pt I	624	Ambicapur Pt VII	888	Sonapur
97	Chandipur (Chondipur)	361	Gorer Bond Pt I	625	Ambicapur Pt II	889	Borosalganga T.V.
98	Icha Chara (Jehachera Garden)	362	Pangram Pt II	626	Monipur Pt I	890	Barjalenga Pt IV
99	Laibong Punji (Haibongpunji)	363	Jagadishpur Pt V	627	Badripar Pt IV	891	Rukni Pt IV
100	Mati Chara T.E.	364	U.S. Natun Chandrapur	628	Niz-Lakhipur Pt III	892	Thankimnagar Pt IV
101	Lailong Chara Punji	365	Niz Katigorah Pt II	629	Lakhichera F.V. Pt II	893	Gopinathpur Khasia Punji
102	Gua Bari	366	Siddeswar Pt I (Sidheswar-I)	630	Digorsrikona Pt II	894	Rakhaltila
103	Saligram (Choligram)	367	Bhola Punji	631	Howkip Punji	895	Taranathpur Pt I
104	Noonchuri Boro Punjee	368	Mohanpur Pt II	632	Singerbond Pt III	896	Bhubannagar Pt VII
105	Lailong Chara	369	Kalinagar Pt II	633	Ambicapur Pt XI	897	Ganganagar Pt IV
106	Nuton Suka Punji	370	Gobindapur Pt II	634	Bajantipur Pt II	898	Duarbond Grant
107	Kaiyajani	371	Chandpur Pt I	635	Lakhinagar Ext. F.V.	899	Taranathpur Pt II
108	Abongchara Grant Pt II	372	Jagadishpur Pt IV	636	Chalitartol	900	Ganganagar Pt III
109	Bhatt Gram	373	U.S. Harinagar	637	Singerbond Pt II	901	Ganganagar Pt II
110	Langkhal Punji	374	Salamatpur Pt I	638	Gobindapur Pt III	902	Thankimnagar Pt II
111	Rajyeswarpur Pt II(Rajeswarpur	375	Badarpur Pt I	639	Gangapur	903	Gopinathpur T.E.
112	Noonchuri Punjee	376	Bandhu Cha Bagicha	640	Lowarjiri P.T.V.	904	Chotosalganga F.V.
113	Maugram	377	Sidhipur	641	Elgin Grant	905	Malugram
114	Khelma Pt VIII	378	Tarinipur Pt I	642	Nayagram	906	Ganganagar Pt V
115	Mahadevpur Pt I	379	Scotpur Cha Bagicha	643	Niz-Lakhipur Pt II	907	Jogirbond Grant
116	Nishchinta Pur	380	U.S. Dikcha	644	Digor Fulertol Pt II	908	Chotojalenga T.V.
117	Madhurapur Grant	381	Ardvallik	645	Ambicapur Pt III	909	Thankimnagar Pt III

118	Aina Chara T.E.	382	Jaipur Grant Pt I	646	Jirighat Cha Bagicha Pt I	910	Ganganagar Pt I
119	Ratanpur	383	Pratapi Para	647	Badripar Pt III	911	Ganganagar Pt XIII
120	Karkari Pt II	384	Baladhan Grant	648	Badripar Pt II	912	Bor Jalenga Pt VIII
121	Niz-Jalalpur Pt II	385	Sarail	649	Khairabad Fv(Old Khairabad Fv)	913	Dharmikhal Grant
122	Rema Punji	386	Pangram Pt III	650	Lakhipur	914	Ganganagar Pt VII
123	Rangpur	387	Gobindapur Pt III	651	Chirirpar Pt II	915	Jalengachara Grant
124	Talkar Beel	388	Doyapore Pt I	652	Durgapur	916	Ganganagar Pt VI
125	Paikan	389	Tarinipur Pt II	653	Neairgram Pt I	917	Chotojalenga Pt IV
126	Sundeura	390	Doyapore Grant	654	Niz-Lakhipur Pt I	918	Noarbond Grant
127	Gorer Iltor Pt I	391	Niz Hari Tikar Pt I	655	Alubaja	919	Ganganagar Pt VIII
128	Jorju Punji	392	Latigram (Lathigram)	656	Singerbond Pt I	920	Bag-O-Bahar T.E.
129	Hatichara Grant	393	U.S. Durga Nagar Khasia Punji	657	Digor Fulertol Pt III	921	Garultolaekth F.V.
130	Subang Garden	394	Dubag	658	Singerbond Pt IV	922	Dulalgram
131	Karkari Pt I	395	Chandpur Pt II	659	Ambicapur Pt VI	923	Ramprasadpur
132	Nagadung Bhudharbond	396	Badarpur Pt II	660	Bajantipur Pt III	924	Sukhtala
133	Nagadung Agustnagar	397	Noon Nagar (Nurnagar)	661	New Khairabad F.V.	925	Baluchari F.V.
134	Khuli Cherra U.S.	398	U.S Molong	662	Algapur Pt I	926	Ganganagar Pt IX
135	Soraipur	399	Majargram Grant	663	Fulertol	927	Duarbond Basti (Duarbond)
136	Dinanathpur Bagicha	400	Karai Kandi Pt II	664	Ambicapur Pt IV	928	Sentcatherine
137	Saraspur	401	Kanakpur Pt II	665	Sibpur Pt I	929	Lantugram
138	Niz-Jalalpur Pt I	402	Teli Tikar Pt II(Talitikar II)	666	Niz-Rupairbali	930	Bharampur
139	Haroi Punji	403	Chandpur Pt V	667	Singer Bond Pt V	931	Sonachera Pt I
140	Narainchara Grant	404	Buribali Pt I	668	Binnakandi Pt II	932	Tupidahar F.V.
141	Daralcherra	405	Hari Nagar Pt II	669	Pachim Biroinhowar	933	Ganganagar Pt XI

142	Khelma Pt VI	406	Durga Nagar Part-V	670	Lakhipur Grant	934	Ramprasabpur
143	Gorer Iltor Pt II	407	Siddeswar Pt II	671	Bagpur Pt II	935	Ganganagar Pt X
144	Mainachara (Moirachara)	408	Masimpur Pt II	672	Dhamalia	936	Bhubandahar Pt I
145	Bichitrapur	409	Peladahar	673	Chengduar Pt I	937	Bag-O-Bahar Pt IV
146	Chandighat Grant	410	Dudhpatil Pt II	674	Ambicapur Pt V	938	Bag-O-Bahar Pt II
147	Mamad Pur	411	Jaipur Pt II	675	Binnakandi Pt I	939	Bhubandahar Pt II
148	Chandranath Pur	412	Niz-Joynagar	676	Kaptanpur Pt VII	940	Mohankhal
149	Mahadevpur Pt II	413	Masimpur Grant	677	Alambag	941	Rajanikhal
150	Pirnagar	414	Hari Nagar Pt III	678	Gobindapur Pt II	942	Loharbond
151	Dinanath Pur Grant	415	Lahamali	679	Algapur Pt II	943	Darmitol F.V. (Darmi)
152	Chirirpar Kachari Punji	416	Durganagar Pt VI	680	Dilkhosh Grant	944	Sadagram (Sapagram)
153	Kachari Gaon	417	Sibnarain Pur	681	Kaptanpur Pt VI	945	Mahadevpur
154	Brahman Gram	418	Niz Hari Tikar Pt II	682	Lalpani	946	Bag-O-Bahar Pt III
155	Khelma Pt VII	419	Niz Katigorah Pt III	683	Neairgram Pt II	947	Loharbond F.V.
156	Mahadevpur Pt IV	420	Durganagar	684	Jaifarpur	948	Bag-O-Bahar Pt V
157	Khelma Pt I	421	Dulalgram Grant	685	Lowerjiri T.V.	949	Sonachera Pt II
158	Marchakhal Punji	422	Dudpur Pt I	686	Sibpur Pt II	950	Sonachera Pt III
159	Dumkar	423	Dudpur Pt III	687	Natun Fulertol	951	Ganganagar Pt XII
160	Karkari Pt III	424	Durganagar Pt I	688	Kaptanpur Pt IV	952	Gurudayalpur
161	Patichara T.E. (Puthicharagrant	425	Chalita Kandi	689	Merua Grant	953	Tupidahar Pt I
162	Tarapur	426	Diglang Phailen Punji	690	Kaptanpur Pt III	954	Newbag Bahar F.V.
163	95 Bsf Camp Damchera	427	Masimpur Bagicha	691	Bagpur Pt III	955	Unsurvey Nimaipur
164	Molong Punji	428	Durganagar Pt II	692	Kaptanpur Pt.	956	Arjanpur
165	Behara Pt I (Bihara Pt I)	429	Buribali Pt II	693	Alni F.V.	957	Debipur

166	Balichara Grant Pt I	430	Raipur	694	Dakhin Krishnapur	958	Nagathal F.V.
167	Burunga Pt II	431	Durganagar Pt IV	695	Satkarakandi Pt I	959	Old Bagbahar
168	Lakhipur Pt I(Lakshanipur Pt I	432	Panch Gram	696	Roberpur	960	Bhubankhal F.V.
169	Balichara Grant Pt II	433	Tarinipur Pt III	697	Sabashpur (Sabujpur)	961	Rammaniayapur
170	Dipuchera	434	Doyapore Pt II	698	Saidpur Pt I	962	Bag-O-Bahar Pt I
171	Khelma Pt II	435	Lathimara (Latimara)	699	Bagpur Pt I	963	Maniyarkhal Chabagicha
172	Kartul Pahar	436	Masimpur Pt I (Maohimpur)	700	Kaptanpur Pt V	964	Ikrathal F.V.
173	Jinam Paithe Punji	437	Dudhpatil Pt III	701	Tarutajabari Pt I	965	Saptagram
174	Burunga Pt I	438	Dudhpatil Pt VIII	702	Kathal Grant	966	Nagakhal
175	Bijung Punji	439	Majhargram Basti (Masurgram)	703	Silcoorie Grant	967	Bhubandhar
176	Bhairabpur Pt V	440	Dudhpatil Grant	704	Gobindapur Pt I	968	Gurudayalpur F.V.
177	Anwarpur	441	Durganagar Pt III	705	Uttar Krishnapur Pt III	969	Boro Salganga F.V.
178	Bhairabpur Pt I	442	Kanakpur Pt I	706	Kaptanpur Pt I	970	Pratappur F.V.
179	Dhalchara Grant	443	Barthal Grant	707	Chotomanda T.E.	971	Tupidahar Pt II
180	Sibnagar	444	Narainpur Grant Pt II	708	Uttar Krishnapur Pt IV	972	Gajalghat
181	Harinchara Grant	445	Latigram Grant (Lathigram)	709	Niz Chatla Howar	973	Nuwagang F.V.
182	Choto Kumbi	446	Buribali Pt III	710	Chengduar Pt II	974	Bhubankhal
183	Patimara T.E. (Puthimaragrant)	447	Balirbond	711	Chibitabichia Pt VI	975	Nokafella F.V.
184	Bren Nagar (Boren Nagar)	448	Ganirgram Pt IV	712	Kaptanpur Pt X	976	Katanpur Grant
185	Natanpur	449	Niz-Fulbari Pt II	713	Dakhin Fulertol	977	Jibangram
186	Ujan Nagar	450	Phailen Punji (Phaigal Punji)	714	Sonabarighat Pt II	978	Smitnagar F.V.
187	Abongchara Grant Pt I	451	Gossaipur Pt V	715	Saidpur Pt II	979	Loknathpur
188	Taligram	452	Madar Pur	716	Baramanda Grant	980	Islamabad
189	Niz Leverpute Pt II (Lavarputa	453	Lediachara Grant	717	Tilka Grant (Tika T.E.)	981	Hatalmara F.V.

190	Bhangerpar	454	Jaipur Pt I	718	Kaptanpur Pt VIII	982	Anandakhal
191	Gora Gram	455	Kalinagar	719	Dhanehari Pt I	983	Tilanagar
192	Chotorampur Grant	456	Tuker Gram	720	Jhanjarbali (Jhanjambali)	984	Joydhanpur
193	Uttar Dipu	457	Durganagar Pt VII	721	Gangapur	985	Mathurapur
194	Mahadevpur Pt III	458	Gossaipur Pt IV	722	Monkhosh Grant	986	Karkat Basti F.V.
195	Khelma Pt III	459	Niz-Fulbari Pt I	723	Sonabarighat Pt I	987	Rajghat
196	Lakhipur Pt II	460	Nazat Pur	724	Tapang Pt II	988	Jabha F.V.
197	Khelma Pt V	461	Masughat	725	Borakhai Grant	989	Saraspur
198	Baraitoli Pt I	462	Simla Dikchamukh	726	Kaptanpur Pt Xvii	990	Raraipunjee
199	Rampur Garden	463	Gossaipur Pt II	727	Baghkhal F.V.	991	Bangram
200	Bijoypur Grant	464	Dudpur Pt II	728	Chibitabichia Pt IV	992	Hathikhal F.V.
201	Boro Tulpi Punji	465	Tupkhana Pt I	729	Dungripar Pt II	993	Khashpur
202	Manipur Pt I	466	Balighat	730	Kaptanpur Pt Xv	994	Gorkhal F.V.
203	Karkari Pt IV	467	Kumarpara	731	Kaptanpur Pt XIv	995	Howaithang
204	Barabond	468	Purba Doyapore	732	Kaptanpur Pt IX	996	Rajnagar
205	Paschim Dipu	469	Nischintapur	733	Kaptanpur Pt.XI	997	Laylapur
206	Behara Pt II	470	Doyapore Pt IV	734	Kaptanpur Pt Xviii	998	Rajgobindapur
207	Tikalpar Basti	471	Narainpur Grant Pt I	735	Binnakandi Grant	999	Bishnupur
208	Bhairabpur Pt II	472	Manikpur	736	Alni Grant	1000	Metnathal F.V.
209	Behara Pt III	473	Doyapore Pt III	737	Bariknagar Pt I	1001	Bidyaratanpur
210	Sewti Pt I (Santi Pt I)	474	Sibpur Pt II	738	Satkarakandi Pt II	1002	Shymacharanpur
211	Kumbha T.E. (Kumbhir T.E.)	475	Istampur Grant (Estampurgrant)	739	Saidpur Pt III	1003	Channighat
212	Digartali Gram	476	Dudhpatil Pt VII	740	Saidpur Pt IV	1004	Chekavcham F.V.

213	Dalu Grant	477	Rakhal Khaler Par Pt I	741	Dungripar Pt I	1005	Dhalakhal F.V.
214	Khelma Pt IV	478	Niz-Fulbari Pt III	742	Bariknagar Pt II	1006	Narayanpur
215	Bhiairabpur	479	Gossaipur Pt III	743	Tapang Pt I	1007	Frenchnagar
216	Bijoypur	480	U.S. Diglang Punji	744	Kaptanpur Pt XIII	1008	Aradhanpur
217	Digabar Grant	481	Chappanahal Grant	745	Tundurkandi (Jundurkandi)	1009	Machkhal F.V.
218	Tikalpar Grant	482	Tarapur Pt I	746	Chibitabichia Pt VII	1010	Anandakhal F.V.
219	Baigajigni (Balgagni)	483	Gossaipur Pt I	747	Kaptanpur Pt XII	1011	Krishnapur F.V.
220	Borokumbi Punji	484	Dudhpatil Pt VI	748	Lileanpur	1012	Jamalpur
221	Bhatarchak	485	Algapur	749	Kaptanpur Pt Xvi	1013	Gamalpur
222	Rampur	486	Lalang Grant	750	Chibitabichia Pt V	1014	Bhubanhill F.V.
223	Boro Kumbi	487	Dudhpatil Pt IV	751	Majhirgram	1015	French Nagar F.V.
224	Saidpur Pt I	488	U.S. Durga Nagar	752	Saidpur Pt V	1016	Khulichora F.V.
225	Suna Tula T.E.	489	Ganirgram Pt III	753	Dhanipur	1017	Sewrartol F.V.
226	Sunapur Pt II	490	Badri Par	754	Tulargram Pt I (Julorgram Pt I	1018	Sonitnagar F.V.
227	Bhitor Gangapur Pt I	491	Diglang Punji	755	Uttar Mohanpur	1019	Kalakhal F.V.
228	Choto Tulpi Punji	492	Budhan Nagar	756	Robipur F.V.	1020	Chandikhal F.V. (Chandghat Fv)
229	Sunapur Pt I (Sonapur Pt I)	493	Palerbond Grant(P.B.Grant T.E)	757	Barsangan Grant	1021	Hadma
230	U.S. Mutrachara	494	Patheri Gram	758	Chibitabichia Pt VIII	1022	Tulartal F.V.
231	Larsingpar Grant	495	Bahadurpur	759	Robipur Grant	1023	Bhubankhal Pt I F.V.
232	Dalu Gram	496	Digar Khasipur Grant	760	Rangirghat Pt II	1024	Khulichara
233	Niz-Borkhola Pt I	497	Hatirhar Pt I(Matirhar Pt I)	761	Nutanramnagar Pt II	1025	Napitkhal Panjum F.V.
234	Niz Leverpute Pt I(Lavarputa I	498	Arcuttepur Grant	762	Chibitabichia Pt III	1026	Punihowar F.V.
235	Behara Pt IV	499	Kamranga Bond Pt I	763	Machkhal Pt III	1027	Bagewallah F.V.
236	Bhitor Gangapur Pt II	500	Tarapur Pt VI	764	Dhanehari Pt II	1028	Borkhal F.V

237	Boro Rampur	501	U.S Budhan Nagar	765	Dhanehari Pt III	1029	Satkarakandi
238	Baraitoli Pt II	502	Ganirgram Pt II	766	Kapakhal F.V.	1030	Jamirkhal F.V.
239	Lakhipur Pt III	503	Mahadevpur	767	Nutanramnagar Pt I	1031	Bhutankhal Pt II F.V.
240	Burunga Pt III	504	Digli Grant	768	Tulargram Pt II	1032	Phainung F.V.
241	Saidpur Pt III	505	Dudhpatil Pt V	769	Rangirghat Pt I	1033	Suparikhal F.V.
242	U.S. Digor Mutrachera	506	Sigli Chur Punji	770	Gobindanagar Pt I	1034	Mohanpur
243	Dipu	507	Rakhalkhalerpar Pt II	771	Kajidahar Pt I	1035	Nagakhal
244	Bhairabpur Pt III	508	Dikcha Punji	772	Rangirghat Pt III	1036	Dhalaikhal F.V.
245	U.S. Anandapur	509	Monipur Kitta Uttar Sonapur	773	Robipur Punji	1037	Radhanagar F.V.
246	Siberbond	510	Sripur Pt I	774	Menipur Pt I	1038	Dhanipur
247	Uttar Doloichara	511	Dikcha Grant	775	Chibitabichia Pt IX	1039	Lailapur
248	Sewti Pt III	512	U.S Kamranga Punji	776	Gurkhakhal F.V.	1040	Garultala F.V.
249	Kashipur	513	Tupkhana Pt II	777	Gobindanagar Pt II	1041	Khulichara Mizo Sec
250	Purba Salganga	514	Srikona Pt I	778	Chibitabichia Pt X	1042	Barmannagar F.V.
251	Manipur Pt II	515	Ganirgram Pt I	779	Tarutazabari Pt II	1043	Kalahawar F.V.
252	Salganga Grant	516	Boma Punji (Dona Punji)	780	Sabughat F.V.	1044	Bishnupur F.V.
253	Bhangarpar-I	517	Silchar	781	Ulai Punji	1045	Pancherrah F.V.
254	Sunapur Pt III	518	Rangpur Pt III	782	Sildubi Grant	1046	Natacherrah F.V.
255	Bhairabpur Pt VI	519	Tarapur Pt II	783	Kajidahar Pt II	1047	Dhalakhal F.V.
256	Niz-Borkhola Pt II	520	Kamranga Bond Pt II	784	Nutanramnagar Pt III	1048	Soranagar (Goranagar)
257	U.S. Uttar Doloichara	521	Rongpur Pt II	785	Naraindhar P.T.V.	1049	Tulartol F.V. (Fulertol F.V.)
258	Salganga Par	522	Silchar Part-X	786	Kajidahar Pt III	1050	Barail R.F.
259	Sewti Pt II	523	U.S Dikcha Basti	787	Dakshin Mohanpur Pt XI	1051	Forest
260	Salimabad	524	Laboc Grant	788	Dakshin Mohanpur Pt IX	1052	Forest

261	Kanakpur Pt V	525	Rongpur Pt I	789	Chibitabichia Pt II	1053	Forest
262	Saidpur Pt II	526	Hatirhar Pt II	790	Dakshin Mohanpur Pt X		
263	Tuiset Punji	527	Singa Punji (Suiga Punji)	791	Dakshin Mohanpur Pt II		
264	Chandi Ghat Pt I	528	Sridharpur	792	Hatiguri		

Table 2. Villages in Hailakandi District

S No	NAME	S No	NAME	S No	NAME	S No	NAME
1054	Uttarbadarpur	1139	Bisnughar	1224	Purbo Kitterbond Pt II	1309	Telecherra N.C.
1055	Thandapur	1140	Chakchandpur	1225	Rajyeswarpur Pt III	1310	Dhancherra N.C.
1056	Badarpur Grant	1141	Nitainagar Pt III	1226	Chandrapur Pt I	1311	Harishnagar Pt II
1057	Uttar Kanchanpur Pt I	1142	Lakhirbond Pt I	1227	Aynakhal	1312	Lalpani N.C.
1058	Dakhin Badarpur	1143	Purba-Sonapur	1228	Uttarjashabad Pt II	1313	Dholai Molai Pt IX
1059	Panchgram	1144	Ujankupa Pt II	1229	Rajyeswarpur Pt VIII	1314	Dholai Molai Pt X
1060	Polaspur	1145	Gangpar Dhonkar Pt III	1230	Chandrapur Pt II	1315	Dholai Molai Pt VII T.E.
1061	Kalinagar Pt I	1146	Itorkandi Grant	1231	Lalamukh Grant	1316	Alaicherra Pt II
1062	Kalinagar Pt II	1147	Gangpar Dhonkar Pt IV	1232	Bhabanipur	1317	Bipincherra
1063	Bakori Hawar Pt I	1148	Chandpur	1233	Behul	1318	Dholai Molai Pt III
1064	Kalinagar Pt III	1149	Narainpur Pt I	1234	Umednagar	1319	Maharpur
1065	Dholidahar Grant	1150	Bahadurpur Pt II	1235	Joynagar-Punjee N.C.	1320	Harishnagar Pt III
1066	Uttar Kanchanpur Pt II	1151	Ratanpur Pt II	1236	Saidpur	1321	Dholai Molai Pt XII
1067	Bakri Howar Pt III	1152	Lakhirbond Pt II	1237	Joynagar	1322	Shyampur
1068	Bakri Howar Pt II	1153	Bilpar Dhumkar	1238	Jalalpur	1323	Dholai Molai Pt VIII
1069	Dholidahar	1154	Chepti Brojapur	1239	Lala Pt I	1324	Paglacherra N.C.

1070	Kalinagar Pt IV	1155	Narainpur Pt II	1240	Lala	1325	Nehal Chandpur
1071	Bakri Howar Pt IV	1156	Hailakandi	1241	Bangalpur Grant	1326	Alaicherra Pt I
1072	Chiparsangam Pt I	1157	Rangauti Pt III	1242	Uttarjasnabad Pt I	1327	Bhagabanpur
1073	Bakri Howar Pt VI	1158	Itorkandi Pt I	1243	Kaiya Grant	1328	Baruncherra Pt II
1074	Bakri Howar Pt VII	1159	Itorkandi Pt II	1244	Dhanipur	1329	Ramsantipur
1075	Chandipur Pt I	1160	Ratanpur Pt I	1245	Bishnupur	1330	Alaicherra Pt VII
1076	Kalinagar Pt V	1161	Narainpur Pt III	1246	Bangalpur	1331	Alaicherra Pt VI
1077	Chandipur Grant	1162	Rangauti Pt I	1247	Lalachera Grant	1332	Ahyalapur N.C.
1078	Chiparsangan Pt II	1163	Bondukmara	1248	Tantoo	1333	Baruncherra F.V.
1079	Bakri Howar Pt V	1164	Bahadurpur Pt I	1249	Niamatpur	1334	Alaicherra Pt V
1080	Bakri Howar Pt VIII	1165	Narainpur Pt V	1250	Nizvesnupur Pt II	1335	Baruncherra Pt I
1081	Kalinagar Pt VI	1166	Narainpur Pt IV	1251	Sarbanandapur	1336	Pratap Nagar
1082	Chiparsangan Pt III	1167	Rangauti Pt II	1252	Ramchandi N.C.	1337	Kukicherra Grant
1083	Kalinagar Pt VIII	1168	Brojapur Pt I	1253	Ramchandi Pt II	1338	Alaicherra Pt III
1084	Narainpur Pt III	1169	Borhailakandi Pt II	1254	Sheralipur	1339	Durgapur
1085	Bakri Howar Pt IX	1170	Brojapur Pt II	1255	Dakhinjansbad Pt I	1340	Lochanpur
1086	Narainpur Pt IV	1171	Purbagool	1256	Abdullapur Pt I	1341	Dharapur N.C.
1087	Chandipur Pt II	1172	Bashdahar Pt II	1257	Dakhin Jansbad Pt II	1342	Alaicherra Pt IV
1088	Bakri Howar Pt XI	1173	Tupkhana	1258	Abdullapur Pt II	1343	Sultanicherra T.E.
1089	Bhatisang Jurai	1174	Kanchanpur Pt I	1259	Nizvesnupur Pt I	1344	Karichera
1090	Bakri Howar Pt X	1175	Bandukmara Grant	1260	Ramchandi Pt I	1345	Bhai-Bonti
1091	Kalinagar Pt VII	1176	Vichingcha Pt II	1261	Kulicherra N.C.	1346	Krishnapur N.C.
1092	Burni Brease Grant	1177	Paikan	1262	Apin Pt II	1347	Rampur
1093	Narainpur Pt II	1178	Kanchanpur Pt II	1263	Ramchandi Pt III	1348	Madhabpur

1094	Nabin Sonapur	1179	Chandrapur	1264	Joykrishnapur	1349	Kukicherra F.V.
1095	Bakri Howar Pt XII	1180	Borhailakandi Pt III	1265	Rongpur Pt V	1350	Dariaghat Grant
1096	Narainpur Pt I	1181	Vichingcha Pt I	1266	Mahamadpur Pt I	1351	Boldaboldi Pt III
1097	Chandipur Pt III	1182	Borhailakandi Pt I	1267	Nunaikhal Grant	1352	Panch Pirar Mukam
1098	Kapnarpar	1183	Dudpur	1268	Rongpur Pt I	1353	Raifalmara
1099	Padmarpar	1184	Matijuri	1269	Lalachera F.V.	1354	Kalyanpur N.C.
1100	Algapur Pt II	1185	Kanchanpur Grant	1270	Mulapur N.C.	1355	Sultani
1101	Chandipur Pt IV	1186	Kuchila Grant	1271	Dinanathpur Pt II	1356	Kanchiwala F.V.
1102	Mohanpur Pt V	1187	Bowarghat Pt I	1272	Mahamadpur Pt II	1357	Boldaboldi Pt II
1103	Mohanpur Pt IV	1188	Borbond Pt III	1273	Rongpur Pt VI	1358	Gollacherra
1104	Algapur Pt I	1189	Bashdahar Pt I	1274	Apin Pt I	1359	Katanala N.C.
1105	Bornagad	1190	Dakhin Sonapur Pt II	1275	Dinanathpur Pt I	1360	Boldaboldi Pt I
1106	Bansbari Pt II	1191	Kanchanpur Pt III	1276	Lalpani F.V.	1361	Kachurthal
1107	HPCL Town	1192	Borbond Pt I	1277	Rongpur Pt II	1362	Jamira Pt V
1108	Mohanpur Pt III	1193	Bowarghat Pt II	1278	Kacharital F.V.	1363	Palaicherra Pt II
1109	Algapur Pt III	1194	Nischintapur Pt I	1279	Borthal F.V.	1364	Bagmara
1110	Bansbari Grant	1195	Borbond Pt II	1280	Bilaipur F.V.	1365	Bangla Vasha
1111	Bhatirkupa Pt I	1196	Dakhin Sonapur Pt I	1281	Rongpur Pt VII	1366	Palaicherra Pt I
1112	Mohanpur Pt VI	1197	Rongpur	1282	Sahabad Pt I	1367	Jalnacherra Grant
1113	Algapur Pt IV	1198	Sudorshonpur Pt I	1283	Apin Grant (Lata Kandi Gra	1368	Janira Bagan Bosti
1114	Balikandi Pt II	1199	Sudorshonpur Pt II	1284	Nunai F.V.	1369	Gendacherra
1115	Bansbari Pt I	1200	Lakshinagar Pt I	1285	Sahabad Pt II	1370	Jalnacherra F.V.
1116	Matirgram	1201	Nischintapur Pt II	1286	Rupacherra Tea Garden	1371	Jamira Pt VI
1117	Sayedbond Pt I	1202	Lakshinagar Pt II	1287	Rongpur Pt III	1372	Jamira Pt I

1118	Algapur Pt V	1203	Nimaichandpur Pt I	1288	Rupacherra Punjee	1373	Nandagram N.C. Pt I
1119	Mohanpur Grant	1204	Nityanandapur Pt I	1289	Rongpur Pt VIII	1374	Nandagram N.C. Pt II
1120	Bhatirkupa Pt II	1205	Nischintapur Pt III	1290	Rongpur Pt IV	1375	Jamira Pt VII
1121	Balikandi Pt I	1206	Monachura Grant	1291	Digar Apin	1376	Jamira Pt II
1122	Boalipar Pt I	1207	Kalachera Grant	1292	Kaliganj N.C.	1377	Sahabmara F.V.
1123	Mohanpur Pt I	1208	Nimaichandpur Pt II	1293	Rangabak Pt II	1378	Jamira Pt III
1124	Mohanpur Pt II	1209	Sudorshonpur Pt III	1294	Araynapur	1379	Jamira PtIv
1125	Sayedbond Pt III	1210	Rajyeswarpur Pt I	1295	Alexanderpur Grant	1380	Bathcherra F.V.
1126	Sayedbond Pt II	1211	Nityanandapur Pt II	1296	Dhalchera F.V.	1381	Gutguti (Pakuwa) F.V.
1127	Sibuttar	1212	Paschim Kitterbond Pt I	1297	Makengipur	1382	Bagcherra F.V.
1128	Bhatirkupa Pt III	1213	Bongalnagar Grant	1298	Rangabak Pt I	1383	Garmura F.V.
1129	Balikandi Grant	1214	Rajyeswarpur Pt VI	1299	Santipur N.C.	1384	Damcherra F.V.
1130	Boalipar Pt II	1215	Gobil	1300	Dholai Molai Pt VI	1385	Jakabpur F.V.
1131	Nitainagar Pt II	1216	Rajyeswarpur Pt V	1301	Dholai Molai Pt IV	1386	Duttapur
1132	Boalipar Pt III	1217	Rajyeswarpur Pt II	1302	Harishnagar Pt I	1387	Ramnathpur F.V.
1133	Nitainagar Pt I	1218	Rajyeswarpur Pt VII	1303	Dhalchera Tripura Punjee	1388	Katakhal R.F.
1134	Ujankupa Pt I	1219	Purbo Kitterbond Pt I	1304	Katlicherra Grant	1389	Inner Line R.F.
1135	Bhajantipur Pt I	1220	Paschim Kitterbond Pt II	1305	Dholai Molai Pt I	1390	Katakhal R.F.
1136	Barjurai	1221	Rajyeswarpur Pt IX	1306	Dholai Molai Pt II	1391	Inner Line R.F.
1137	Bhajantipur Pt II	1222	Rajyeswarpur Pt IV	1307	Dholai Molai Pt XI	1392	Inner Line R.F.
1138	Ujankupa Pt III	1223	Gaglachera Grant	1308	Dholai Molai Pt V	1393	Inner Line R.F.

Table 3. Villages in Karimganj District

S No	NAME	S No	NAME	S No	NAME	S No	NAME
1394	Vitargool	1632	Ranigram Pt I	1870	Chayabari	2108	Ankapai Punjee
1395	Achiura	1633	Paulkapan	1871	Satghori Pt III	2109	Latitilla
1396	Gangpar	1634	Dattapur	1872	Srinagar	2110	Bhairabnagar
1397	Dakhinbond	1635	Ratanpur Pt I	1873	Kandigram Pt II	2111	Shephinjuri T.E.
1398	Lafasail Pt III	1636	Srimanthakanisha	1874	Rakhal Basti	2112	Medli Grant
1399	Lafasail Pt II	1637	Bagan	1875	Danirbond	2113	Kachu Khouri
1400	Narikuli	1638	Baleswar	1876	Kandigram Pt I	2114	Baroputni
1401	Serulbhag	1639	Balirbond	1877	Paschim Lakshipu	2115	Beratuk
1402	Bagarsangan	1640	Khola Pt I	1878	Deodhar	2116	Harinagar Pt II
1403	Keshorkapan Pt I	1641	Barthal Pt XI	1879	Satghori Pt II	2117	Awalala (T.S.)
1404	Shikarpur	1642	Ranibari	1880	Eral IV	2118	Andurpar
1405	Marera Pt II	1643	Ratanpur Pt II	1881	Barcharra	2119	Radhanagar
1406	Sadarashi Pt I	1644	Ramanikrishna T.	1882	Satghori Pt I	2120	Chunaligul Cha B
1407	Keshorkapan Pt I	1645	Barapunjee Pt I	1883	Lakshipur	2121	Bethubari
1408	Dhit	1646	Brahmanshasan Ch	1884	Kabaribond Pt I	2122	Chunaligul Cha B
1409	Sadarashi Pt II	1647	Lamabahadurpur P	1885	Duhalia Pt IV	2123	Amarkhal
1410	Lafasail Pt I	1648	Meda Pt I	1886	Eral Pt III	2124	Sarkaribari
1411	Keshorkapan 9	1649	Sekikanishail Ch	1887	Kalacherra	2125	Satrishhal
1412	Umapati (T.S.)	1650	Baniargool	1888	Uzan Lakshipur	2126	Hulashnagar Pt
1413	Banamali	1651	Rauthgram Pt I	1889	Anandapur	2127	Bidyanagar T.E.
1414	Chandsrikuna	1652	Khagkandi	1890	Nizkhali	2128	Chunaligul Cha B
1415	Bar Purahuria Pt	1653	Umarpur Pt II	1891	Dowki	2129	Dakshin Balaigao

1416	Adhakandi	1654	Meda Pt II	1892	Durlovpur Pt IV	2130	Awalala (P.S.)
1417	Kalacherra	1655	Umarpur Pt III	1893	Durlovpur Pt V	2131	Bidyanagar T.E.
1418	Jarapata	1656	Mahakal Pt VI	1894	Saija Nagar	2132	Salgoi T.E.
1419	Bar Purahuria Pt	1657	Brahmansashan Pt	1895	Farid Kuna	2133	Muliala Pt I
1420	Batarashi	1658	Lokdas	1896	Bager Sangan	2134	Hailam Charra
1421	Dhit-Chak 4	1659	Dasgram Pt II	1897	Eraligool Pt VII	2135	Uttor Hailamchar
1422	Faridpur	1660	Krishnanagar Pt	1898	Dargarbond Pt II	2136	Harinagar Pt I
1423	Maizgram Pt I	1661	Rauthgram Pt II	1899	Nalugaon	2137	Krishnagar
1424	Chandsrikuna Cha	1662	Kartikdas	1900	Dargarbond Pt I	2138	Kharkana Putni
1425	Jabda	1663	Bagbari	1901	Bhubrighat T.E.	2139	Panchdali Pt II
1426	Keshorkapan Chak	1664	Robbania Pt II T	1902	Hatkhala Kitte A	2140	Bidyanagar T.E.
1427	Khudra Purahuria	1665	Mugrapur	1903	Bilbari T.S.	2141	Chuto Putni
1428	Dhit Chak 8	1666	Loharpara Pt II	1904	Kadmacherra	2142	Panchdali Pt I
1429	Marera Pt I	1667	Mahakal Pt V	1905	Durlovpur Pt I	2143	Paschim Salgoi
1430	Kandigram Chaita	1668	Brahmanshasan Pt	1906	Sonbil Pt I	2144	Purbo Hailamchar
1431	Chapra	1669	Rauthgram Pt III	1907	Purbogool	2145	Muliala Pt II
1432	Suprakandi	1670	Hizim Madanpur	1908	Defolala	2146	Behairdala
1433	Karimganj	1671	Loharpara Pt I	1909	Kamarbond	2147	Lila Chila Grant
1434	Alakulipur	1672	Brahmanshasan Pt	1910	Khaser Gaon	2148	Patiala (P.S.)
1435	Umarpur Pt I	1673	Nayagram Pt II	1911	Dargarbond Jungl	2149	Achairghat
1436	Maizgram Pt II	1674	Pankshankar	1912	Durlovpur Pt II	2150	Indurali Punjee
1437	Karnamadhu Pt II	1675	Lamabahadurpur P	1913	Rajbari	2151	Purbo Achairghat
1438	Ulukandi	1676	Umarpur Pt IV	1914	Duhalia Pt III	2152	Dhengarbond
1439	Tazpur	1677	Loharpara Pt III	1915	Purbo Purbogool	2153	Tarbin Cherra Gr

1440	Gandhak Chak	1678	Rampasha Pt I	1916	Bargul	2154	Rupagram Pt I
1441	Cherakuri	1679	Kuchilargool	1917	Patherkandi Pt I	2155	Bidyanagar T.E.
1442	Nandanbond	1680	Barthal Pt X	1918	Bishnunagar Colo	2156	Purbo Pecharghat
1443	Badarpur Rly Town	1681	Bahartadbir	1919	Durlovpur Pt III	2157	Bidyanagar T.E.
1444	Karnamadhu Pt II	1682	Barthal Pt VII(S	1920	Jummahal Pt II	2158	Trimti T.E.
1445	Naharpur	1683	Bahar	1921	Samriddhipur	2159	Bidyanagar T.E.
1446	Jabda Chak	1684	Hizimangura Pt I	1922	Haitorkha Pt II	2160	Rupagram Pt II
1447	Sutarkandi	1685	Dalfa	1923	Kalyanpur	2161	Kachari Gaon
1448	Mirjapur Pt I	1686	Nandibari	1924	Gamaria Pt I	2162	Chamtilla
1449	Srigauri	1687	Barantar	1925	Purba Faridkuna	2163	Purbo Indurali
1450	Karnamadhu Pt V	1688	Madanpur T.E.	1926	Nayanabin	2164	Hulashnagar Pt I
1451	Jarua	1689	Kutnipara	1927	Purbo Tatirbond	2165	Uttor Hatikhira
1452	Amtoli	1690	Khangter	1928	Barcharrapunjee	2166	Purbo Pecharghat
1453	Jatua Pt I	1691	Dasgram Pt I	1929	Chinanal	2167	Patiala (T.S.)
1454	Mosli Pt I	1692	Berajal	1930	Eraligool Pt II	2168	Paschim Krishna
1455	Lamajuar Pt I	1693	Barthal Pt VIII	1931	Baruail	2169	Pecharghat
1456	Panaragarh	1694	Khagail	1932	Haitorkha Pt I	2170	Pechala (T.S.)
1457	Patharkandi	1695	Nayagram Hizim A	1933	Tatirbond	2171	Pachim Tarbin Ch
1458	Maizgram Pt III	1696	Barkapan	1934	Dhupa Gamaria Ki	2172	Kunagram
1459	Niz Malua	1697	Chandkhani	1935	Adamtilla T.E.	2173	Daluachera Grant
1460	Sarang Dewpur	1698	Hizimangura Pt I	1936	Kabaribond Pt II	2174	Anipur Grant
1461	Sunadari	1699	Barthal Pt V	1937	Sonbil Pt Iii	2175	Jungal Block
1462	Barbhadri	1700	Meghna Pt I	1938	Eraligool Pt IX	2176	Marugaon
1463	Mirjapur Pt II	1701	Ghorardhap	1939	Swastipur	2177	Damcherra T.E. P

1464	Kankalesh Pt I	1702	Khudrakandi	1940	Sontoshpur	2178	Uttor Tilbhum
1465	Prasadpur	1703	Bharibond	1941	Defolala Charra	2179	Kalachera Grant
1466	Hamindpur	1704	Barthal Pt. IX	1942	Chotokona	2180	Mukamcherra T.E.
1467	Jum Pt VII	1705	Firujee	1943	Kabaribond Pt I	2181	Kurti Gaon
1468	Kamargram	1706	Sonatola	1944	Chengjur	2182	Dengura Charra
1469	Kandigram Malua	1707	Hizim	1945	Sontoshpur Bagan	2183	Damcherra T.E. P
1470	Dharakuna	1708	Chaykut	1946	Mukamtilla Punje	2184	Damcherra T.E. P
1471	Dimpur	1709	Rampasha Pt II	1947	Dakshin Defolala	2185	Mukamcherra T.E.
1472	Karnamadhu Pt IV	1710	Barthal Pt I	1948	Duhalia Hill Kit	2186	Pechala (P.S.)
1473	Karuria	1711	Chandrapur	1949	Gamaria Pt II	2187	Hatikhira T.E.
1474	Mosli Pt II	1712	Barthal Pt III	1950	Kachubari P.S.	2188	Damcherra T.E.
1475	Supnargool Pt II	1713	Kamargram	1951	Duhalia Hill Ki	2189	Damcherra T.E. P
1476	Lakarkhai	1714	Alamkhani Pt IV	1952	Rajar Gaon	2190	Damcherra T.E. P
1477	Kankalesh Pt II	1715	Chandkhani Chak	1953	Patherkandi Pt I	2191	Mukamcherra T.E.
1478	Banamali Pt I	1716	Brahmanshasan Pt	1954	Sulonagar Bagant	2192	Baskaltilla
1479	Banamali Pt II	1717	Robbania Pt I T.	1955	Sonbil Pt Ii	2193	Dargarbond
1480	Pechakuna	1718	Rauthgram Chak	1956	Sripur	2194	Purbo Lowairpoa
1481	Umapati	1719	Angura Dunguri	1957	Duhalia Pt II	2195	Hatairbond
1482	Sajpur Pt I	1720	Bhuja	1958	Gopikanagar	2196	Lowairpoa
1483	Mahakal Pt I	1721	Bacharbond Pt I	1959	Mangalpur	2197	Mukamcherra Pt I
1484	Badarpur	1722	Sharishakuri	1960	Pekurgaon	2198	Bagan Gaon
1485	Kujab	1723	Taltala	1961	Sonaicherra Pt I	2199	Dullavecherra T.E. Pt Iv
1486	Maizgram	1724	Haldigool	1962	Satirsaugan	2200	Sarjul Punjee
1487	Sarisa	1725	Mauzkuri Pt I	1963	Sonbil Pt V	2201	Fetipath

1488	Kamarkhai	1726	Konabagargool P	1964	Kodali	2202	Singlacherra Gra
1489	Karnamadhu Pt I	1727	Barthal Pt IV	1965	Bilbari P.S.	2203	Veterbond
1490	Jatua (T.S.)	1728	Hizimangura Pt I	1966	Jamirala	2204	Dullavcherra T.E
1491	Fatepur	1729	Parbat Hizim Ang	1967	Sonaicherra Pt Ii	2205	Dakshin Hatikhir
1492	Kurikhala	1730	Angura	1968	Unamgaon	2206	Dhupanpur (T.S.)
1493	Jabainpur Pt II	1731	Mauzkurichak	1969	Khalagaon	2207	Dullavcherra T.E
1494	Harikhai	1732	Barthal Pt II (S	1970	Gandhinagar	2208	Balirbond Grant
1495	Gandhak	1733	Barthal Pt VI	1971	Dhigalikandi	2209	Barbari
1496	Dasgram	1734	Fatepur Pt I	1972	Singhariah	2210	Pachim Singla
1497	Medal Pt I	1735	Chandidas	1973	Nagendra Nagar	2211	Dullavecherra T.
1498	Chandanpur	1736	Singaria Pt III	1974	Duhalia Hill Kit	2212	Kanikhai F.V.
1499	Alongjuri	1737	Bacharbond Pt II	1975	Duhalia Hill Kit	2213	Dullavcherra Gra
1500	Ambarkhana	1738	Promodnagar T.E.	1976	Daloo Pt I	2214	Chamtilla
1501	Hasanpur	1739	Dalgram	1977	Maniknagar Chaba	2215	Barbazari Kitte
1502	Jabainpur Pt I	1740	Mauzkuri Pt II	1978	Champabari Grant	2216	Maneswarpur (P.S
1503	Raj Pasha	1741	Duliakhal	1979	Dalua Charra	2217	Hatai Charra
1504	Lamajuar Pt II	1742	Alamkhani Pt II	1980	Duhalia Pt I	2218	Purbo Bazari
1505	Medalbeel	1743	Bacharbond Pt II	1981	Netajinagar	2219	Dullavcherra T.E
1506	Kewtala Sankarpu	1744	Adarkona Pt IV	1982	Champabari Gaon	2220	Singlacherra Gra
1507	Inathpur	1745	Konabagargool Pt	1983	Kalkalimukh	2221	Sibergool
1508	Supnargool Pt I	1746	Patharia Block	1984	Niznabin	2222	Maneswarpur K.P.
1509	Arengabad	1747	Ghugrakona Pt II	1985	Binnatikari Pt I	2223	Dullavcherra T.E
1510	Biskut	1748	Ghugrakona Pt I	1986	Garerbond	2224	Gajadharpur Pt I
1511	Kalakuri	1749	Ishwarshree	1987	Longai T.E.	2225	Pachim Lalcherra

1512	Umarpur Pt II	1750	Adarkona Pt III	1988	Nayadasgram	2226	Gajadharpur Pt I
1513	Medal Pt II	1751	Keutkona Pt I	1989	Chipacharra	2227	Dhupanpar (P.S.)
1514	Umarpur Pt III	1752	Farampasha Pt II	1990	Binnatikari Pt I	2228	Maneswarpur K.P.
1515	Lalbhaturi	1753	Farampasha Pt II	1991	Maniknagar Chaba	2229	Dakshin Ahmedpur
1516	Tajpur Pt I	1754	Goyalkandi	1992	Basantapur	2230	Fanairbond
1517	Bhatgram	1755	Adarkona Pt II	1993	Daloo Pt II	2231	Ahmedpur
1518	Latu	1756	Ghugrakona Pt IV	1994	Kachubari T.S.	2232	Kalacharra
1519	Rahatpur	1757	Rampasha Pt III	1995	Dalurbond	2233	Muralibond
1520	Kaibarthakapan	1758	Alamkhani Pt I	1996	Sripur	2234	Rampur
1521	Dakshin Gram	1759	Dubri(Bsf Camp)	1997	Pachim Jarail Ba	2235	Juitpur
1522	Chaliyadi	1760	Khagail Pt II	1998	Krishnanagar Col	2236	Bazarghat F.V.
1523	Saidambar Pt II	1761	Fatepur Pt III	1999	Bhurunga	2237	Purbo Lalcherra
1524	Tajpur Pt II	1762	Keutkona Pt III	2000	Duhaliahill Kitt	2238	Fanai Cherra Gra
1525	Kanisail Pt II	1763	Gangpar	2001	Nalibari	2239	Makundarbond
1526	Bakarshal Pt II	1764	Farampasha Pt I	2002	Panchgram	2240	Dhukupur
1527	Nagkapan Pt II	1765	Konabagargool Pt	2003	Duhalia Hill Kit	2241	Dakshin Bazari
1528	Hazipur	1766	Adarkona Pt I	2004	Duhaliahill Kitt	2242	Fanaicherra Punj
1529	Nathupur Pt I	1767	Fatepur Pt II	2005	Kalkali	2243	Dakshin Rampur
1530	Jum Pt VI	1768	Khagail Pt I	2006	Birgram	2244	Mahabirganj
1531	Mahakal Pt III	1769	Khagail Pt III	2007	Nayatilla	2245	Balicherra Grant
1532	Maizgram Pt IV	1770	Kaysthagram Pt I	2008	Singirpar	2246	Purba Fanai
1533	Panchas	1771	Maizbagargool Pt	2009	Ghilaitikar Pt I	2247	Paglacherra Punj
1534	Pathu Pt I	1772	Keutkona Pt II	2010	Galla Sail	2248	Wangirbond
1535	Lamajuar	1773	Kanakpur	2011	Singlarpar	2249	Sakalpur

1536	Kamalpur	1774	Uttarbandarkona	2012	Champaknagar	2250	Daulatpur
1537	Bargool	1775	Baraituk	2013	Kurikala	2251	Uttor Chagolmar
1538	Lamajuar Pt II	1776	Meghna Pt III	2014	Krishna Mantri G	2252	Maguragrant
1539	Sajpur Pt II	1777	Saidpur	2015	Purbo Jarail Bar	2253	Srirampur
1540	Jum Pt V	1778	Eraligool Pt I	2016	Kurtacharra	2254	Radhamadhabpur K
1541	Nairgram	1779	Beelbari	2017	Bhurunga Cherrag	2255	Barbali
1542	Nagkapan Pt I	1780	Gopinather Akhra	2018	Bazarghat Pt II	2256	Old Solamona F.V
1543	Balidara	1781	Alamkhani Pt III	2019	Nalarpar	2257	Purbo Gombira
1544	Chinipatan	1782	Kaysthagram Pt I	2020	Kalinagar Cha Ba	2258	Purba Gombira Gr
1545	Tikarpara	1783	Nagharia Pt II	2021	Uttar Bhurunga K	2259	Uttar Olivia
1546	Lamajuar Pt III	1784	Choudhurytilla	2022	Pachim Baruala	2260	Chagolmar Bond
1547	Medamail	1785	Ghugrakona Pt II	2023	Kalapani	2261	Jumtilla
1548	Alekargool	1786	Hafania Kitte Ba	2024	Dalurpar	2262	Isaipunjee Kitte
1549	Lamajuar Pt I	1787	Maizbagargool Pt	2025	Gazardingi	2263	Amtilla
1550	Bedrong Pt III	1788	Uttarbandarkona	2026	Pailamuli	2264	Isabeel
1551	Jum Pt IV	1789	Bhitargool	2027	Ichakhouri	2265	Gombira Grant
1552	Barbari	1790	Duliakhal Karaib	2028	Bazarghat Pt I	2266	Dakshin Olivia T
1553	Basail	1791	Andharibond	2029	Padmarpar	2267	Purba Magura
1554	Bakarshal Pt I	1792	Kaysthagram Pt I	2030	Kachubari P.S.	2268	Wangirbill
1555	Mahakal Pt IV	1793	Changjurirpar	2031	Maligaon	2269	Dakshin Sagolmar
1556	Kanisail Pt I	1794	Maizbagargool Pt	2032	Hafanigool Grant	2270	Pachim Magura
1557	Medal Pt III	1795	Meghna Pt II	2033	Sonakhira	2271	Purbo Isabeel
1558	Pathu Pt II	1796	Niyamat Khani	2034	Kalinagar Pt Iv	2272	Uttar Khegragool
1559	Mazar Gool	1797	Tegharia Kitte Tehurbeel	2035	Chamela	2273	Roypur

1560	Bakarshal Pt IV	1798	Dhalcherra	2036	Chandkhira T.E.	2274	Purba Khegra Goo
1561	Nagkapan	1799	Sonatola	2037	Saizanagar Pt I	2275	Dakshin Khegrago
1562	Bargool	1800	Nayagram	2038	Saizanagar Pt II	2276	Pata Khauri
1563	Mahakal Pt II	1801	Mahamadpur Pt I	2039	Thengargul	2277	Purba Butucherra
1564	Piratikar	1802	Bataiya	2040	Ratabari Pt II	2278	N/S Solamona F.V
1565	Lamajuar Pt IV	1803	Hafania Kitte Ka	2041	Ratabari Pt I	2279	Uttor Isarpar Ki
1566	Bhagichagi	1804	Eraligool Pt V	2042	Saizanagar Pt II	2280	Isarpar
1567	Nathupur Pt II	1805	Asalkandi	2043	Jangibari Pt III	2281	Teracherra
1568	Jatkapan	1806	Singaria Pt II	2044	Pachim Sonai Kit	2282	Pachim Butucherr
1569	Jum Pt II	1807	Khagail Pt IV	2045	Saizanagar Pt IV	2283	Radhamadhabpur K
1570	Bedrong Pt I	1808	Serpur Pt II	2046	Patharia Forest F.V.	2284	Zahanpur F.V.
1571	Kamargram	1809	Durganagar T.E.	2047	Purbo Piplagool	2285	Bhudaikuri
1572	Tesuya	1810	Madanduri	2048	Maniknagar Cha B	2286	Kalanpur
1573	Basla	1811	Duttapara	2049	Paschim Hafanigo	2287	Zerjheri
1574	Ghoramara Pt I	1812	Bhug	2050	Kalinagar Pt I	2288	Pachim Cheragirb
1575	Chandpur	1813	Mahamadpur Pt II	2051	Kalinagar Pt II	2289	Dhakshin Cheragi
1576	Bakarshal Pt III	1814	Singaria Pt I	2052	Purbo Hafanigool	2290	Cheragirbond
1577	Ayalabari T.E.	1815	Bazaibala	2053	Katabari	2291	Bhutupunjee (Tri
1578	Ranigram Pt III	1816	Hafania	2054	Chand Khani	2292	Bhutukuchi
1579	Saidambar Pt I	1817	Mahamadpur Pt II	2055	Purbo Katabari	2293	North Maguna F.V
1580	Jinahabra	1818	Bahadurpur	2056	Maniknagar Cha B	2294	Dakshin Cheragir
1581	Barbari	1819	Ilaspur	2057	Baithakhal T.E.	2295	Kamalpur
1582	Jikar	1820	Eral Pt IV	2058	Gulal Kandi	2296	Hempur
1583	Goabari	1821	Gandarua Khani	2059	Chandroy	2297	Maguna Punjee F.

1584	Prakashpur	1822	Chayabari Pt II	2060	Piplagool T.E.	2298	Kakura Punjee
1585	Surigram Pt I	1823	Kalakhauri	2061	Ramkrishnanagar	2299	Proper Magura F.
1586	Mubarakpur	1824	Serpur Kitte Cho	2062	Lakshminagar	2300	Hataiyerbond
1587	Alampur	1825	Baraigram	2063	Mahadevpur	2301	Chotobalia
1588	Umarpur Pt V	1826	Serpur Pt I	2064	Tangibari Pt II	2302	Pachim Kamalpur
1589	Jalalnagar T.E.	1827	Eraligool Pt X	2065	Lalkhira Sonakhi	2303	Bhutupunjee (Man
1590	Kamargram Pt I	1828	Nabipur	2066	Kalinagar Pt III	2304	Kishorepur
1591	Marjat Kandi	1829	Eraligool Pt III	2067	Dhalgram Pt I	2305	Barbalia
1592	Humak	1830	Dakshinbandorkon	2068	Kalinagar Cha Ba	2306	Dakshin Lalargao
1593	Medal Chak	1831	Maina Pt II	2069	Shivbari Krishna	2307	Rengmong Lalarga
1594	Mahishasan	1832	Ghilaitikar Pt I	2070	Dhalgram Pt II	2308	Dakshin Hataiyer
1595	Umarpur Pt I	1833	Chayabari Pt I	2071	Ramkrishnanagar	2309	Birajapur
1596	Harinadik	1834	Balirbond Pt III	2072	Paschim Lalkhira	2310	Kalamagura
1597	Tundurail	1835	Uttarbandarkona	2073	Purba Baruala	2311	Shambu Nagar F.V
1598	Krishnanagar Pt	1836	Nagharia Pt I	2074	Pachim Jangibari	2312	Bhutupunjee (Daw
1599	Kamargram Pt II	1837	Dakshinbandorkon	2075	Rengbook Tilla	2313	Manik Bond Mahi
1600	Ranigram Pt II	1838	Sonbil Pt Iv	2076	Dhalibil Pt I	2314	Tilbhum Forest
1601	Dewakuri	1839	Maina Pt I	2077	Dhalibil Pt II	2315	Akshoypur
1602	Anicherra	1840	Dhalchurra Kitte	2078	Saruchalita	2316	Cheragi Nagar
1603	Barkatpur	1841	Mahamadpur T.E.	2079	Tangibari Pt IV	2317	South Magura F.V
1604	Dewakuri Jhapur	1842	Balirbond Pt II	2080	Badshahi Forest	2318	Kanakpur F.V.
1605	Jum Pt I	1843	Hatirgool	2081	Kalinagar Jungle	2319	Rajendrapur
1606	Ghoramara Pt II	1844	Madanmohan T.E.	2082	Bargool	2320	Bijoypur
1607	Surigram Pt II	1845	Eraligool West L	2083	Ramkrishnanagar	2321	Manikbond Punjee

1608	Gharua Chak	1846	Bhairabnagar Pt	2084	Chanala	2322	Khagragura F.V.
1609	Surjyadas	1847	Balirbond Pt I	2085	Putni T.E.	2323	Nurkha F.V.
1610	Latu Chak	1848	Chandpur	2086	Saruchalitar Pur	2324	Nandigram F.V.
1611	Gharua	1849	Singua Kitte Nal	2087	Chagi Khouri	2325	Baruatilla
1612	Brahmansashan Pt	1850	Eraligool Pt VI	2088	Ramkrishnanagar	2326	Nilkantapur F.V.
1613	Kulcherra Pt I	1851	Maina Pt III	2089	Uttor Gopalpur	2327	Rongpur
1614	Bedrong Pt II	1852	Singua (Singua P	2090	Damcherra Tripur	2328	Tarapur F.V.
1615	Brahmanshasan Pt	1853	Bhairabnagar Pt	2091	Tangibari Pt I	2329	Jacobnagar F.V.
1616	Ghatudaram	1854	Maraura	2092	Longai Forest	2330	Bara Bhubirbond
1617	Nagkapan Chak	1855	Bataiya Punjee	2093	Nayagram	2331	Batiapunjee F.V.
1618	Barthal Pt XII	1856	Bhairabnagar Pt	2094	Baithakhal Basti	2332	Rangamati F.V.
1619	Kapurpur	1857	Chataiya Punjee	2095	Dullavpur	2333	Piplapunjee F.V.
1620	Nagkapan	1858	Dhalcharra Kitte	2096	Kalinagar Jungle	2334	Aditya Nagar F.V
1621	Sekikanishail	1859	Paschim Bhubrighat	2097	Tangibari Pt V	2335	Balipipla F.V.
1622	Kulcherra Pt II	1860	Eraligool Pt VII	2098	Dumabaroi	2336	Dewali F.V.
1623	Kurtab Dewtali	1861	Bakalkandi	2099	Gopalpur	2337	Piplacharra F.V.
1624	Sirajdhipur	1862	Singua Pt II	2100	Nitainagar	2338	Patharia Hill Reserved Forest
1625	Nayagram Pt I	1863	Lahirbond	2101	Basattihal	2339	Pathara Hill Reserved Forest
1626	Siberchak	1864	Jummahal Pt I	2102	Dakshin Sonakhir	2340	Dohalia Forest
1627	Khola Pt II	1865	Eral V	2103	Uttor Shephinjur	2341	Badsahi Tila Reserved Forest
1628	Dayabasana	1866	Nankar	2104	Kalachup	2342	Tilbhum Reseved Forest
1629	Kunapara	1867	Singua Pt I	2105	Akaidum	2343	Badsahi Tila Reserved Forest
1630	Barapunjee Pt II	1868	Bhairabnagar Pt	2106	Balaigaon	2344	Singla Reserved Forest
1631	Mahakal Pt VII	1869	Mendibari	2107	Madanpur	2345	Langai Reserved Forest

Census variables and Socio-economic indicators

Basic concepts and some census variables relevant for the current work are explained below (Based on Srinivasan, 2011; DCHB-Cachar, 2011).

Variable: Underlying and unobservable processes in the study of demography can be better understood by studying the characteristics of the population. Value of this characteristic which may vary from individual to individual and over time and space is called a variable. For example, age of the individual.

Ratio and Rate: In demographic analysis, denominator data is required, most often these are size and characteristics of the base population, resulting in computation of ratios and rates. Information on the absolute numbers can convey only a limited meaning in demographic analysis. A ratio is the result of dividing the size of one of the two non-overlapping groups possessing some common characteristics by that of the other. For example, sex ratio. A ratio is an index helpful in comparing the relative strength of each group in populations at different times and territories. Rates express the number of events, say E, which occur in a population of size P as a fraction E/P.

Census house: A 'census house' is a building or part of a building used or recognized as a separate unit because of having a separate main entrance from the road or common courtyard or staircase, etc. It may be occupied or vacant. It may be used for residential or non- residential purpose or both. If a building has a number of Flats or Blocks/Wings, which are independent of one another having separate entrances of their own from the road or a common staircase or a common courtyard leading to a main gate, these are considered as a separate Census house.

Village: The basic unit for rural areas is the revenue village, which has definite surveyed boundaries. The revenue village may comprise of one or more hamlets but the entire village is treated as one unit for presentation of data. In un surveyed areas, like villages within forest areas, each habitation area with locally recognized boundaries is treated as one village.

Household: A 'household' is usually a group of persons who normally live together and take their meals from a common kitchen unless the exigencies of work prevent any of them from doing so. Persons in a household may be related or unrelated or a mix of both. However, if a group of unrelated persons live in a census house but do not take their meals from the common kitchen, then they are not constituent of a common household. Each such person was to be treated as a separate household. The important link in finding out whether it was a household or not was a common kitchen/common cooking. There may be one member households, two member households or multi-member households.

Literate: A person aged 7 years and above who can both read and write with understanding in any language is taken as literate. A person who can only read but cannot write is not literate. It is not necessary that to be considered as literate, a person should have received any formal education or passed any minimum educational standard. Literacy could have been achieved through adult literacy classes or through any non-formal educational system. People who are blind and can read in Braille are treated as literates.

Literacy rate: Literacy rate of the population is defined as the percentage of literates in the age-group seven years and above. For different age-groups the percentage of literates in that age-group gives the literacy rate.

Work: Work is defined as participation in any economically productive activity with or without compensation, wages or profit. Such participation may be physical and/or mental in nature. Work involves not only actual work but also includes effective supervision and direction of work. It even includes part time help or unpaid work on farm, family enterprise or in any other economic activity. All persons engaged in 'work' as defined above are workers. The main point to note is that the activity should be economically productive. Reference period for determining a person as worker and non-worker is one year preceding the date of enumeration.

Main worker: A person who has worked for major part of the reference period (i.e. six months or more during the last one year preceding the date of enumeration) in any economically productive activity is termed as 'Main worker'.

Marginal worker: A person who worked for 3 months or less but less than six months of the reference period (i.e. in the last one year preceding the date of enumeration) in any economic activity is termed as 'Marginal worker'.

Non-worker: A person who has not worked at all in any economically productive activity during the reference period (i.e. last one year preceding the date of enumeration) is termed as 'Non worker'.

Cultivator: For purposes of the Census, a person is classified as cultivator if he or she is engaged in cultivation of land owned or from government or from private persons or institutions for payment in money, kind or share. Cultivation also includes effective supervision or direction in cultivation. Cultivation involves ploughing, sowing, harvesting and production of cereals and millet crops such as wheat, paddy, jowar, bajra, ragi, etc., and other crops such as sugarcane, tobacco, ground-nuts, tapioca, etc., and pulses, raw jute and kindred fiber crop, cotton, cinchona and other medicinal plants, fruit growing, vegetable growing or keeping orchards or groves, etc. Cultivation does not include the plantation crops like– tea, coffee, rubber, coconut and betel nuts (areca). The workers engaged in Plantation crops are recorded under "other workers".

Agricultural labourer: A person who works on another person's land for wages in cash or kind or share is regarded as an agricultural labourer. She/he has no risk in the cultivation, but merely works on another person's land for wages. An agricultural labourer has no right of lease or contract on land on which she/he works.

Household industry worker: Household industry is defined as an industry conducted by one or more members of the household at home or within the village in rural areas and only within the precincts of the house where the household lives in urban areas. The larger proportion of workers in household industry should consist of members of the household. The industry should not be run on the scale of a registered factory which would qualify or has to be registered under the Indian Factories Act and should be engaged in manufacturing, processing, servicing and repairs of goods. The activity relate to production, processing, servicing, repairing or making and selling of goods. It does not include professions such as a pleader, Doctor, Musician, Dancer, Waterman, Astrologer, Dhobi, Barber, etc. or merely trade or business, even if such professions, trade or services are run at home by members of the household.

Other worker: A person, who has been engaged in some economic activity during the last year of reference period but not as a cultivator or agricultural labourer or worker in Household Industry. The type of workers that come under this category include all government servants, municipal employees, teachers, factory workers, plantation workers, those engaged in trade, commerce, business, transport, banking, mining, construction, political or social work, priests, entertainment artists, etc. In fact, all those workers other than cultivators or agricultural labourers or household industry workers are 'Other Workers'.

Work participation rate: Percentage of Workers (Main + Marginal) to total population.

Population density: Population density is the number of persons inhabited per square kilometer of the area.

Sex Ratio: Number of females per 1,000 males in a population.

Persons enumerated (MoSPI 2012): Persons who were present in the household during the entire period of enumeration or who were known to be usual residents of the household and had stayed there for part of the enumeration period, or who were not present at the time of visit of the enumerator but were expected to return by 28 February 2001 (or 28 February 2011, for 2011 census) were eligible to be enumerated.

Household size: The number of persons living together in one house is commonly called household size.

Indicators: The socio-economic indicators are in the form of rates, ratios, proportions, averages, indices, or some other function of basic data. Some of the socio-economic indicators particularly used for multilevel planning in India are percentage of scheduled caste population, percentage of scheduled tribe population, percentage of working population, percentage of cultivators to total working population, percentage of agricultural labourer to to total working population, percentage of agricultural workers to total working population, percentage of literates to total population, and density of population, among others (Rao 1976). Some other indicators which can be used to present a comparative picture of pace, progress, and pattern of development are females per 1000 males, size of household, percentage of female workers to total workers, etc. (Rao 1976).

As per NITI Ayog (2023), Hailakandi, Karimganj, and Cachar, are the top three poorest districts in Assam with percentage of population who are multidimensionally poor are 36.22%, 32.93%, and 30.58% respectively. Multidimentional poverty index (MPI) is calculated with the help of indicators of health, eduation, and standard of living.

Workforce in India: Many important demographic and socio-economic data are provided by the Indian census at village level. The change in the concept of literacy by changing age group of 4+ to 7+ was one of the features in 1991 census (Census of India, 2011). Along with this, the sex wise population of children below seven years of age was added to calculate literacy rate in a more practical sense. In the census of 2011, the males include 'males' and 'others' (MHA 2011). The male, female, and total literacy rate in India as per 2011 census is observed to be 80%, 64.63%, and 72.98% respectively. Women in rural India exhibited significant hike in the literacy rate in 2011 (MoSPI 2019). In the 1991 census the population was divided into Main worker, Marginal worker, and Non-worker. The main worker was the one involved in work for one hundred eighty-three or more days. This involved economically productive work (physical or mental) or effective supervision or direction of work. The marginal worker was the worker involved in work for less than one hundred eighty-three days. In 1991 census, unpaid workers on farm or family enterprise were also incorporated among workers. The non-worker was the person who has not done any work at any time in last one year (MoSPI 2012). In the 1991 census in India, apart from the usual information such as village and town directory, primary census abstract (PCA) of village/town, and amenities, nine-fold industrial classification of main workers were added. These are Cultivators, Agricultural laborers, Livestock Forestry Fishing etc and allied activities workers, Mining and Quarying workers, Manufacturing and Processing in household industry workers, Manufacturing and processing in other than household industry workers, Construction workers, Trade and Commerce workers, Transport Storage and Communication workers. This nine-fold industrial category upto village level was one of the special features of 1991 census (Census of India, 2011). In 2001 census, workers were divided into Cultivators, Agricultural laborers, Household industry workers, and Other workers. This fourfold division or fourfold occupational category continued in 2011 census also. One of the new features in 2001 census was dropping of question on secondary work of main workers (Census of India, 2011). In 2001 census, people involved in cultivation and milk production for self use were incorporated as workers (Kasturi 2015). Among the non-workers, those who confirms availability for the work are considered unemployed in 2011 (Kasturi 2015). Motkuri and Naik (2016) in a study suggested that between 2001 and 2011 there is a decline in workforce in general and females in particular in India. Marginal wokers have increased comparatively more than the main workers. Motkuri et al. (2019) suggests that increasing marginal category is an indicator of under employment. Evidences also suggest that male population is shifting towards marginal workforce category in India. On one hand the cultivators are reducing, while on the other hand agricultural laborers are increasing in India. Motkuri and Naik (2016) mention that workforce is growing more in non-agricultural work as compared to in the agriculture sector. Rural India is witnessing a gradual diversification of workforce away from agricultural activity; many a times this is due to out-migration to urban areas, dispossession from their land, and reducing profitability from agriculture (Motkuri et al. 2019). They have also mentioned about 'extinction of farmers', particularly after implementation of economic reforms. Regarding relationship between work participation rate, workforce, and population, Motkuri et al. (2019) mentions that if work participation rate remains constant, workforce remains lower than population, and if the population growth rate remains constant, workforce growth rate depends on work participation rate, and hence change in participation rate changes the growth of workforce. In India, between 1991 and 2011, there has been a decline of WPR with respect to main workers particularly in rural areas. WPR of marginal workers have increased, which has led to the increase in marginal workforce in rural india (Motkuri et al. 2019).

Thomas and Jayesh (2016) have argued that after 1991, there has been a decline of main cultivators, and increase in marginal agricultural labourers. Workforce participation rates are also lower in India. In 2013 the participation rate was around 52% in the country whereas it was 71% in China and 65.5% in Brazil. In north east India in particular, the participation rate for main worker (males) was 48.2%, 42.5%, and 44.1% in the years 1991, 2001, and 2011 respectively. For marginal workers it was 1%, 7.1%, and 9.1% respectively. The participation rate for main worker (females) was 16.7%, 13.6%, and 14.3% in the years 1991, 2001, and 2011 respectively in north east India. Thomas and Jayesh (2016) further mention that between 2001 and 2011, change in employment in different sectors such as a)All workers, b)Workers other than cultivators and agricultural labourers, c)Cultivators and agricultural labourers, d) Agricultural labourers, and e)Cultivators are as follows; 79.9%, 50.9%, 28.9%, 37.6%, and Minus 8.6% respectively. The Economic Times noted, citing the economic survey of 2024 (The Economic Times 2024) that India's workforce is nearly 56.5 crore with 45% employed in agriculture. Female workforce is shifting towards self-employment, whereas its male counterpart is relatively stable. Work participation is witnessing an increase in last couple of years, particularly the female labour force participation.

Details of variables and indicators used in this work is given below (Table 4 to Table 9).

Table 4. Census variables used in the study for the year 1991

S. No.	Variable	Code used for spatial analysis
1	No of households	HOUSEHOLDS
2	Total population	T_POPLN
3	Total male population	T_M_POPLN
4	Total female population	T_F_POPLN
5	Male population below age 7	POPLN_M6
6	Female population below age 7	POPLN_F6
7	Male SC population	M_SC

8	Female SC population	F_SC
9	Male ST population	M_ST
10	Female ST Population	F_ST
11	Male literates	M_LITERATE
12	Female literates	F_LITERATE
13	Total main workers Male	T_M_WORKER
14	Total main workers Female	T_F_WORKER
15	Cultivators Male	M_INDCAT1
16	Cultivators Female	F_INDCAT1
17	Agricultural labourers Male	M_INDCAT2
18	Agricultural labourers Female	F_INDCAT2
19	Livestock Forestry Fishing etc and allied activities workers Male	M_INDCAT3
20	Livestock Forestry Fishing etc and allied activities workers Female	F_INDCAT3
21	Mining and Quarying workers Male	M_INDCAT4
22	Mining and Quarying workers Female	F_INDCAT4
23	Manufacturing and Processing in household industry workers Male	M_INDCAT5A
24	Manufacturing and Processing in household industry workers Female	F_INDCAT5A
25	Manufacturing and processing in other than household industry workers Male	M_INDCAT5B
26	Manufacturing and processing in other than household industry workers Female	F_INDCAT5B
27	Construction workers Male	M_INDCAT6
28	Construction workers Female	F_INDCAT6
29	Trade and Commerce workers Male	M_INDCAT7
30	Trade and Commerce workers Female	F_INDCAT7
31	Transport Storage and Communication workers Male	M_INDCAT8
32	Transport Storage and Communication workers Female	F_INDCAT8
33	Other services workers Male	M_INDCAT9
34	Other services workers Female	F_INDCAT9
35	Marginal workers Male	M_MARGINAL
36	Marginal workers Female	F_MARGINAL
37	Non Workers Male	M_NON_WORK
38	Non Workers Female	F_NON_WORK

Table 5. Census variables used in the study for the year 2001 & 2011

S. No.	Variable	Code used for spatial analysis
1	Number of Households	No_HH
2	Total Population	TOT_P
3	Total Male Population	TOT_M
4	Total Female Population	TOT_F
5	0-6 Age Group Persons	P_06
6	0-6 Age Group Males	M_06
7	0-6 Age Group Females	F_06
8	Scheduled Caste Persons	P_SC
9	Scheduled Caste Males	M_SC
10	Scheduled Caste Females	F_SC
11	Scheduled Tribe Persons	P_ST
12	Scheduled Tribe Males	M_ST
13	Scheduled Tribe Females	F_ST
14	Person Literates	P_LIT
15	Male Literates	M_LIT
16	Female Literates	F_LIT
17	Person Illiterates	P_ILL
18	Male Illiterates	M_ILL
19	Female Illiterates	F_ILL
20	Total Workers (Main + Marginal) Persons	TOT_WORK_P
21	Total Workers (Main + Marginal) Males	TOT_WORK_M
22	Total Workers (Main + Marginal) Females	TOT_WORK_F
23	Main Workers - Persons	MAINWORK_P
24	Main Workers - Males	MAINWORK_M
25	Main Workers - Females	MAINWORK_F
26	Main Workers Cultivators - Persons	MAIN_CL_P
27	Main Workers Cultivators - Males	MAIN_CL_M
28	Main Workers Cultivators - Females	MAIN_CL_F
29	Main Workers Agricultural Laborers - Persons	MAIN_AL_P
30	Main Workers Agricultural Laborers - Males	MAIN_AL_M
31	Main Workers Agricultural Laborers - Females	MAIN_AL_F
32	Main Workers Household Industry - Persons	MAIN_HH_P
33	Main Workers Household Industry - Males	MAIN_HH_M
34	Main Workers Household Industry - Females	MAIN_HH_F
35	Main Workers Other - Persons	MAIN_OT_P

36	Main Workers Other - Males	MAIN_OT_M
37	Main Workers Other - Females	MAIN_OT_F
38	Marginal Workers - Persons	MARGWORK_P
39	Marginal Workers - Males	MARGWORK_M
40	Marginal Workers - Females	MARGWORK_F
41	Marginal Workers Cultivators - Persons	MARG_CL_P
42	Marginal Workers Cultivators - Males	MARG_CL_M
43	Marginal Workers Cultivators - Females	MARG_CL_F
44	Marginal Workers Agricultural Laborers - Persons	MARG_AL_P
45	Marginal Workers Agricultural Laborers - Males	MARG_AL_M
46	Marginal Workers Agricultural Laborers - Females	MARG_AL_F
47	Marginal Workers Household Industry - Persons	MARG_HH_P
48	Marginal Workers Household Industry - Males	MARG_HH_M
49	Marginal Workers Household Industry - Females	MARG_HH_F
50	Marginal Workers Other - Persons	MARG_OT_P
51	Marginal Workers Other - Males	MARG_OT_M
52	Marginal Workers Other - Females	MARG_OT_F
53	Non Workers - Persons	NON_WORK_P
54	Non Workers - Males	NON_WORK_M
55	Non Workers - Females	NON_WORK_F

Table 6. Census variables used in the study for the year 2011 only

S. No.	Variable	Code used for spatial analysis
1	Marginal worker (3 to 6 months) - Total	MARGWORK_3
2	Marginal worker (3 to 6 months) - Male	MARGWORK_1
3	Marginal worker (3 to 6 months) - Female	MARGWORK_2
4	Marginal worker (3 to 6 months), cultivator - Total	MARG_CL_3_
5	Marginal worker (3 to 6 months), cultivator - Male	MARG_CL__1
6	Marginal worker (3 to 6 months), cultivator - Female	MARG_CL__2
7	Marginal worker (3 to 6 months), agricultural labourer - Total	MARG_AL_3_
8	Marginal worker (3 to 6 months), agricultural labourer - Male	MARG_AL__1
9	Marginal worker (3 to 6 months), agricultural labourer - Female	MARG_AL__2
10	Marginal worker (3 to 6 months), household industry - Total	MARG_HH_3_
11	Marginal worker (3 to 6 months), household industry - Male	MARG_HH__1
12	Marginal worker (3 to 6 months), household industry - Female	MARG_HH__2

13	Marginal worker (3 to 6 months), other - Total	MARG_OT_3_
14	Marginal worker (3 to 6 months), other - Male	MARG_OT__1
15	Marginal worker (3 to 6 months), other - Female	MARG_OT__2
16	Marginal worker (0 to 3 months) - Total	MARGWORK_0
17	Marginal worker (0 to 3 months) - Male	MARGWORK_4
18	Marginal worker (0 to 3 months) - Female	MARGWORK_5
19	Marginal worker (0 to 3 months), cultivator - Total	MARG_CL_0_
20	Marginal worker (0 to 3 months), cultivator - Male	MARG_CL__3
21	Marginal worker (0 to 3 months), cultivator - Female	MARG_CL__4
22	Marginal worker (0 to 3 months), agricultural labourer - Total	MARG_AL_0_
23	Marginal worker (0 to 3 months), agricultural labourer - Male	MARG_AL__3
24	Marginal worker (0 to 3 months), agricultural labourer - Female	MARG_AL__4
25	Marginal worker (0 to 3 months), household industry - Total	MARG_HH_0_
26	Marginal worker (0 to 3 months), household industry - Male	MARG_HH__3
27	Marginal worker (0 to 3 months), household industry - Female	MARG_HH__4
28	Marginal worker (0 to 3 months), other - Total	MARG_OT_0_
29	Marginal worker (0 to 3 months), other - Male	MARG_OT__3
30	Marginal worker (0 to 3 months), other - Female	MARG_OT__4

Table 7. Expression used in QGIS 'Expression Builder' for calculation of indicators - 1991

S. No	Indicator	Spatial display mode	Expression
1	Household size	Equal Count (Quantile)	("T_POPLN" / "RES_HOUSE")
2	Population density	Equal Count (Quantile)	("T_POPLN" / "Area(Sqkm)")
3	Population sex ratio	Equal Count (Quantile)	(("T_F_POPLN" / "T_M_POPLN") * 1000)
4	Child sex ratio	Equal Count (Quantile)	(("POPLN_F6" / "POPLN_M6") * 1000)
5	SC percentage	Natural Breaks (Jenks)	(("F_SC" + "M_SC") / "T_POPLN") * 100
6	ST percentage	Natural Breaks (Jenks)	(("F_ST" + "M_ST") / "T_POPLN") * 100
7	Literacy rate	Natural Breaks (Jenks)	(("M_LITERATE" + "F_LITERATE") / ("T_POPLN" - ("POPLN_M6" + "POPLN_F6"))) * 100
8	Workforce sex ratio – Non worker	Natural Breaks (Jenks)	("F_NON_WORK" / "M_NON_WORK") * 1000
9	Workforce sex ratio (Cultivators + Agricultural Labourers)	Natural Breaks (Jenks)	((("F_INDCAT1" + "F_INDCAT2") / ("M_INDCAT1" + "M_INDCAT2")) * 1000)
10	Workforce sex ratio (Livestock Forestry Fishing etc and allied activities workers)	Natural Breaks (Jenks)	(("F_INDCAT3" / "M_INDCAT3") * 1000)
11	Workforce sex ratio (Mining and Quarying workers)	Natural Breaks (Jenks)	(("F_INDCAT4" / "M_INDCAT4") * 1000)
12	Workforce sex ratio (Manufacturing and Processing in household industry workers)	Natural Breaks (Jenks)	(("F_INDCAT5A" / "M_INDCAT5A") * 1000)
13	Workforce sex ratio (Manufacturing and Processing in other than household industry workers)	Natural Breaks (Jenks)	(("F_INDCAT5B" / "M_INDCAT5B") * 1000)
14	Workforce sex ratio (Construction workers)	Natural Breaks (Jenks)	(("F_INDCAT6" / "M_INDCAT6") * 1000)
15	Workforce sex ratio (Trade and Commerce workers)	Natural Breaks (Jenks)	(("F_INDCAT7" / "M_INDCAT7") * 1000)
16	Workforce sex ratio (Transport Storage and Communication workers)	Natural Breaks (Jenks)	(("F_INDCAT8" / "M_INDCAT8") * 1000)
17	Workforce sex ratio (Other services workers)	Natural Breaks (Jenks)	(("F_INDCAT9" / "M_INDCAT9") * 1000)

18	Workforce sex ratio (Main + Marginal workers)	Natural Breaks (Jenks)	((("T_F_WORKER" + "F_MARGINAL") / ("T_M_WORKER" + "M_MARGINAL")) * 1000)
19	Workforce sex ratio (Main workers)	Natural Breaks (Jenks)	(("T_F_WORKER" / "T_M_WORKER") * 1000)
20	Workforce sex ratio (Marginal workers)	Equal Count (Quantile)	(("F_MARGINAL" / "M_MARGINAL") * 1000)
21	Work Participation Rate (Main - Male)	Natural Breaks (Jenks)	((("T_M_WORKER") / ("T_POPLN")) * 100)
22	Work Participation Rate (Main - Female)	Natural Breaks (Jenks)	((("T_F_WORKER") / ("T_POPLN")) * 100)
23	Work Participation Rate (Main - Total)	Natural Breaks (Jenks)	((("T_M_WORKER" + "T_F_WORKER") / ("T_POPLN")) * 100)
24	Work Participation Rate (Main+Marginal-Total)	Natural Breaks (Jenks)	((("T_M_WORKER" + "T_F_WORKER" + "M_MARGINAL" + "F_MARGINAL") / ("T_POPLN")) * 100)
25	Work Participation Rate (Main+Marginal-Male)	Natural Breaks (Jenks)	((("T_M_WORKER" + "M_MARGINAL") / ("T_POPLN")) * 100)
26	Work Participation Rate (Main+Marginal-Female)	Natural Breaks (Jenks)	((("T_F_WORKER" + "F_MARGINAL") / ("T_POPLN")) * 100)
27	Work Participation Rate (Marginal - Male)	Natural Breaks (Jenks)	((("M_MARGINAL") / ("T_POPLN")) * 100)
28	Work Participation Rate (Marginal - Female)	Natural Breaks (Jenks)	((("F_MARGINAL") / ("T_POPLN")) * 100)
29	Work Participation Rate (Marginal - Total)	Natural Breaks (Jenks)	((("M_MARGINAL" + "F_MARGINAL") / ("T_POPLN")) * 100)
30	Work Participation Rate (Cultivators - Total)	Natural Breaks (Jenks)	(("M_INDCAT1" + "F_INDCAT1") / "T_POPLN") * 100
31	Work Participation Rate (Cultivators - Male)	Natural Breaks (Jenks)	(("M_INDCAT1") / "T_POPLN") * 100
32	Work Participation Rate (Cultivators - Female)	Natural Breaks (Jenks)	(("F_INDCAT1") / "T_POPLN") * 100
33	Work Participation Rate (Agricultural labourer - Male)	Natural Breaks (Jenks)	(("M_INDCAT2") / "T_POPLN") * 100
34	Work Participation Rate (Agricultural labourer - Female)	Natural Breaks (Jenks)	(("F_INDCAT2") / "T_POPLN") * 100
35	Work Participation Rate (Agricultural labourer - Total)	Natural Breaks (Jenks)	(("M_INDCAT2" + "F_INDCAT2") / "T_POPLN") * 100
36	Work Participation Rate (Livestock Forestry Fishing etc and allied activities - Total)	Natural Breaks (Jenks)	(("M_INDCAT3" + "F_INDCAT3") / "T_POPLN") * 100
37	Work Participation Rate (Livestock Forestry Fishing etc and allied activities - Male)	Natural Breaks (Jenks)	(("M_INDCAT3") / "T_POPLN") * 100

38	Work Participation Rate (Livestock Forestry Fishing etc and allied activities - Female)	Natural Breaks (Jenks)	(("F_INDCAT3") / "T_POPLN") * 100
39	Work Participation Rate (Mining and Quarying workers - Male)	Natural Breaks (Jenks)	(("M_INDCAT4") / "T_POPLN") * 100
40	Work Participation Rate (Mining and Quarying workers - Female)	Natural Breaks (Jenks)	(("F_INDCAT4") / "T_POPLN") * 100
41	Work Participation Rate (Mining and Quarying workers - Total)	Natural Breaks (Jenks)	(("M_INDCAT4" + "F_INDCAT4") / "T_POPLN") * 100
42	Work Participation Rate (Manufacturing and Processing in household industry workers - Total)	Natural Breaks (Jenks)	(("M_INDCAT5A" + "F_INDCAT5A") / "T_POPLN") * 100
43	Work Participation Rate (Manufacturing and Processing in household industry workers - Male)	Natural Breaks (Jenks)	(("M_INDCAT5A") / "T_POPLN") * 100
44	Work Participation Rate (Manufacturing and Processing in household industry workers - Female)	Natural Breaks (Jenks)	(("F_INDCAT5A") / "T_POPLN") * 100
45	Work Participation Rate (Manufacturing and Processing in other than household industry workers - Male)	Natural Breaks (Jenks)	(("M_INDCAT5B") / "T_POPLN") * 100
46	Work (Manufacturing and Processing in other than household industry workers - Female) Participation Rate	Natural Breaks (Jenks)	(("F_INDCAT5B") / "T_POPLN") * 100
47	Work Participation Rate (Manufacturing and Processing in other than household industry workers - Total)	Natural Breaks (Jenks)	(("M_INDCAT5B" + "F_INDCAT5B") / "T_POPLN") * 100
48	Work Participation Rate (Construction workers - Total)	Natural Breaks (Jenks)	(("M_INDCAT6" + "F_INDCAT6") / "T_POPLN") * 100
49	Work Participation Rate (Construction workers - Male)	Natural Breaks (Jenks)	(("M_INDCAT6") / "T_POPLN") * 100
50	Work Participation Rate (Construction workers - Female)	Natural Breaks (Jenks)	(("F_INDCAT6") / "T_POPLN") * 100
51	Work Participation Rate (Trade and Commerce workers - Male)	Natural Breaks (Jenks)	(("M_INDCAT7") / "T_POPLN") * 100
52	Work Participation Rate (Trade and Commerce workers - Female)	Natural Breaks (Jenks)	(("F_INDCAT7") / "T_POPLN") * 100

53	Work Participation Rate (Trade and Commerce workers - Total)	Natural Breaks (Jenks)	((“M_INDCAT7” + “F_INDCAT7”) / “T_POPLN”) * 100
54	Work Participation Rate (Transport Storage and Communication workers - Total)	Natural Breaks (Jenks)	((“M_INDCAT8” + “F_INDCAT8”) / “T_POPLN”) * 100
55	Work Participation Rate (Transport Storage and Communication workers - Male)	Natural Breaks (Jenks)	((“M_INDCAT8”) / “T_POPLN”) * 100
56	Work Participation Rate (Transport Storage and Communication workers - Female)	Natural Breaks (Jenks)	((“F_INDCAT8”) / “T_POPLN”) * 100
57	Work Participation Rate (Other services workers - Male)	Natural Breaks (Jenks)	((“M_INDCAT9”) / “T_POPLN”) * 100
58	Work Participation Rate (Other services workers - Female)	Natural Breaks (Jenks)	((“F_INDCAT9”) / “T_POPLN”) * 100
59	Work Participation Rate (Other services workers - Total)	Natural Breaks (Jenks)	((“M_INDCAT9” + “F_INDCAT9”) / “T_POPLN”) * 100
60	Work Participation Rate (Non workers - Total)	Natural Breaks (Jenks)	((“M_NON_WORK” + “F_NON_WORK”) / “T_POPLN”) * 100
61	Work Participation Rate (Non workers - Male)	Natural Breaks (Jenks)	(“M_NON_WORK” / “T_POPLN”) * 100
62	Work Participation Rate (Non workers - Female)	Natural Breaks (Jenks)	(“F_NON_WORK” / “T_POPLN”) * 100

Table 8. Expression used in QGIS ‘Expression Builder’ for calculation of indicators - 2001

S. No	Indicator	Spatial display mode	Expression
1	Household size	Natural Breaks (Jenks)	“TOT_P” / “No_HH”
2	Population density	Equal Count (Quantile)	“TOT_P” / “Area_1”
3	Population sex ratio	Equal Count (Quantile)	(“TOT_F” / “TOT_M”) * 1000
4	Child sex ratio	Equal Count (Quantile)	(“F_06” / “M_06”) * 1000
5	SC percentage	Natural Breaks (Jenks)	(“P_SC” / “TOT_P”) * 100
6	ST percentage	Natural Breaks (Jenks)	(“P_ST” / “TOT_P”) * 100
7	Literacy rate	Natural Breaks (Jenks)	(“P_LIT” / (“TOT_P” - “P_06”)) * 100

8	Workforce sex ratio (Main + Marginal worker)	Natural Breaks (Jenks)	(“TOT_WORK_F” / “TOT_WORK_M”) * 1000
9	Workforce sex ratio (Main worker)	Natural Breaks (Jenks)	(“MAINWORK_F” / “MAINWORK_M”) * 1000
10	Workforce sex ratio – Cultivators (Main worker)	Natural Breaks (Jenks)	(“MAIN_CL_F” / “MAIN_CL_M”) * 1000
11	Workforce sex ratio – Agricultural laborers (Main worker)	Natural Breaks (Jenks)	(“MAIN_AL_F” / “MAIN_AL_M”) * 1000
12	Workforce sex ratio – Household industry (Main worker)	Natural Breaks (Jenks)	(“MAIN_HH_F” / “MAIN_HH_M”) * 1000
13	Workforce sex ratio – Other (Main worker)	Natural Breaks (Jenks)	(“MAIN_OT_F” / “MAIN_OT_M”) * 1000
14	Workforce sex ratio (Marginal worker)	Equal Count (Quantile)	(“MARGWORK_F” / “MARGWORK_M”) * 1000
15	Workforce sex ratio – Cultivators (Marginal workers)	Natural Breaks (Jenks)	(“MARG_CL_F” / “MARG_CL_M”) * 1000
16	Workforce sex ratio – Agricultural laborers (Marginal worker)	Natural Breaks (Jenks)	(“MARG_AL_F” / “MARG_AL_M”) * 1000
17	Workforce sex ratio – Household industry (Marginal workers)	Natural Breaks (Jenks)	(“MARG_HH_F” / “MARG_HH_M”) * 1000
18	Workforce sex ratio – Other (Marginal workers)	Natural Breaks (Jenks)	(“MARG_OT_F” / “MARG_OT_M”) * 1000
19	Workforce sex ratio – Non worker	Natural Breaks (Jenks)	(“NON_WORK_F” / “NON_WORK_M”) * 1000
20	Work participation rate (Main+Marginal – Male)	Natural Breaks (Jenks)	(“TOT_WORK_M” / “TOT_P”) * 100
21	Work participation rate (Main+Marginal – Female)	Natural Breaks (Jenks)	(“TOT_WORK_F” / “TOT_P”) * 100
22	Work participation rate (Main+Marginal -Total)	Natural Breaks (Jenks)	(“TOT_WORK_P” / “TOT_P”) * 100
23	Work participation rate (Main – Total)	Natural Breaks (Jenks)	(“MAINWORK_P” / “TOT_P”) * 100
24	Work participation rate (Main – Male)	Natural Breaks (Jenks)	(“MAINWORK_M”/”TOT_P”) * 100
25	Work participation rate (Main – Female)	Natural Breaks (Jenks)	(“MAINWORK_F”/”TOT_P”) * 100
26	Work participation rate (Main –Cultivators-Male)	Natural Breaks (Jenks)	(“MAIN_CL_M” /”TOT_P”) * 100
27	Work participation rate (Main –Cultivators-Female)	Natural Breaks (Jenks)	(“MAIN_CL_F” / “TOT_P”) * 100
28	Work participation rate (Main – Cultivators-Total)	Natural Breaks (Jenks)	(“MAIN_CL_P” /”TOT_P”) * 100
29	Work participation rate (Main – Agricultural laborers-Total)	Natural Breaks (Jenks)	(“MAIN_AL_P” / “TOT_P”) * 100
30	Work participation rate (Main – Agricultural Laborers- Male)	Natural Breaks (Jenks)	(“MAIN_AL_M” / “TOT_P”) * 100
31	Work participation rate (Main – Agricultural Laborers- Female)	Natural Breaks (Jenks)	(“MAIN_AL_F” / “TOT_P”) * 100

32	Work participation rate (Main – Household Industry-Male)	Natural Breaks (Jenks)	(“MAIN_HH_M” / “TOT_P”) * 100
33	Work participation rate (Main – Household Industry-Female)	Natural Breaks (Jenks)	(“MAIN_HH_F” / “TOT_P”) * 100
34	Work participation rate (Main – Household Industry-Total)	Natural Breaks (Jenks)	(“MAIN_HH_P” / “TOT_P”) * 100
35	Work participation rate (Main – Other - Total)	Natural Breaks (Jenks)	(“MAIN_OT_P” / “TOT_P”) * 100
36	Work participation rate (Main – Other - Male)	Natural Breaks (Jenks)	(“MAIN_OT_M”/ “TOT_P”) * 100
37	Work participation rate (Main – Other - Female)	Natural Breaks (Jenks)	(“MAIN_OT_F” / “TOT_P”) * 100
38	Work participation rate (Marginal – Male)	Natural Breaks (Jenks)	(“MARGWORK_M” / “TOT_P”) * 100
39	Work participation rate (Marginal – Female)	Natural Breaks (Jenks)	(“MARGWORK_F” / “TOT_P”) * 100
40	Work participation rate (Marginal – Total)	Natural Breaks (Jenks)	(“MARGWORK_P” / “TOT_P”) * 100
41	Work participation rate (Marginal – Cultivators-Total)	Natural Breaks (Jenks)	(“MARG_CL_P” / “TOT_P”) * 100
42	Work participation rate (Marginal –Cultivators-Male)	Natural Breaks (Jenks)	(“MARG_CL_M” / “TOT_P”) * 100
43	Work participation rate (Marginal –Cultivators-Female)	Natural Breaks (Jenks)	(“MARG_CL_F” / “TOT_P”) * 100
44	Work participation rate (Marginal – Agricultural Laborers- Male)	Natural Breaks (Jenks)	(“MARG_AL_M” / “TOT_P”) * 100
45	Work participation rate (Marginal – Agricultural Laborers- Female)	Natural Breaks (Jenks)	(“MARG_AL_F” / “TOT_P”) * 100
46	Work participation rate (Marginal – Agricultural Laborers-Total)	Natural Breaks (Jenks)	(“MARG_AL_P” / “TOT_P”) * 100
47	Work participation rate (Marginal – Household Industry- Total)	Natural Breaks (Jenks)	(“MARG_HH_P” / “TOT_P”) * 100
48	Work participation rate (Marginal – Household Industry- Male)	Natural Breaks (Jenks)	(“MARG_HH_M” / “TOT_P”) * 100
49	Work participation rate (Marginal – Household Industry- Female)	Natural Breaks (Jenks)	(“MARG_HH_F” / “TOT_P”) * 100
50	Work participation rate (Marginal – Other - Male)	Natural Breaks (Jenks)	(“MARG_OT_M”/ “TOT_P”) * 100
51	Work participation rate (Marginal – Other - Female)	Natural Breaks (Jenks)	(“MARG_OT_F”/ “TOT_P”) * 100
52	Work participation rate (Marginal – Other - Total)	Natural Breaks (Jenks)	(“MARG_OT_P” / “TOT_P”) * 100
53	Work participation rate (Non workers –Total)	Natural Breaks (Jenks)	(“NON_WORK_P”/ “TOT_P”) * 100
54	Work participation rate (Non workers –Male)	Natural Breaks (Jenks)	(“NON_WORK_M”/ “TOT_P”) * 100
55	Work participation rate (Non workers –Female)	Natural Breaks (Jenks)	(“NON_WORK_F”/ “TOT_P”) * 100

Table 9. Expression used in QGIS 'Expression Builder' for calculation of indicators - 2011

S. No	Indicator	Spatial display mode	Expression
1	Household size	Natural Breaks (Jenks)	"TOT_P" / "No_HH"
2	Population density	Equal Count (Quantile)	"TOT_P" / "Area"
3	Population sex ratio	Equal Count (Quantile)	("TOT_F" / "TOT_M") * 1000
4	Child sex ratio	Equal Count (Quantile)	("F_06" / "M_06") * 1000
5	SC percentage	Natural Breaks (Jenks)	("P_SC" / "TOT_P") * 100
6	ST percentage	Natural Breaks (Jenks)	("P_ST" / "TOT_P") * 100
7	Literacy rate	Natural Breaks (Jenks)	("P_LIT" / ("TOT_P" - "P_06")) * 100
8	Workforce sex ratio (Main + Marginal worker)	Natural Breaks (Jenks)	("TOT_WORK_F" / "TOT_WORK_M") * 1000
9	Workforce sex ratio (Main worker)	Natural Breaks (Jenks)	("MAINWORK_F" / "MAINWORK_M") * 1000
10	Workforce sex ratio – Cultivators (Main worker)	Natural Breaks (Jenks)	("MAIN_CL_F" / "MAIN_CL_M") * 1000
11	Workforce sex ratio – Agricultural laborers (Main worker)	Natural Breaks (Jenks)	("MAIN_AL_F" / "MAIN_AL_M") * 1000
12	Workforce sex ratio – Household industry (Main worker)	Natural Breaks (Jenks)	("MAIN_HH_F" / "MAIN_HH_M") * 1000
13	Workforce sex ratio – Other (Main worker)	Natural Breaks (Jenks)	("MAIN_OT_F" / "MAIN_OT_M") * 1000
14	Workforce sex ratio (Marginal worker)	Equal Count (Quantile)	("MARGWORK_F" / "MARGWORK_M") * 1000
15	Workforce sex ratio – Cultivators (Marginal worker)	Natural Breaks (Jenks)	("MARG_CL_F" / "MARG_CL_M") * 1000
16	Workforce sex ratio – Agricultural laborers (Marginal worker)	Natural Breaks (Jenks)	("MARG_AL_F" / "MARG_AL_M") * 1000
17	Workforce sex ratio – Household industry (Marginal worker)	Natural Breaks (Jenks)	("MARG_HH_F" / "MARG_HH_M") * 1000
18	Workforce sex ratio – Other (Marginal worker)	Natural Breaks (Jenks)	("MARG_OT_F" / "MARG_OT_M") * 1000
19	Workforce sex ratio – Non worker	Natural Breaks (Jenks)	("NON_WORK_F" / "NON_WORK_M") * 1000
20	Work participation rate (Main+Marginal – Male)	Natural Breaks (Jenks)	("TOT_WORK_M" / "TOT_P") * 100
21	Work participation rate (Main+Marginal – Female)	Natural Breaks (Jenks)	("TOT_WORK_F" / "TOT_P") * 100

22	Work participation rate (Main+Marginal -Total)	Natural Breaks (Jenks)	(“TOT_WORK_P” / “TOT_P”) * 100
23	Work participation rate (Main – Total)	Natural Breaks (Jenks)	(“MAINWORK_P”/ “TOT_P”) * 100
24	Work participation rate (Main – Male)	Natural Breaks (Jenks)	(“MAINWORK_M” /”TOT_P”) * 100
25	Work participation rate (Main – Female)	Natural Breaks (Jenks)	(“MAINWORK_F” / “TOT_P”) * 100
26	Work participation rate (Main –Cultivators-Male)	Natural Breaks (Jenks)	(“MAIN_CL_M” / “TOT_P”) * 100
27	Work participation rate (Main –Cultivators-Female)	Natural Breaks (Jenks)	(“MAIN_CL_F” / “TOT_P”) * 100
28	Work participation rate (Main – Cultivators-Total)	Natural Breaks (Jenks)	(“MAIN_CL_P” / “TOT_P”) * 100
29	Work participation rate (Main – Agricultural laborers-Total)	Natural Breaks (Jenks)	(“MAIN_AL_P” / “TOT_P”) * 100
30	Work participation rate (Main – Agricultural Laborers- Male)	Natural Breaks (Jenks)	(“MAIN_AL_M” / “TOT_P”) * 100
31	Work participation rate (Main – Agricultural Laborers- Female)	Natural Breaks (Jenks)	(“MAIN_AL_F” / “TOT_P”) * 100
32	Work participation rate (Main – Household Industry-Male)	Natural Breaks (Jenks)	(“MAIN_HH_M” / “TOT_P”) * 100
33	Work participation rate (Main – Household Industry-Female)	Natural Breaks (Jenks)	(“MAIN_HH_F” / “TOT_P”) * 100
34	Work participation rate (Main – Household Industry-Total)	Natural Breaks (Jenks)	(“MAIN_HH_P” / “TOT_P”) * 100
35	Work participation rate (Main – Other - Total)	Natural Breaks (Jenks)	(“MAIN_OT_P” / “TOT_P”) * 100
36	Work participation rate (Main – Other - Male)	Natural Breaks (Jenks)	(“MAIN_OT_M”/ “TOT_P”) * 100
37	Work participation rate (Main – Other - Female)	Natural Breaks (Jenks)	(“MAIN_OT_F” / “TOT_P”) * 100
38	Work participation rate (Marginal – Male)	Natural Breaks (Jenks)	(“MARGWORK_M” / “TOT_P”) * 100
39	Work participation rate (Marginal – Female)	Natural Breaks (Jenks)	(“MARGWORK_F” / “TOT_P”) * 100
40	Work participation rate (Marginal – Total)	Natural Breaks (Jenks)	(“MARGWORK_P” / “TOT_P”) * 100
41	Work participation rate (Marginal – Cultivators-Total)	Natural Breaks (Jenks)	(“MARG_CL_P” / “TOT_P”) * 100
42	Work participation rate (Marginal –Cultivators-Male)	Natural Breaks (Jenks)	(“MARG_CL_M” / “TOT_P”) * 100
43	Work participation rate (Marginal –Cultivators-Female)	Natural Breaks (Jenks)	(“MARG_CL_F” / “TOT_P”) * 100
44	Work participation rate (Marginal – Agricultural Laborers- Male)	Natural Breaks (Jenks)	(“MARG_AL_M” / “TOT_P”) * 100
45	Work participation rate (Marginal – Agricultural Laborers- Female)	Natural Breaks (Jenks)	(“MARG_AL_F” / “TOT_P”) * 100

46	Work participation rate (Marginal – Agricultural Laborers-Total)	Natural Breaks (Jenks)	(“MARG_AL_P” / “TOT_P”) * 100
47	Work participation rate (Marginal – Household Industry- Total)	Natural Breaks (Jenks)	(“MARG_HH_P” / “TOT_P”) * 100
48	Work participation rate (Marginal – Household Industry- Male)	Natural Breaks (Jenks)	(“MARG_HH_M” / “TOT_P”) * 100
49	Work participation rate (Marginal – Household Industry- Female)	Natural Breaks (Jenks)	(“MARG_HH_F” / “TOT_P”) * 100
50	Work participation rate (Marginal – Other - Male)	Natural Breaks (Jenks)	(“MARG_OT_M”/ “TOT_P”) * 100
51	Work participation rate (Marginal – Other - Female)	Natural Breaks (Jenks)	(“MARG_OT_F”/ “TOT_P”) * 100
52	Work participation rate (Marginal – Other - Total)	Natural Breaks (Jenks)	(“MARG_OT_P” / “TOT_P”) * 100
53	Work participation rate (Non workers –Total)	Natural Breaks (Jenks)	(“NON_WORK_P”/ “TOT_P”) * 100
54	Work participation rate (Non workers –Male)	Natural Breaks (Jenks)	(“NON_WORK_M”/ “TOT_P”) * 100
55	Work participation rate (Non workers –Female)	Natural Breaks (Jenks)	(“NON_WORK_F”/ “TOT_P”) * 100
56	Work participation rate (Marginal-3to6 months-Male)	Natural Breaks (Jenks)	(“MARGWORK_1”/ “TOT_P”) * 100
57	Work participation rate (Marginal-3to6 months-Female)	Natural Breaks (Jenks)	(“MARGWORK_2”/ “TOT_P”) * 100
58	Work participation rate (Marginal-3to6 months-Total)	Natural Breaks (Jenks)	(“MARGWORK_3”/ “TOT_P”) * 100
59	Work participation rate (Marginal-3to6 months-Cultivator-Total)	Natural Breaks (Jenks)	(“MARG_CL_3_”/ “TOT_P”) * 100
60	Work participation rate (Marginal-3to6 months-Cultivator-Male)	Natural Breaks (Jenks)	(“MARG_CL__1” / “TOT_P”) * 100
61	Work participation rate (Marginal-3to6 months-Cultivator-Female)	Natural Breaks (Jenks)	(“MARG_CL__2”/ “TOT_P”) * 100
62	Work participation rate (Marginal-3to6 months-Agricultural laborer-Male)	Natural Breaks (Jenks)	(“MARG_AL__1” / “TOT_P”) * 100
63	Work participation rate (Marginal-3to6 months-Agricultural laborer-Female)	Natural Breaks (Jenks)	(“MARG_AL__2” / “TOT_P”) * 100
64	Work participation rate (Marginal-3to6 months-Agricultural laborer-Total)	Natural Breaks (Jenks)	(“MARG_AL_3_” / “TOT_P”) * 100
65	Work participation rate (Marginal-3to6 months-Household Industry-Total)	Natural Breaks (Jenks)	(“MARG_HH_3_” / “TOT_P”) * 100
66	Work participation rate (Marginal-3to6 months-Household Industry-Male)	Natural Breaks (Jenks)	(“MARG_HH__1”/ “TOT_P”) * 100
67	Work participation rate (Marginal-3to6 months-Household Industry-Female)	Natural Breaks (Jenks)	(“MARG_HH__2”/ “TOT_P”) * 100

68	Work participation rate (Marginal-3to6 months-Other-Male)	Natural Breaks (Jenks)	("MARG_OT__1"/ "TOT_P") * 100
69	Work participation rate (Marginal-3to6 months-Other-Female)	Natural Breaks (Jenks)	("MARG_OT__2"/ "TOT_P") * 100
70	Work participation rate (Marginal-3to6 months-Other-Total)	Natural Breaks (Jenks)	("MARG_OT_3_"/ "TOT_P") * 100
71	Work participation rate (Marginal-0to3 months-Total)	Natural Breaks (Jenks)	("MARGWORK_0"/ "TOT_P") * 100
72	Work participation rate (Marginal-0to3 months-Male)	Natural Breaks (Jenks)	("MARGWORK_4"/ "TOT_P") * 100
73	Work participation rate (Marginal-0to3 months-Female)	Natural Breaks (Jenks)	("MARGWORK_5"/ "TOT_P") * 100
74	Work participation rate (Marginal-0to3 months-Cultivator-Male)	Natural Breaks (Jenks)	("MARG_CL__3"/ "TOT_P") * 100
75	Work participation rate (Marginal-0to3 months-Cultivator-Female)	Natural Breaks (Jenks)	("MARG_CL__4"/ "TOT_P") * 100
76	Work participation rate (Marginal-0to3 months-Cultivator-Total)	Natural Breaks (Jenks)	("MARG_CL_0_"/ "TOT_P") * 100
77	Work participation rate (Marginal-0to3 months-Agricultural laborer-Total)	Natural Breaks (Jenks)	("MARG_AL_0_"/ "TOT_P") * 100
78	Work participation rate (Marginal-0to3 months-Agricultural laborer-Male)	Natural Breaks (Jenks)	("MARG_AL__3"/ "TOT_P") * 100
79	Work participation rate (Marginal-0to3 months-Agricultural laborer-Female)	Natural Breaks (Jenks)	("MARG_AL__4"/ "TOT_P") * 100
80	Work participation rate (Marginal-0to3 months-Household Industry-Male)	Natural Breaks (Jenks)	("MARG_HH__3"/ "TOT_P") * 100
81	Work participation rate (Marginal-0to3 months-Household Industry-Female)	Natural Breaks (Jenks)	("MARG_HH__4"/ "TOT_P") * 100
82	Work participation rate (Marginal-0to3 months-Household Industry-Total)	Natural Breaks (Jenks)	("MARG_HH_0_"/ "TOT_P") * 100
83	Work participation rate (Marginal-0to3 months-Other-Total)	Natural Breaks (Jenks)	("MARG_OT_0_"/ "TOT_P") * 100
84	Work participation rate (Marginal-0to3 months-Other-Male)	Natural Breaks (Jenks)	("MARG_OT__3"/ "TOT_P") * 100
85	Work participation rate (Marginal-0to3 months-Other-Female)	Natural Breaks (Jenks)	("MARG_OT__4"/ "TOT_P") * 100

Comparison of census variables and socio-economic indicators of Barak Valley across decades

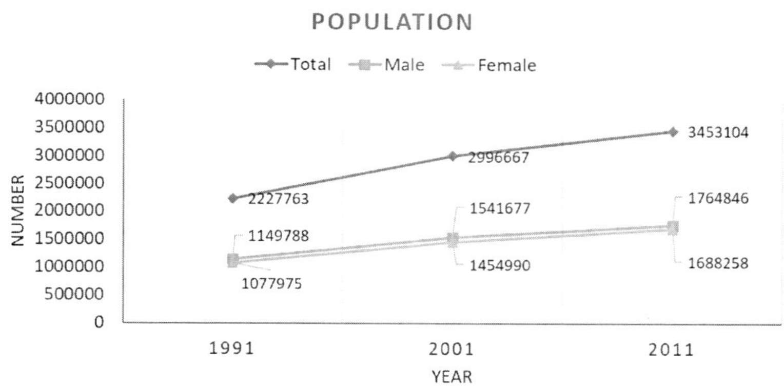

Fig. 1. Population of Barak Valley during the study years.

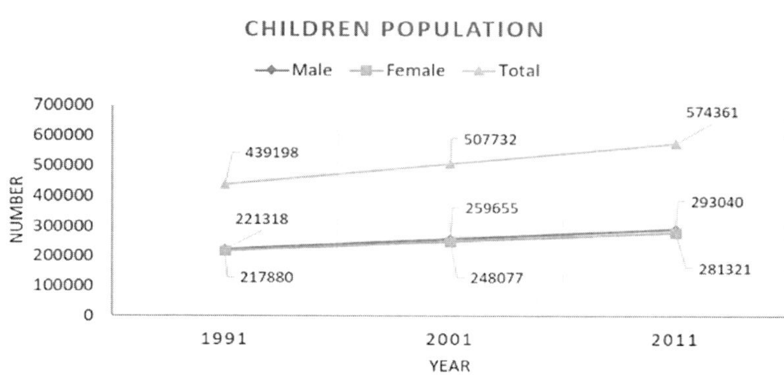

Fig. 2. Children population of Barak Valley during the study years.

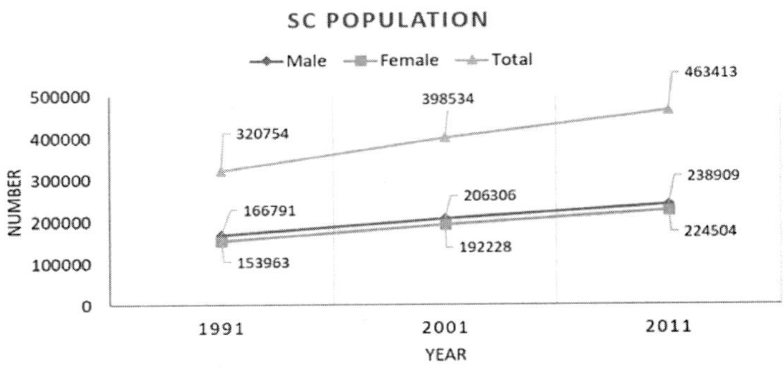

Fig. 3. Scheduled caste (SC) population of Barak Valley during the study years.

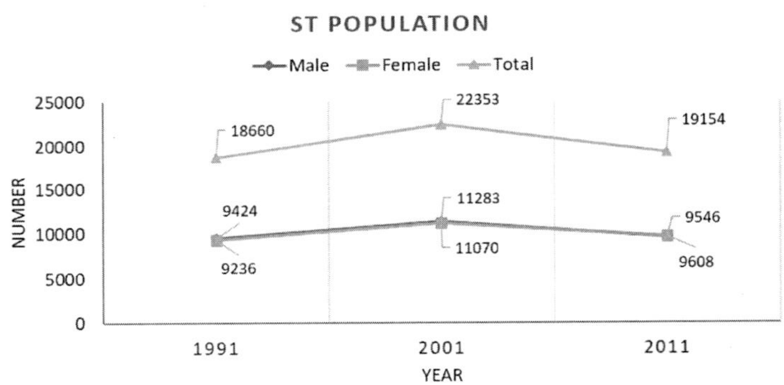

Fig. 4. Scheduled tribe (ST) population of Barak Valley during the study years.

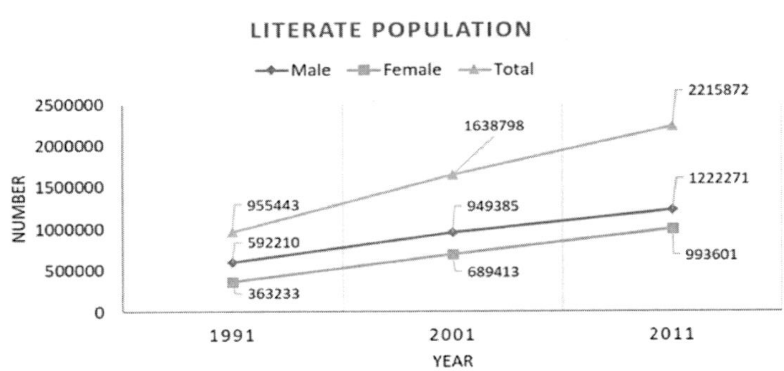

Fig. 5. Literate population of Barak Valley during the study years.

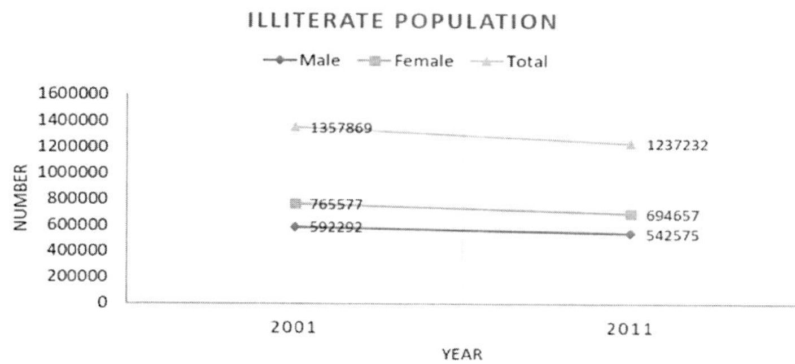

Fig. 6. Illiterate Population of Barak Valley in 2001 & 2011.

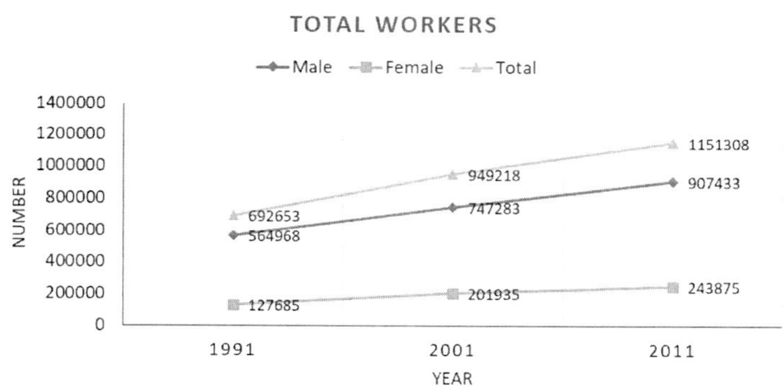

Fig. 7. Total (main and marginal) workers in Barak Valley during the study years.

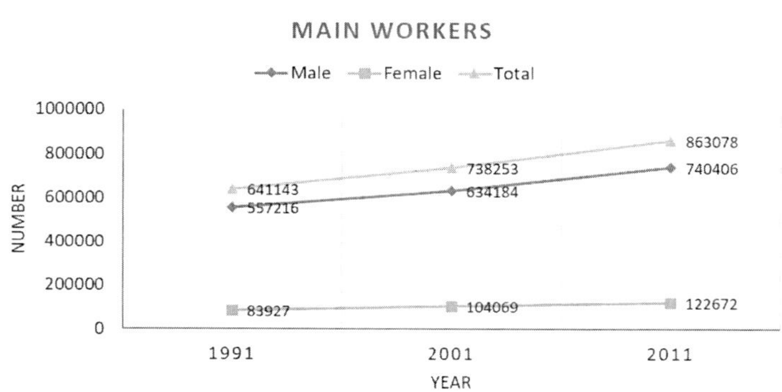

Fig. 8. Main workers in Barak Valley during the study years.

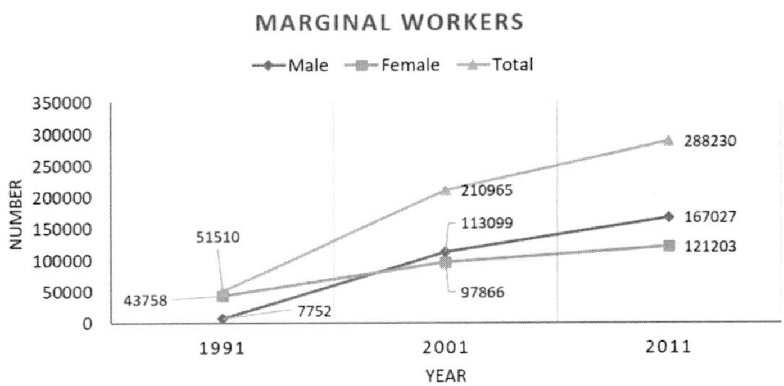

Fig. 9. Marginal workers in Barak Valley during the study years.

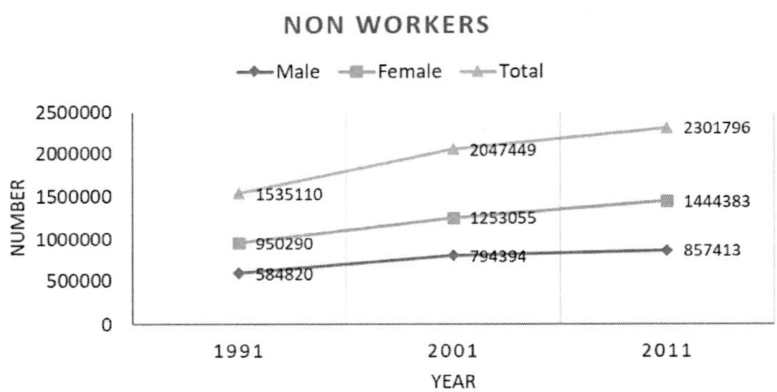

Fig. 10. Non workers in Barak Valley during the study years.

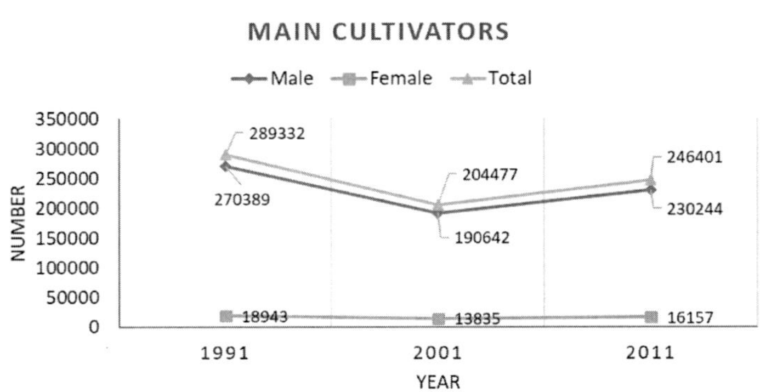

Fig. 11. Main Cultivators in Barak Valley during the study years.

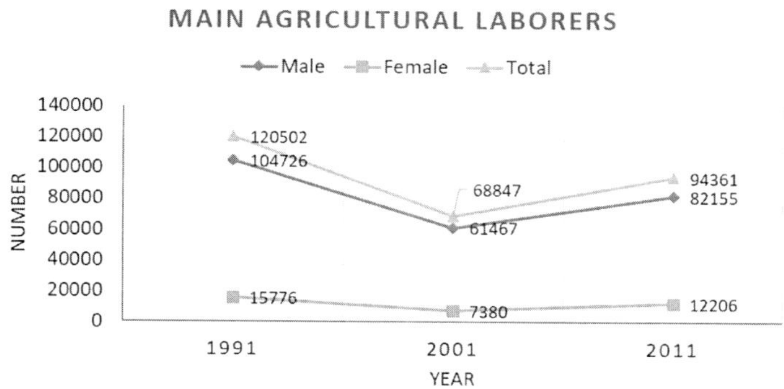

Fig. 12. Main Agricultural laborers in Barak Valley during the study years.

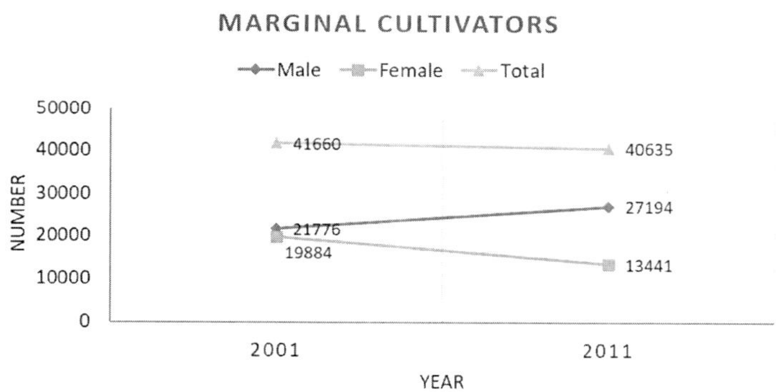

Fig. 13. Marginal Cultivators in Barak Valley in 2001 & 2011.

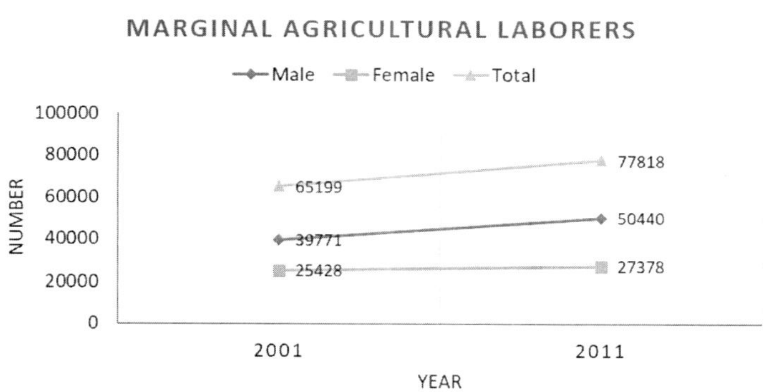

Fig. 14. Marginal Agricultural laborers in Barak Valley in 2001 & 2011.

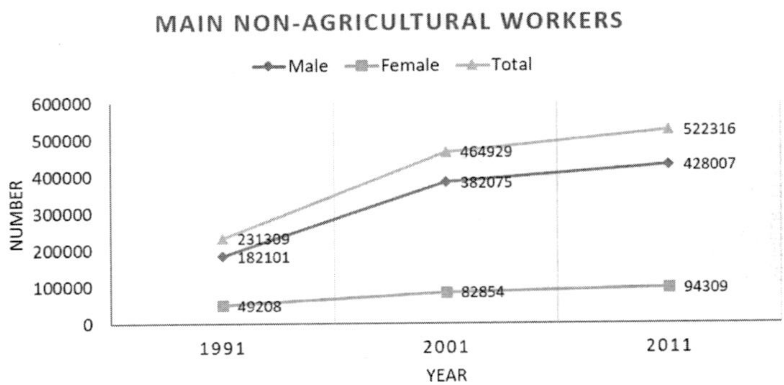

Fig. 15. Main Non-Agricultural (involves household industry and others).

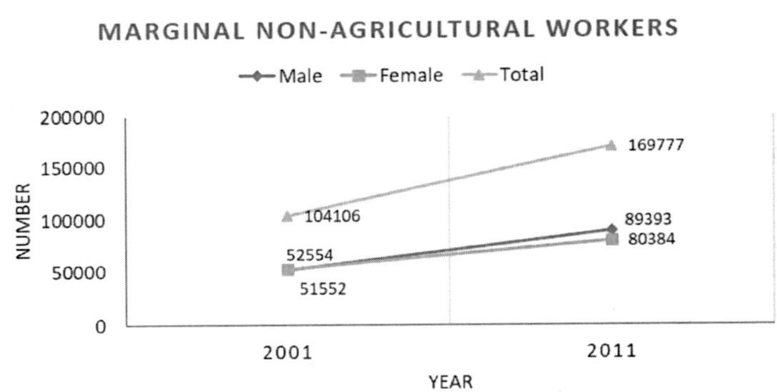

Fig. 16. Marginal Non-Agricultural workers in Barak Valley in 2001 & 2011.

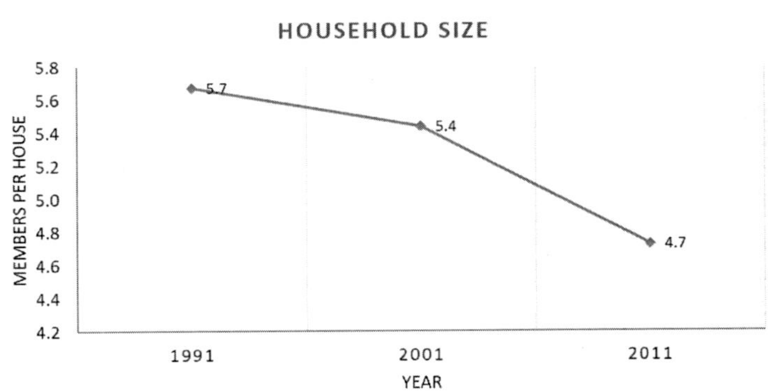

Fig. 17. Change in household size in Barak Valley between 1991 and 2011.

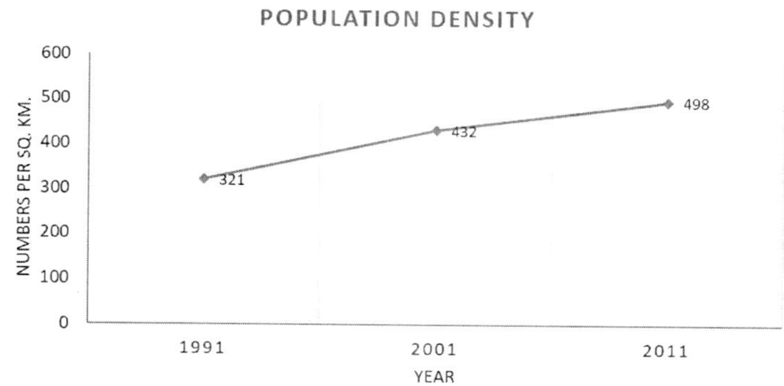

Fig. 18. Change in Population density in Barak Valley between 1991 and 2011.

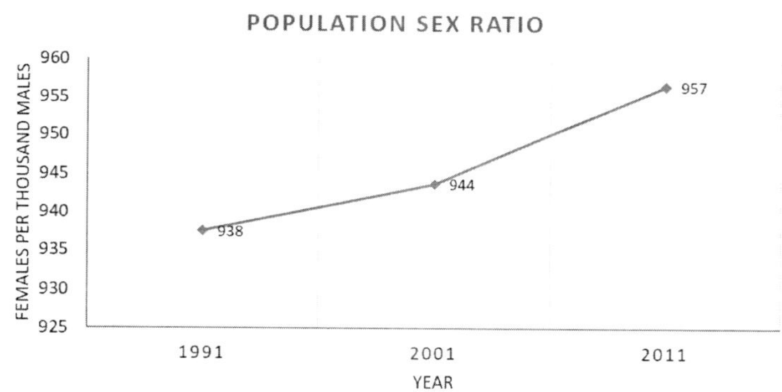

Fig. 19. Change in Population sex ratio in Barak Valley between 1991 and 2011.

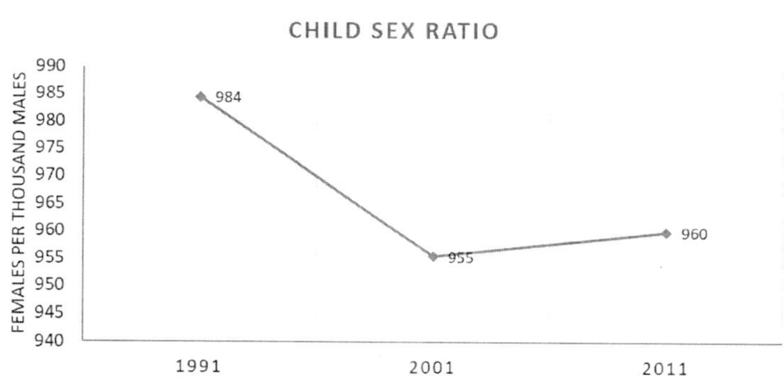

Fig. 20. Change in Child sex ratio in Barak Valley between 1991 and 2011.

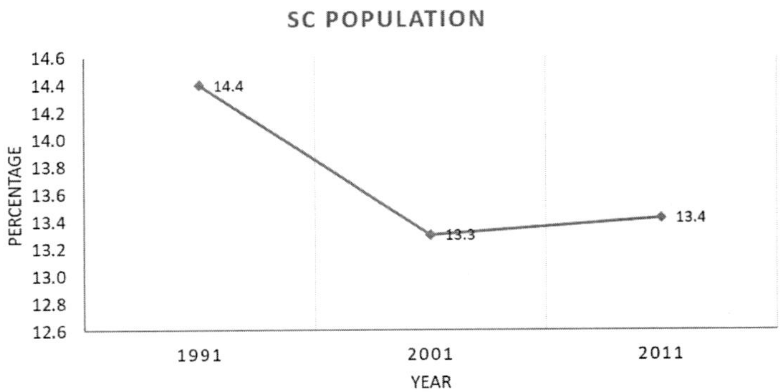

Fig. 21. Percentage of SC Population to total population in Barak Valley.

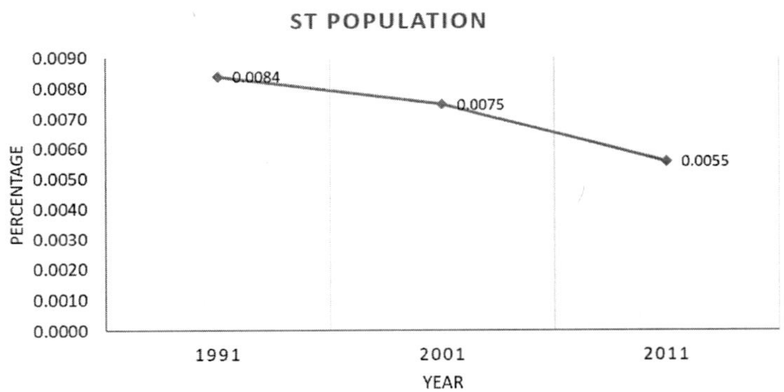

Fig. 22. Percentage of ST Population to total population in Barak Valley.

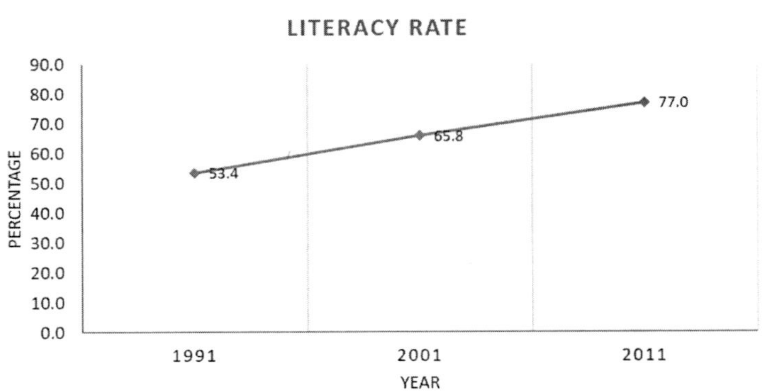

Fig. 23. Change in literacy rate (male + female) in Barak Valley.

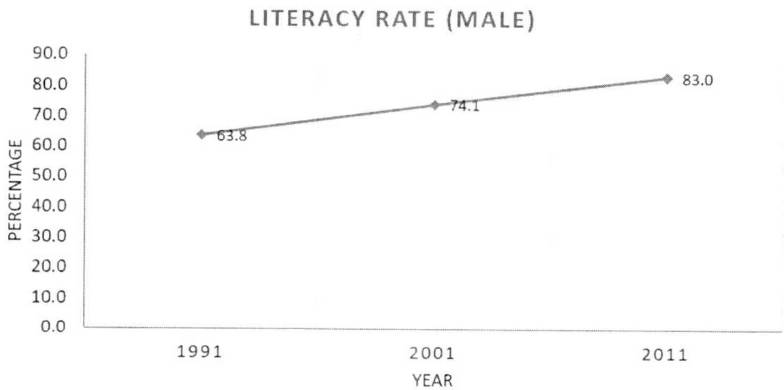

Fig. 24. Change in literacy rate (male) in Barak Valley.

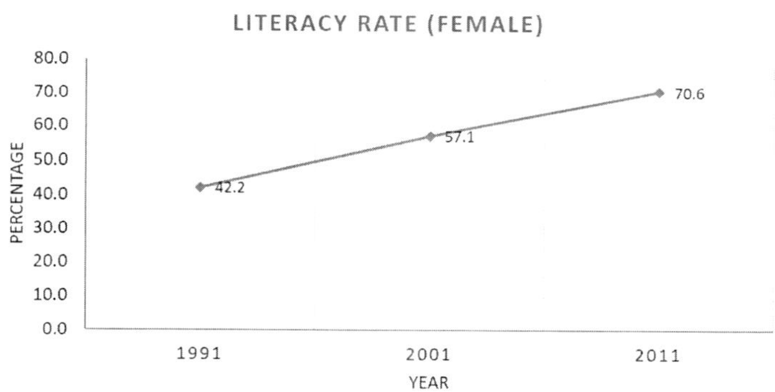

Fig. 25. Change in literacy rate (female) in Barak Valley.

Fig. 26. Total (main + marginal) workforce sex ratio across study years in Barak Valley.

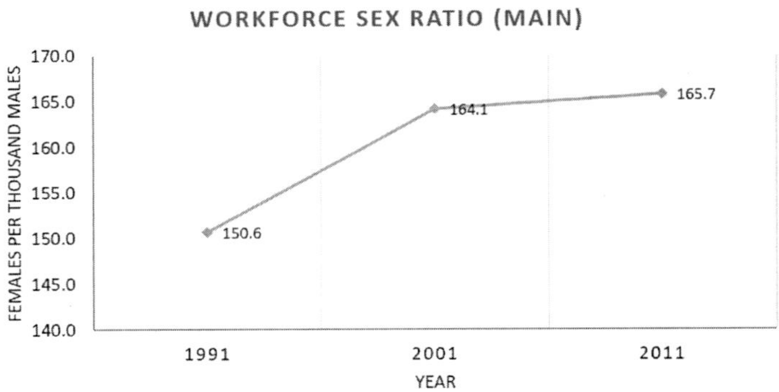

Fig. 27. Main workforce sex ratio across study years in Barak Valley.

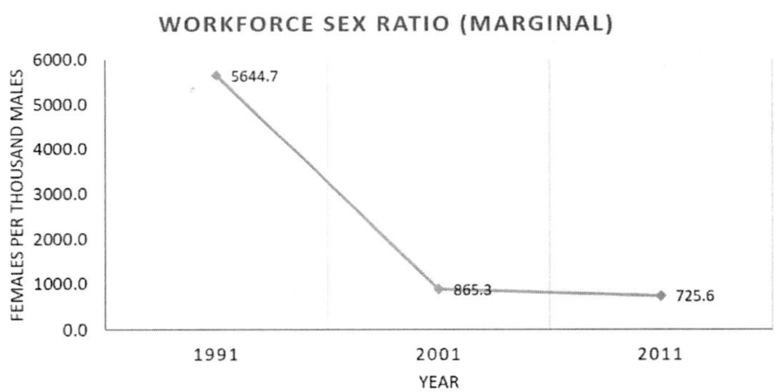

Fig. 28. Marginal workforce sex ratio across study years in Barak Valley.

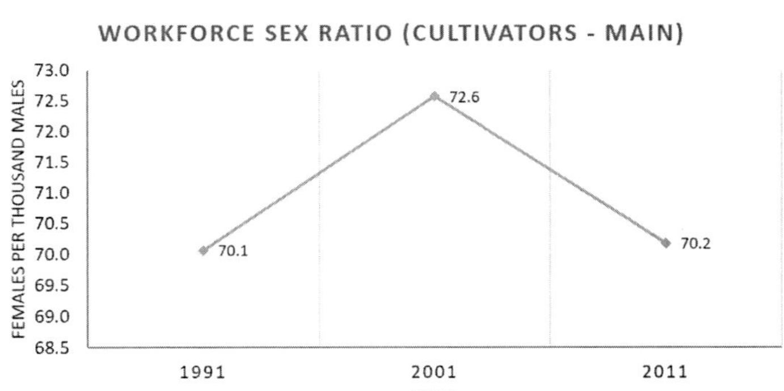

Fig. 29. Workforce sex ratio in cultivators across study years.

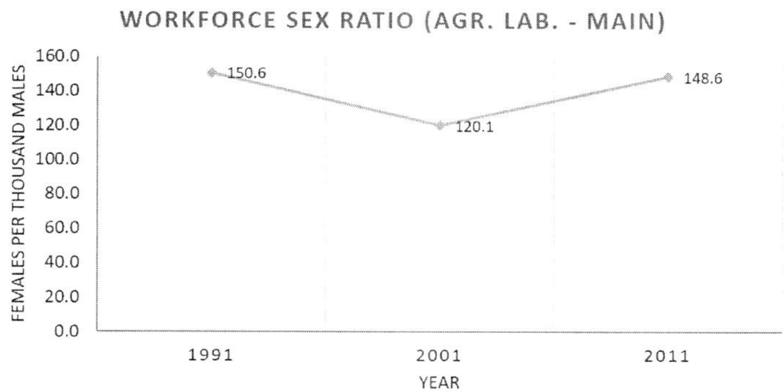

Fig. 30. Workforce sex ratio (Agricultural labourer - Main) across study years in Barak Valley.

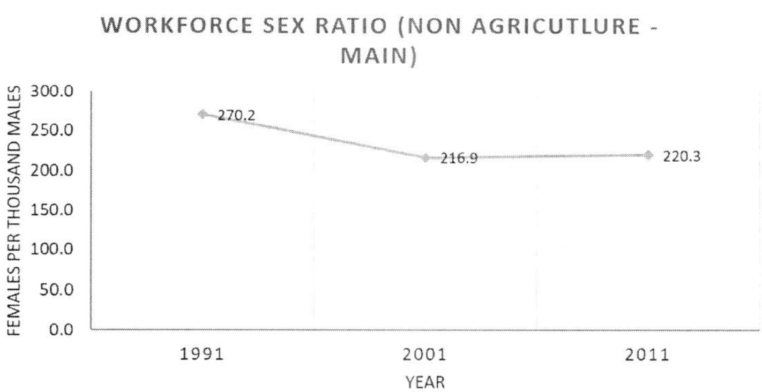

Fig. 31. Workforce sex ratio (Household industry and others - Main) in Barak Valley.

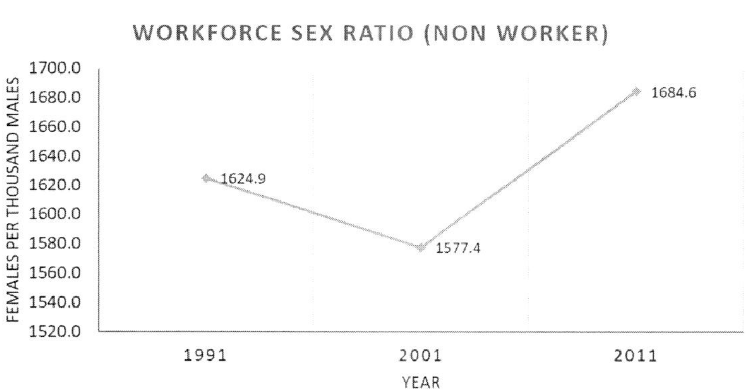

Fig. 32. Workforce sex ratio (Non-workers) across study years in Barak Valley.

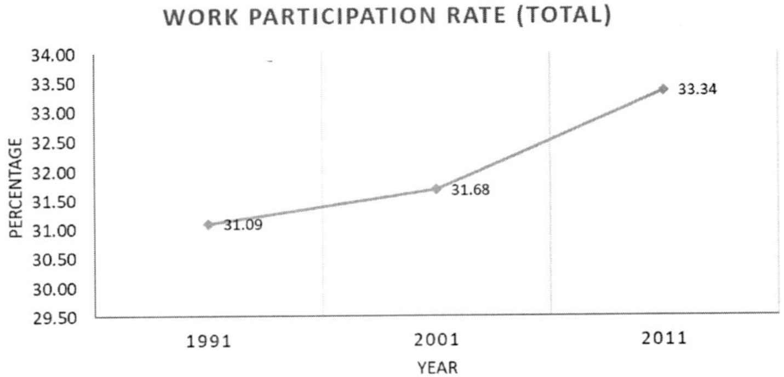

Fig. 33. WPR (Main + Marginal) across study years in Barak Valley.

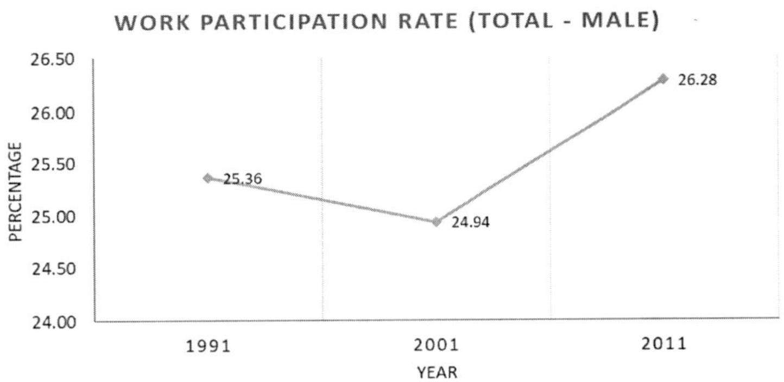

Fig. 34. WPR (Main + Marginal) (Male) across study years in Barak Valley.

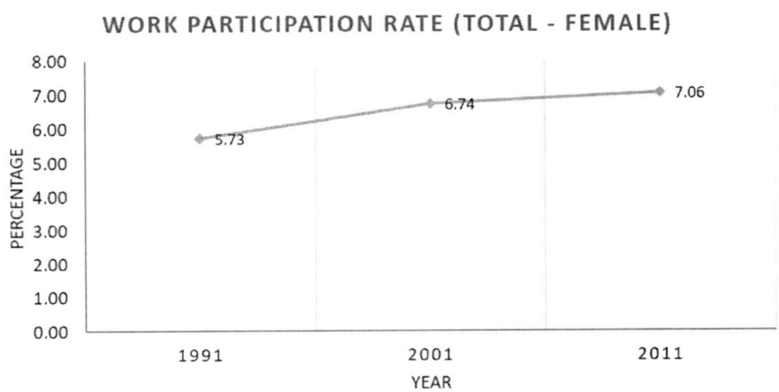

Fig. 35. WPR (Main + Marginal) (Female) across study years in Barak Valley.

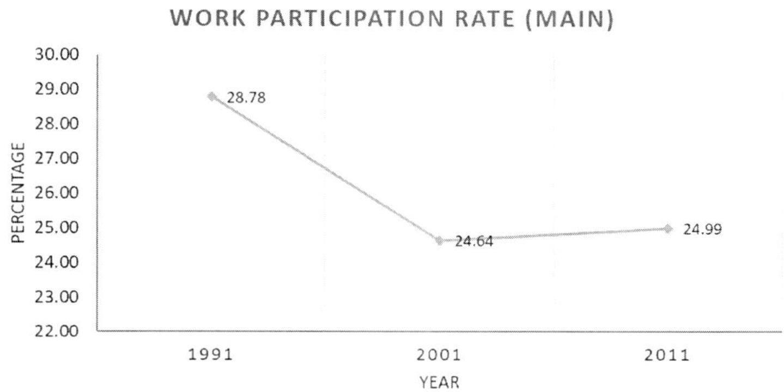

Fig. 36. WPR (Main) (Total) across study years in Barak Valley.

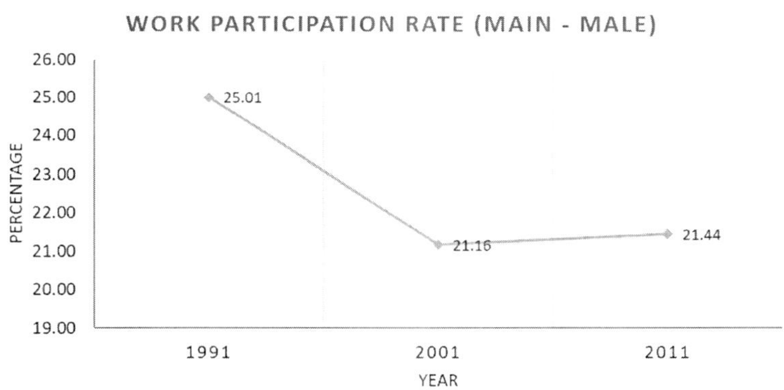

Fig. 37. WPR (Main) (Male) across study years in Barak Valley.

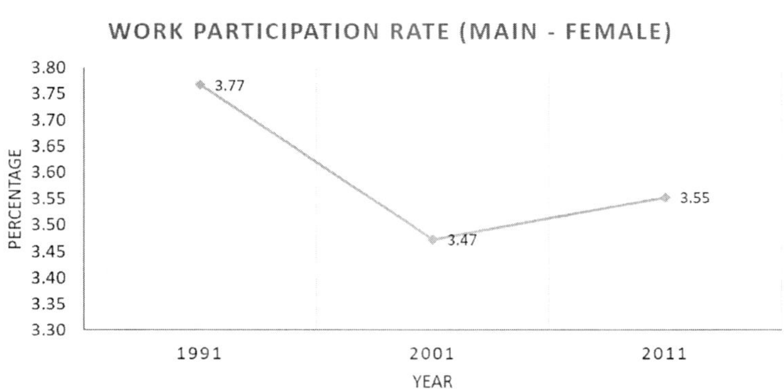

Fig. 38. WPR (Main) (Female) across study years in Barak Valley.

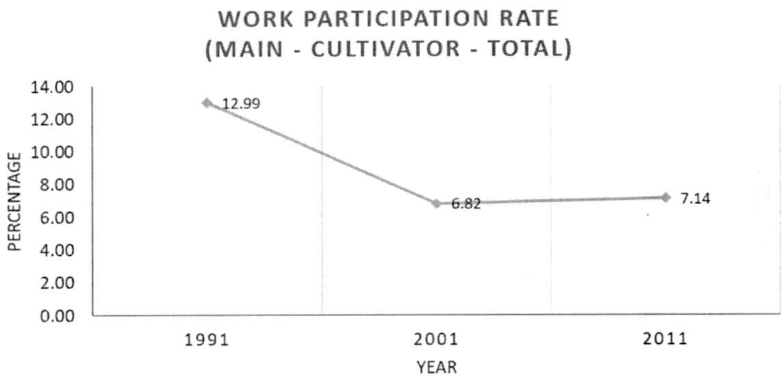

Fig. 39. WPR (Main-Cultivators) (Total) across study years in Barak Valley.

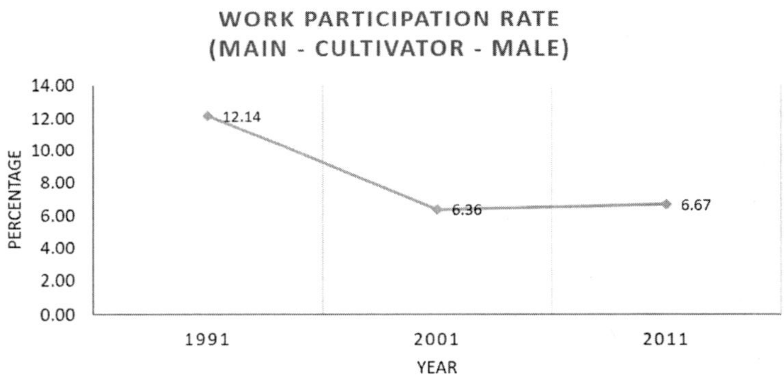

Fig. 40. WPR (Main-Cultivators) (Male) across study years in Barak Valley.

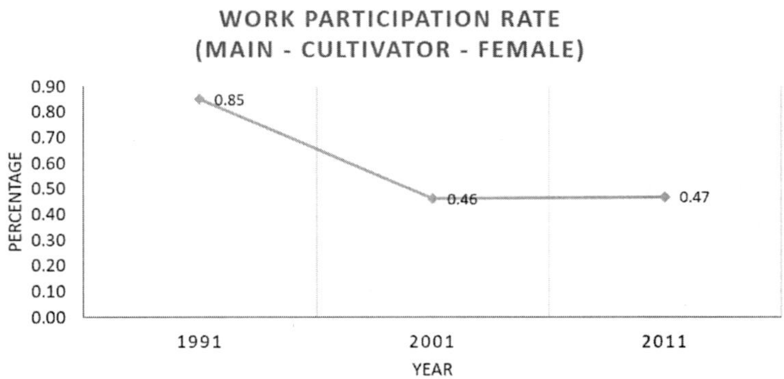

Fig. 41. WPR (Main-Cultivators) (Female) across study years in Barak Valley.

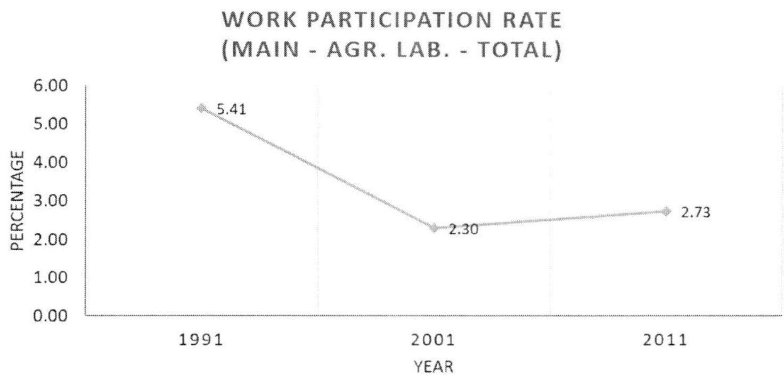

Fig. 42. WPR (Main-Agricultural laborer) (Total) across study years in Barak Valley.

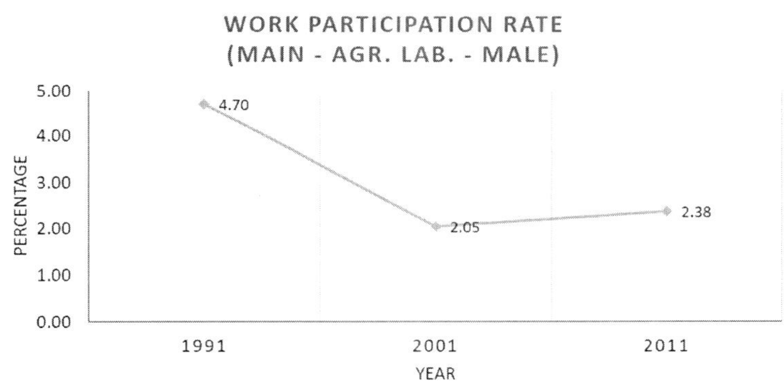

Fig. 43. WPR (Main-Agricultural laborer) (Male) across study years in Barak Valley.

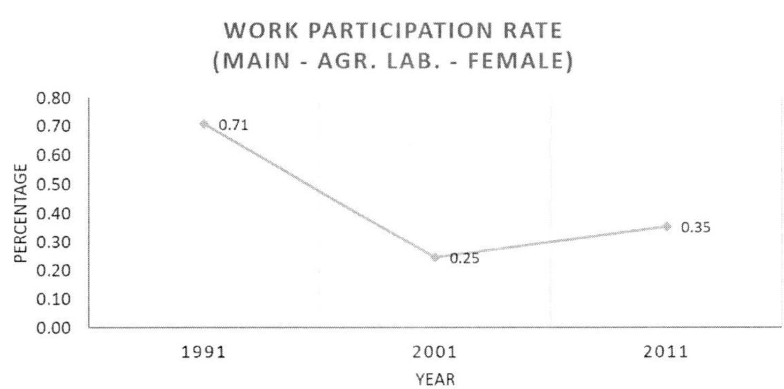

Fig. 44. WPR (Main-Agricultural laborer) (Female) across study years in Barak Valley.

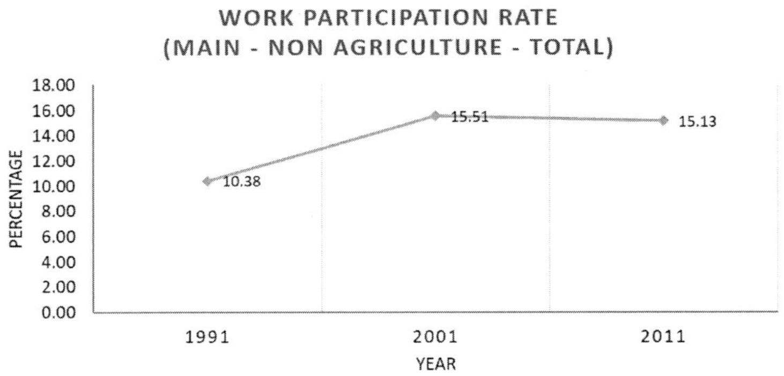

Fig. 45. WPR (Main-Non Agricultural worker) (Total) across study years in Barak Valley.

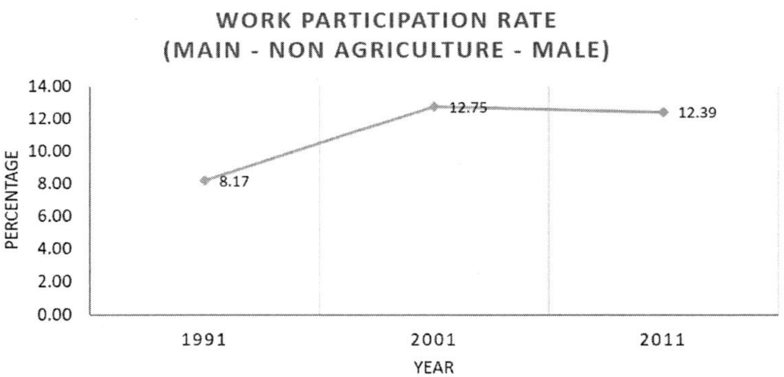

Fig. 46. WPR (Main-Non Agricultural worker) (Male) across study years in Barak Valley.

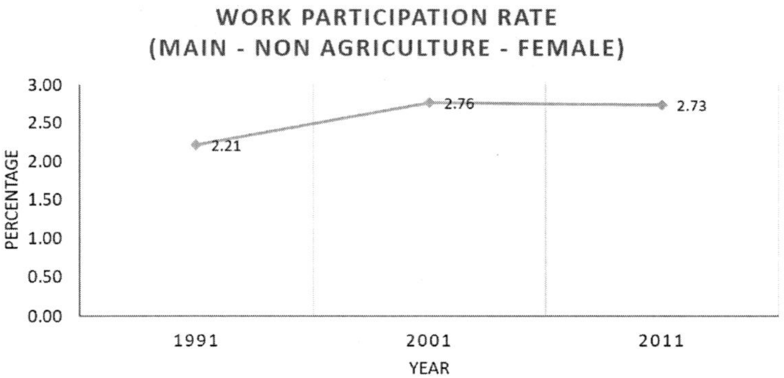

Fig. 47. WPR (Main-Non Agricultural worker) (Female) across study years in Barak Valley.

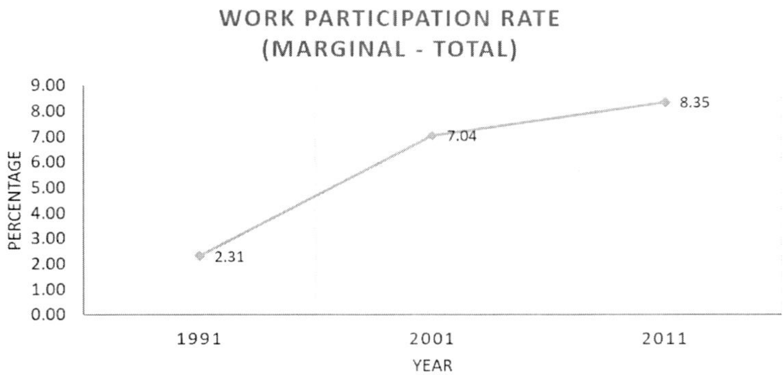

Fig. 48. WPR (Marginal worker) (Total) across study years in Barak Valley.

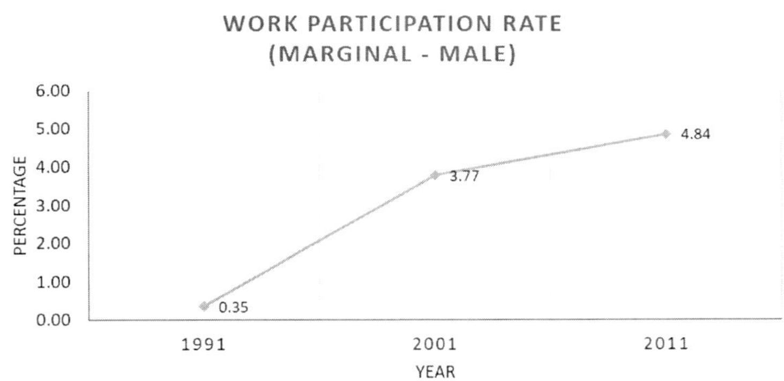

Fig. 49. WPR (Marginal worker) (Male) across study years in Barak Valley.

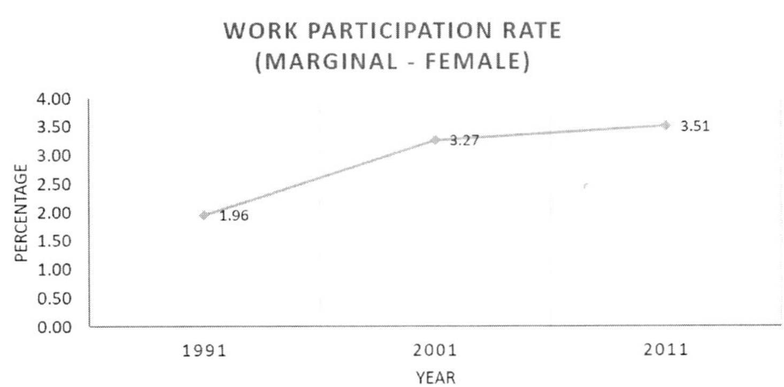

Fig. 50. WPR (Marginal worker) (Female) across study years in Barak Valley.

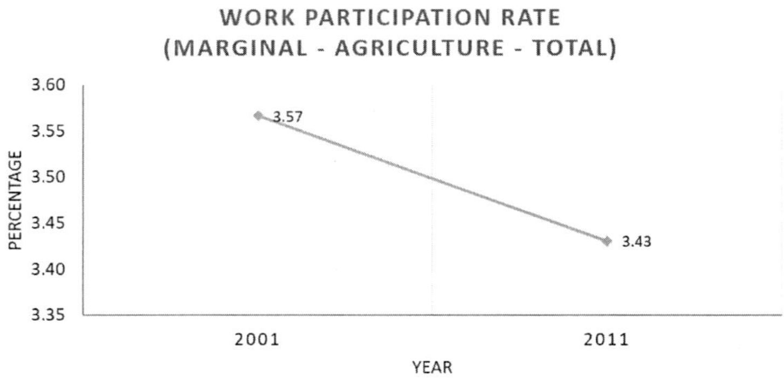

Fig. 51. WPR (Marginal – Agricultural worker) (Total) across study years in Barak Valley.

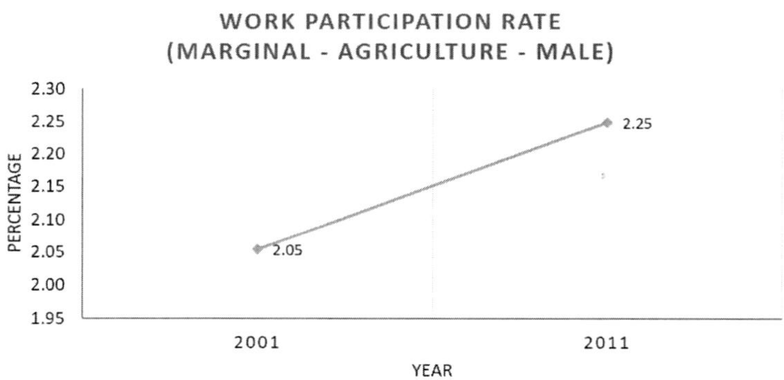

Fig. 52. WPR (Marginal – Agricultural worker) (Male) across study years in Barak Valley.

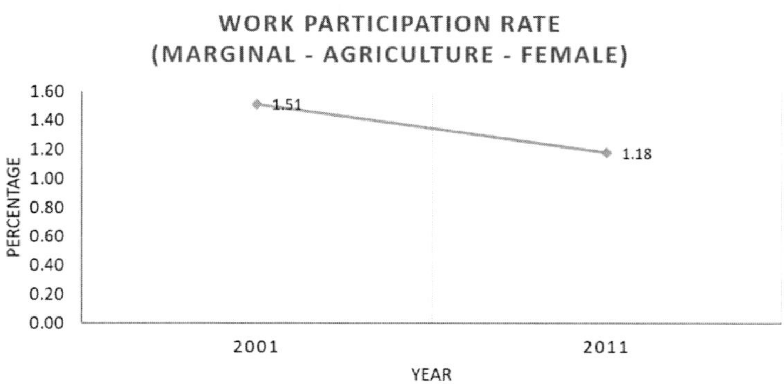

Fig. 53. WPR (Marginal – Agricultural worker) (Female) across study years in Barak Valley.

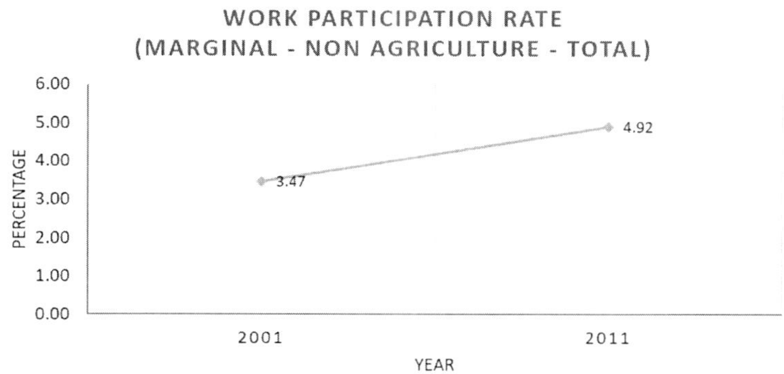

Fig. 54. WPR (Marginal – Non Agricultural worker) (Total) across study years in Barak Valley.

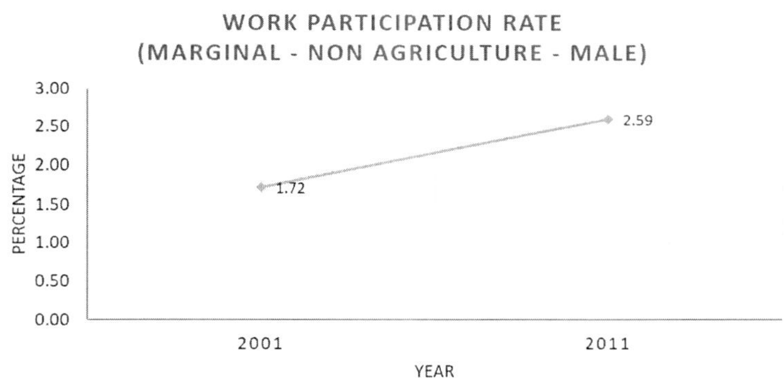

Fig. 55. WPR (Marginal – Non Agricultural worker) (Male) across study years in Barak Valley.

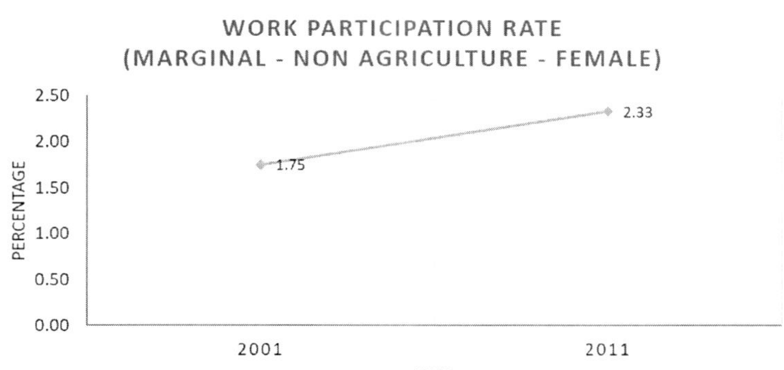

Fig. 56. WPR (Marginal – Non Agricultural worker) (Female) across study years in Barak Valley.

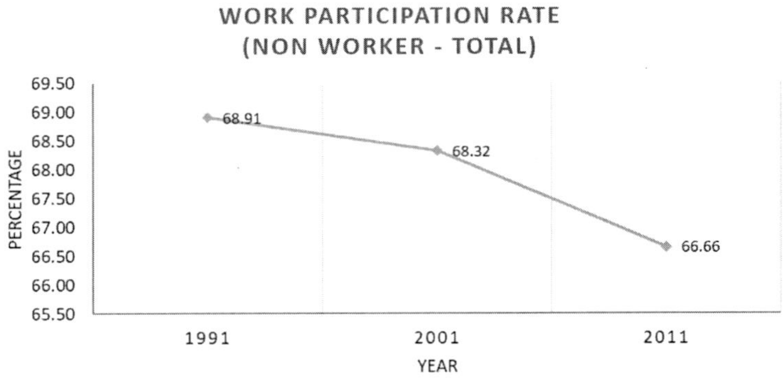

Fig. 57. WPR (Non worker) (Total) across study years in Barak Valley.

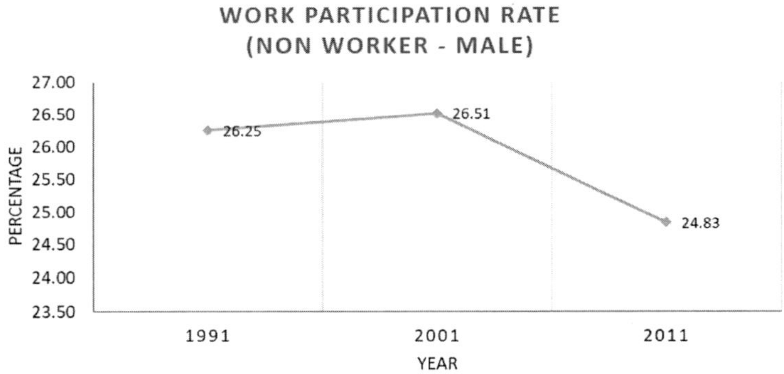

Fig. 58. WPR (Non worker) (Male) across study years in Barak Valley.

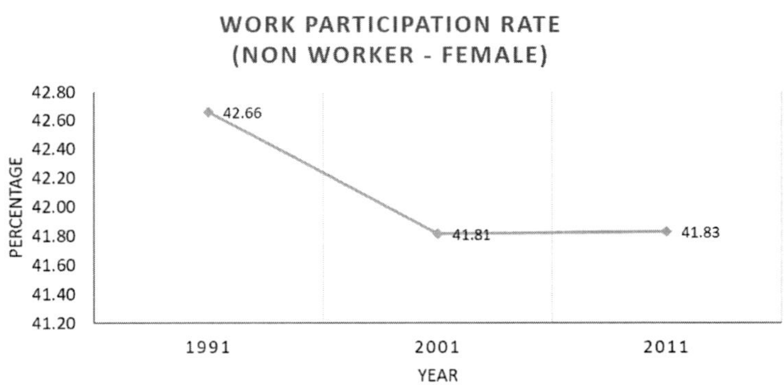

Fig. 59. WPR (Non worker) (Female) across study years in Barak Valley.

Spatial analysis of census variables, 1991

Map 1

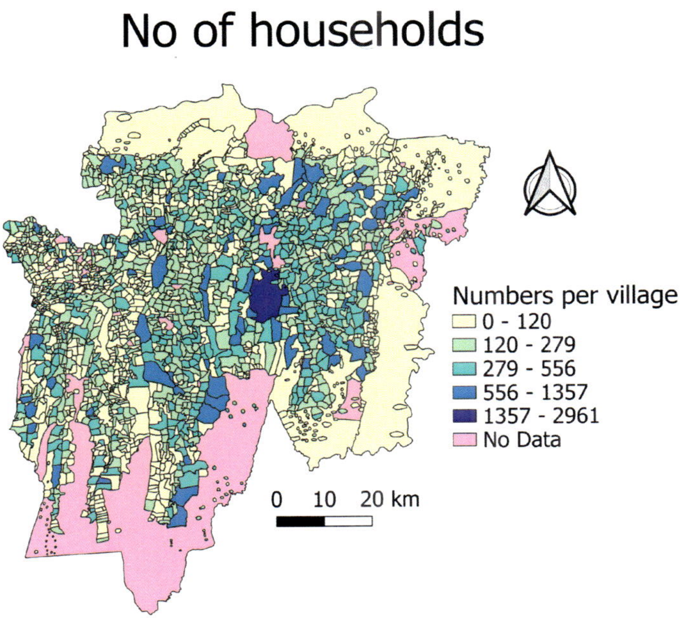

Map 2

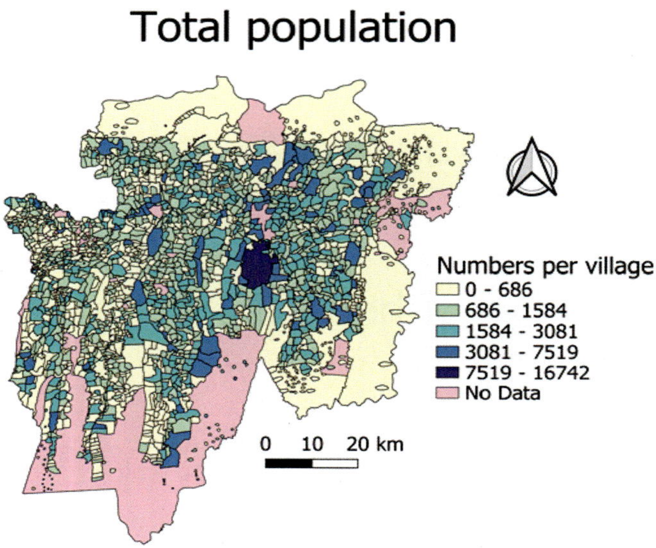
Total population
Numbers per village
0 - 686
686 - 1584
1584 - 3081
3081 - 7519
7519 - 16742
No Data
0 10 20 km

Map 3

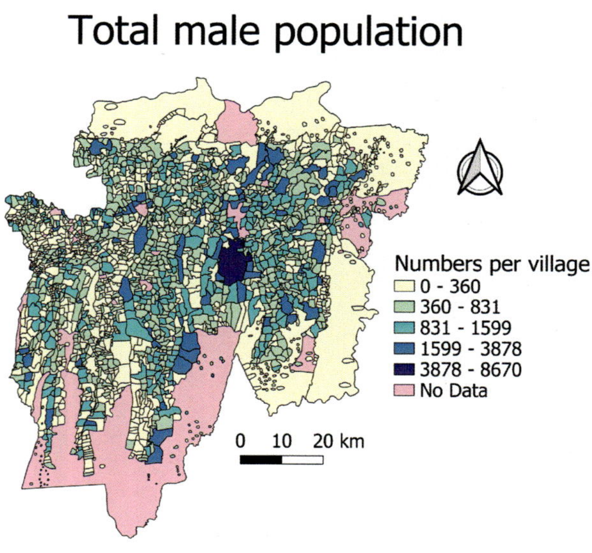
Total male population
Numbers per village
0 - 360
360 - 831
831 - 1599
1599 - 3878
3878 - 8670
No Data
0 10 20 km

Map 4

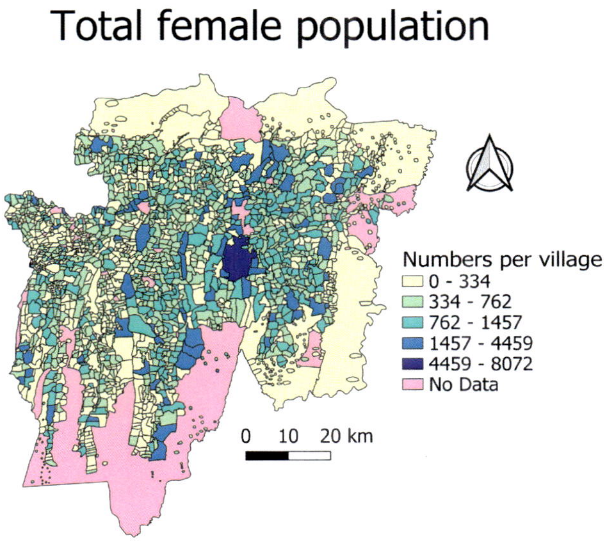
Total female population
Numbers per village
0 - 334
334 - 762
762 - 1457
1457 - 4459
4459 - 8072
No Data
0 10 20 km

Map 5

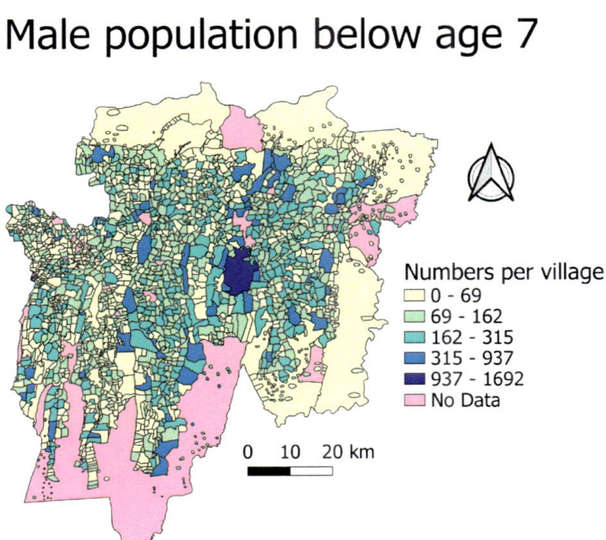
Male population below age 7
Numbers per village
0 - 69
69 - 162
162 - 315
315 - 937
937 - 1692
No Data
0 10 20 km

Map 6

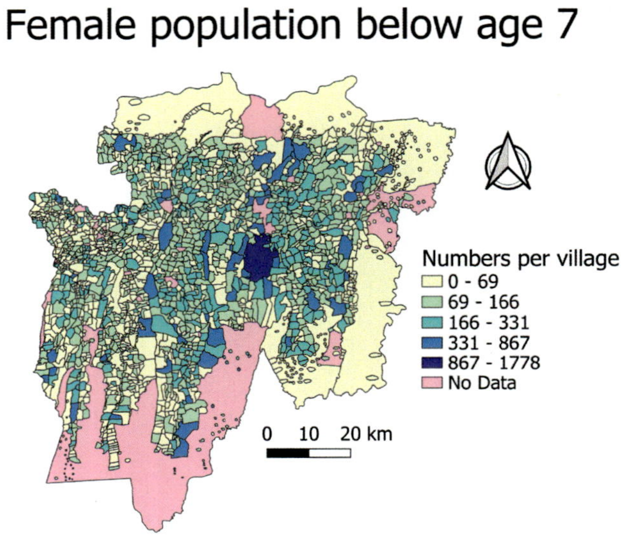
Female population below age 7
Numbers per village
0 - 69
69 - 166
166 - 331
331 - 867
867 - 1778
No Data
0 10 20 km

Map 7

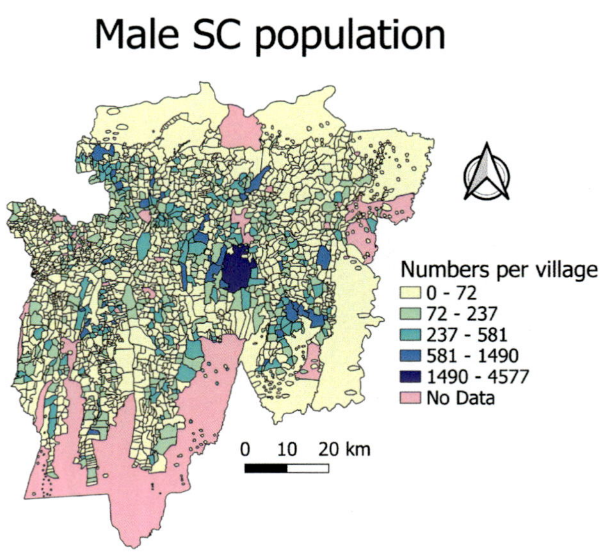
Male SC population
Numbers per village
0 - 72
72 - 237
237 - 581
581 - 1490
1490 - 4577
No Data
0 10 20 km

Map 8

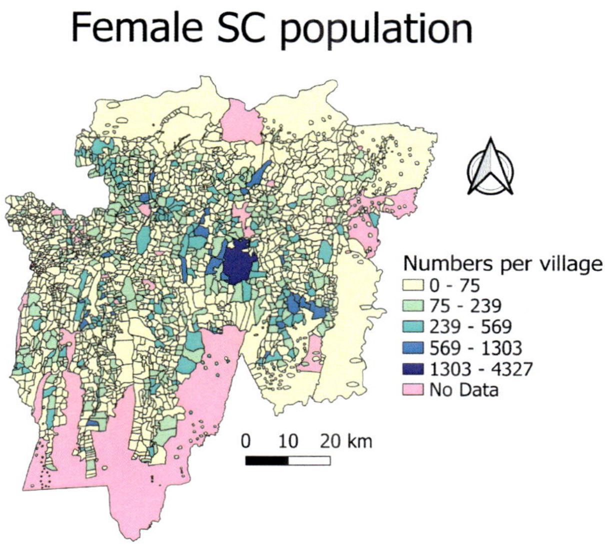
Female SC population
Numbers per village
0 - 75
75 - 239
239 - 569
569 - 1303
1303 - 4327
No Data
0 10 20 km

Map 9

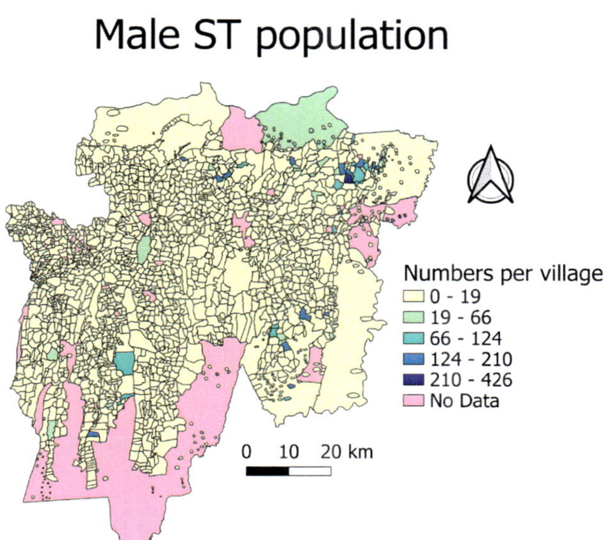
Male ST population
Numbers per village
0 - 19
19 - 66
66 - 124
124 - 210
210 - 426
No Data
0 10 20 km

Map 10

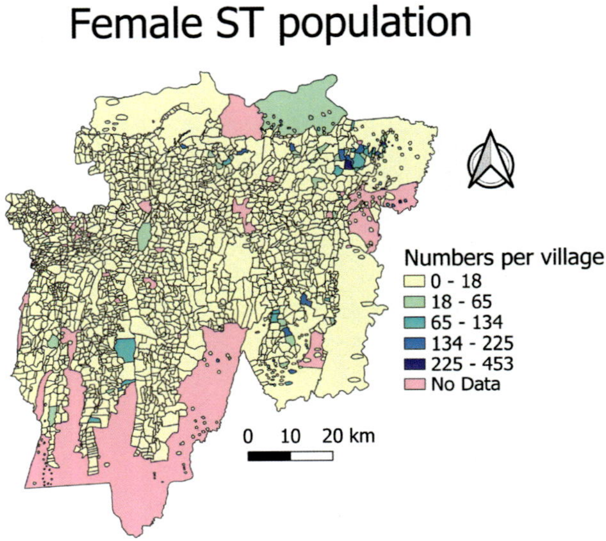
Female ST population
Numbers per village
0 - 18
18 - 65
65 - 134
134 - 225
225 - 453
No Data
0 10 20 km

Map 11

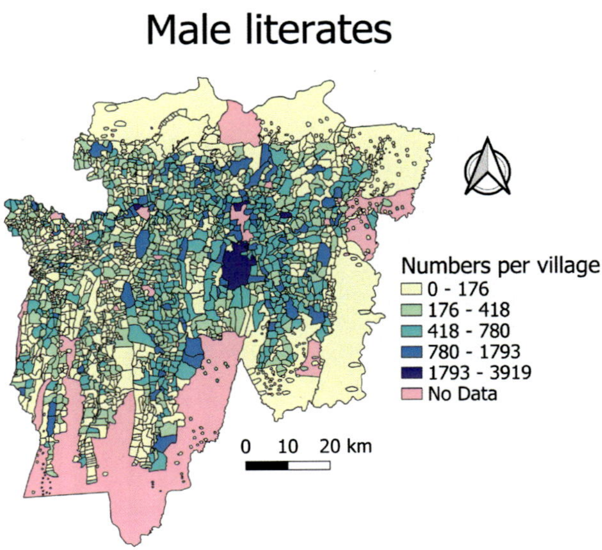
Male literates
Numbers per village
0 - 176
176 - 418
418 - 780
780 - 1793
1793 - 3919
No Data
0 10 20 km

Map 12

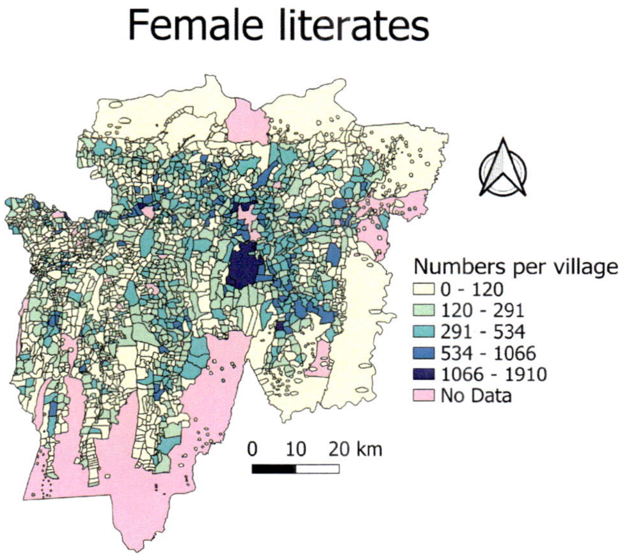
Female literates
Numbers per village
0 - 120
120 - 291
291 - 534
534 - 1066
1066 - 1910
No Data
0 10 20 km

Map 13

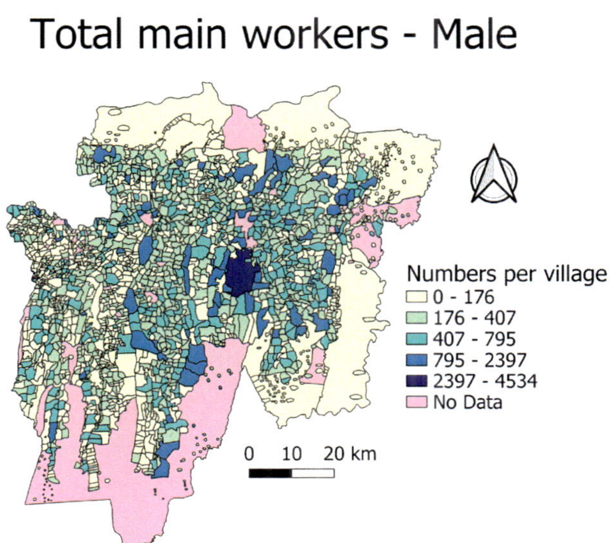
Total main workers - Male
Numbers per village
0 - 176
176 - 407
407 - 795
795 - 2397
2397 - 4534
No Data
0 10 20 km

Map 14

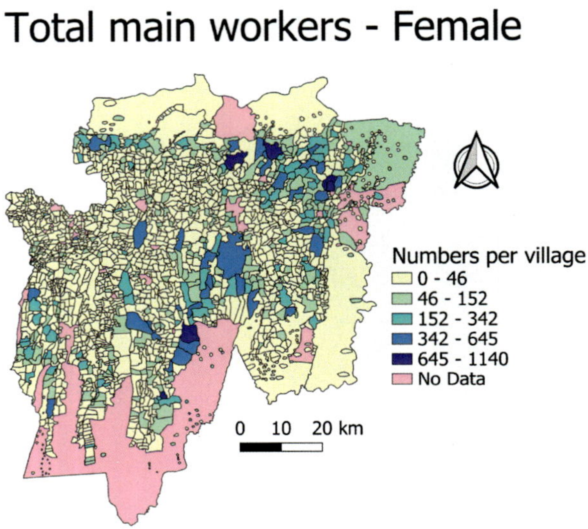
Total main workers - Female
Numbers per village
0 - 46
46 - 152
152 - 342
342 - 645
645 - 1140
No Data
0 10 20 km

Map 15

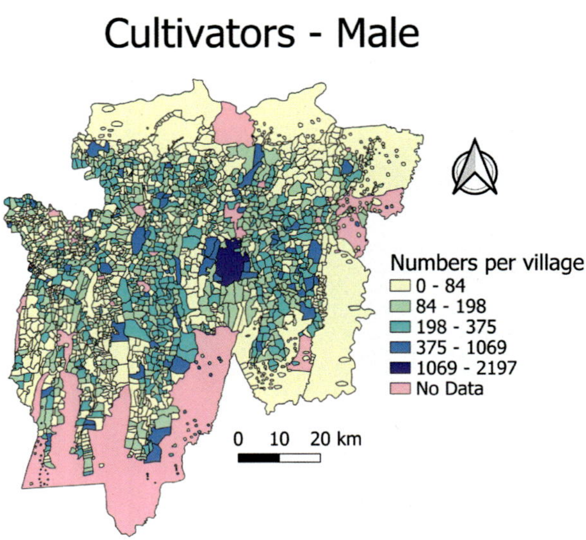
Cultivators - Male
Numbers per village
0 - 84
84 - 198
198 - 375
375 - 1069
1069 - 2197
No Data
0 10 20 km

Map 16

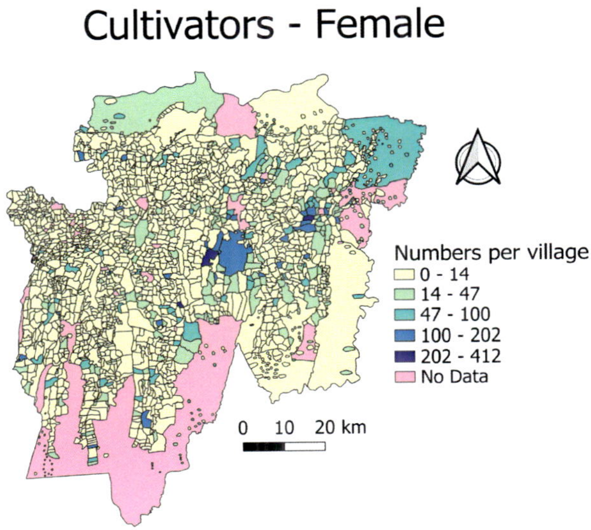
Cultivators - Female
Numbers per village
0 - 14
14 - 47
47 - 100
100 - 202
202 - 412
No Data
0 10 20 km

Map 17

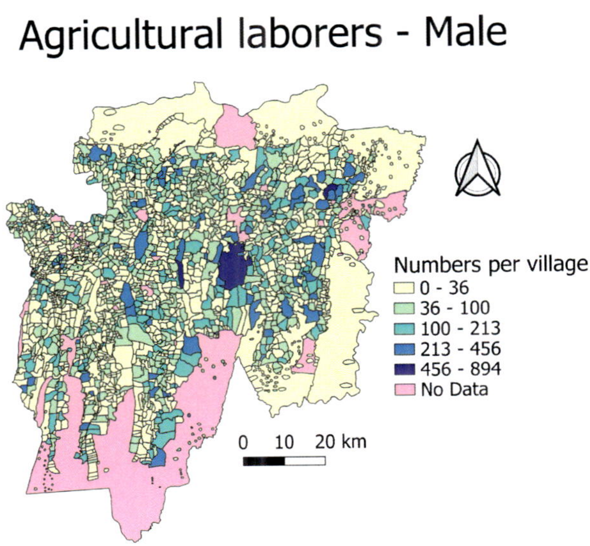
Agricultural laborers - Male
Numbers per village
0 - 36
36 - 100
100 - 213
213 - 456
456 - 894
No Data
0 10 20 km

Map 18

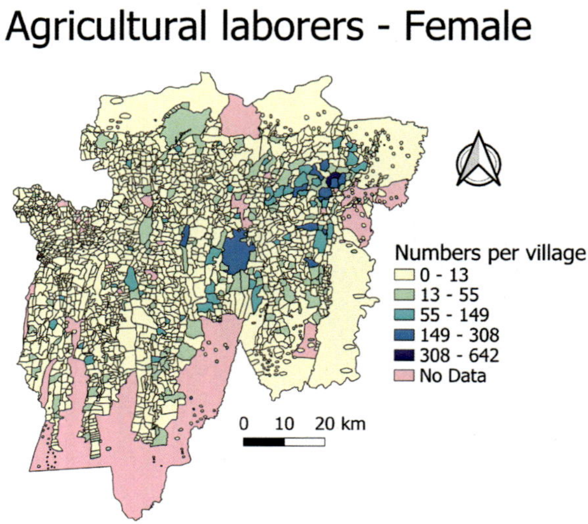
Agricultural laborers - Female
Numbers per village
0 - 13
13 - 55
55 - 149
149 - 308
308 - 642
No Data
0 10 20 km

Map 19

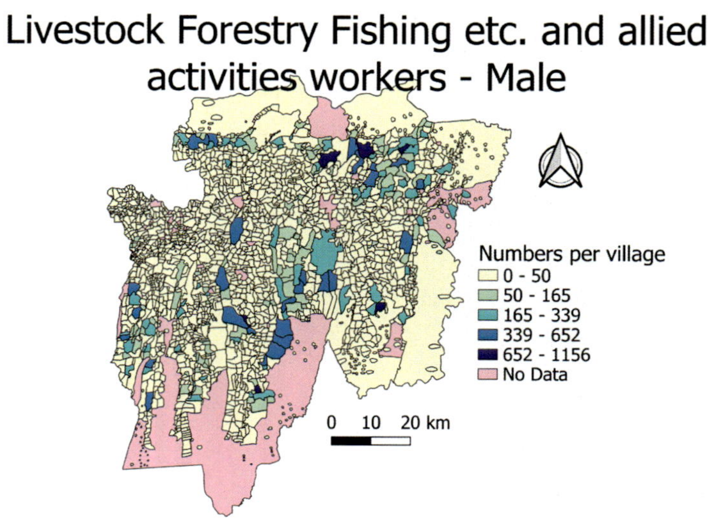
Livestock Forestry Fishing etc. and allied activities workers - Male
Numbers per village
0 - 50
50 - 165
165 - 339
339 - 652
652 - 1156
No Data
0 10 20 km

Map 20

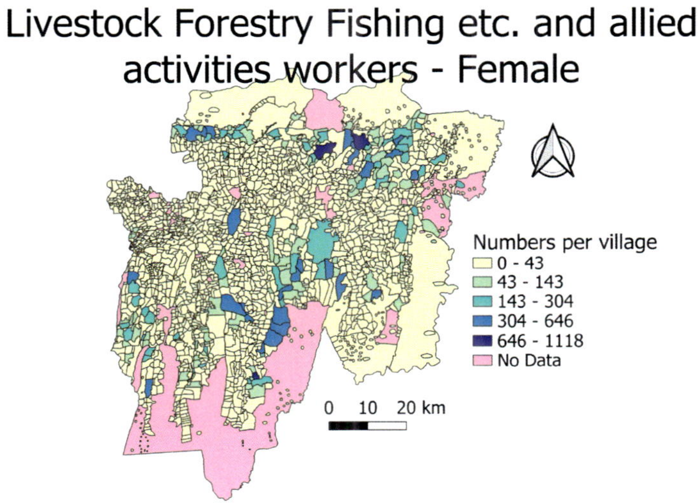
Livestock Forestry Fishing etc. and allied activities workers - Female
Numbers per village
0 - 43
43 - 143
143 - 304
304 - 646
646 - 1118
No Data
0 10 20 km

Map 21

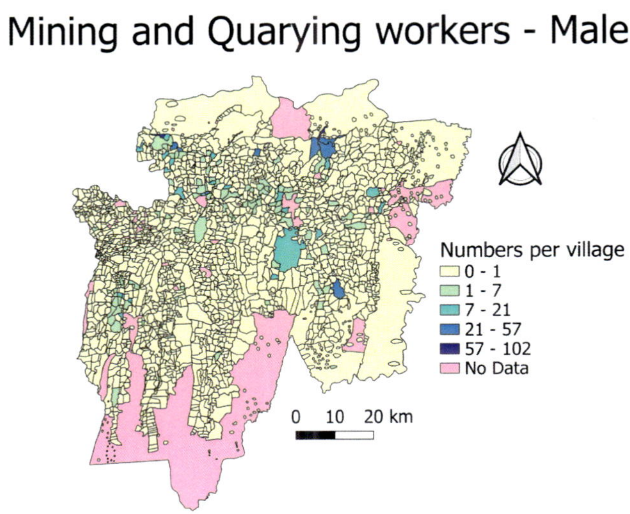
Mining and Quarying workers - Male
Numbers per village
0 - 1
1 - 7
7 - 21
21 - 57
57 - 102
No Data
0 10 20 km

Map 22

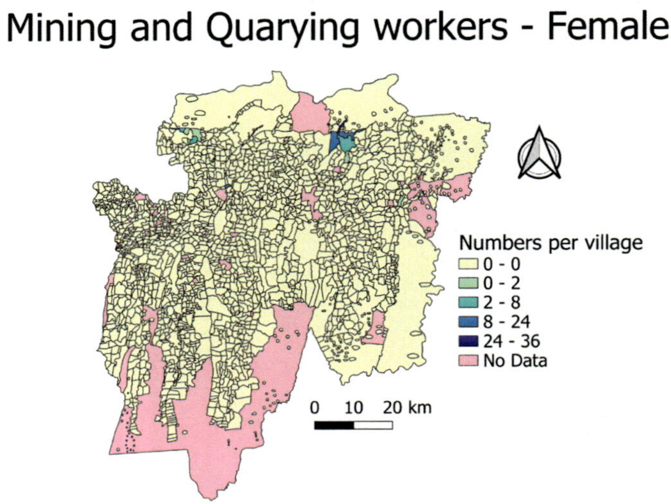
Mining and Quarying workers - Female
Numbers per village
0 - 0
0 - 2
2 - 8
8 - 24
24 - 36
No Data
0 10 20 km

Map 23

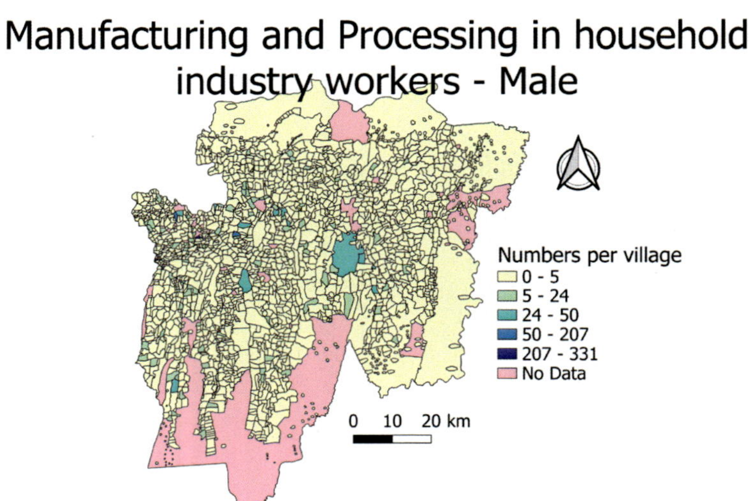
Manufacturing and Processing in household industry workers - Male
Numbers per village
0 - 5
5 - 24
24 - 50
50 - 207
207 - 331
No Data
0 10 20 km

Map 24

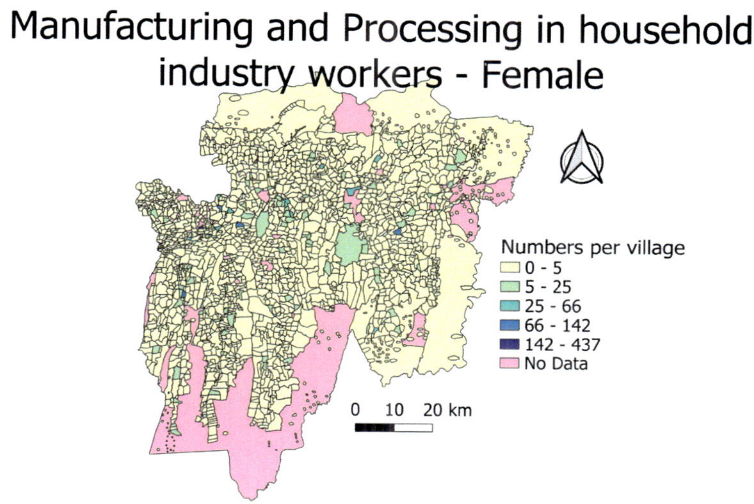
Manufacturing and Processing in household industry workers - Female
Numbers per village
0 - 5
5 - 25
25 - 66
66 - 142
142 - 437
No Data
0 10 20 km

Map 25

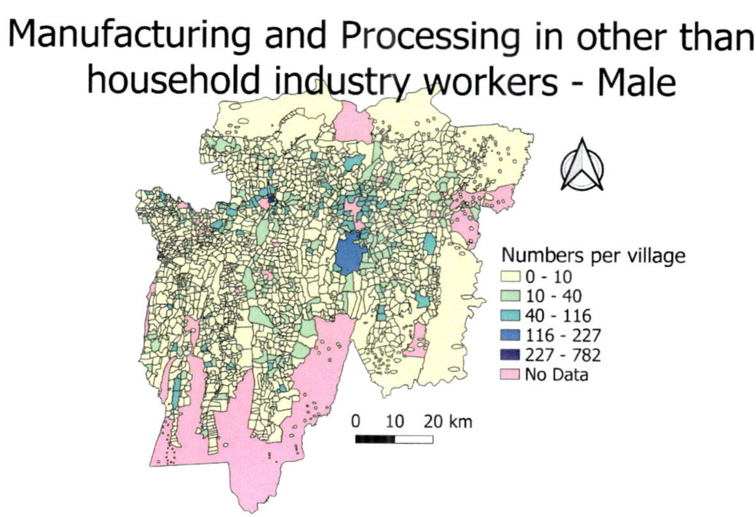
Manufacturing and Processing in other than household industry workers - Male
Numbers per village
0 - 10
10 - 40
40 - 116
116 - 227
227 - 782
No Data
0 10 20 km

Map 26

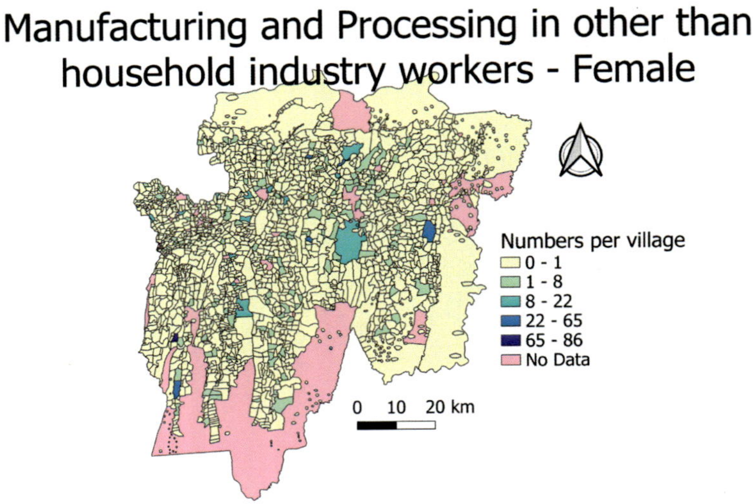
Manufacturing and Processing in other than household industry workers - Female
Numbers per village
0 - 1
1 - 8
8 - 22
22 - 65
65 - 86
No Data
0 10 20 km

Map 27

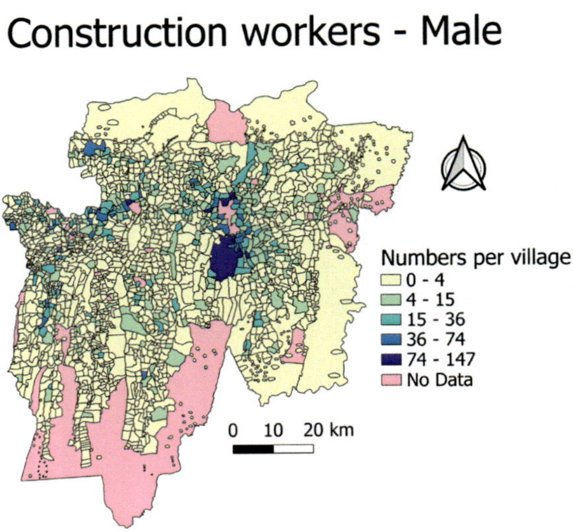
Construction workers - Male
Numbers per village
0 - 4
4 - 15
15 - 36
36 - 74
74 - 147
No Data
0 10 20 km

Map 28

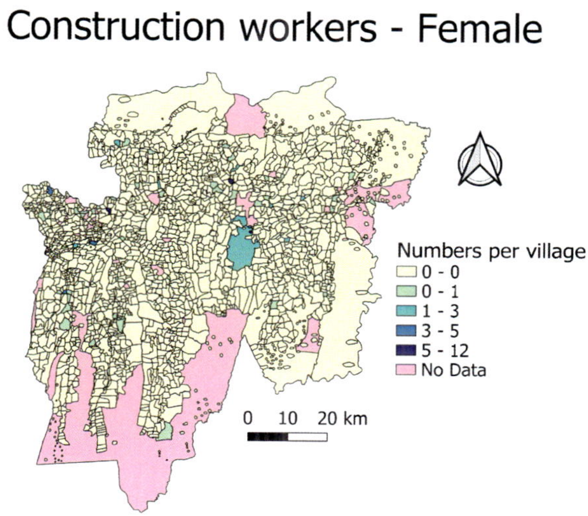
Construction workers - Female
Numbers per village
0 - 0
0 - 1
1 - 3
3 - 5
5 - 12
No Data
0 10 20 km

Map 29

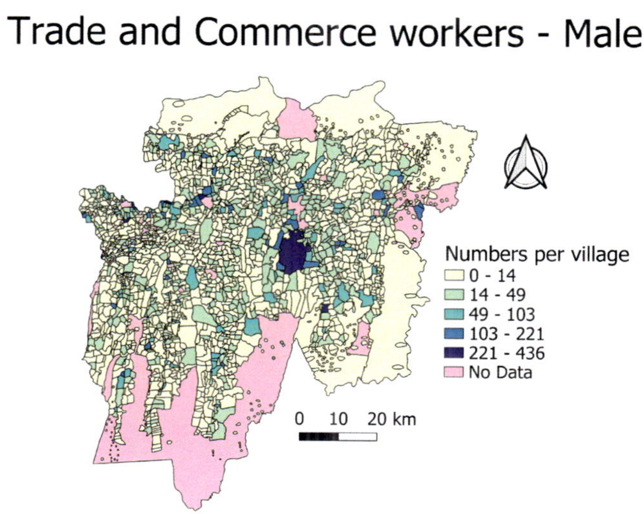
Trade and Commerce workers - Male
Numbers per village
0 - 14
14 - 49
49 - 103
103 - 221
221 - 436
No Data
0 10 20 km

Map 30

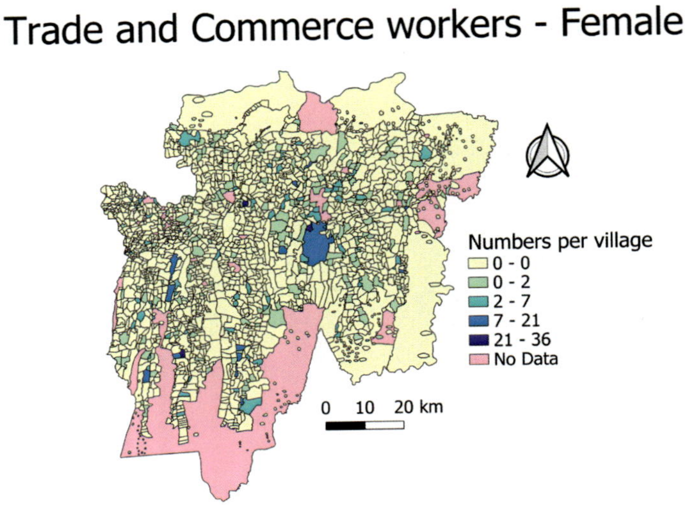
Trade and Commerce workers - Female
Numbers per village
0 - 0
0 - 2
2 - 7
7 - 21
21 - 36
No Data
0 10 20 km

Map 31

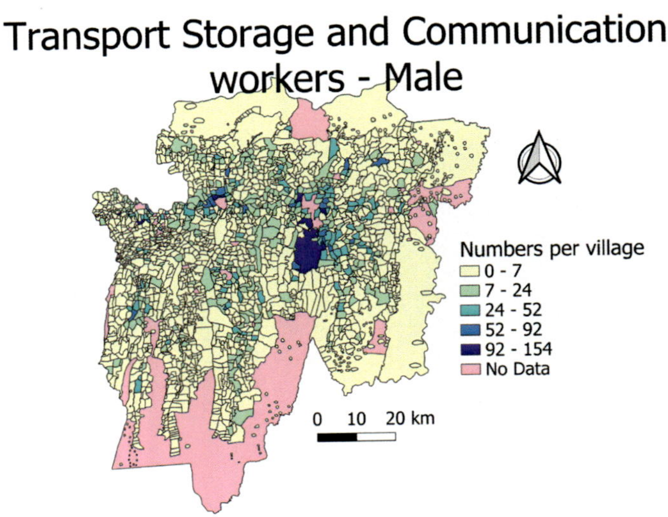
Transport Storage and Communication workers - Male
Numbers per village
0 - 7
7 - 24
24 - 52
52 - 92
92 - 154
No Data
0 10 20 km

Map 32

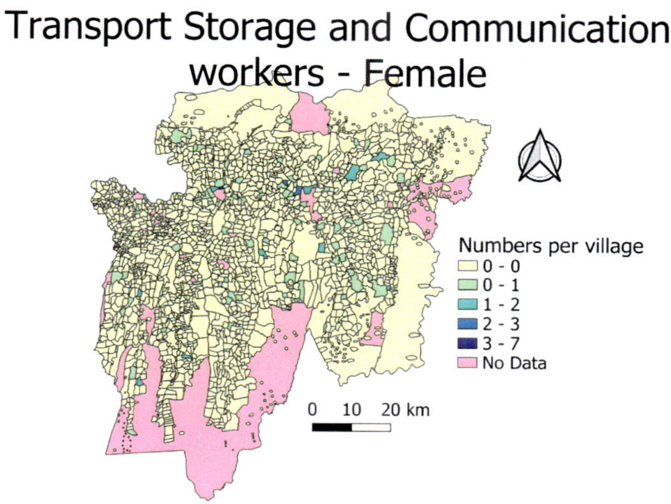
Transport Storage and Communication workers - Female
Numbers per village
0 - 0
0 - 1
1 - 2
2 - 3
3 - 7
No Data
0 10 20 km

Map 33

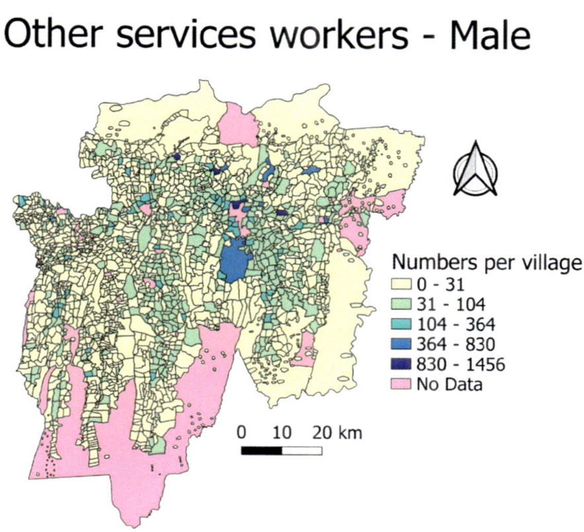
Other services workers - Male
Numbers per village
0 - 31
31 - 104
104 - 364
364 - 830
830 - 1456
No Data
0 10 20 km

Map 34

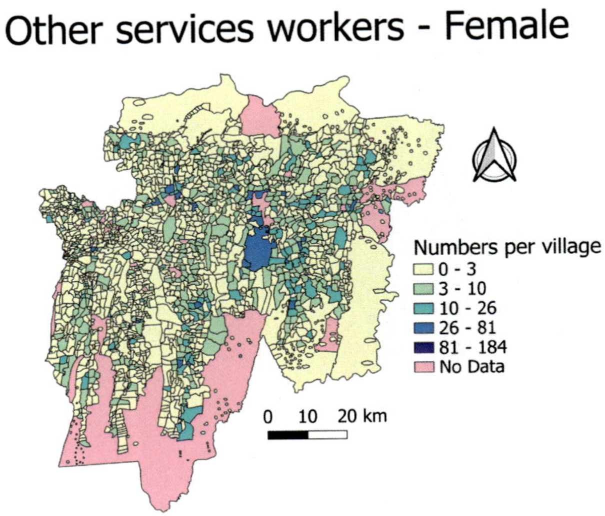
Other services workers - Female
Numbers per village
0 - 3
3 - 10
10 - 26
26 - 81
81 - 184
No Data
0 10 20 km

Map 35

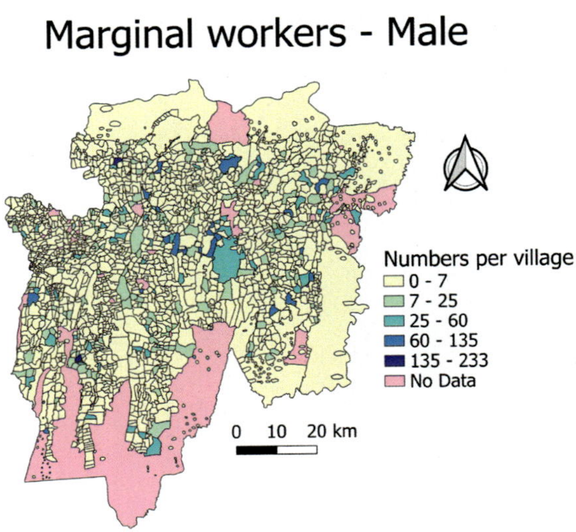
Marginal workers - Male
Numbers per village
0 - 7
7 - 25
25 - 60
60 - 135
135 - 233
No Data
0 10 20 km

Map 36

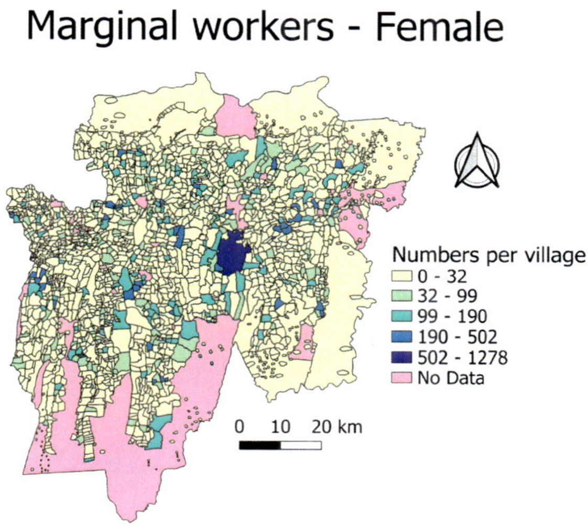
Marginal workers - Female
Numbers per village
0 - 32
32 - 99
99 - 190
190 - 502
502 - 1278
No Data
0 10 20 km

Map 37

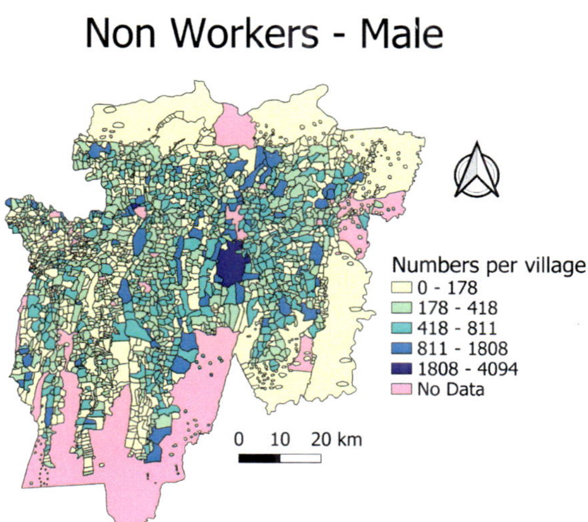
Non Workers - Male
Numbers per village
0 - 178
178 - 418
418 - 811
811 - 1808
1808 - 4094
No Data
0 10 20 km

Map 38

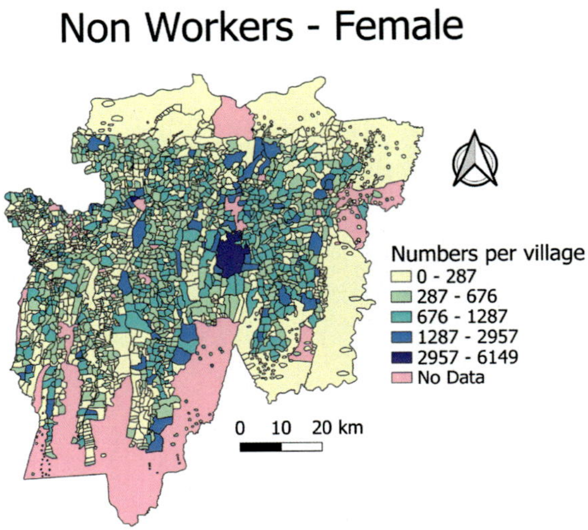
Non Workers - Female
Numbers per village
0 - 287
287 - 676
676 - 1287
1287 - 2957
2957 - 6149
No Data
0 10 20 km

Spatial analysis of socio-economic indicators, 1991

Map 39

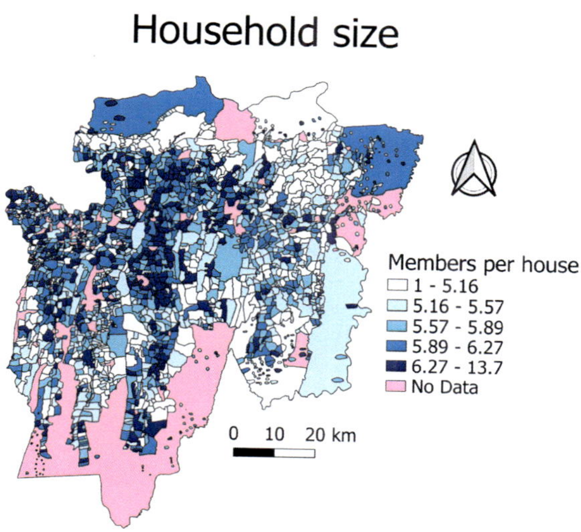

Map 40

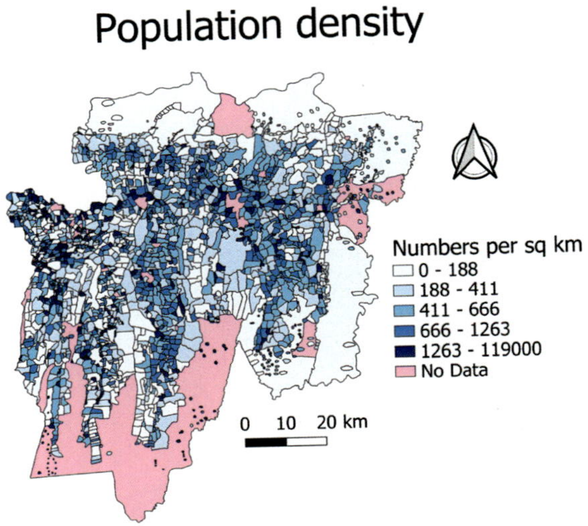
Population density
Numbers per sq km
0 - 188
188 - 411
411 - 666
666 - 1263
1263 - 119000
No Data
0 10 20 km

Map 41

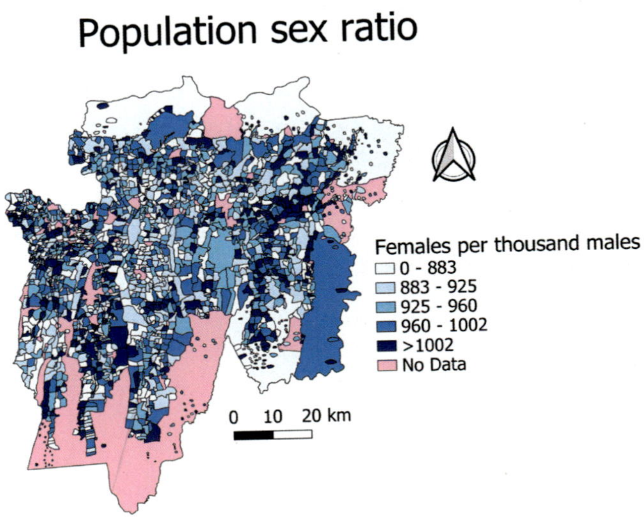
Population sex ratio
Females per thousand males
0 - 883
883 - 925
925 - 960
960 - 1002
>1002
No Data
0 10 20 km

Map 42

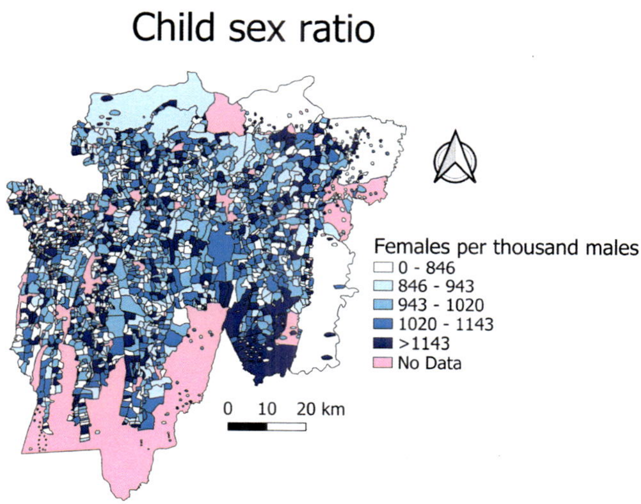
Child sex ratio
Females per thousand males
0 - 846
846 - 943
943 - 1020
1020 - 1143
>1143
No Data
0 10 20 km

Map 43

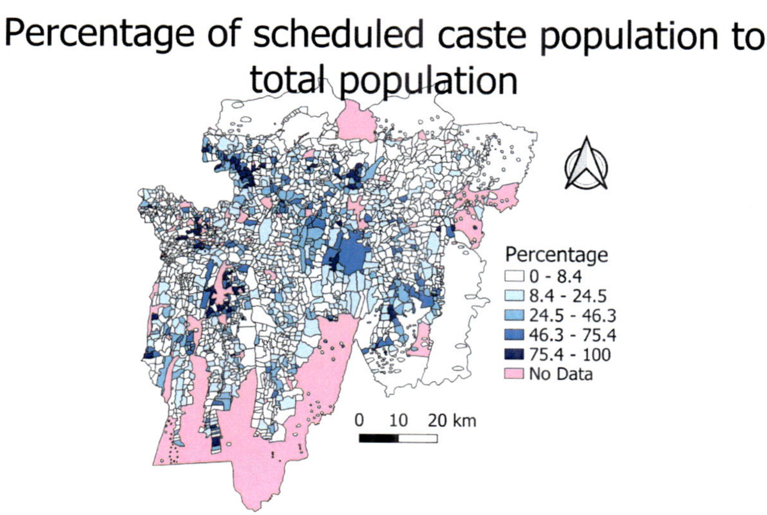
Percentage of scheduled caste population to total population
Percentage
0 - 8.4
8.4 - 24.5
24.5 - 46.3
46.3 - 75.4
75.4 - 100
No Data
0 10 20 km

Map 44

Percentage of scheduled tribe population to total population

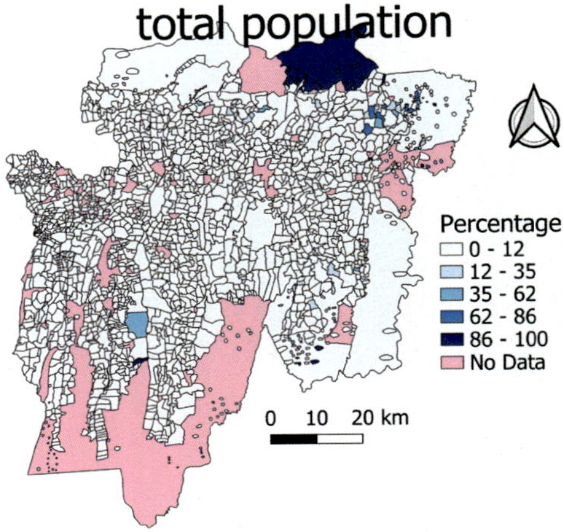

Map 45

Literacy rate

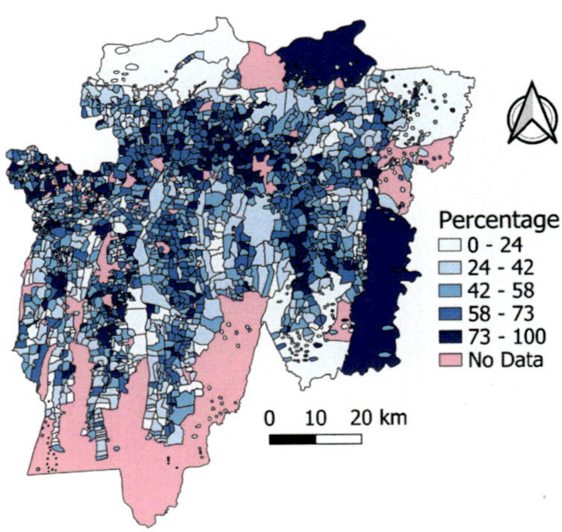

Map 46

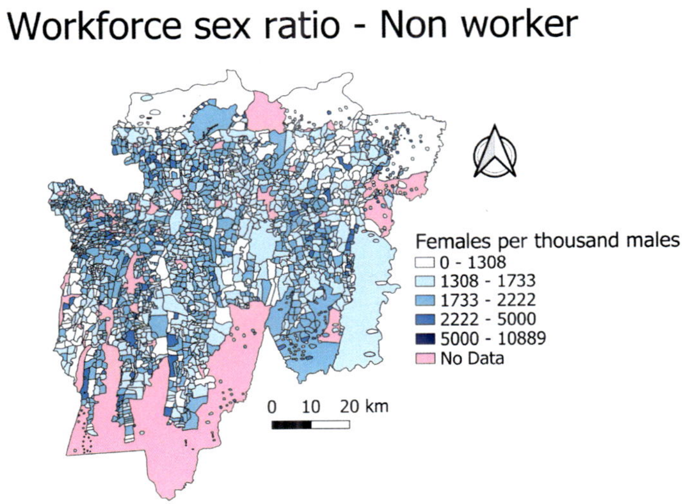
Workforce sex ratio - Non worker
Females per thousand males
0 - 1308
1308 - 1733
1733 - 2222
2222 - 5000
5000 - 10889
No Data
0 10 20 km

Map 47

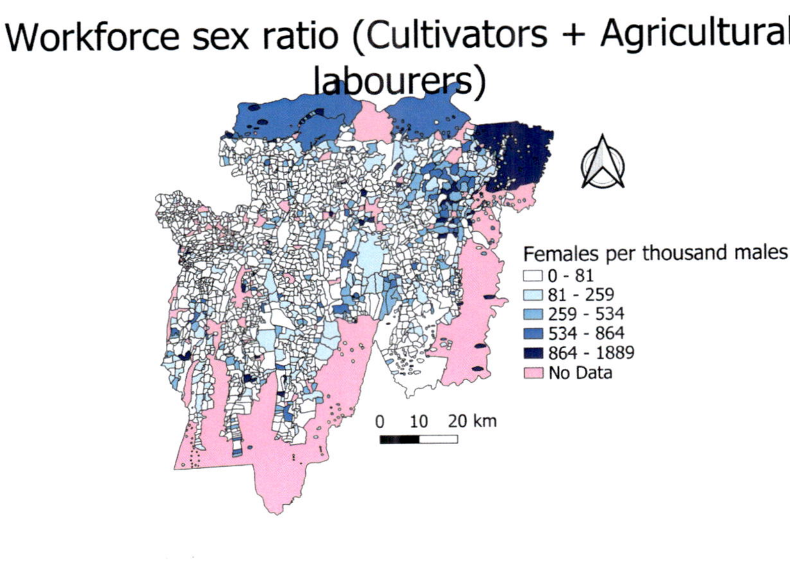
Workforce sex ratio (Cultivators + Agricultural labourers)
Females per thousand males
0 - 81
81 - 259
259 - 534
534 - 864
864 - 1889
No Data
0 10 20 km

Map 48

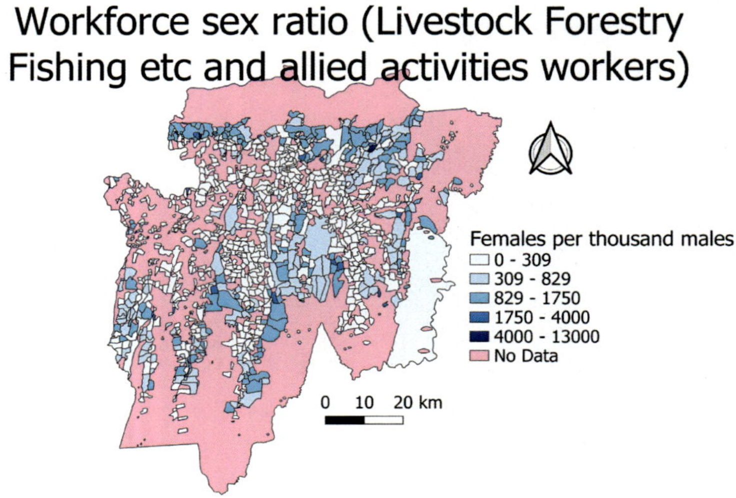
Workforce sex ratio (Livestock Forestry Fishing etc and allied activities workers)
Females per thousand males
0 - 309
309 - 829
829 - 1750
1750 - 4000
4000 - 13000
No Data
0 10 20 km

Map 49

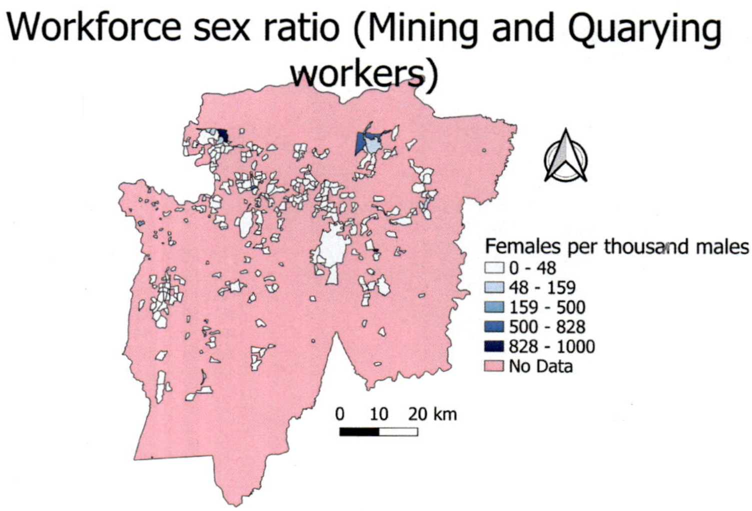
Workforce sex ratio (Mining and Quarying workers)
Females per thousand males
0 - 48
48 - 159
159 - 500
500 - 828
828 - 1000
No Data
0 10 20 km

Map 50

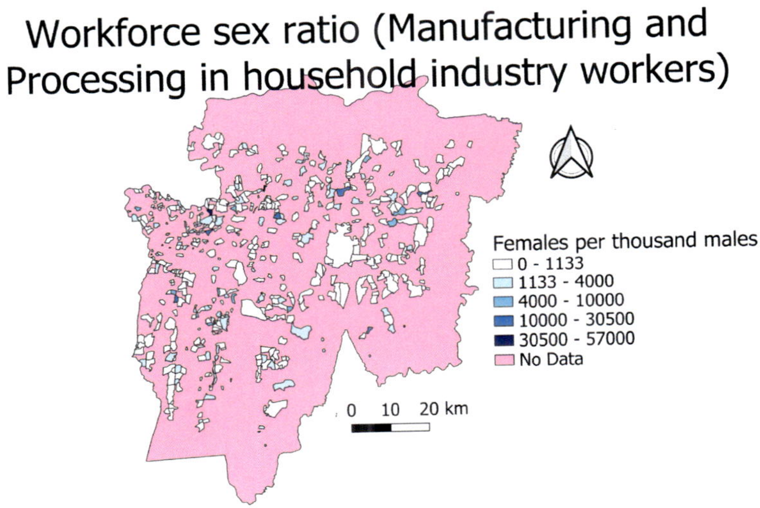
Workforce sex ratio (Manufacturing and Processing in household industry workers)
Females per thousand males
0 - 1133
1133 - 4000
4000 - 10000
10000 - 30500
30500 - 57000
No Data
0 10 20 km

Map 51

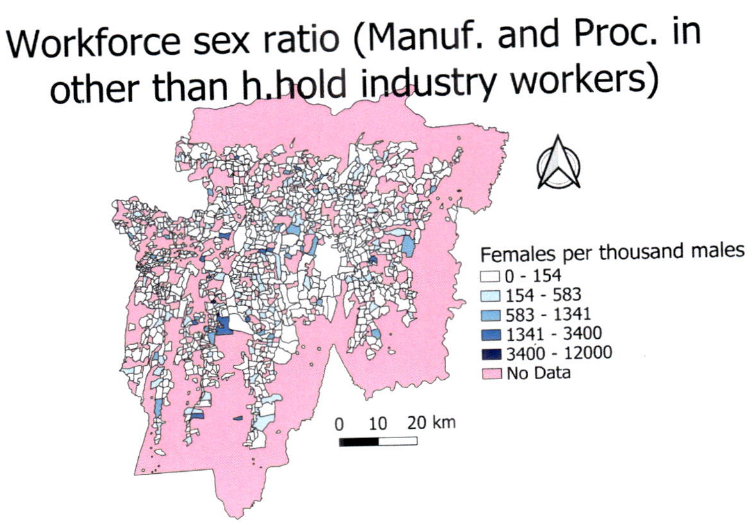
Workforce sex ratio (Manuf. and Proc. in other than h.hold industry workers)
Females per thousand males
0 - 154
154 - 583
583 - 1341
1341 - 3400
3400 - 12000
No Data
0 10 20 km

Map 52

Workforce sex ratio (Construction workers)

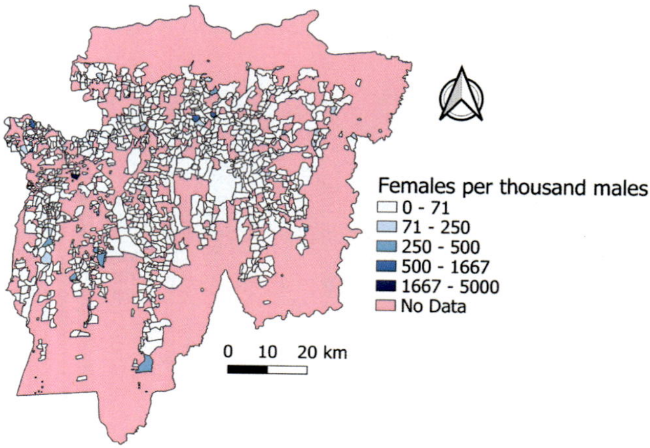

Map 53

Workforce sex ratio (Trade and Commerce workers)

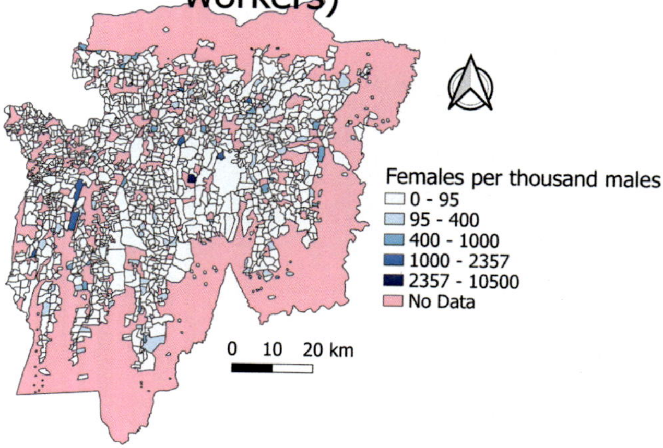

Map 54

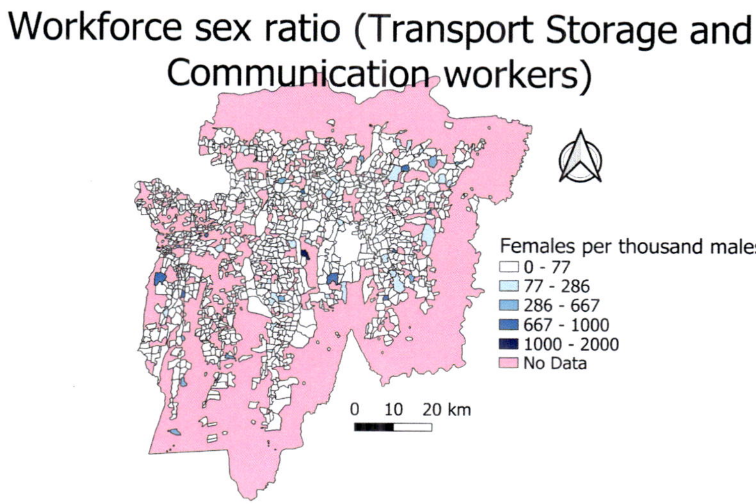
Workforce sex ratio (Transport Storage and Communication workers)
Females per thousand males
0 - 77
77 - 286
286 - 667
667 - 1000
1000 - 2000
No Data
0 10 20 km

Map 55

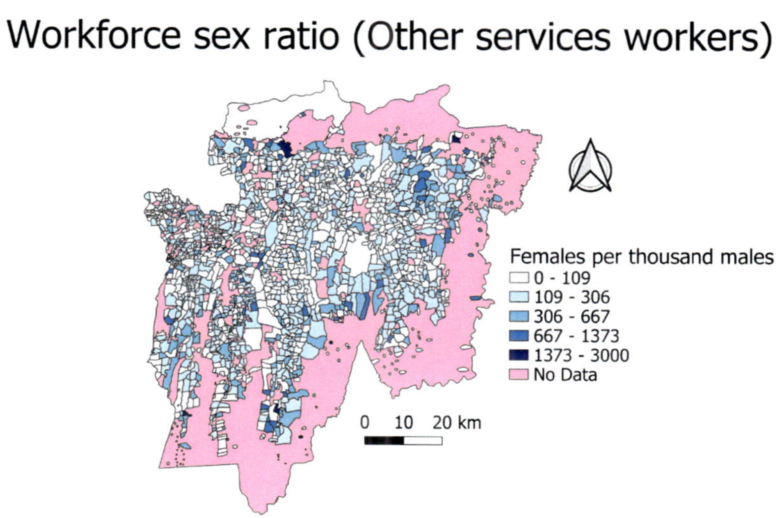
Workforce sex ratio (Other services workers)
Females per thousand males
0 - 109
109 - 306
306 - 667
667 - 1373
1373 - 3000
No Data
0 10 20 km

Map 56

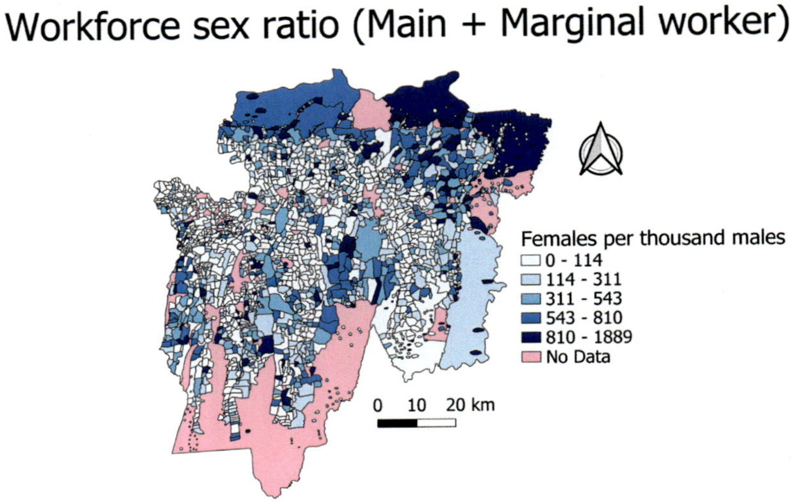
Workforce sex ratio (Main + Marginal worker)
Females per thousand males
0 - 114
114 - 311
311 - 543
543 - 810
810 - 1889
No Data
0 10 20 km

Map 57

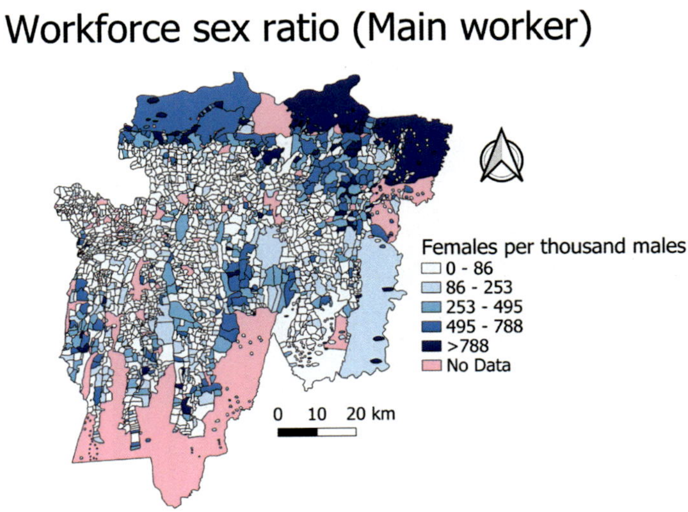
Workforce sex ratio (Main worker)
Females per thousand males
0 - 86
86 - 253
253 - 495
495 - 788
>788
No Data
0 10 20 km

Map 58

Workforce sex ratio (Marginal worker)

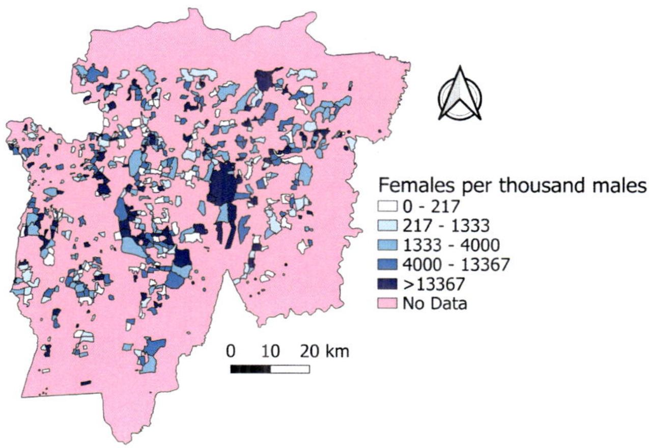

Map 59

Work participation rate (Main - Male)

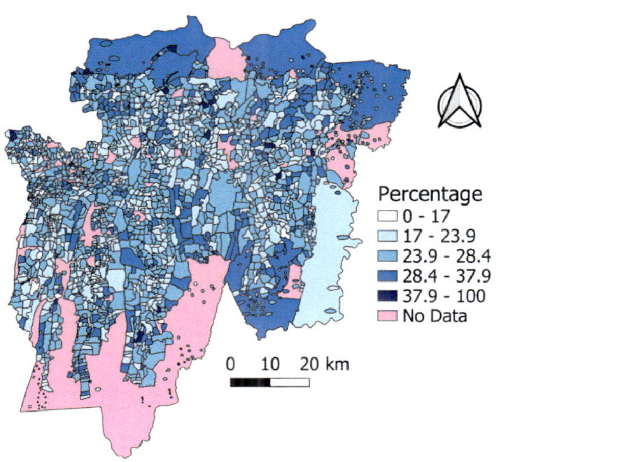

Map 60

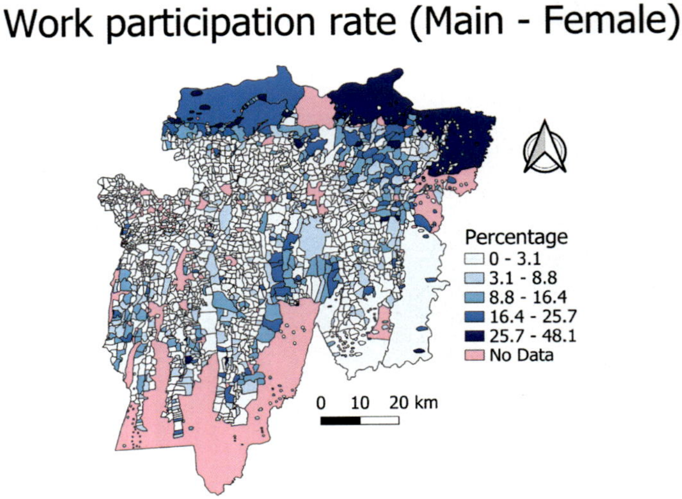
Work participation rate (Main - Female)
Percentage
0 - 3.1
3.1 - 8.8
8.8 - 16.4
16.4 - 25.7
25.7 - 48.1
No Data
0 10 20 km

Map 61

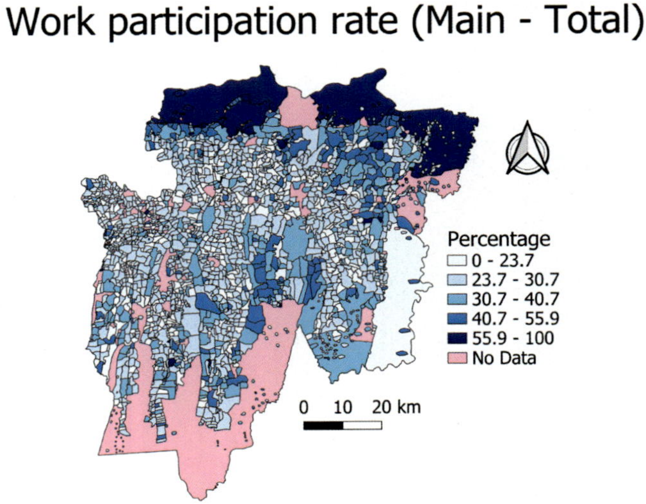
Work participation rate (Main - Total)
Percentage
0 - 23.7
23.7 - 30.7
30.7 - 40.7
40.7 - 55.9
55.9 - 100
No Data
0 10 20 km

Map 62

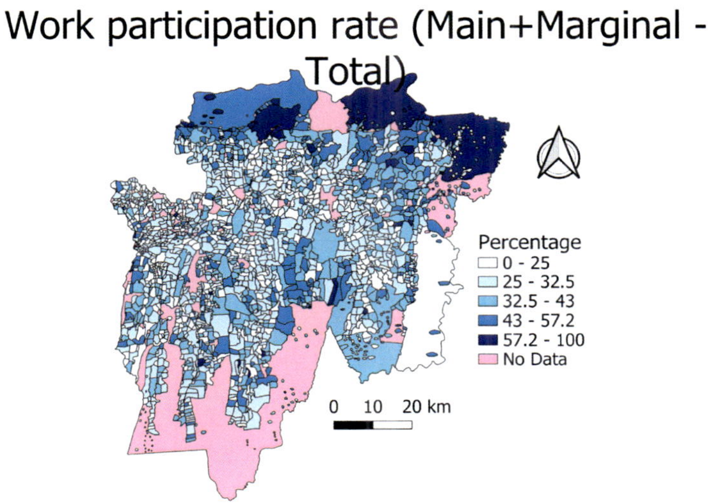
Work participation rate (Main+Marginal - Total)
Percentage
0 - 25
25 - 32.5
32.5 - 43
43 - 57.2
57.2 - 100
No Data
0 10 20 km

Map 63

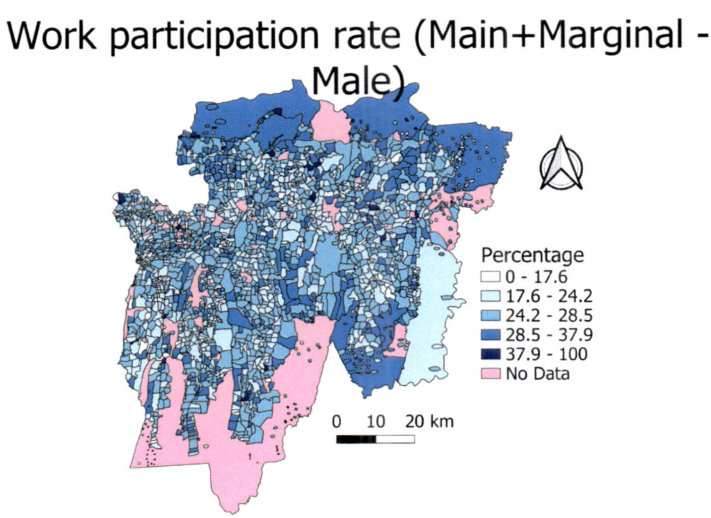
Work participation rate (Main+Marginal - Male)
Percentage
0 - 17.6
17.6 - 24.2
24.2 - 28.5
28.5 - 37.9
37.9 - 100
No Data
0 10 20 km

Map 64

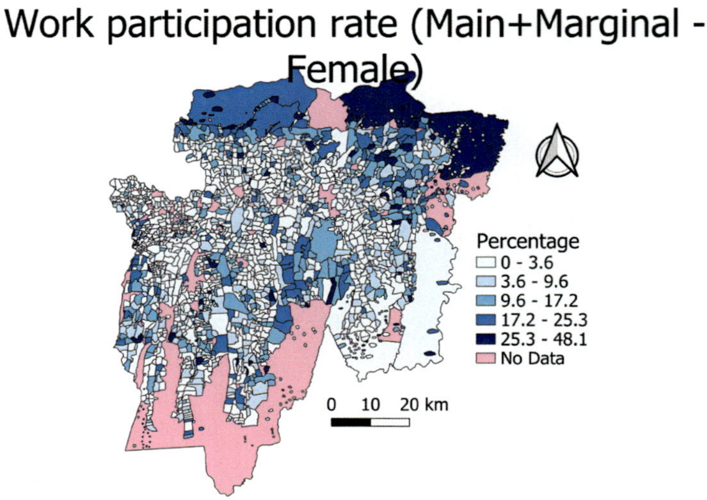
Work participation rate (Main+Marginal - Female)
Percentage
0 - 3.6
3.6 - 9.6
9.6 - 17.2
17.2 - 25.3
25.3 - 48.1
No Data
0 10 20 km

Map 65

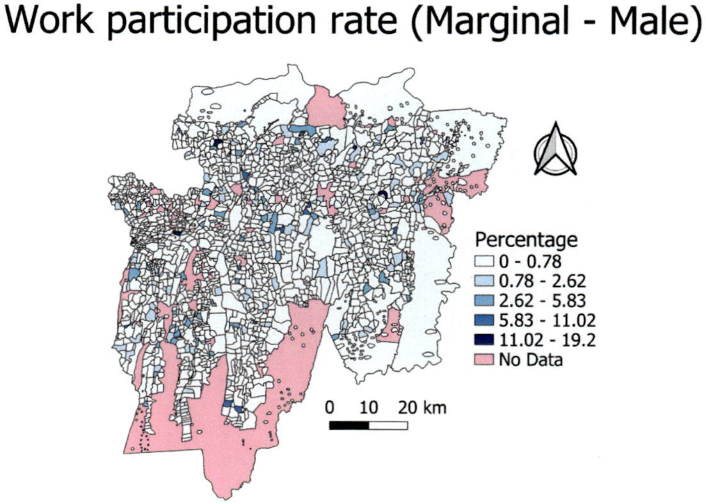
Work participation rate (Marginal - Male)
Percentage
0 - 0.78
0.78 - 2.62
2.62 - 5.83
5.83 - 11.02
11.02 - 19.2
No Data
0 10 20 km

Map 66

Work participation rate (Marginal - Female)

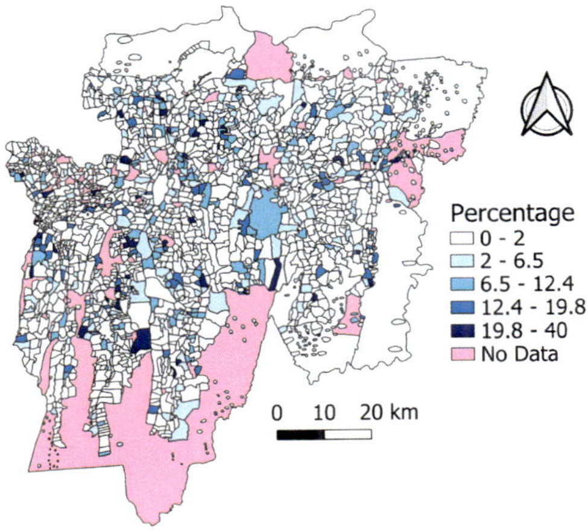

Map 67

Work participation rate (Marginal - Total)

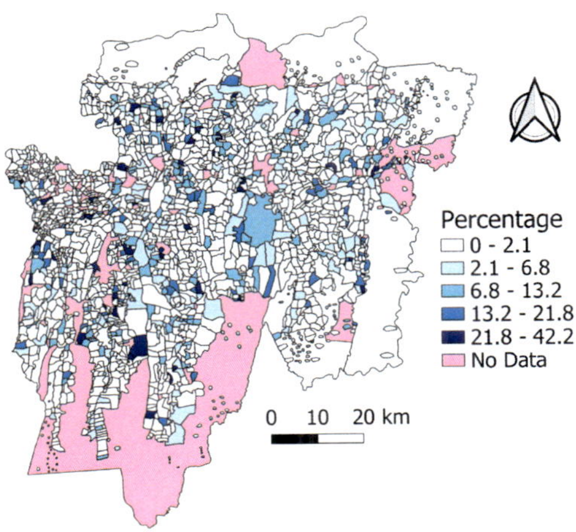

Map 68

Work participation rate (Cultivators - Total)

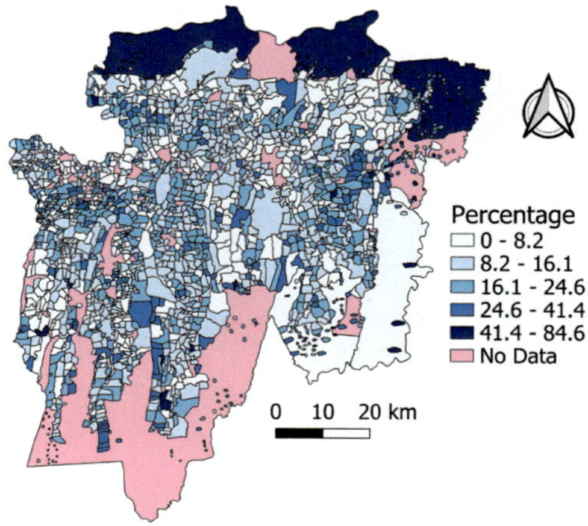

Map 69

Work participation rate (Cultivators - Male)

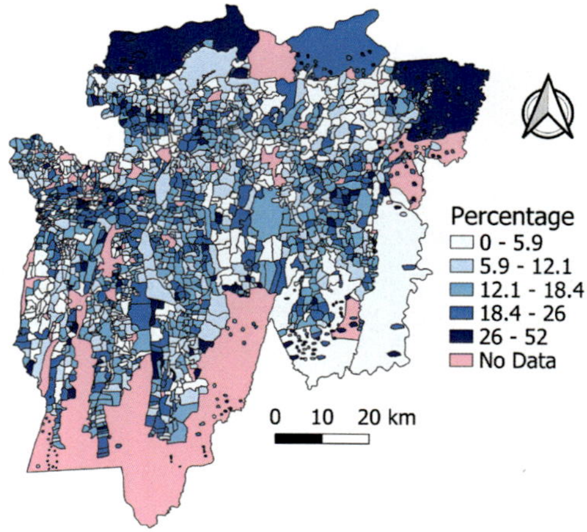

Map 70

Work participation rate (Cultivators - Female)

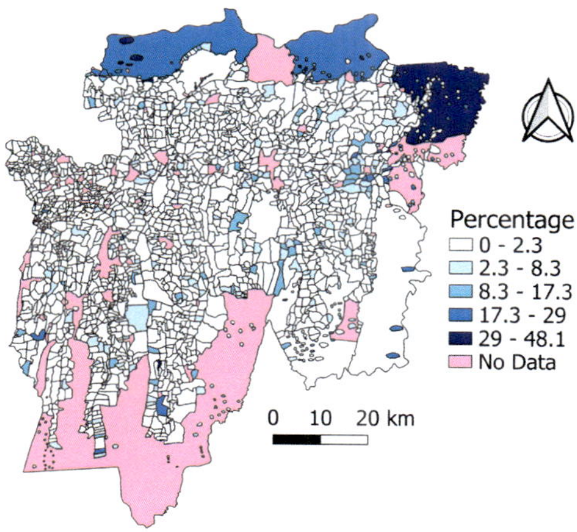

Map 71

Work participation rate (Agricultural laborers - Male)

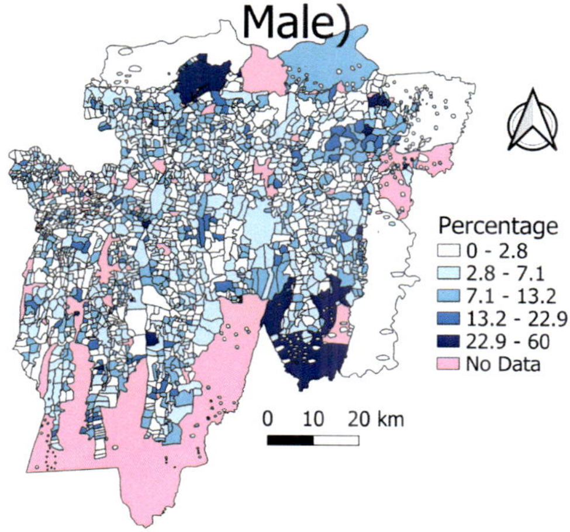

Map 72

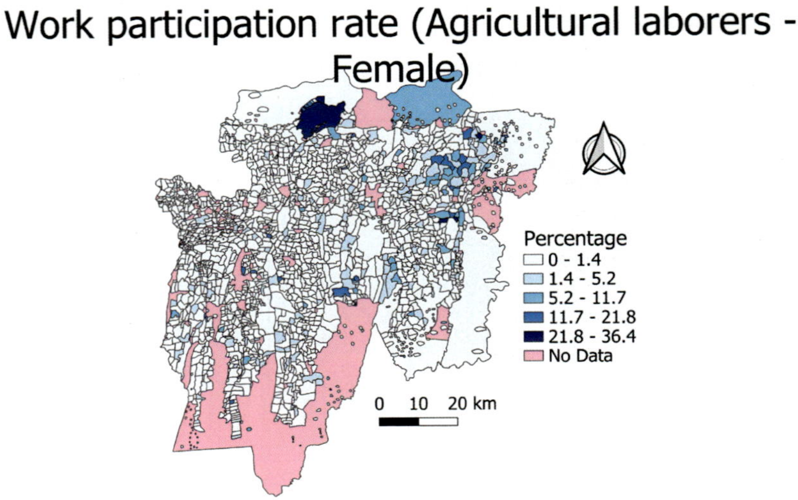
Work participation rate (Agricultural laborers - Female)
Percentage
0 - 1.4
1.4 - 5.2
5.2 - 11.7
11.7 - 21.8
21.8 - 36.4
No Data
0 10 20 km

Map 73

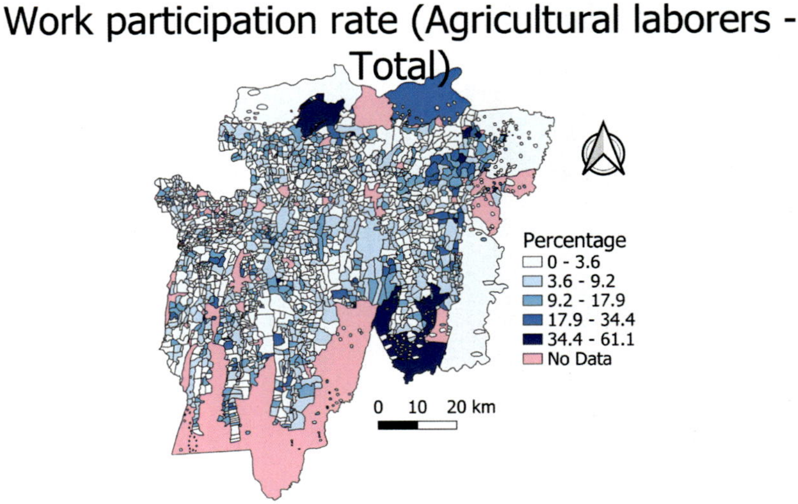
Work participation rate (Agricultural laborers - Total)
Percentage
0 - 3.6
3.6 - 9.2
9.2 - 17.9
17.9 - 34.4
34.4 - 61.1
No Data
0 10 20 km

Map 74

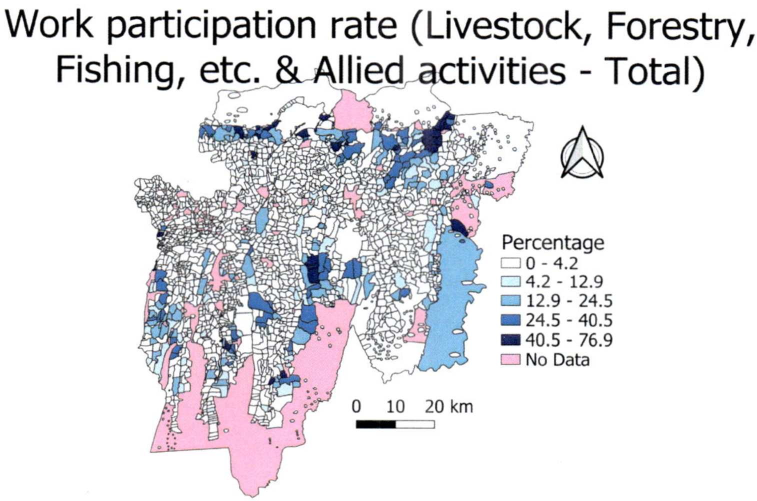
Work participation rate (Livestock, Forestry, Fishing, etc. & Allied activities - Total)
Percentage
0 - 4.2
4.2 - 12.9
12.9 - 24.5
24.5 - 40.5
40.5 - 76.9
No Data
0 10 20 km

Map 75

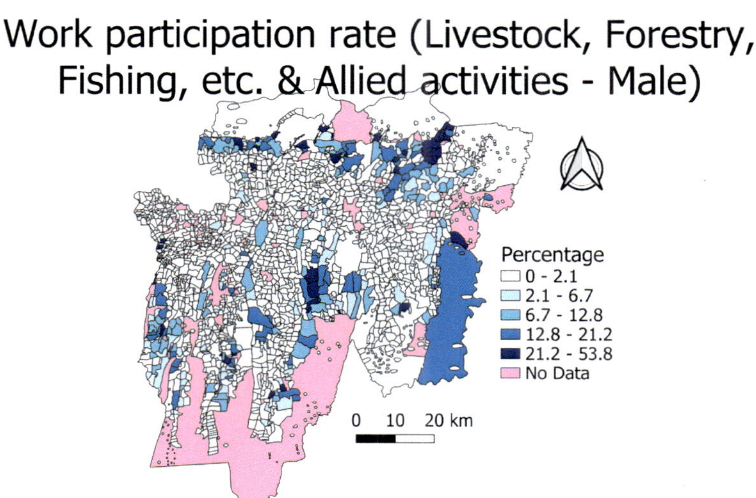
Work participation rate (Livestock, Forestry, Fishing, etc. & Allied activities - Male)
Percentage
0 - 2.1
2.1 - 6.7
6.7 - 12.8
12.8 - 21.2
21.2 - 53.8
No Data
0 10 20 km

Map 76

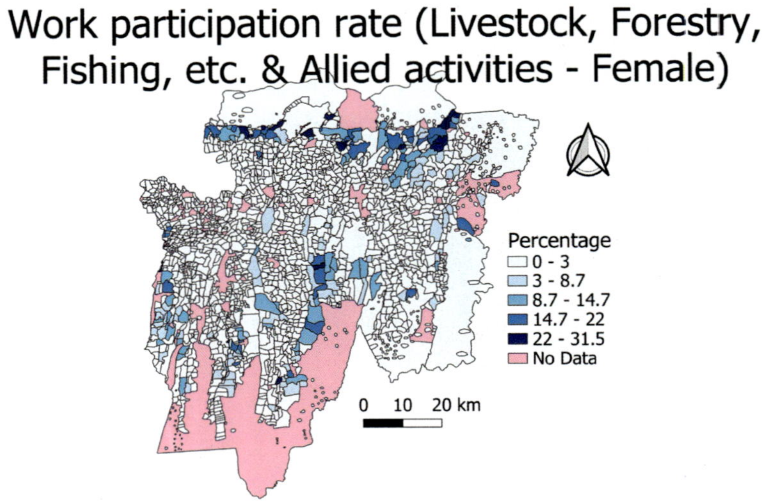
Work participation rate (Livestock, Forestry, Fishing, etc. & Allied activities - Female)
Percentage
0 - 3
3 - 8.7
8.7 - 14.7
14.7 - 22
22 - 31.5
No Data
0 10 20 km

Map 77

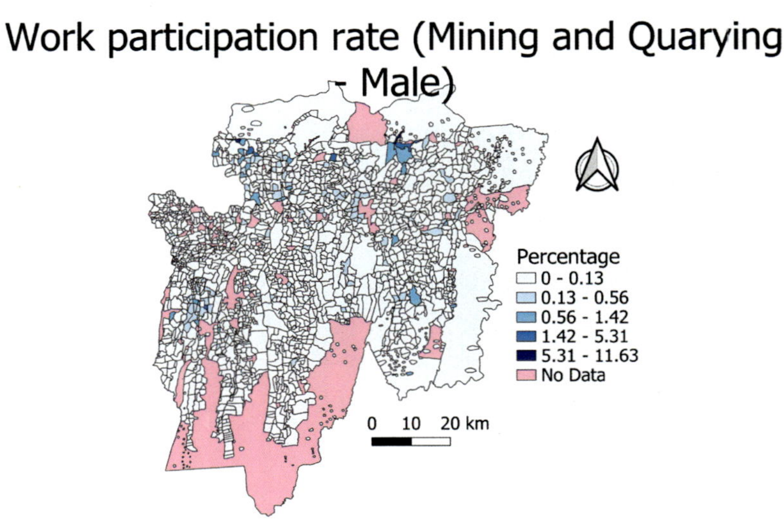
Work participation rate (Mining and Quarying - Male)
Percentage
0 - 0.13
0.13 - 0.56
0.56 - 1.42
1.42 - 5.31
5.31 - 11.63
No Data
0 10 20 km

Map 78

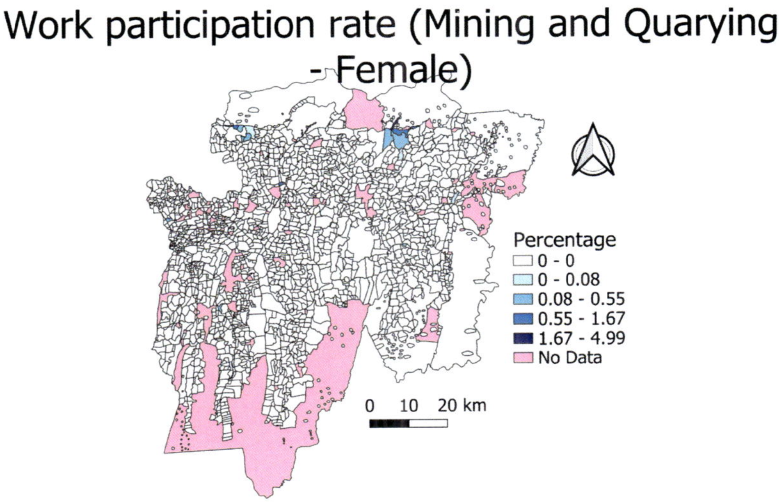
Work participation rate (Mining and Quarying - Female)
Percentage
0 - 0
0 - 0.08
0.08 - 0.55
0.55 - 1.67
1.67 - 4.99
No Data
0 10 20 km

Map 79

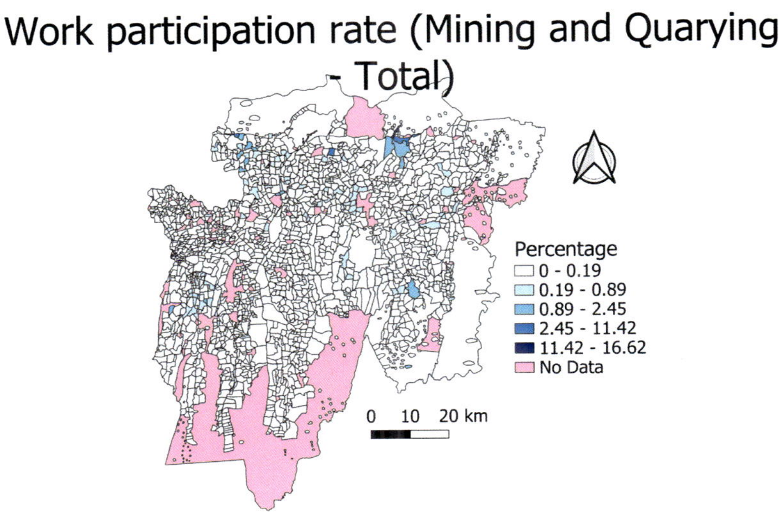
Work participation rate (Mining and Quarying - Total)
Percentage
0 - 0.19
0.19 - 0.89
0.89 - 2.45
2.45 - 11.42
11.42 - 16.62
No Data
0 10 20 km

Map 80

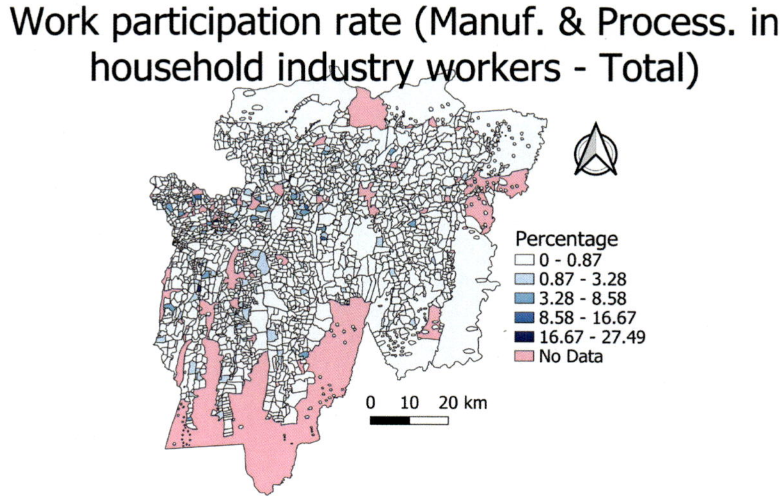
Work participation rate (Manuf. & Process. in household industry workers - Total)
Percentage
0 - 0.87
0.87 - 3.28
3.28 - 8.58
8.58 - 16.67
16.67 - 27.49
No Data
0 10 20 km

Map 81

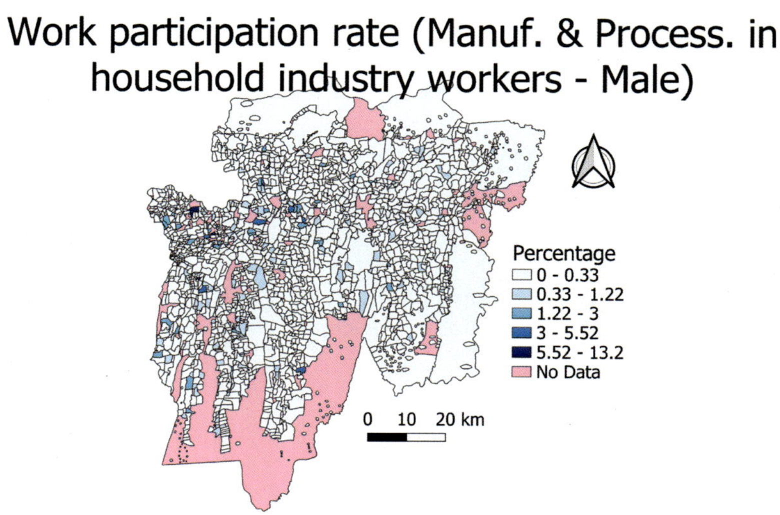
Work participation rate (Manuf. & Process. in household industry workers - Male)
Percentage
0 - 0.33
0.33 - 1.22
1.22 - 3
3 - 5.52
5.52 - 13.2
No Data
0 10 20 km

Map 82

Work participation rate (Manuf. & Process. in household industry workers - Female)

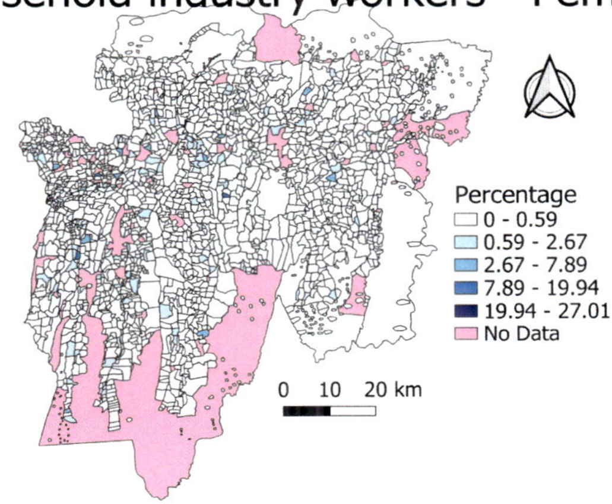

Map 83

Work participation rate (Manuf. & Process. in other than household industry workers - Male)

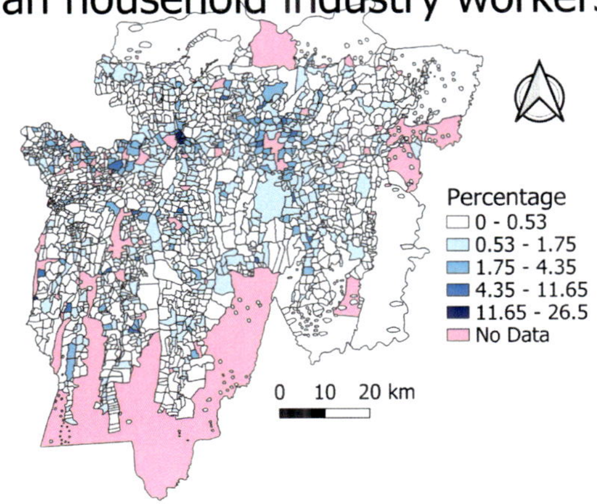

Map 84

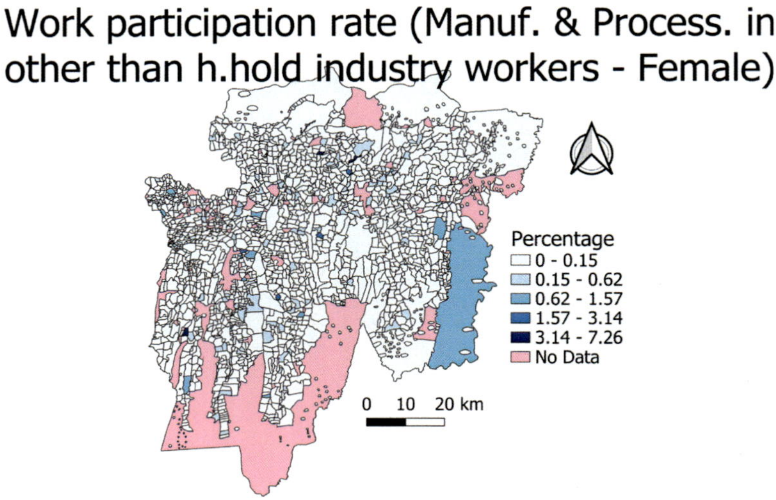
Work participation rate (Manuf. & Process. in other than h.hold industry workers - Female)
Percentage
0 - 0.15
0.15 - 0.62
0.62 - 1.57
1.57 - 3.14
3.14 - 7.26
No Data
0 10 20 km

Map 85

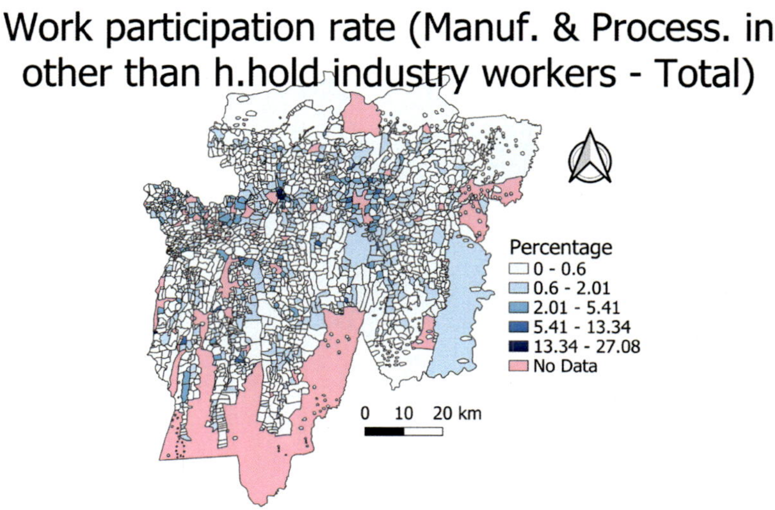
Work participation rate (Manuf. & Process. in other than h.hold industry workers - Total)
Percentage
0 - 0.6
0.6 - 2.01
2.01 - 5.41
5.41 - 13.34
13.34 - 27.08
No Data
0 10 20 km

Map 86

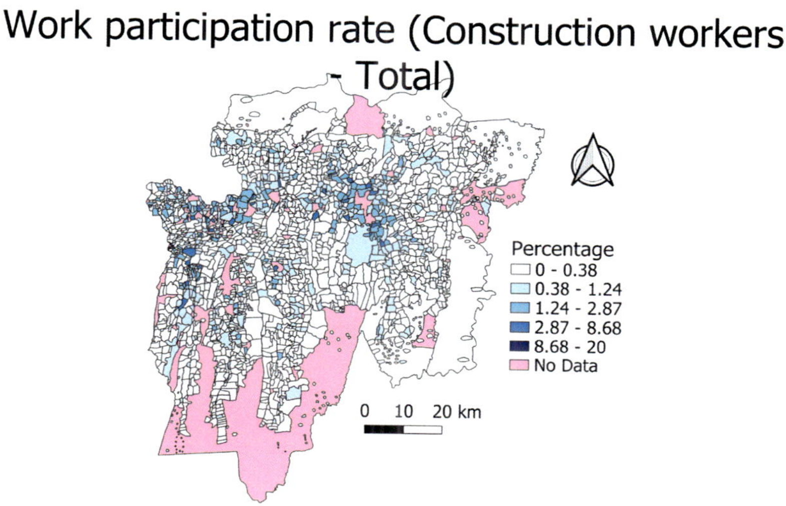
Work participation rate (Construction workers - Total)
Percentage
0 - 0.38
0.38 - 1.24
1.24 - 2.87
2.87 - 8.68
8.68 - 20
No Data
0 10 20 km

Map 87

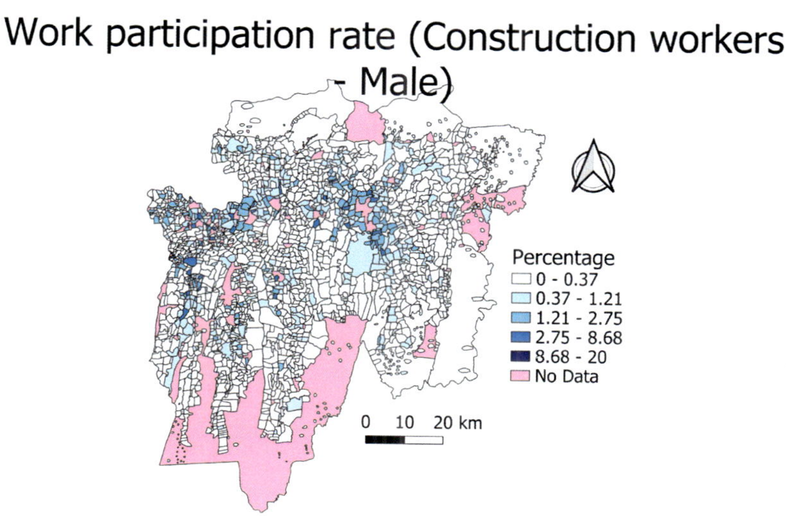
Work participation rate (Construction workers - Male)
Percentage
0 - 0.37
0.37 - 1.21
1.21 - 2.75
2.75 - 8.68
8.68 - 20
No Data
0 10 20 km

Map 88

Work participation rate (Construction workers - Female)

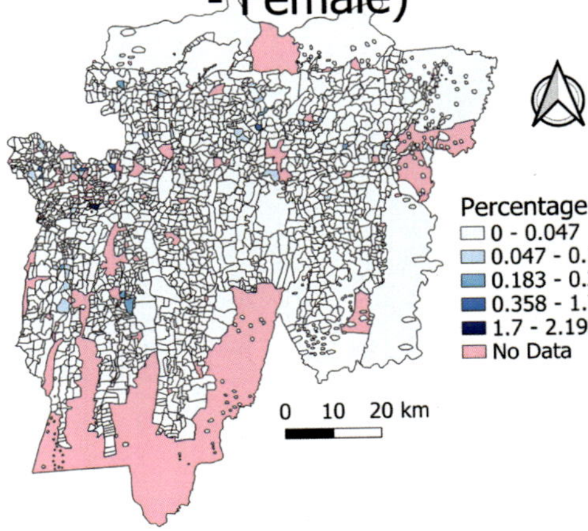

Map 89

Work participation rate (Trade and commerce workers - Male)

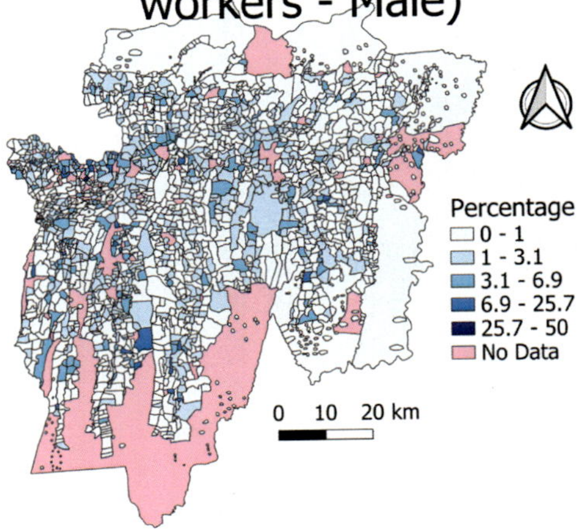

Map 90

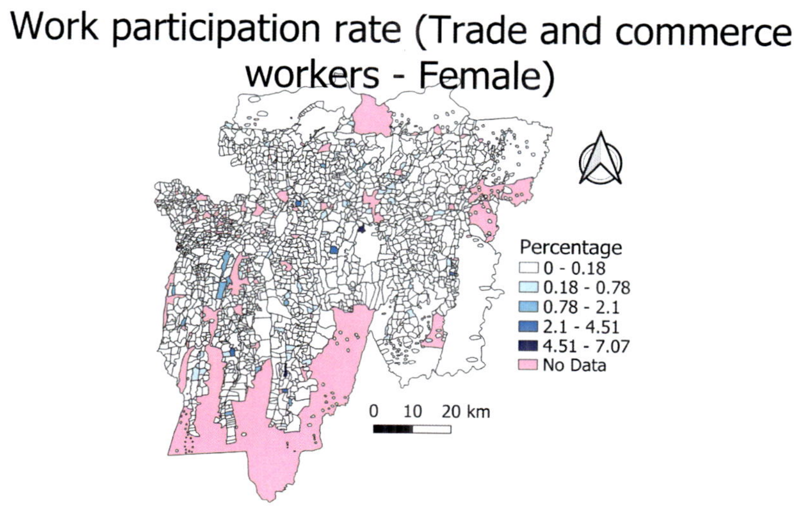
Work participation rate (Trade and commerce workers - Female)
Percentage
0 - 0.18
0.18 - 0.78
0.78 - 2.1
2.1 - 4.51
4.51 - 7.07
No Data
0 10 20 km

Map 91

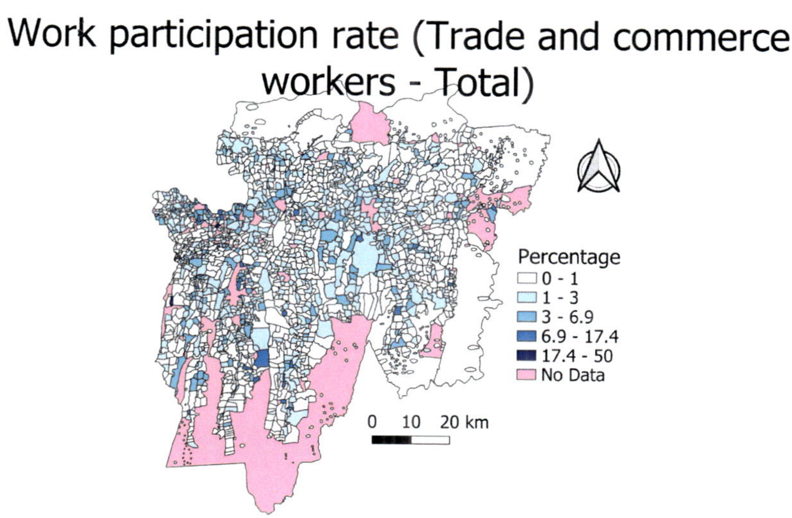
Work participation rate (Trade and commerce workers - Total)
Percentage
0 - 1
1 - 3
3 - 6.9
6.9 - 17.4
17.4 - 50
No Data
0 10 20 km

Map 92

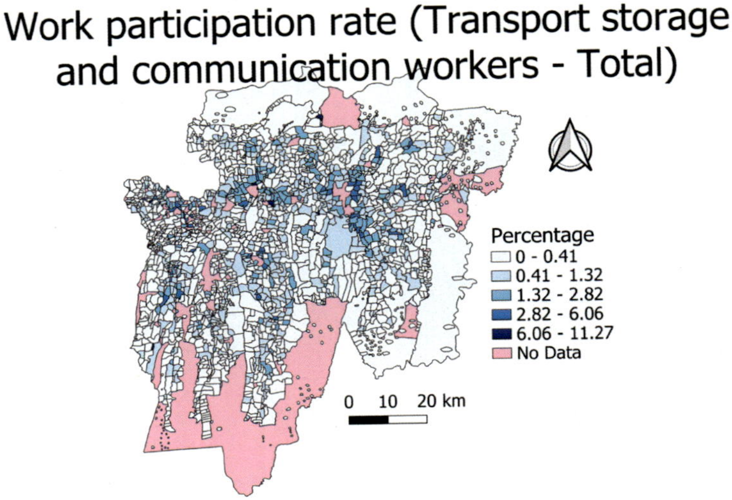
Work participation rate (Transport storage and communication workers - Total)
Percentage
0 - 0.41
0.41 - 1.32
1.32 - 2.82
2.82 - 6.06
6.06 - 11.27
No Data
0 10 20 km

Map 93

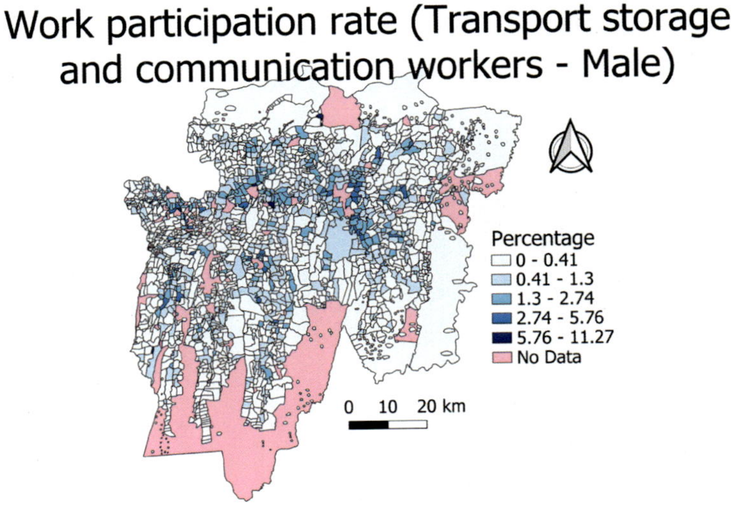
Work participation rate (Transport storage and communication workers - Male)
Percentage
0 - 0.41
0.41 - 1.3
1.3 - 2.74
2.74 - 5.76
5.76 - 11.27
No Data
0 10 20 km

Map 94

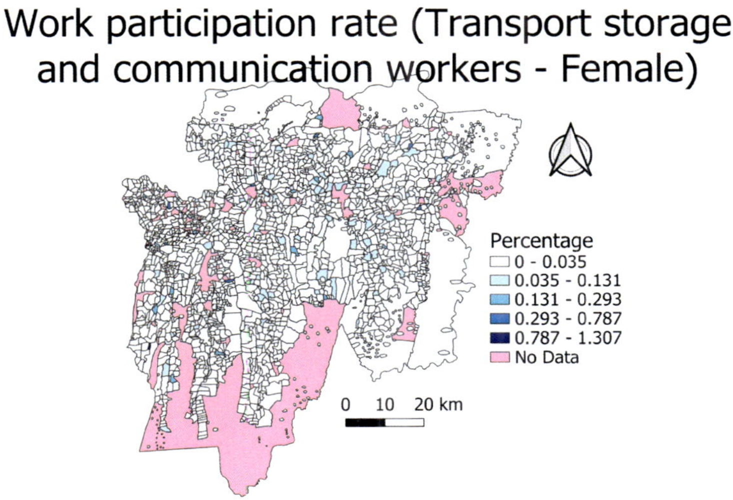
Work participation rate (Transport storage and communication workers - Female)
Percentage
0 - 0.035
0.035 - 0.131
0.131 - 0.293
0.293 - 0.787
0.787 - 1.307
No Data
0 10 20 km

Map 95

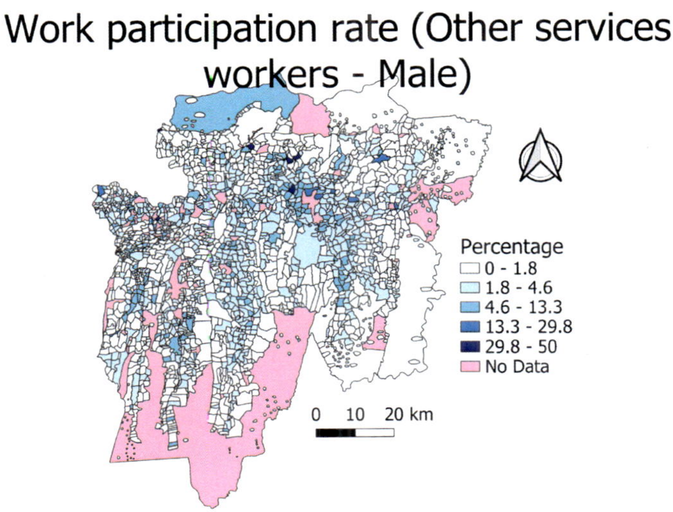
Work participation rate (Other services workers - Male)
Percentage
0 - 1.8
1.8 - 4.6
4.6 - 13.3
13.3 - 29.8
29.8 - 50
No Data
0 10 20 km

Map 96

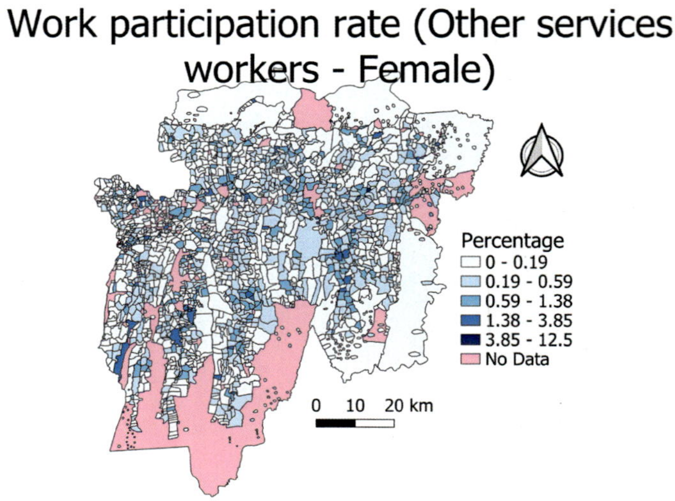
Work participation rate (Other services workers - Female)
Percentage
0 - 0.19
0.19 - 0.59
0.59 - 1.38
1.38 - 3.85
3.85 - 12.5
No Data
0 10 20 km

Map 97

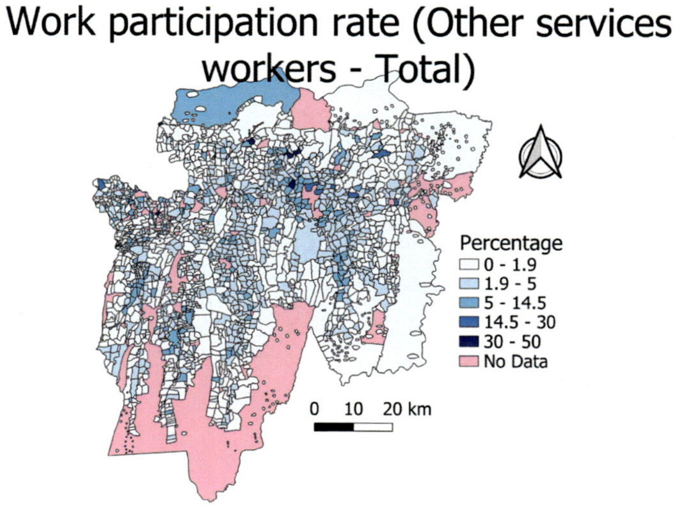
Work participation rate (Other services workers - Total)
Percentage
0 - 1.9
1.9 - 5
5 - 14.5
14.5 - 30
30 - 50
No Data
0 10 20 km

Map 98

Work participation rate (Non workers - Total)

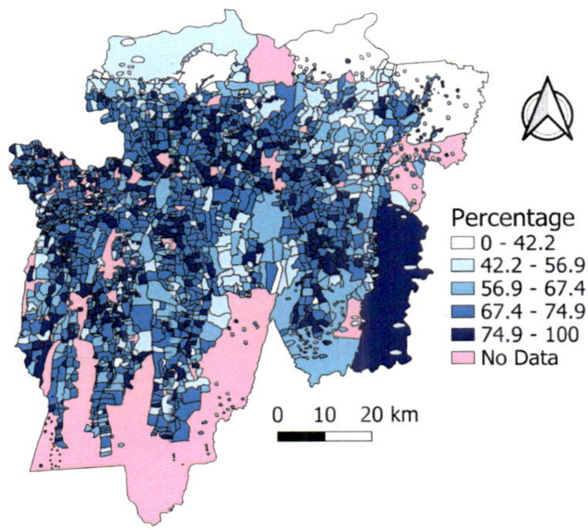

Map 99

Work participation rate (Non workers - Male)

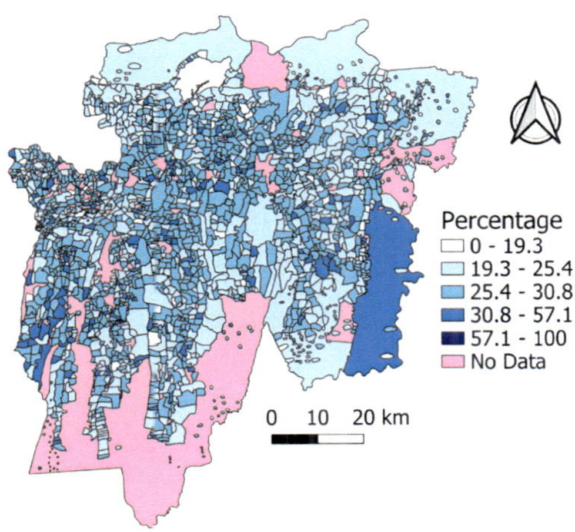

Map 100

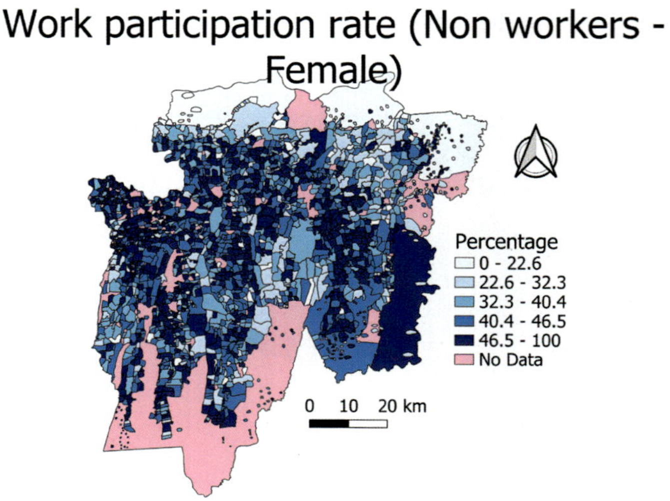
Work participation rate (Non workers - Female)
Percentage
0 - 22.6
22.6 - 32.3
32.3 - 40.4
40.4 - 46.5
46.5 - 100
No Data
0 10 20 km

Spatial analysis of census variables, 2001

Map 101

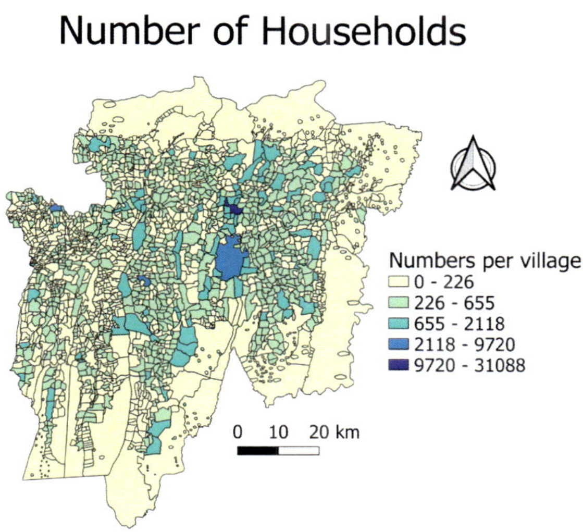

Map 102

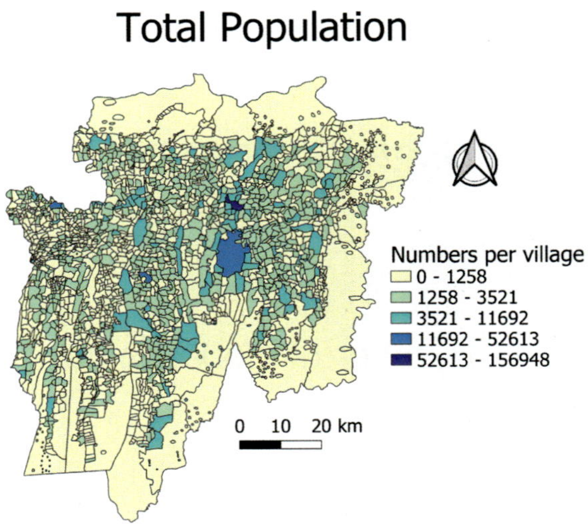

Map 103

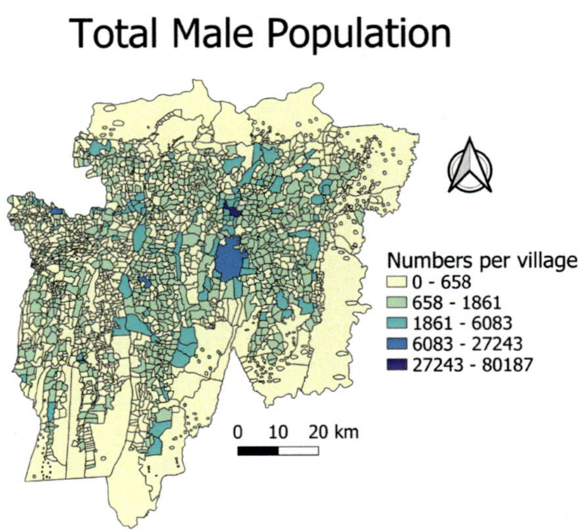

Map 104

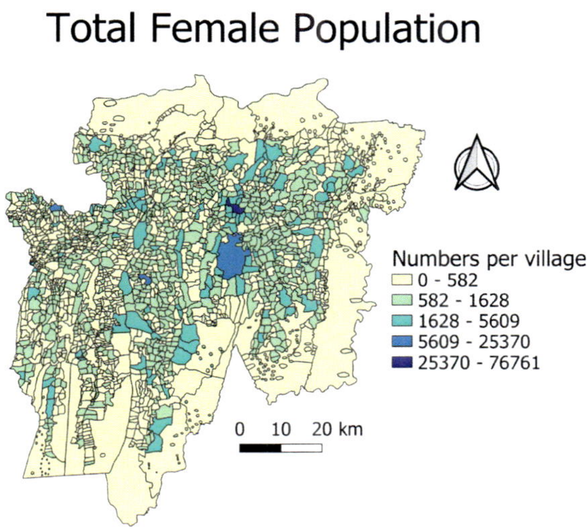

Map 105

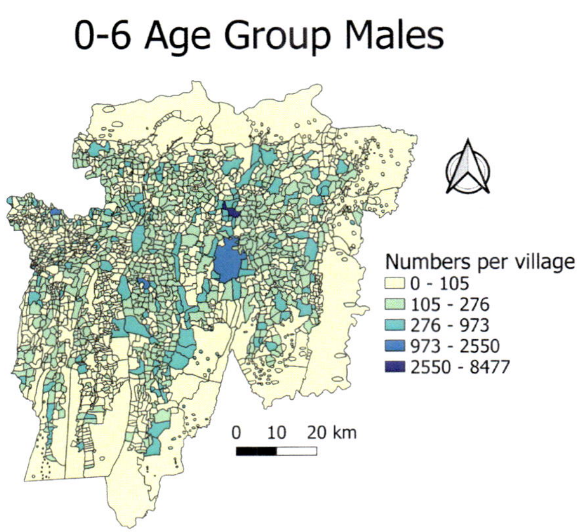

Map 106

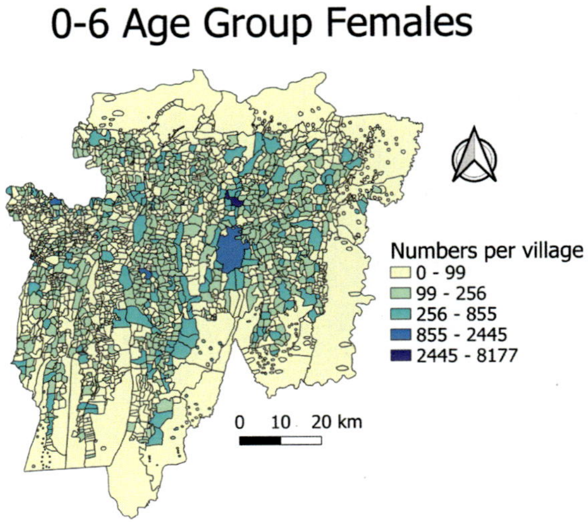

Map 107

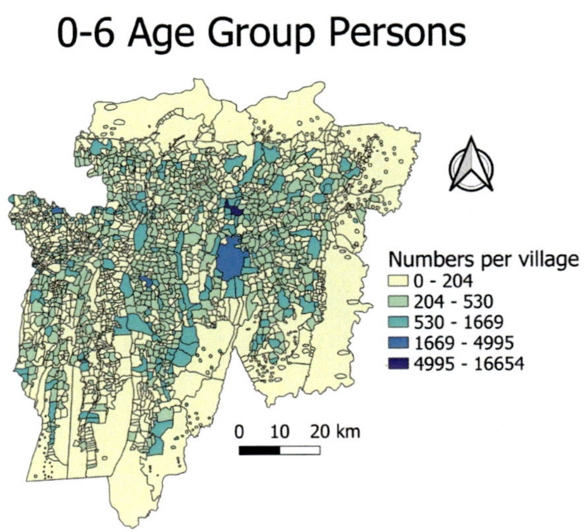

Map 108

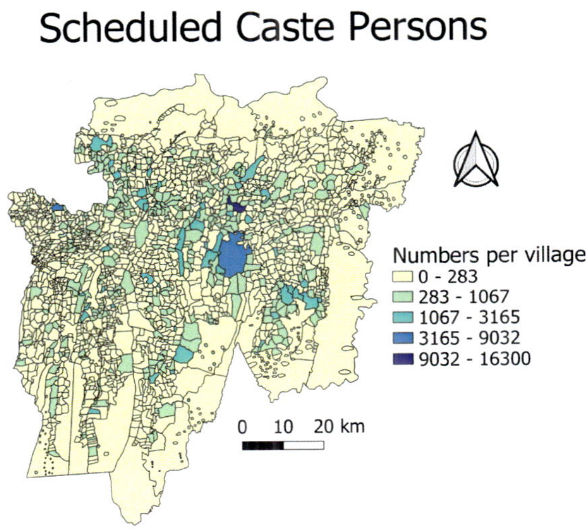

Map 109

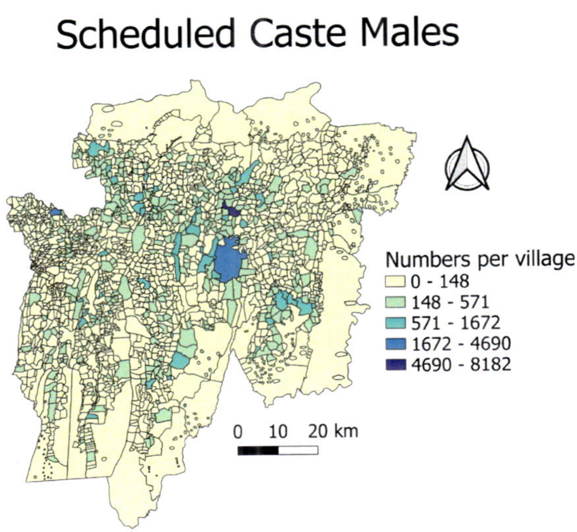

Map 110

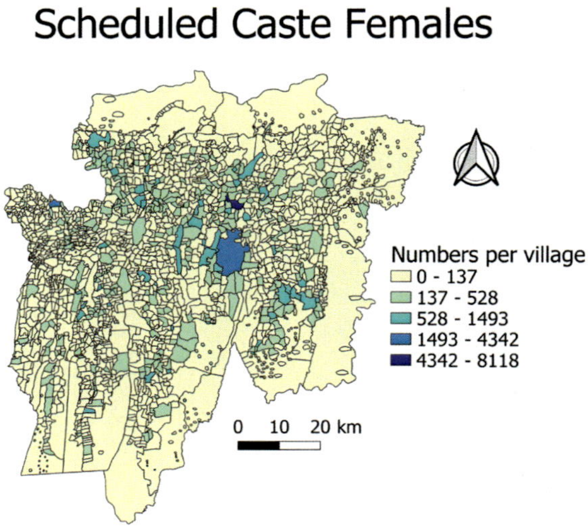

Map 111

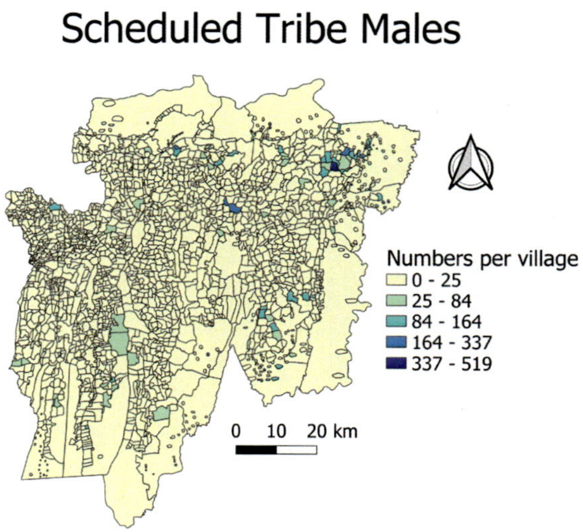

Map 112

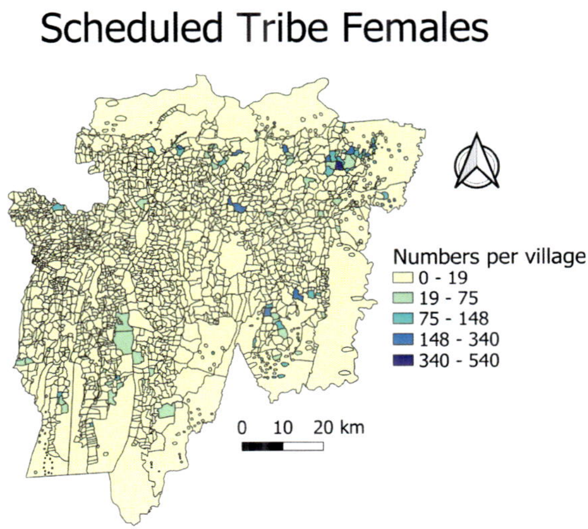

Map 113

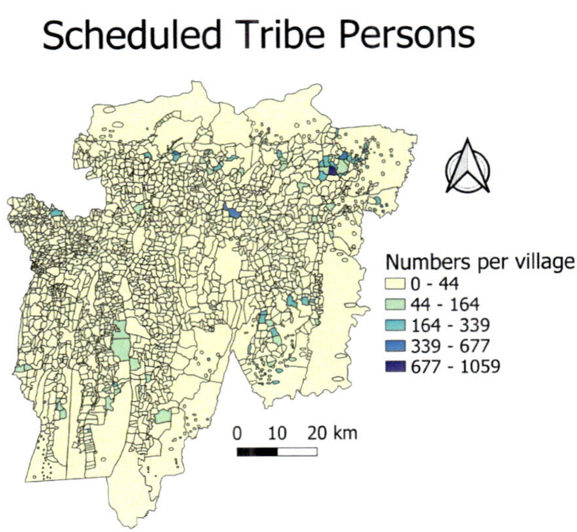

Map 114

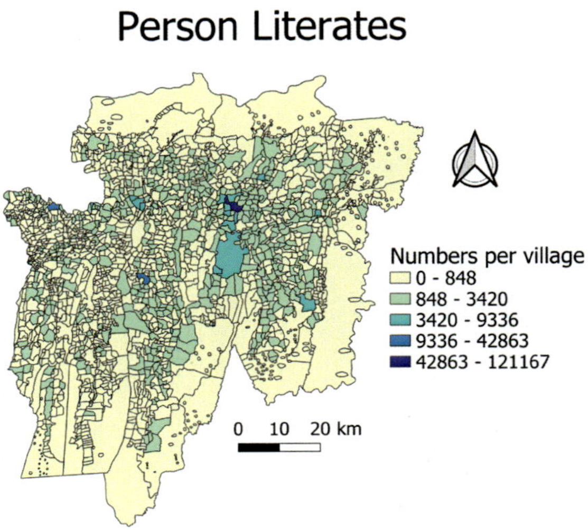

Map 115

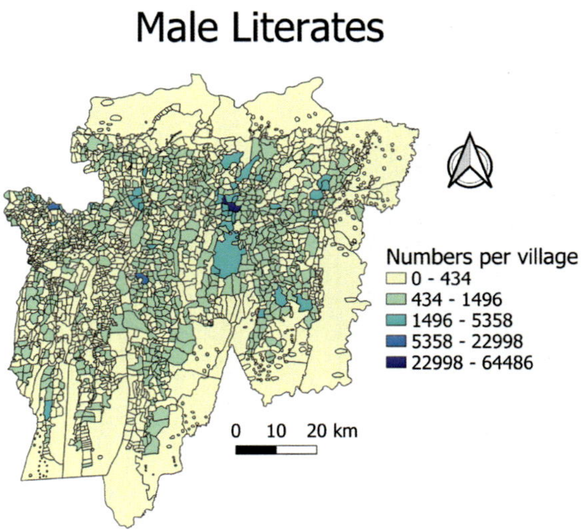

Map 116

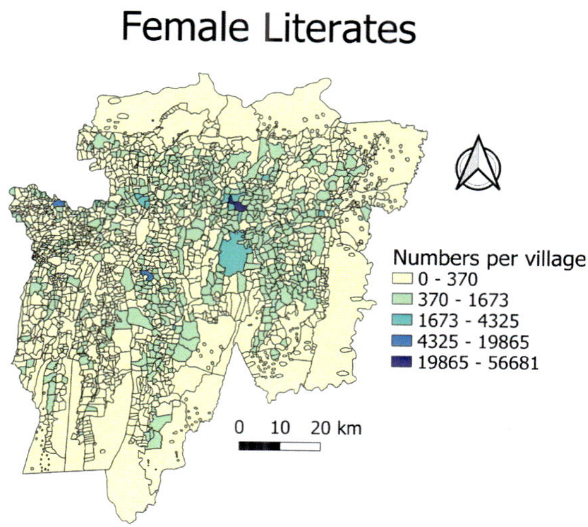

Map 117

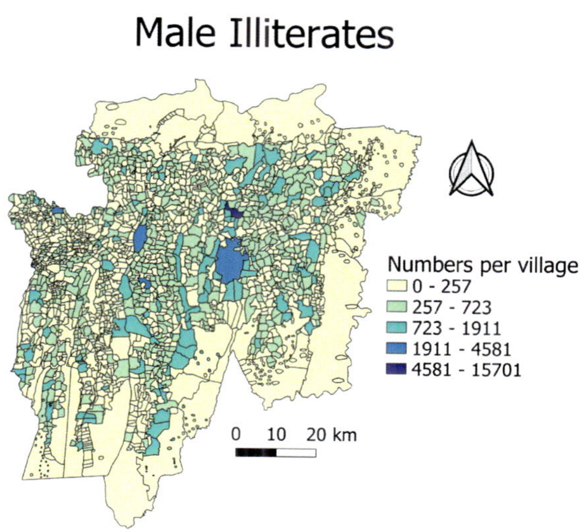

Map 118

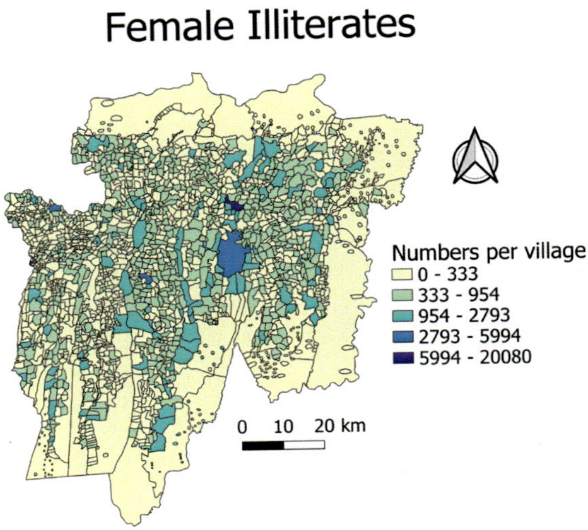

Map 119

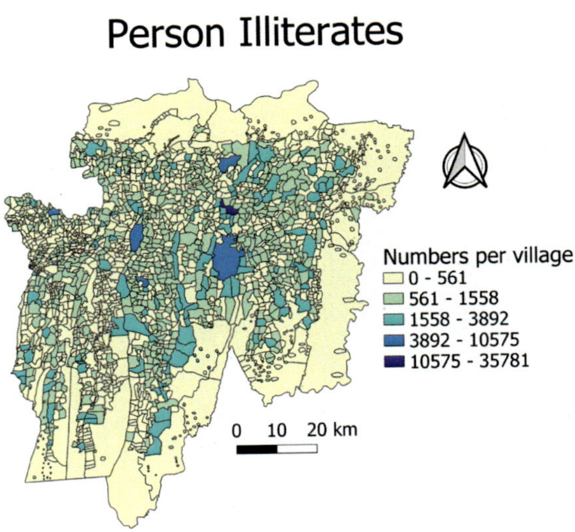

Map 120

Total Workers (Main + Marginal) Persons

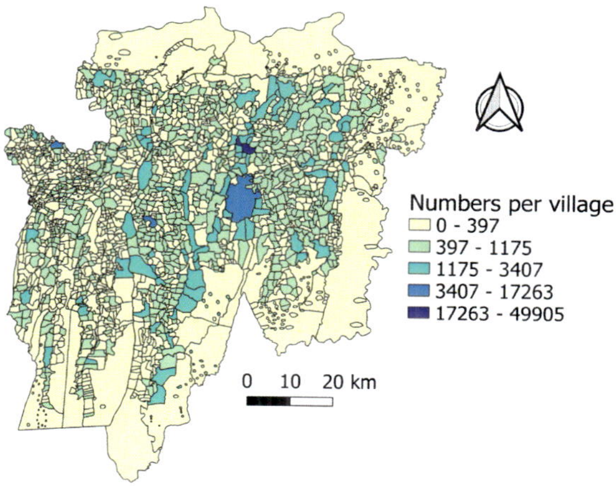

Map 121

Total Workers (Main + Marginal) Males

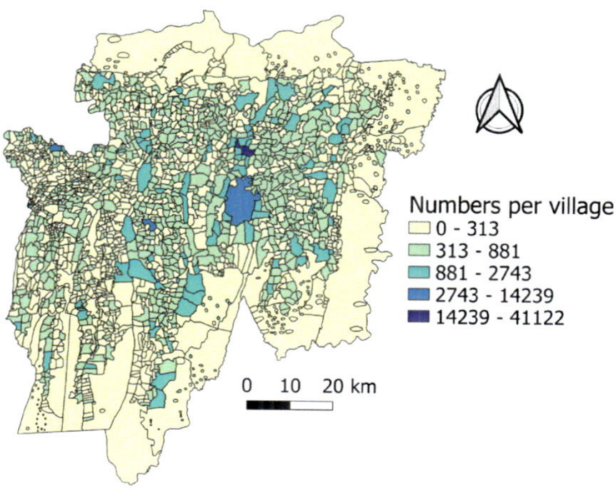

Map 122

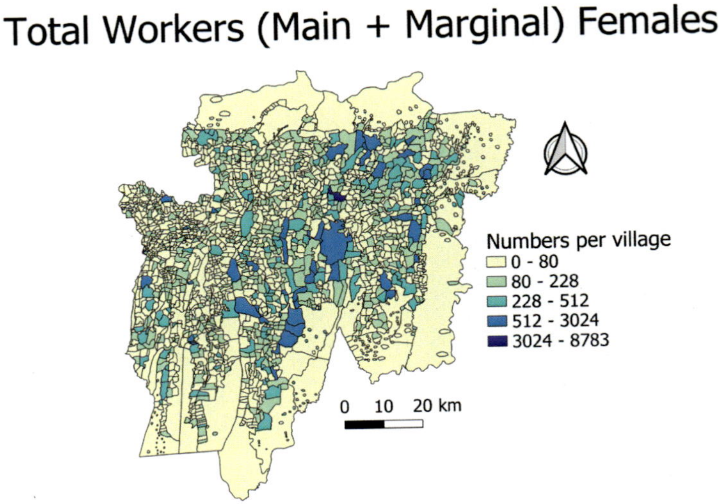

Map 123

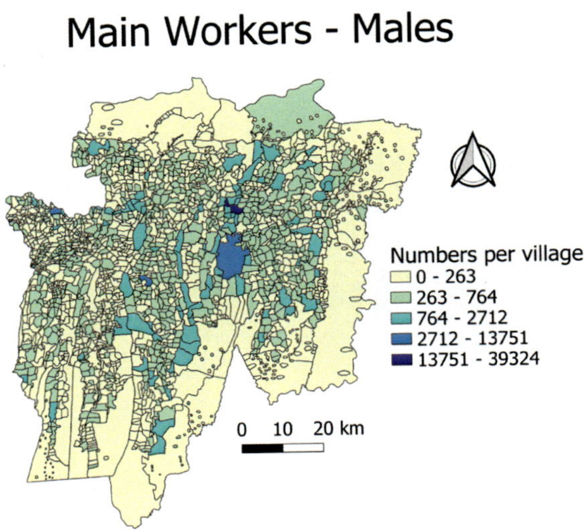

Map 124

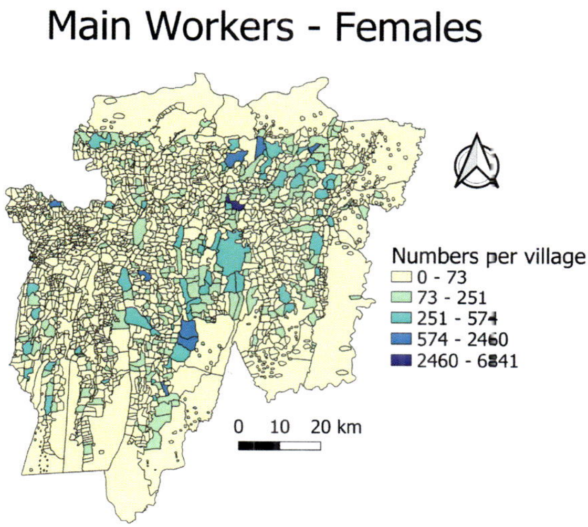

Map 125

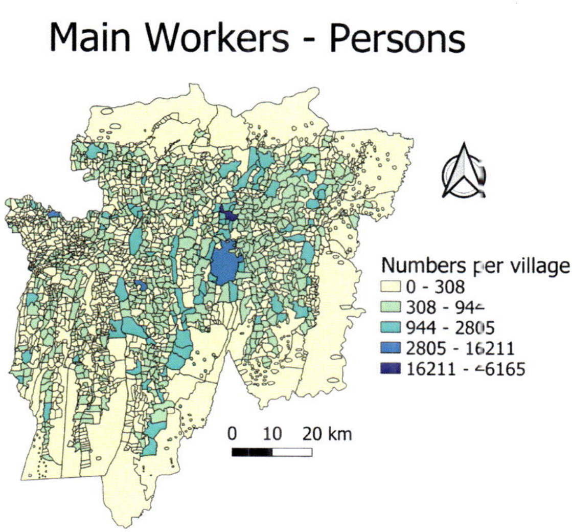

Map 126

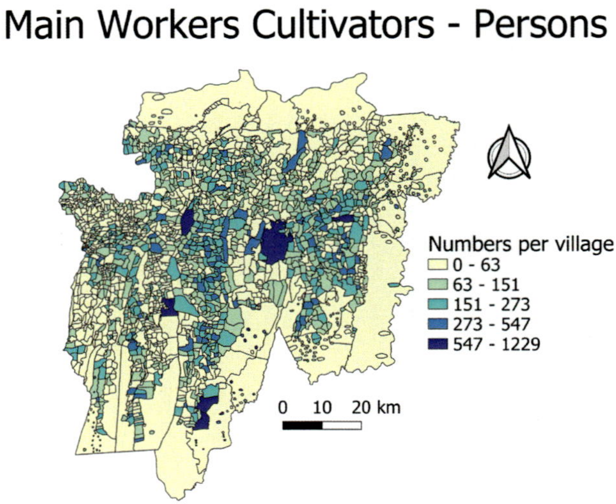

Map 127

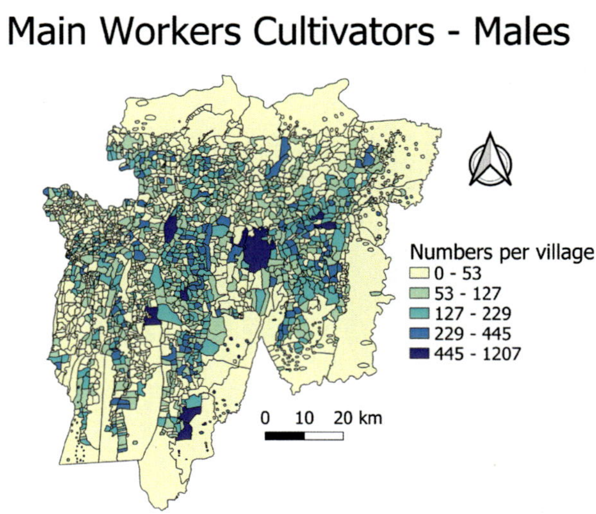

Map 128

Main Workers Cultivators - Females

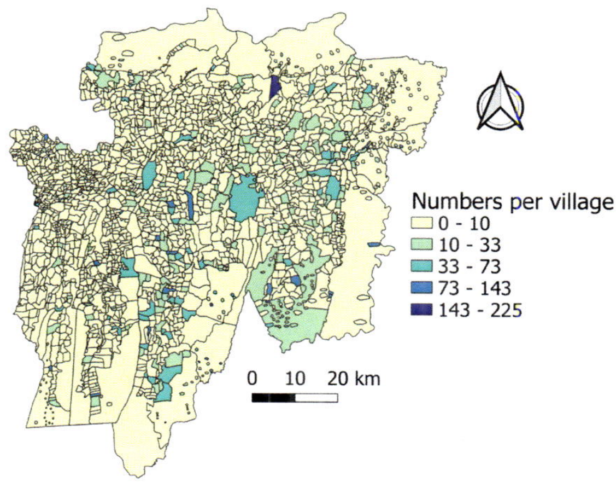

Map 129

Main Workers Agricultural Laborers - Males

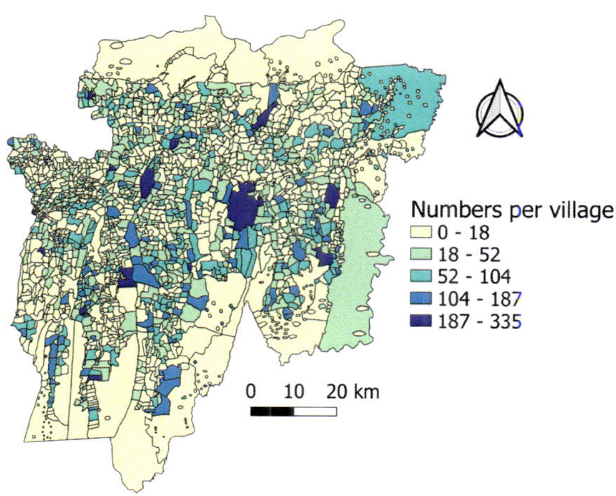

Map 130

Main Workers Agricultural Laborers - Females

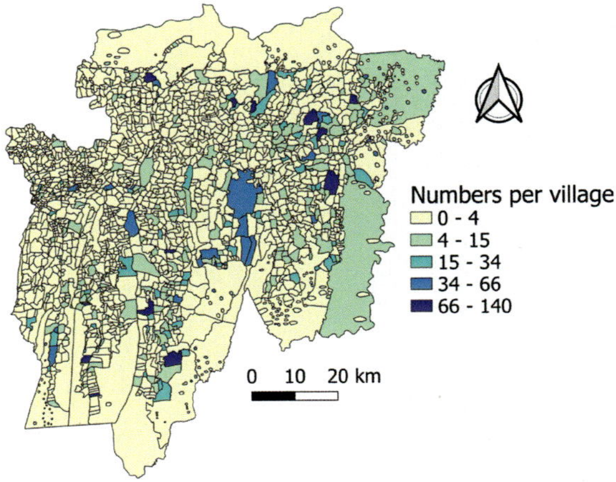

Map 131

Main Workers Agricultural Laborers - Persons

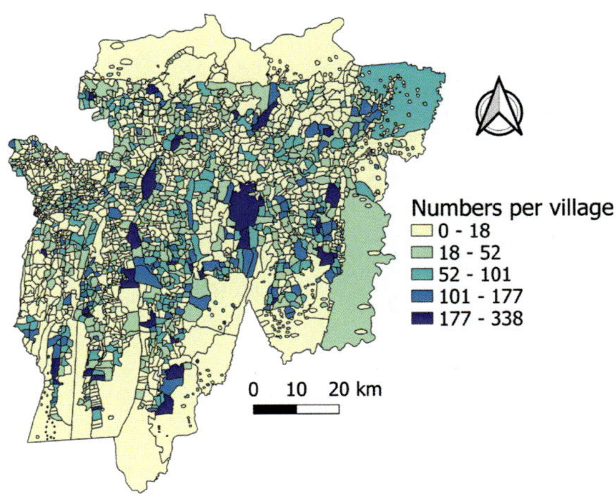

Map 132

Main Workers Household Industry - Persons

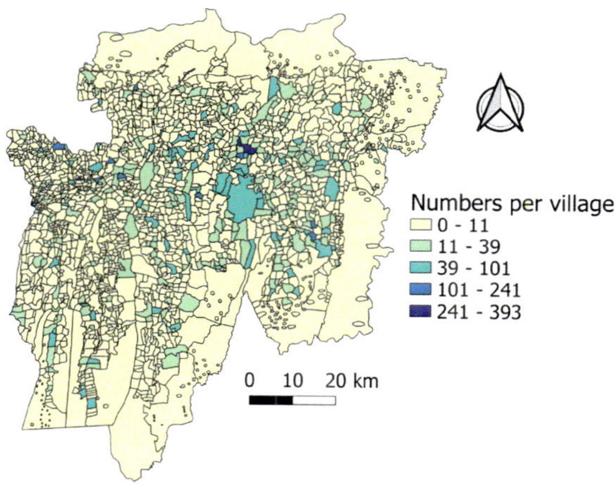

Map 133

Main Workers Household Industry - Males

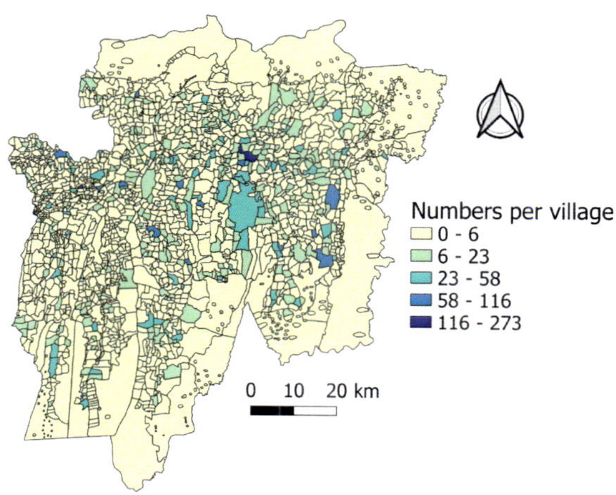

Map 134

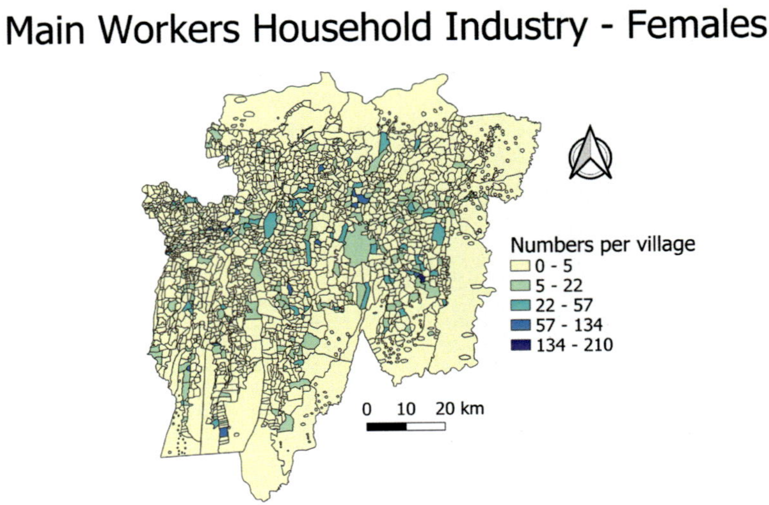

Map 135

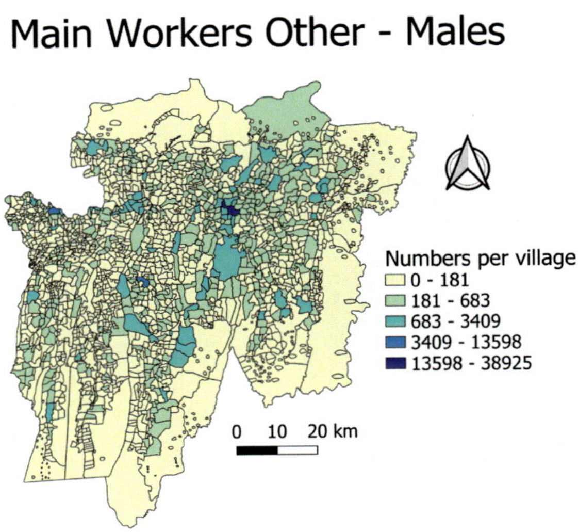

Map 136

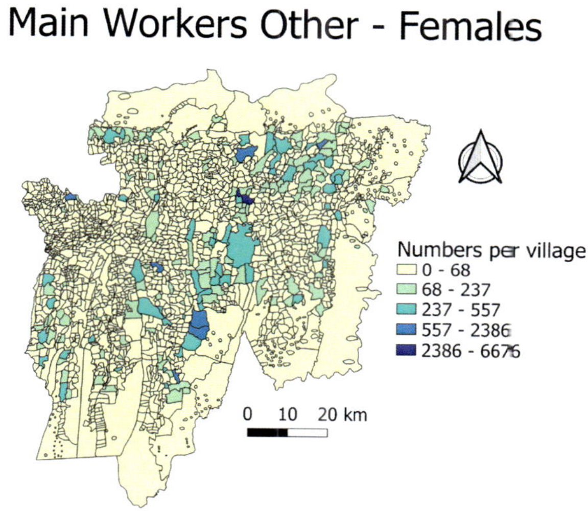

Map 137

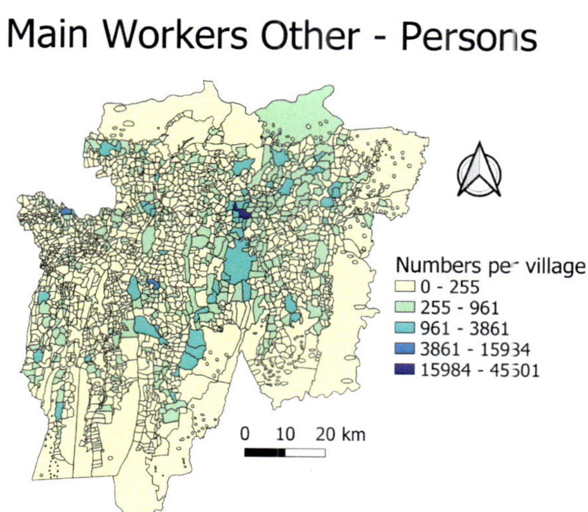

Map 138

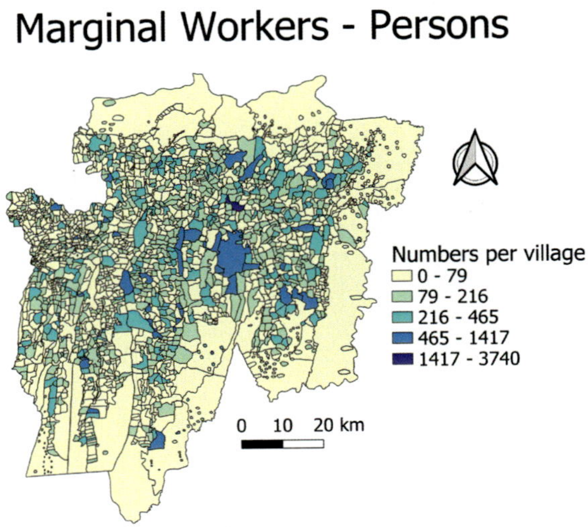

Map 139

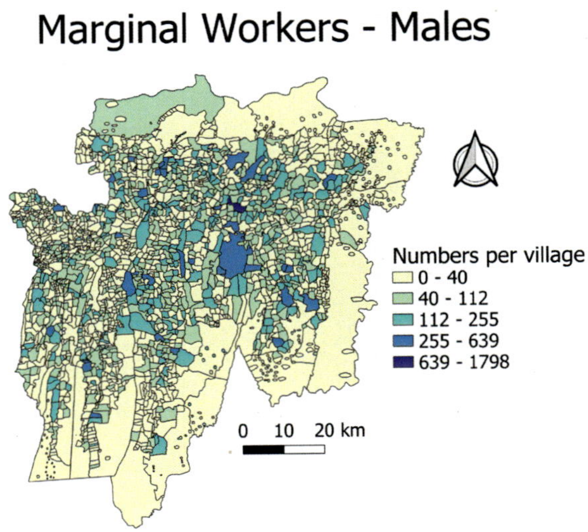

Map 140

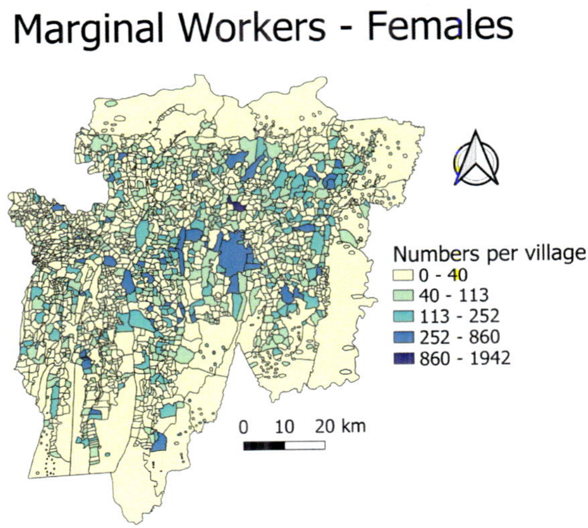

Map 141

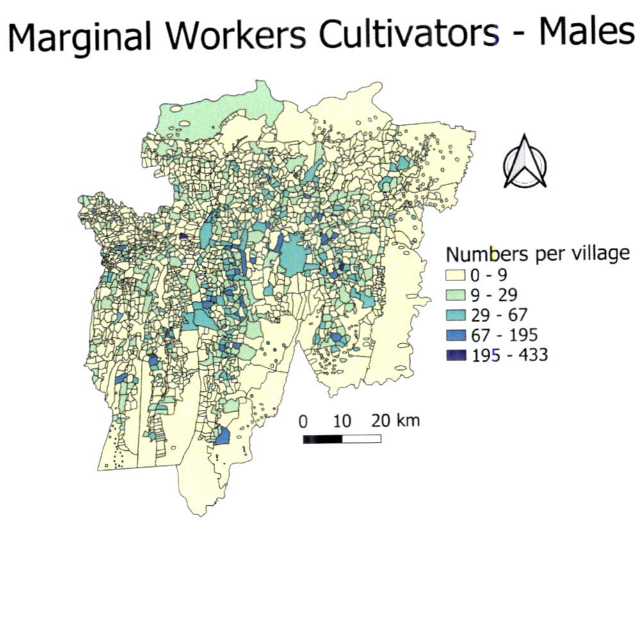

Map 142

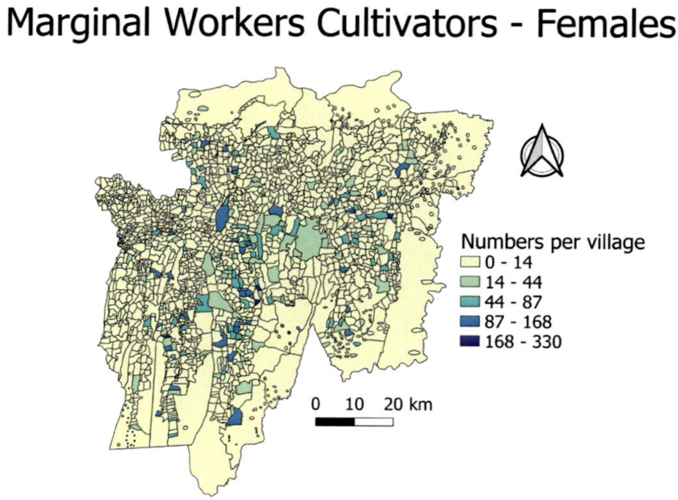

Map 143

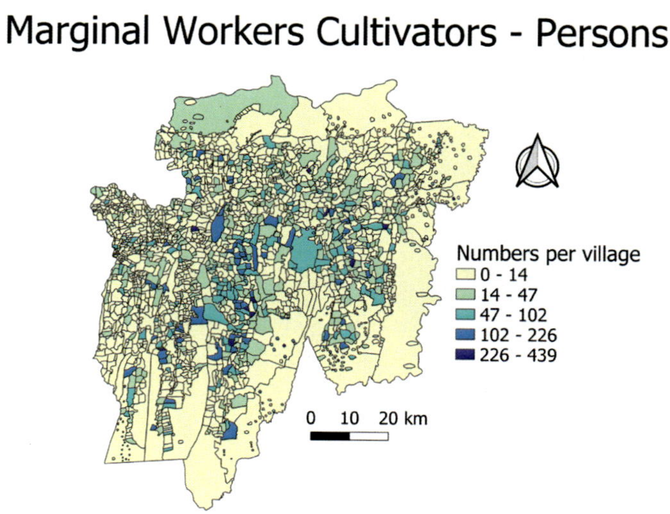

Map 144

Marginal Workers Agri. Laborers - Persons

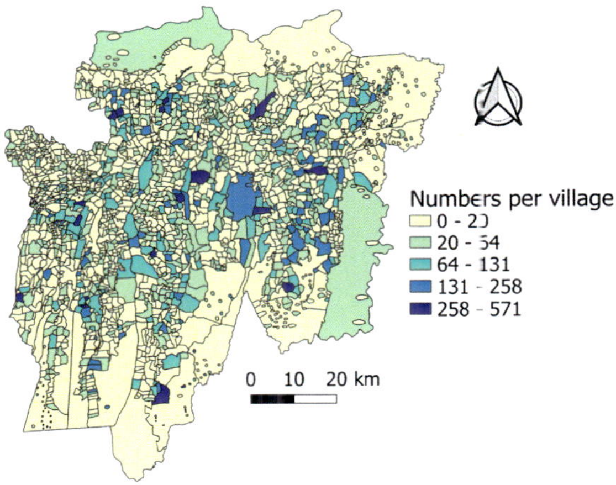

Map 145

Marginal Workers Agri. Laborers - Males

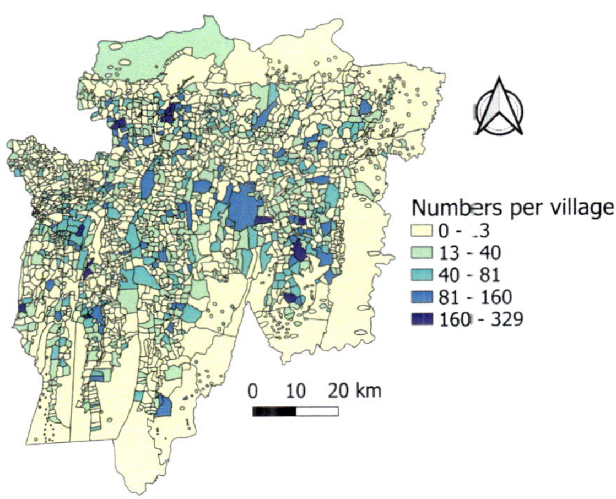

Map 146

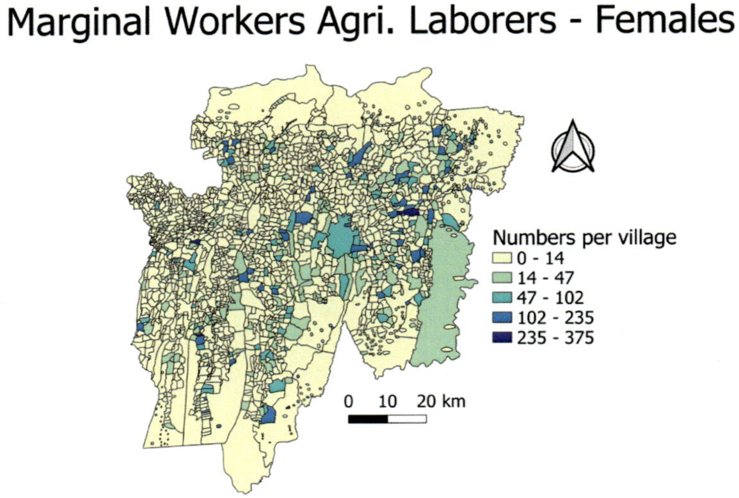

Map 147

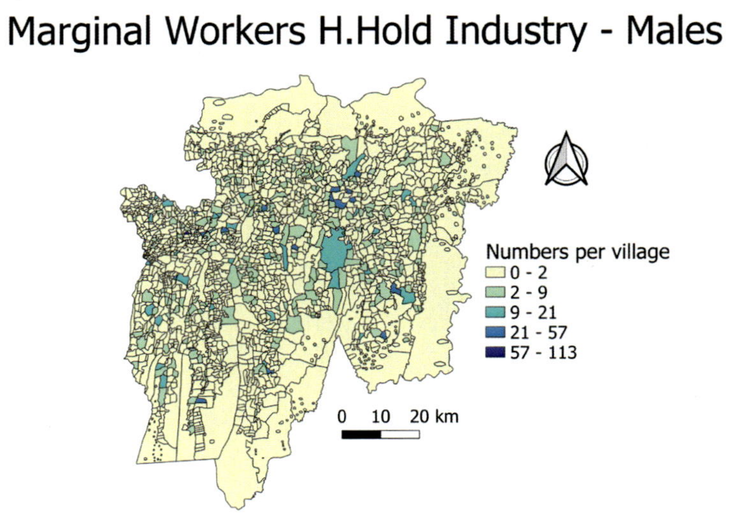

Map 148

Marginal Workers H.Hold Industry - Females

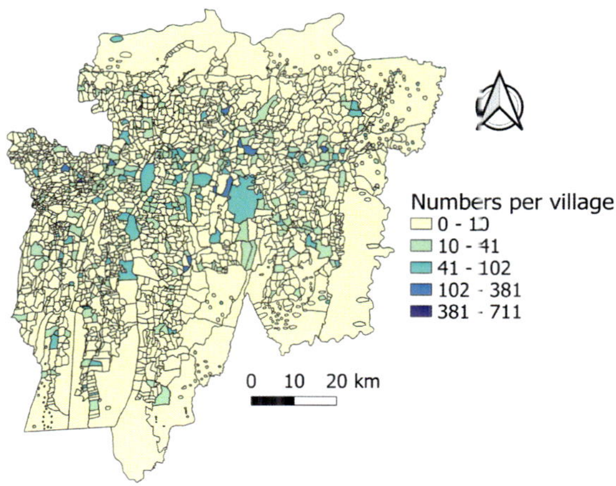

Map 149

Marginal Workers H.Hold Industry - Persons

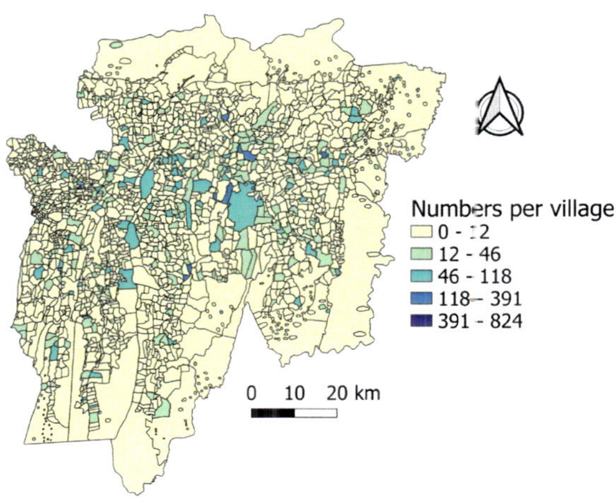

Map 150

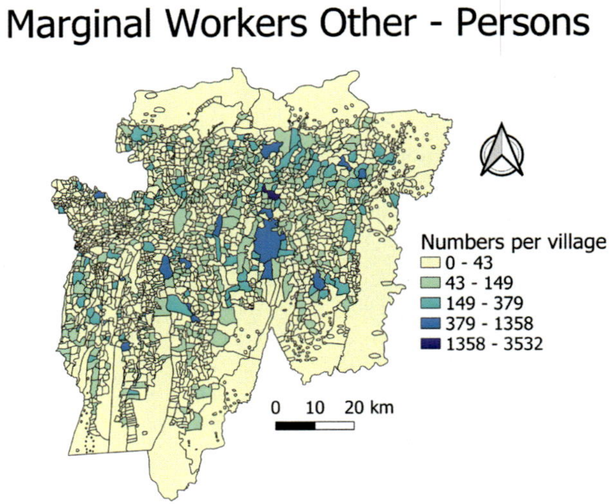

Map 151

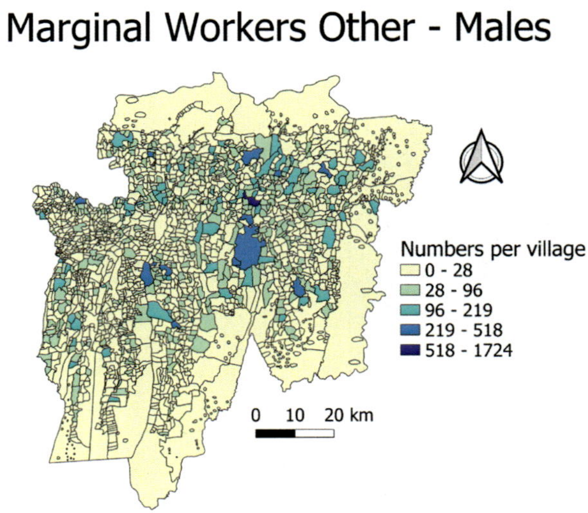

Map 152

Marginal Workers Other - Females

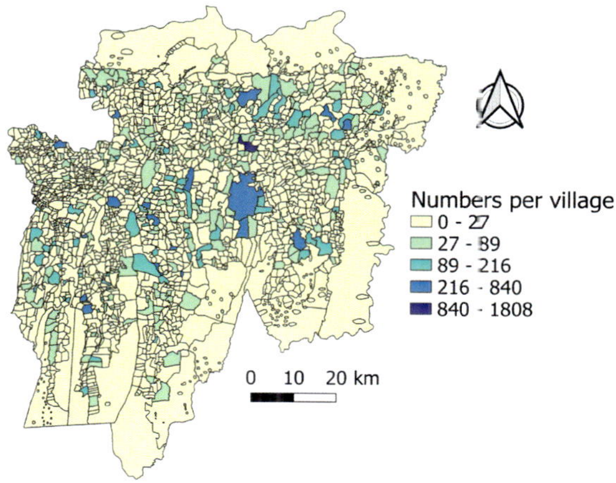

Map 153

Non Workers - Males

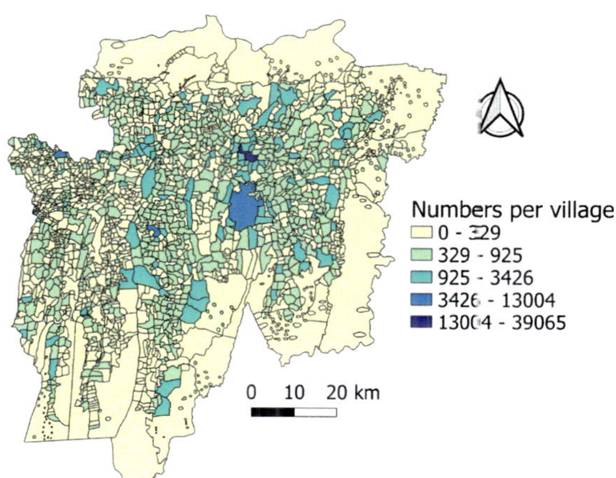

Map 154

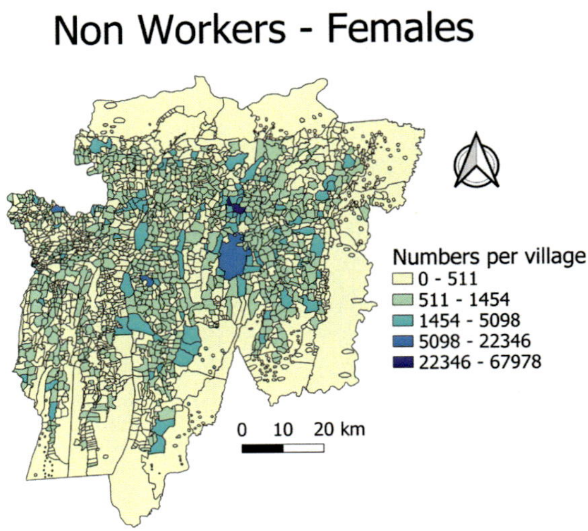

Map 155

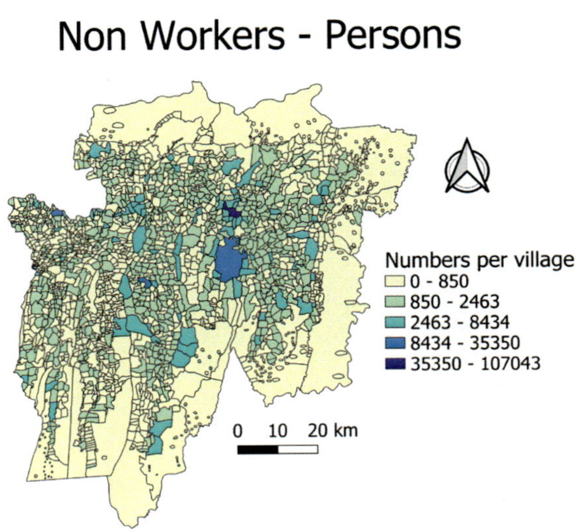

Spatial analysis of socio-economic indicators, 2001

Map 156

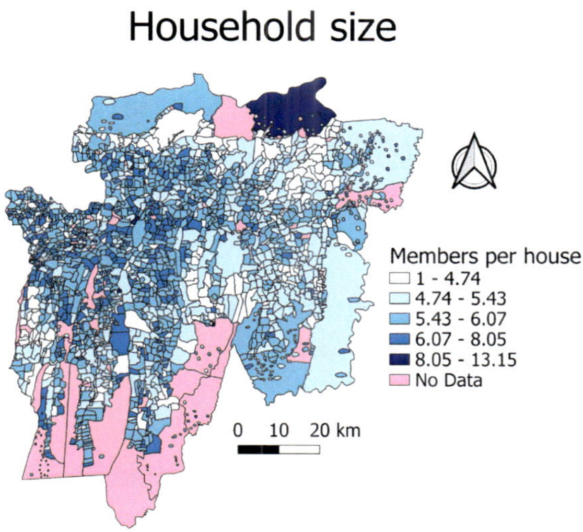

Map 157

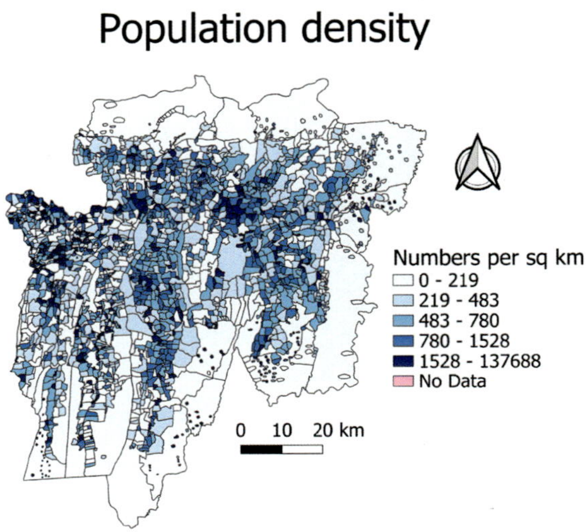

Map 158

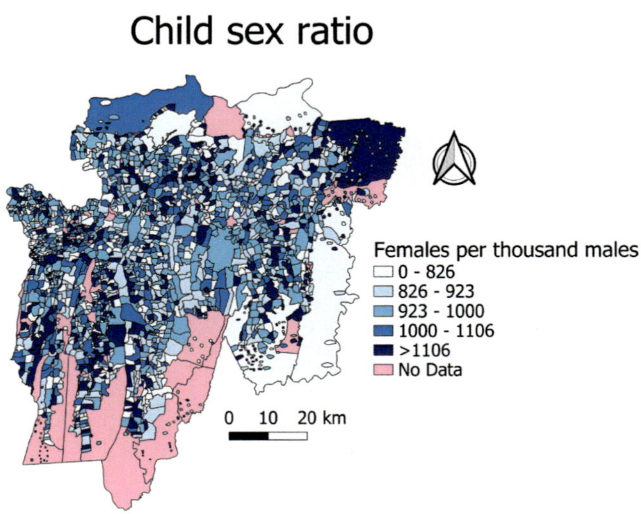

Map 159

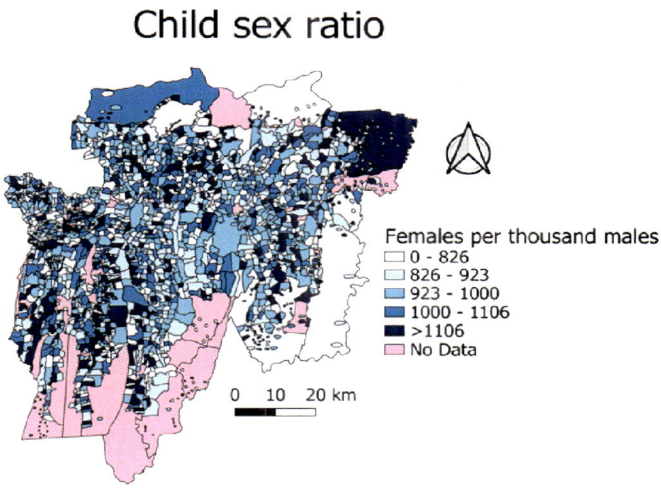

Map 160

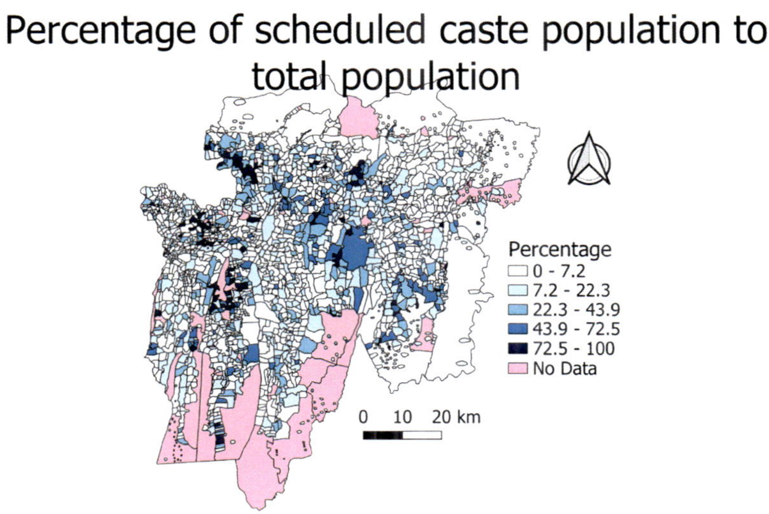

Map 161

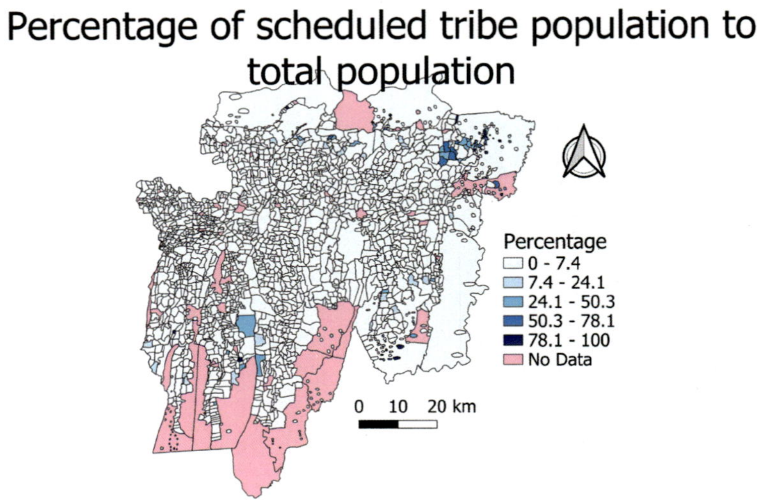

Map 162

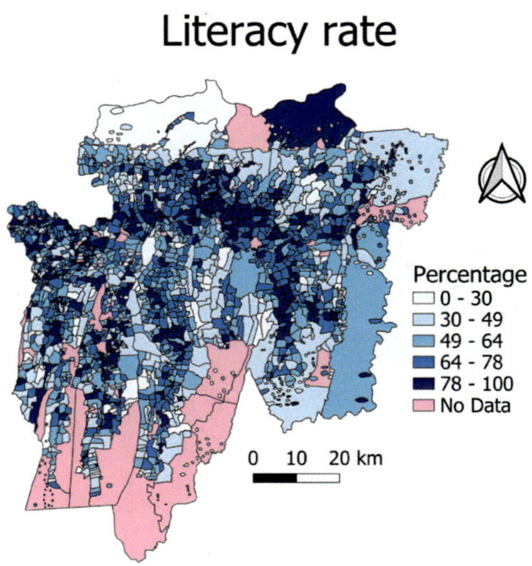

Map 163

Workforce sex ratio (Main + Marginal worker)

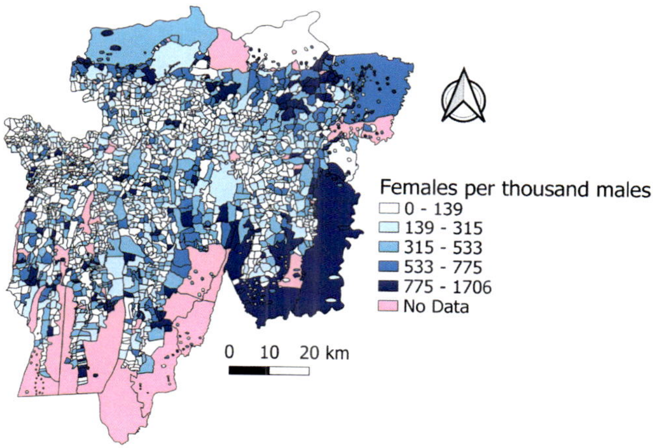

Map 164

Workforce sex ratio (Main worker)

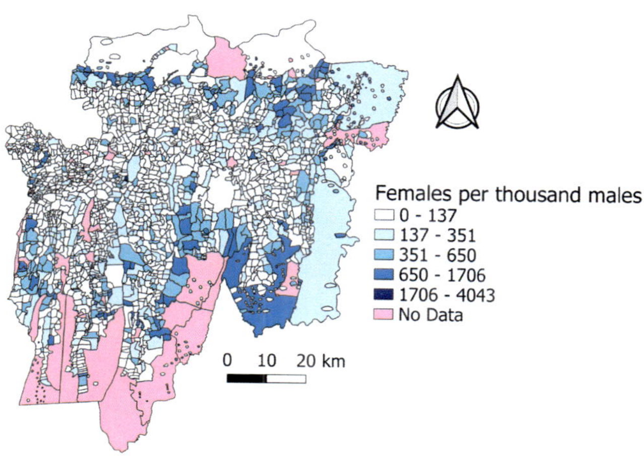

Map 165

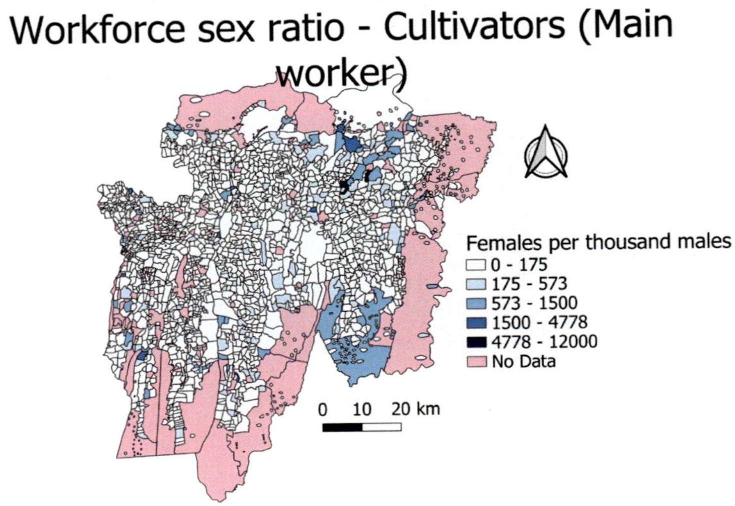

Map 166

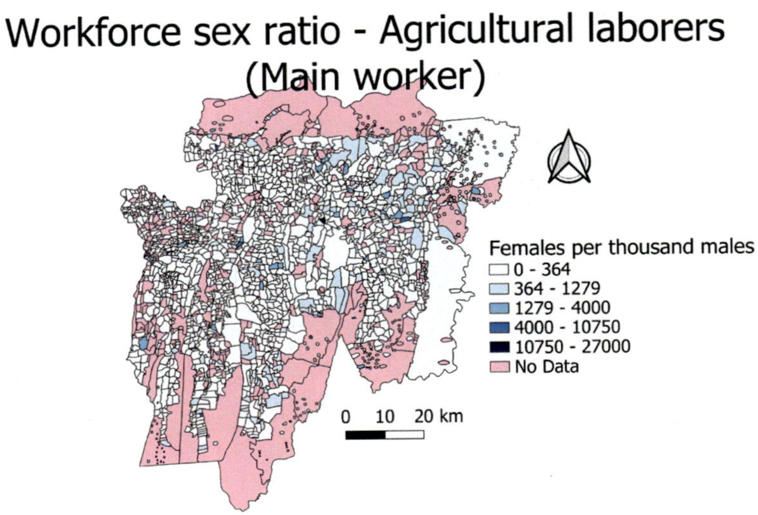

Map 167

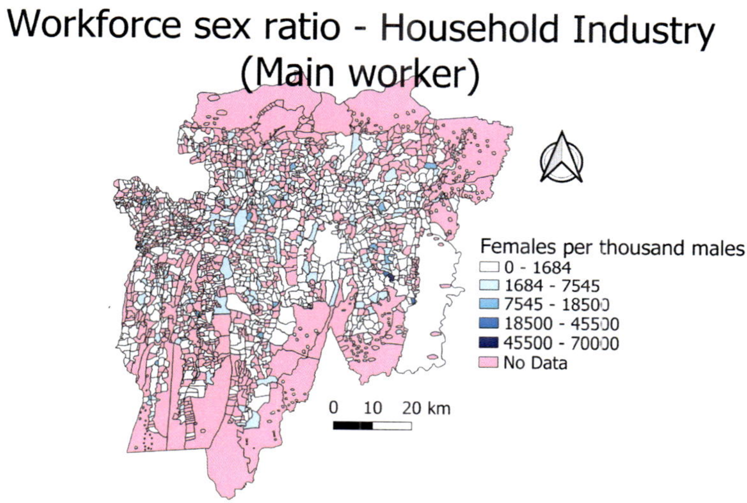

Map 168

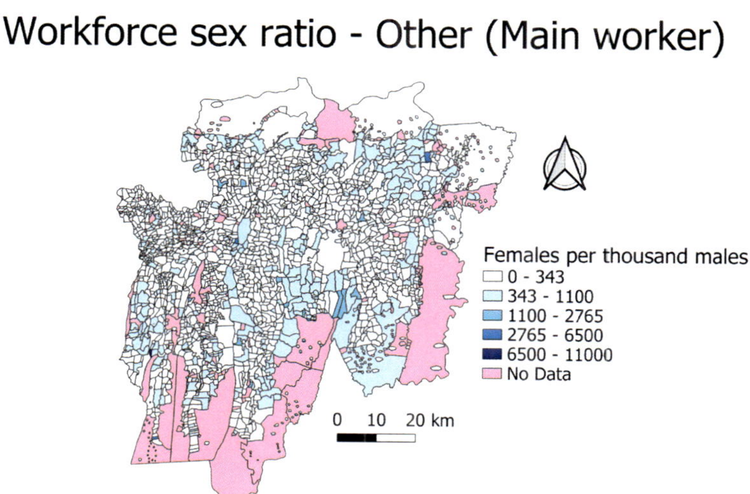

Map 169

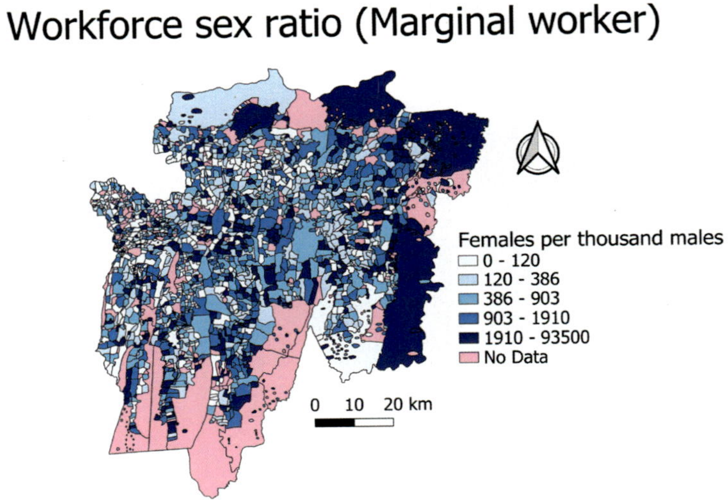

Map 170

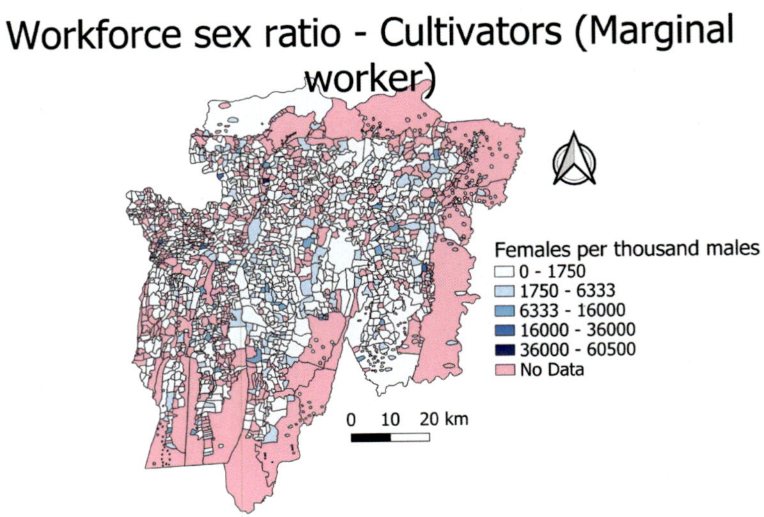

Map 171

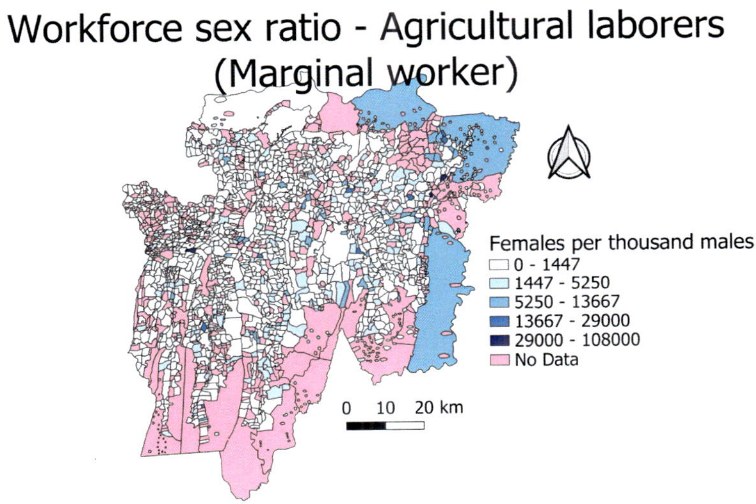

Map 172

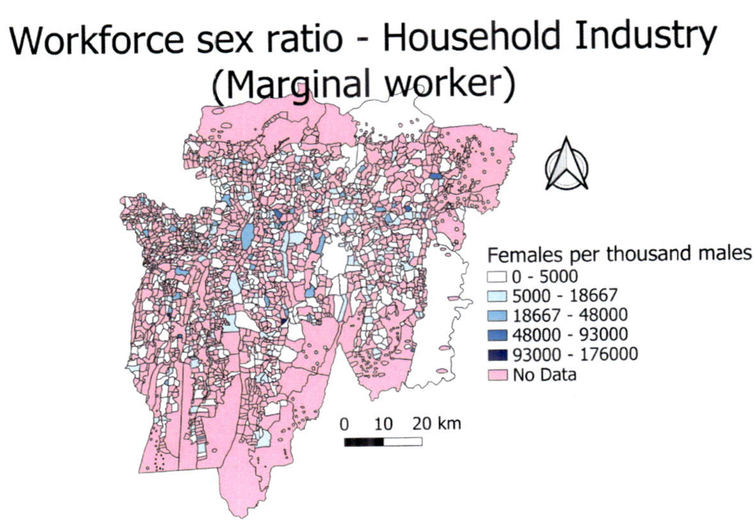

Map 173

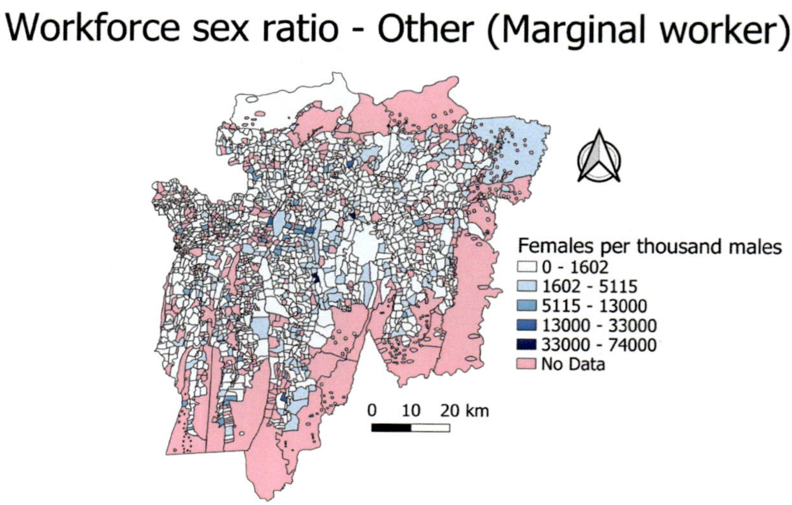

Map 174

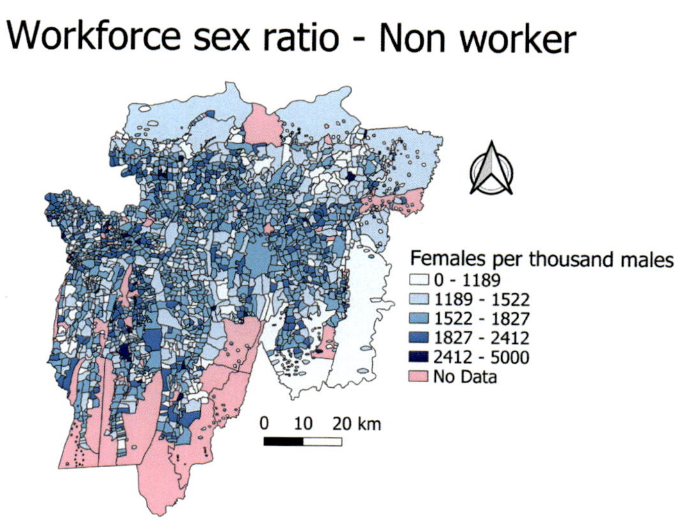

Map 175

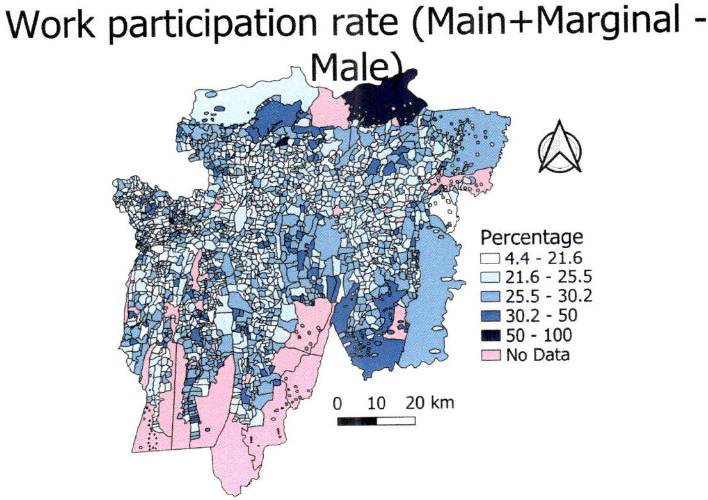

Map 176

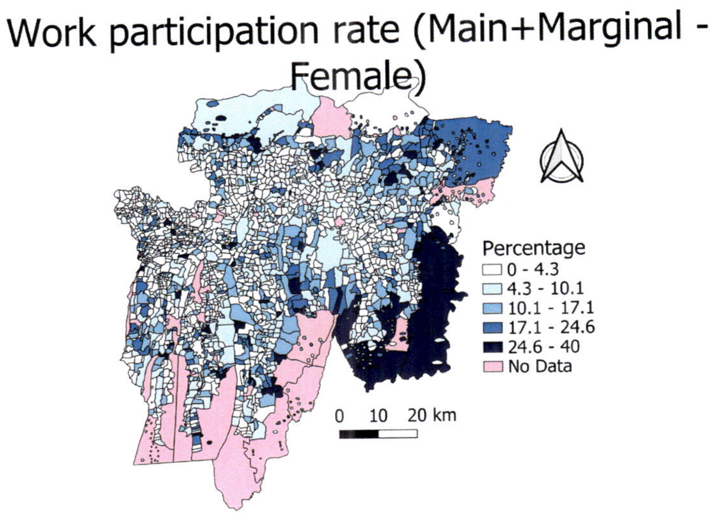

Map 177

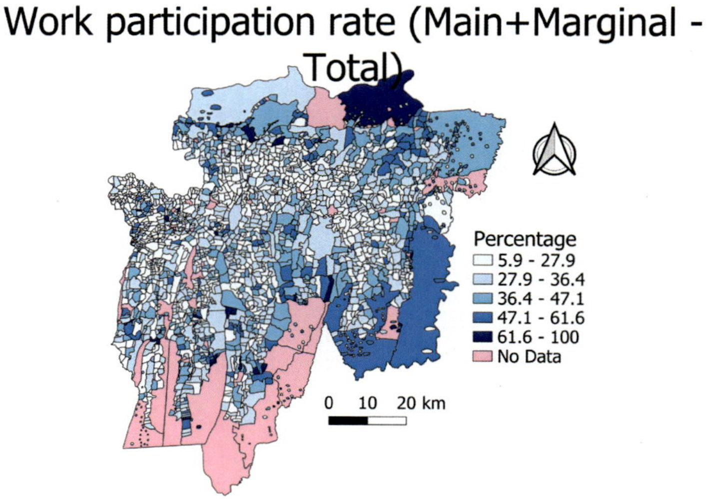

Map 178

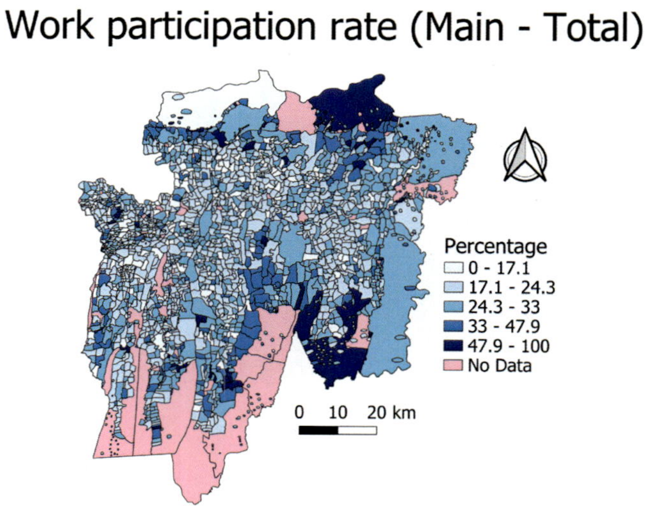

Map 179

Work participation rate (Main - Male)

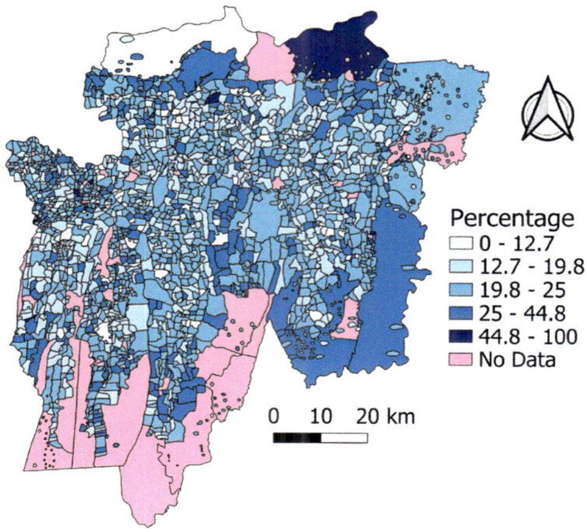

Map 180

Work participation rate (Main - Female)

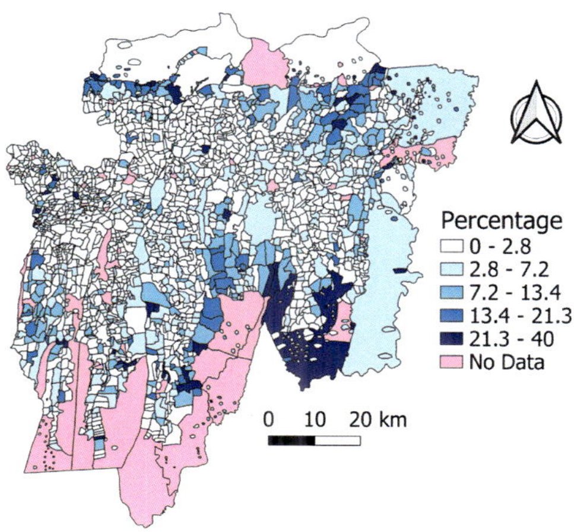

Map 181

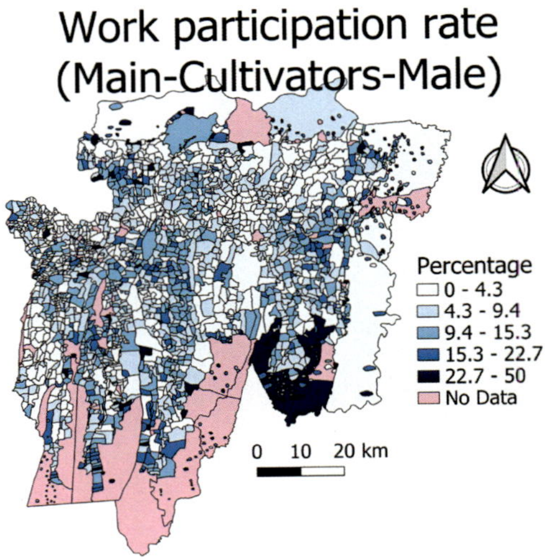

Map 182

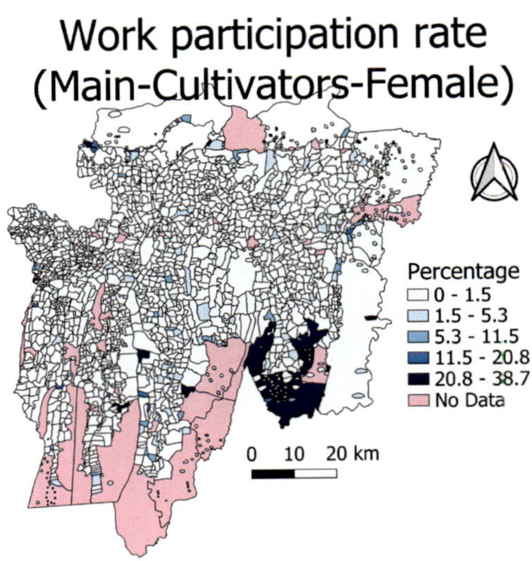

Map 183

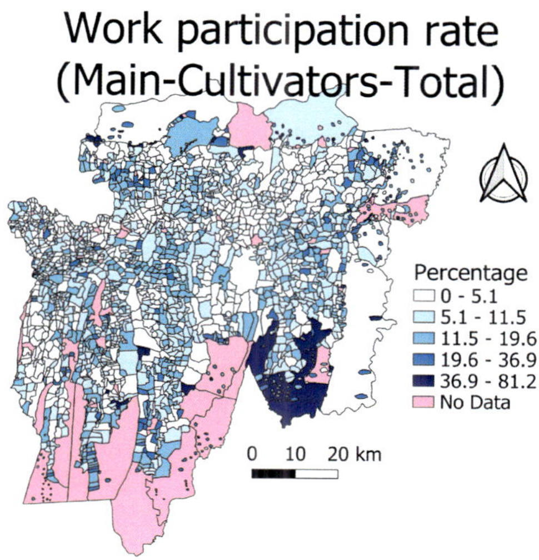

Map 184

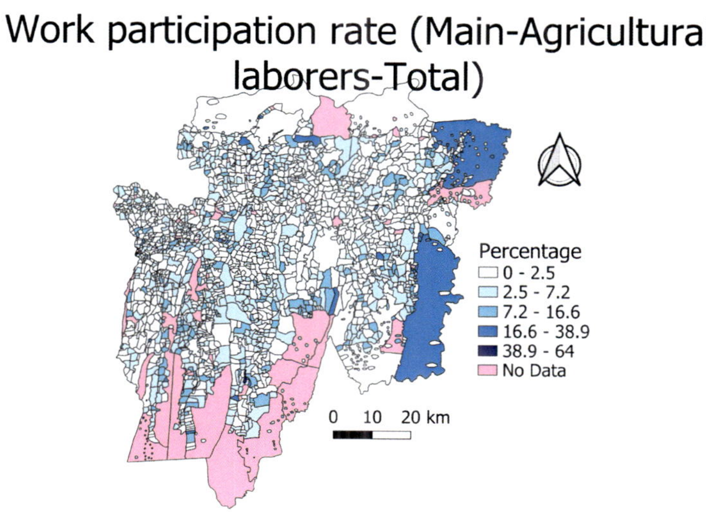

Map 185

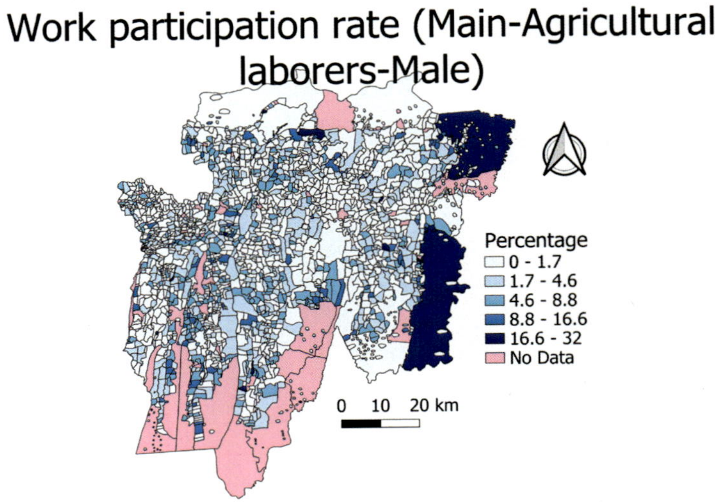

Map 186

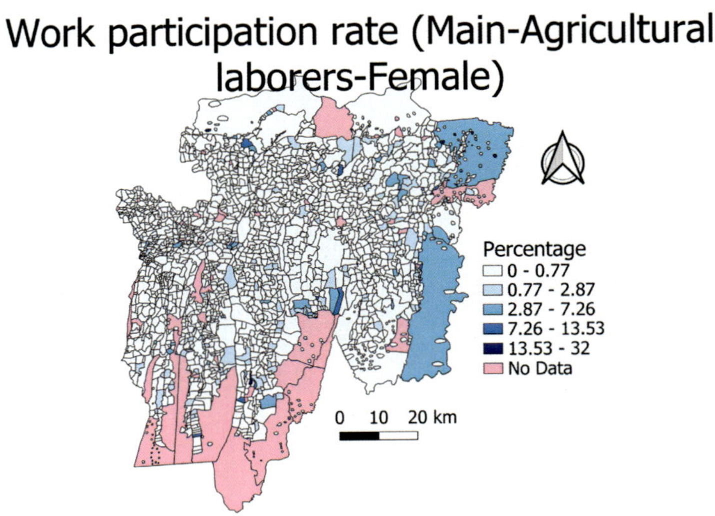

Map 187

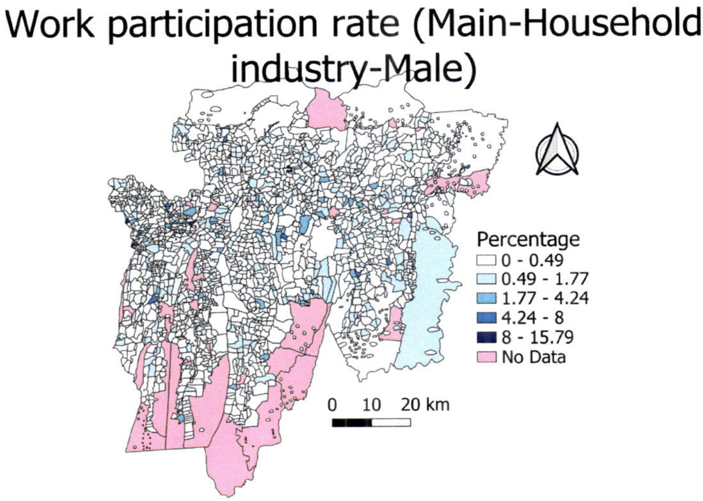

Map 188

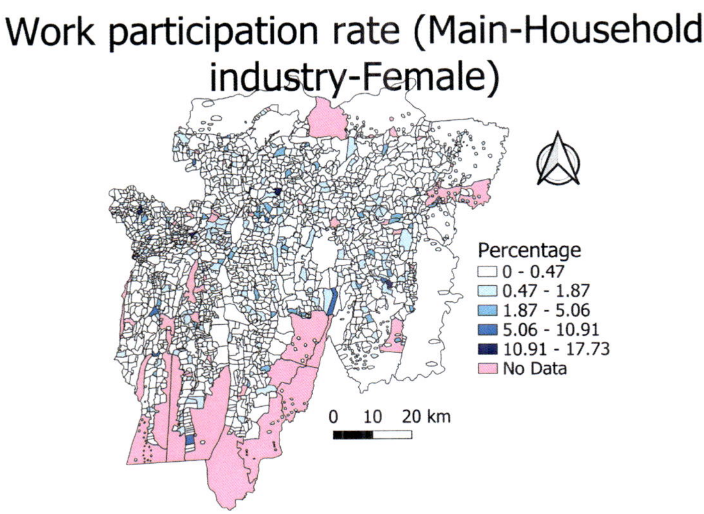

Map 189

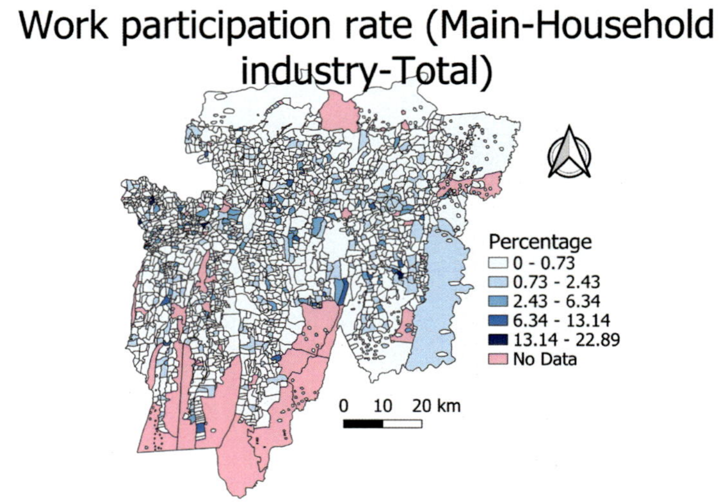

Map 190

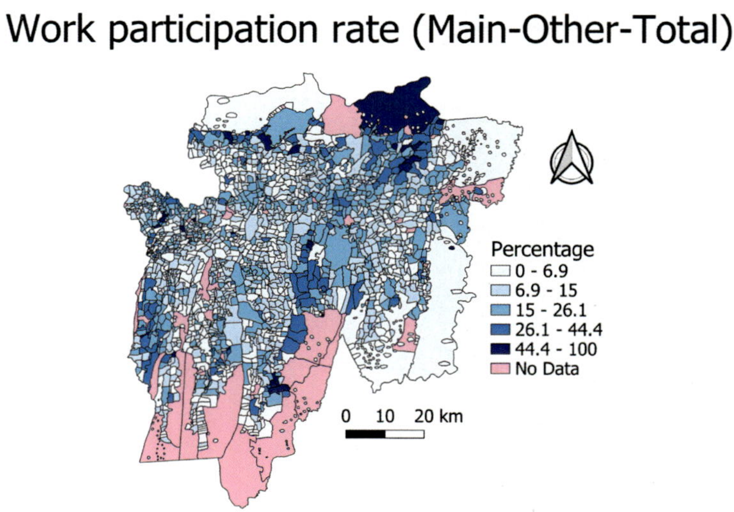

Map 191

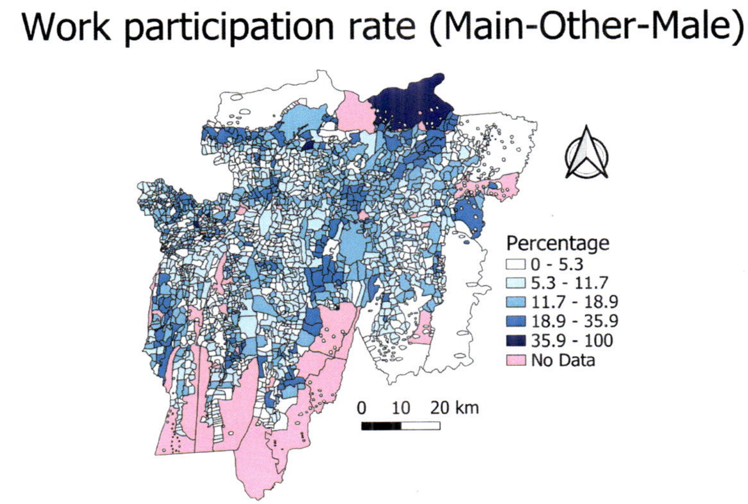

Map 192

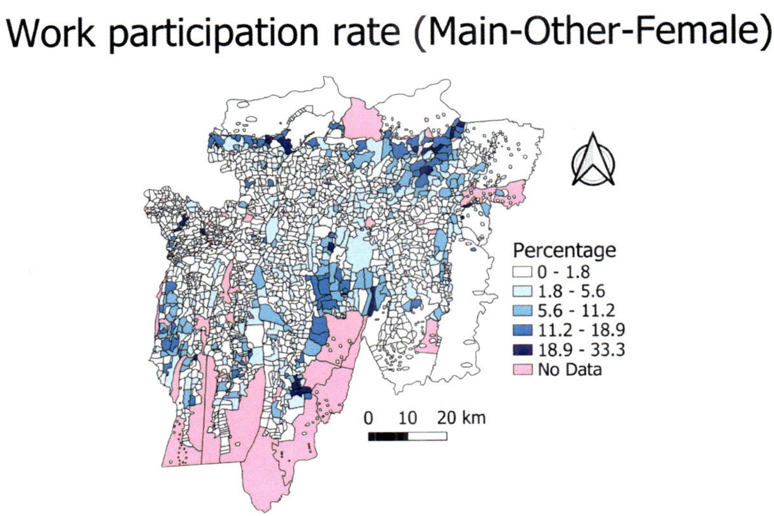

Map 193

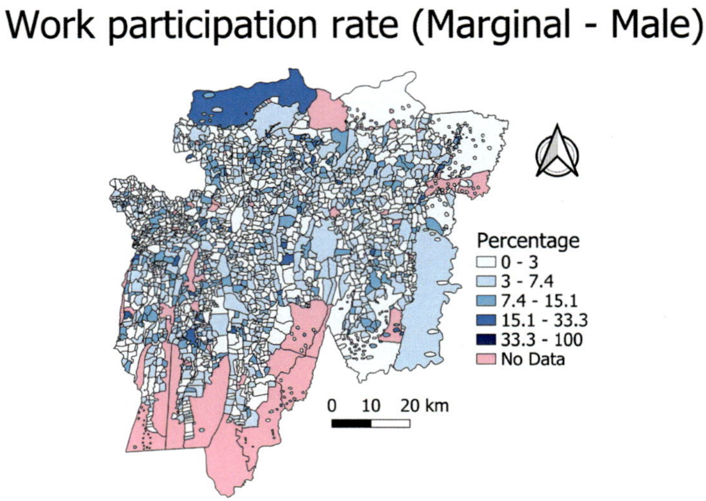

Map 194

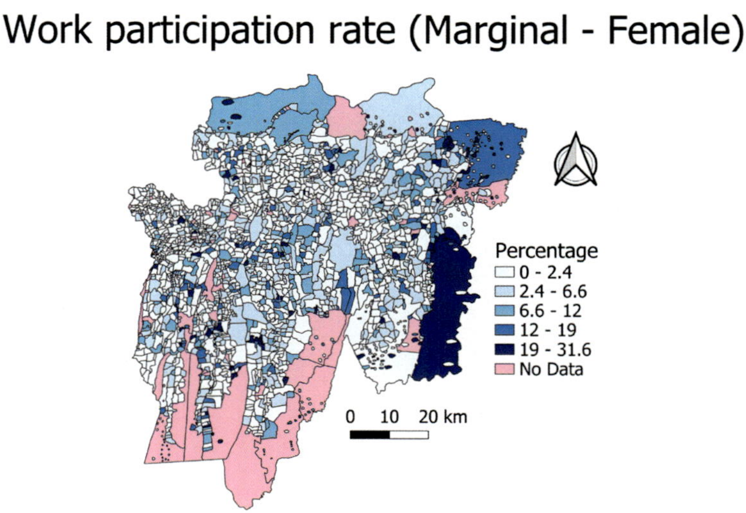

Map 195

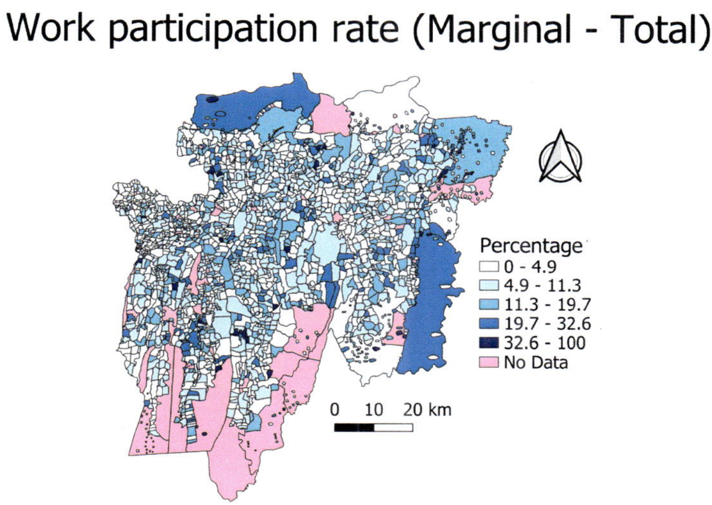

Map 196

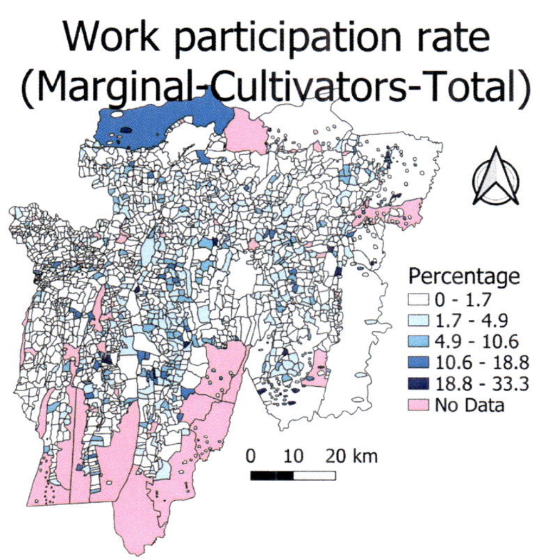

Map 197

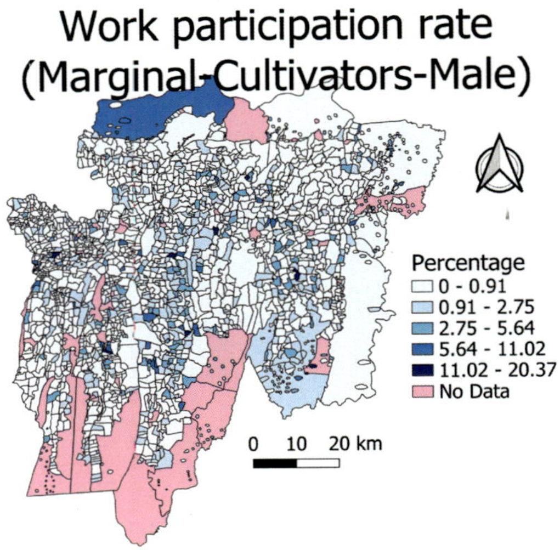

Map 198

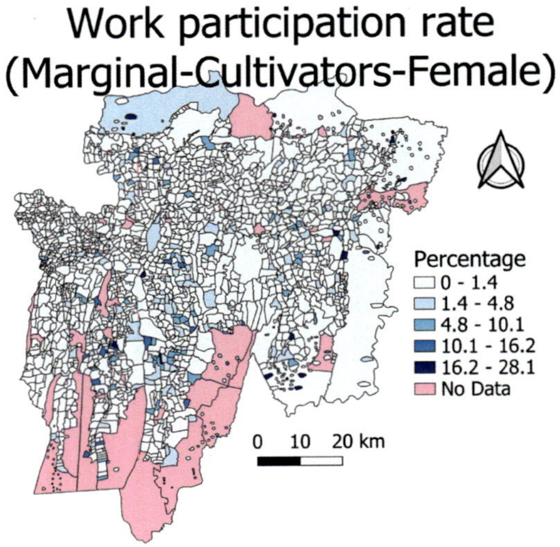

Map 199

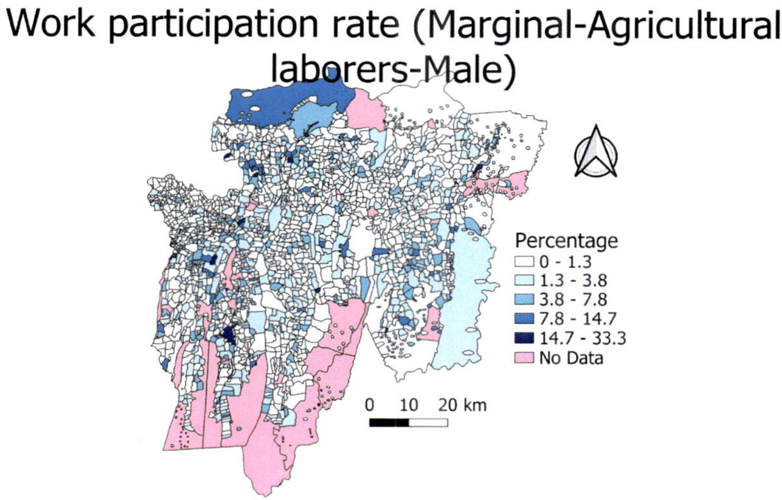

Map 200

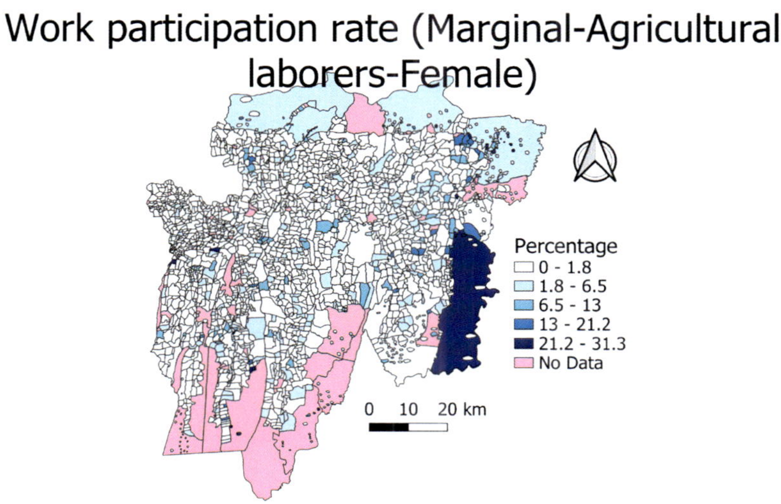

Map 201

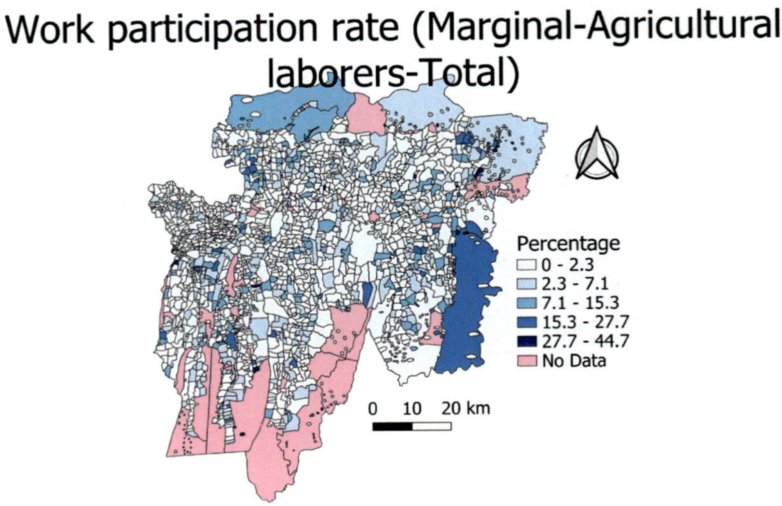

Map 202

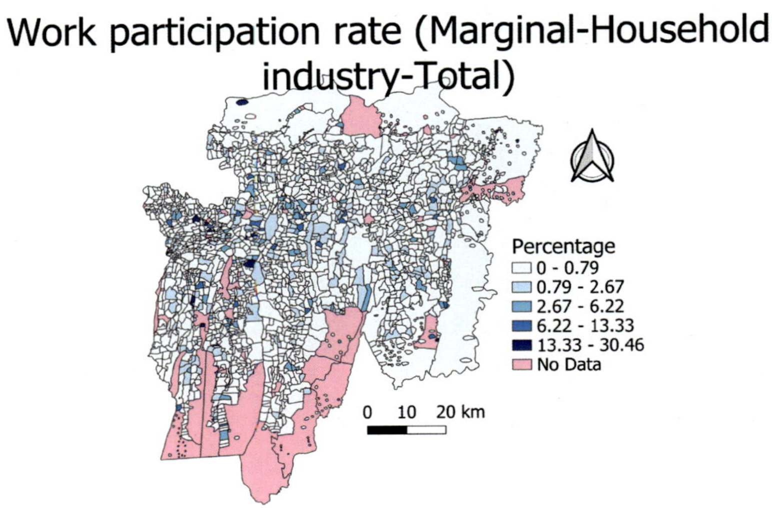

Map 203

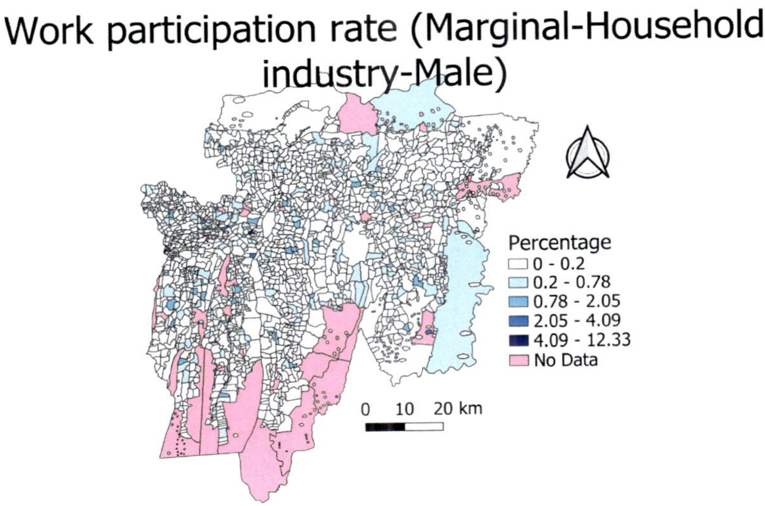

Map 204

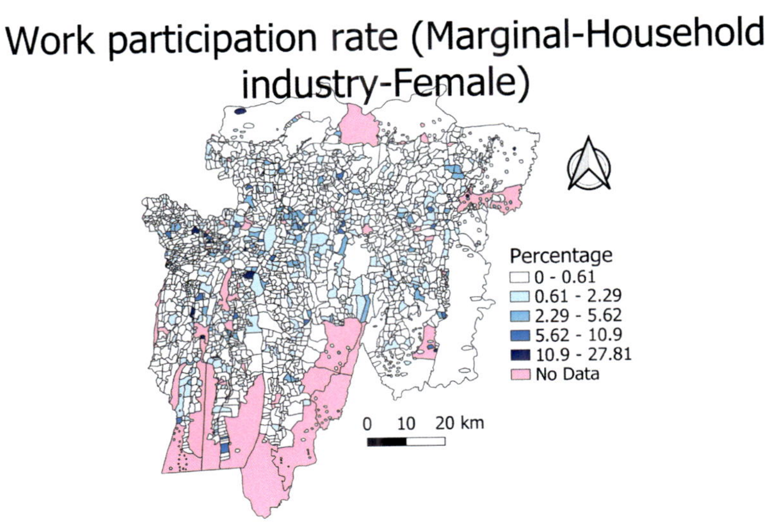

Map 205

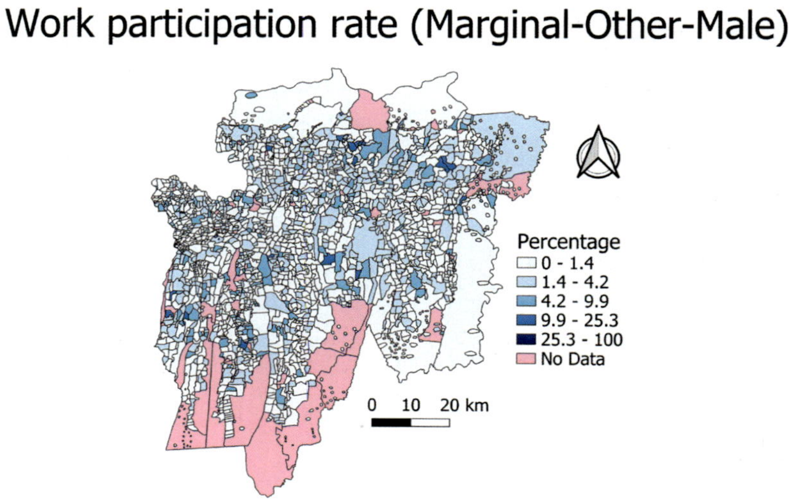

Map 206

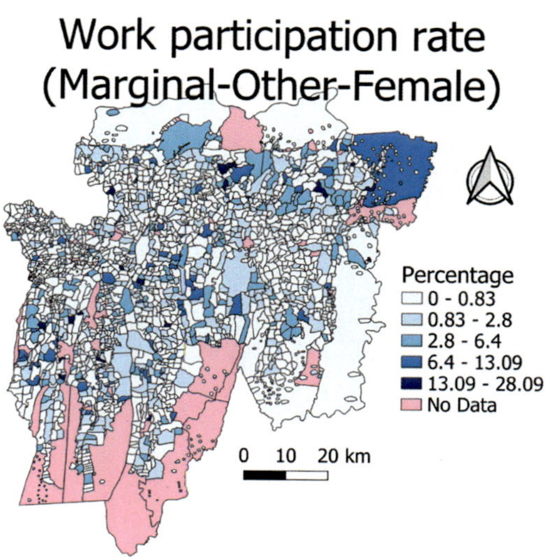

Map 207

Work participation rate (Marginal-Other-Total)

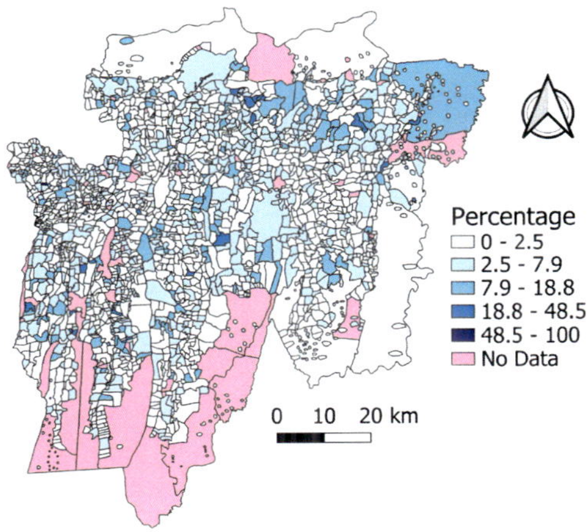

Map 208

Work participation rate (Non workers-Total)

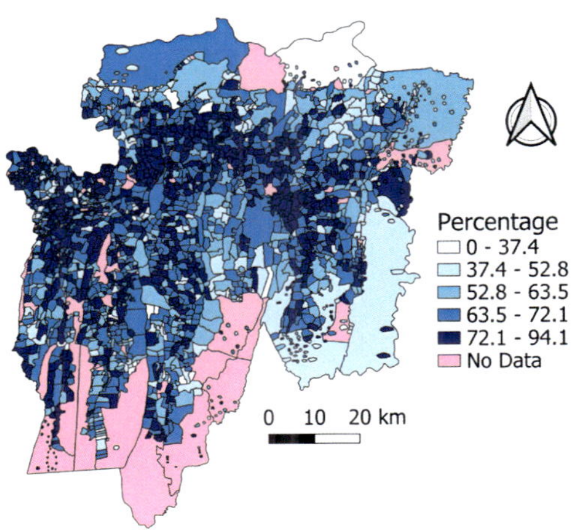

Map 209

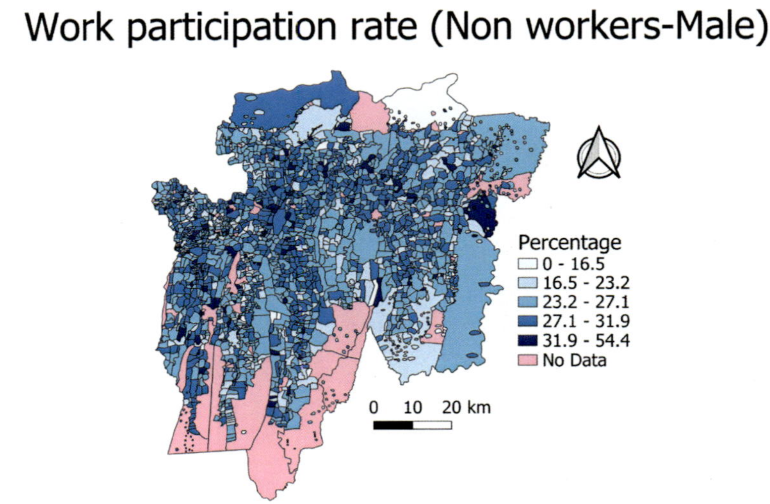

Map 210

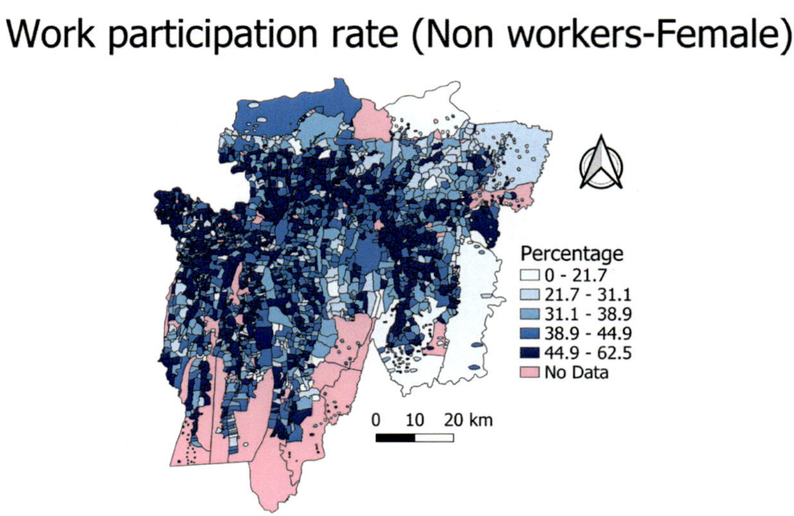

Spatial analysis of census variables, 2011

Map 211

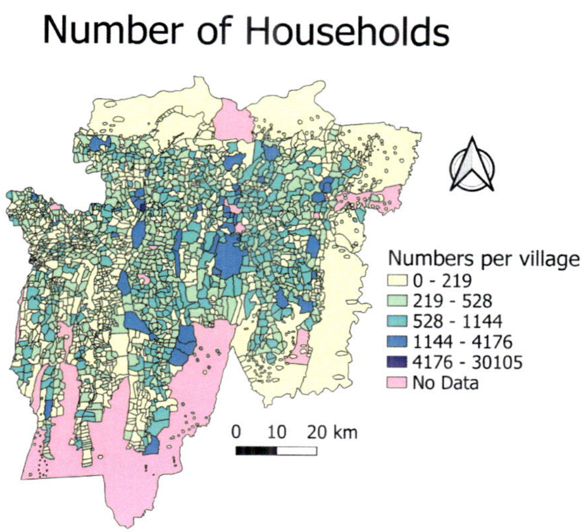

Map 212

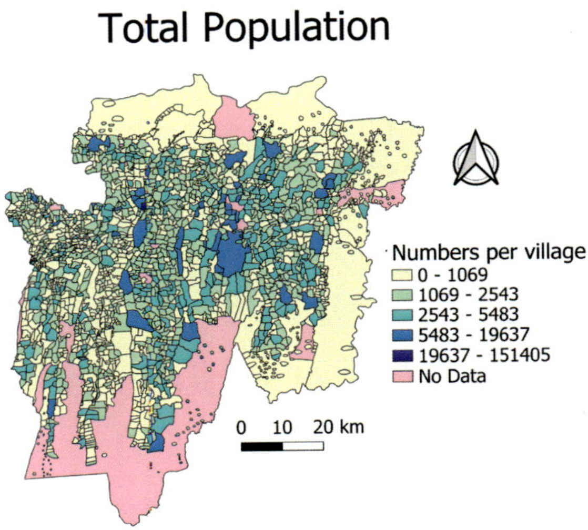

Map 213

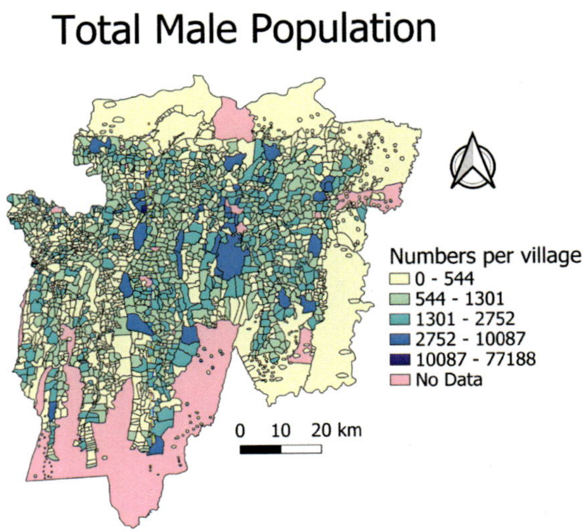

Map 214

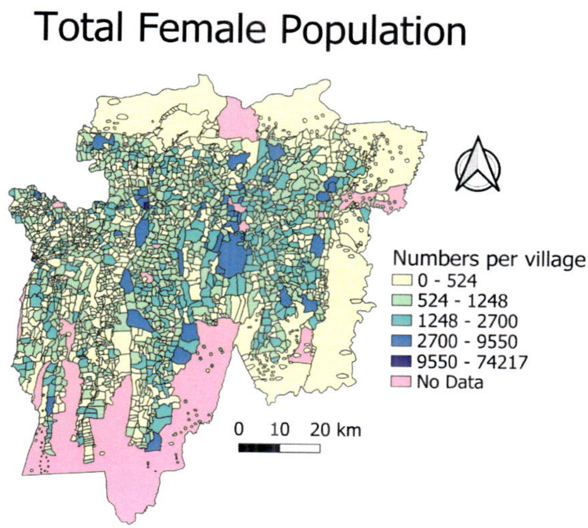

Map 215

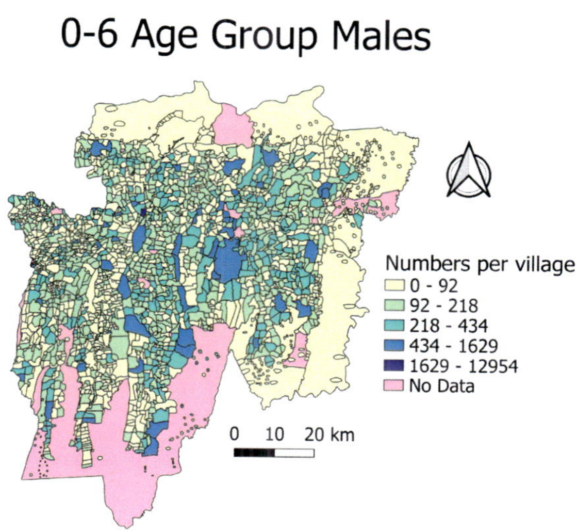

Map 216

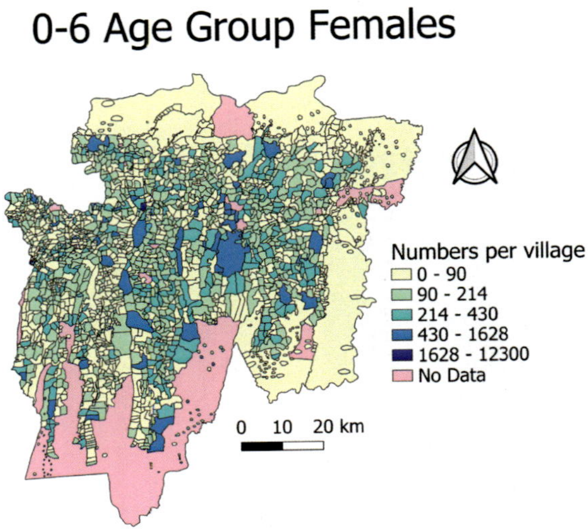

Map 217

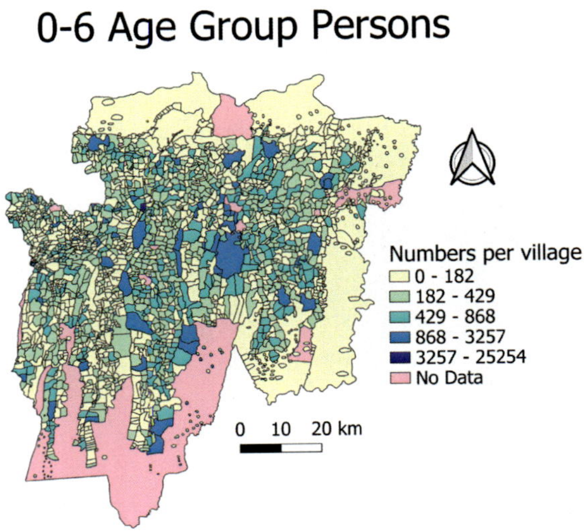

Map 218

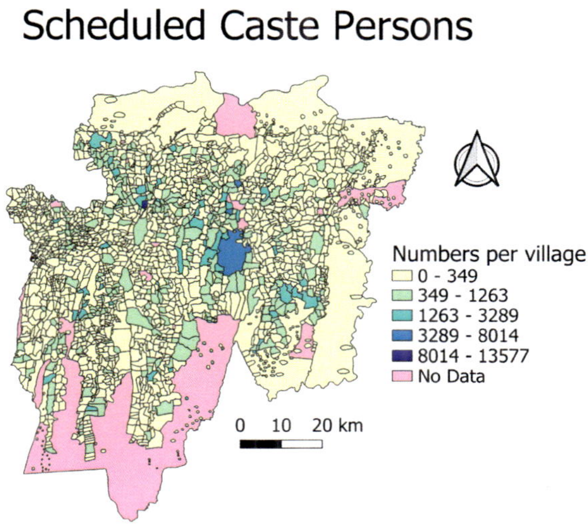

Map 219

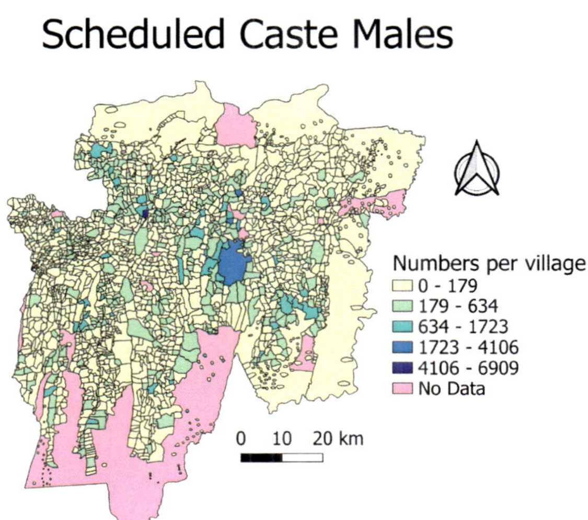

Map 220

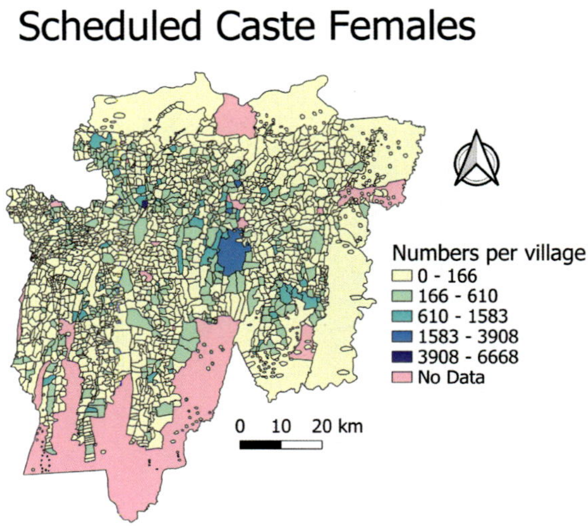

Map 221

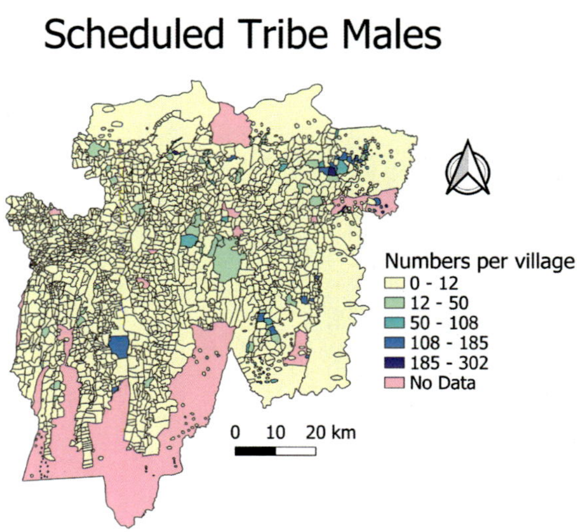

Map 222

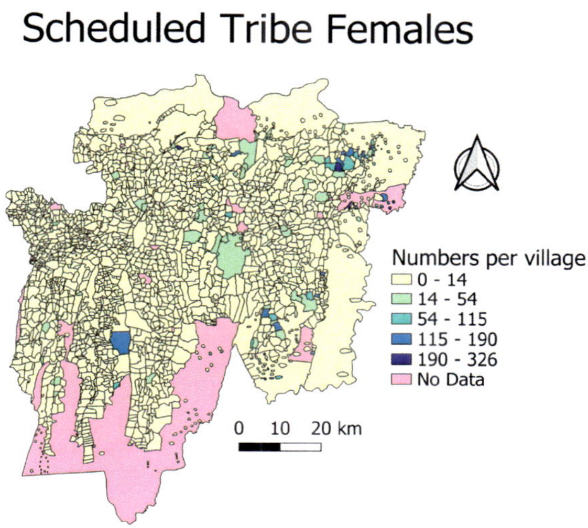

Map 223

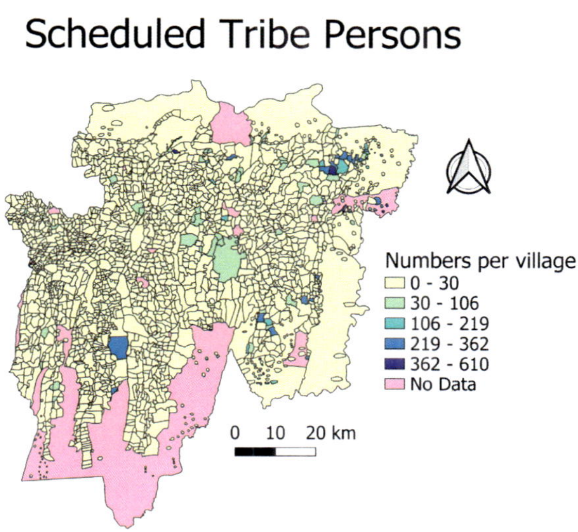

Map 224

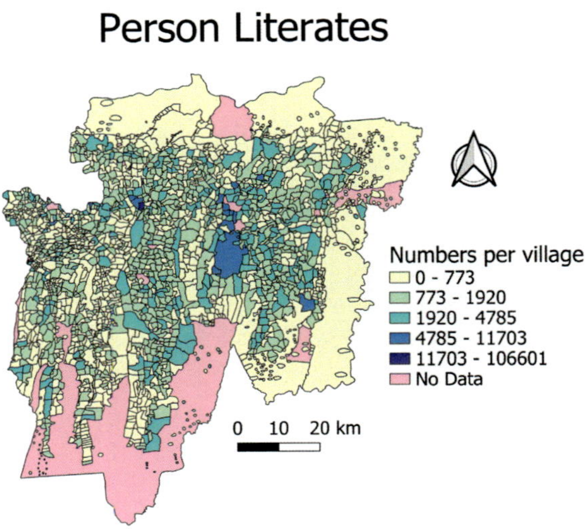

Map 225

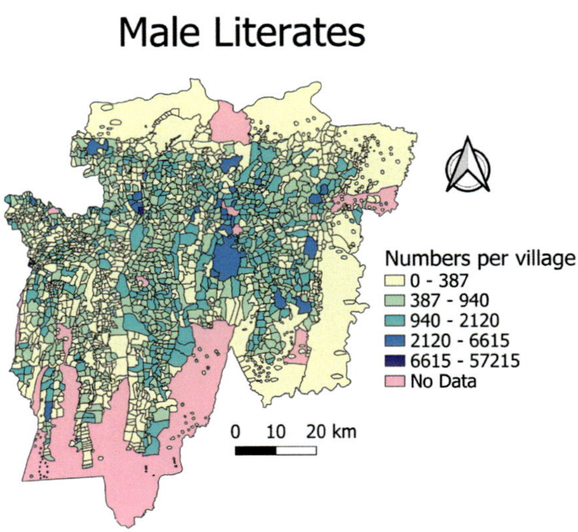

Map 226

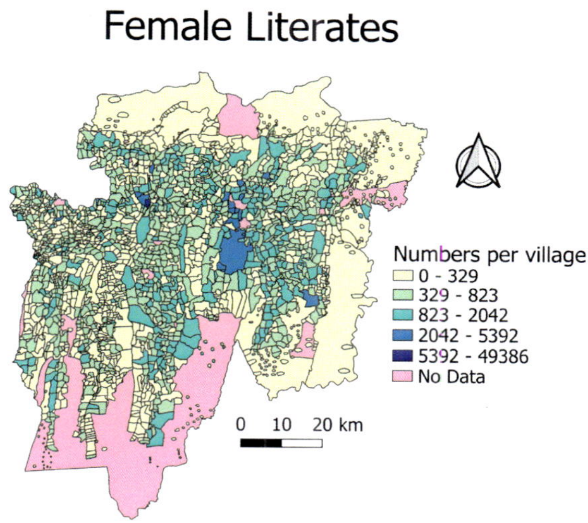

Map 227

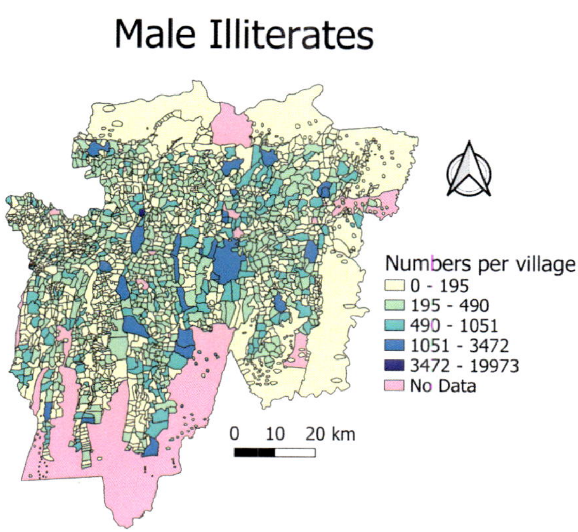

Map 228

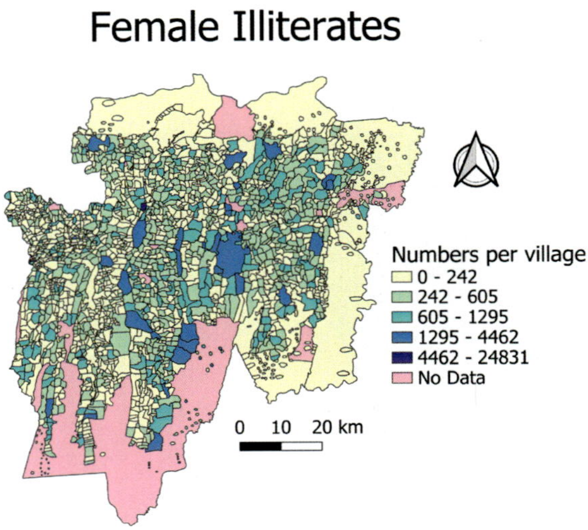

Map 229

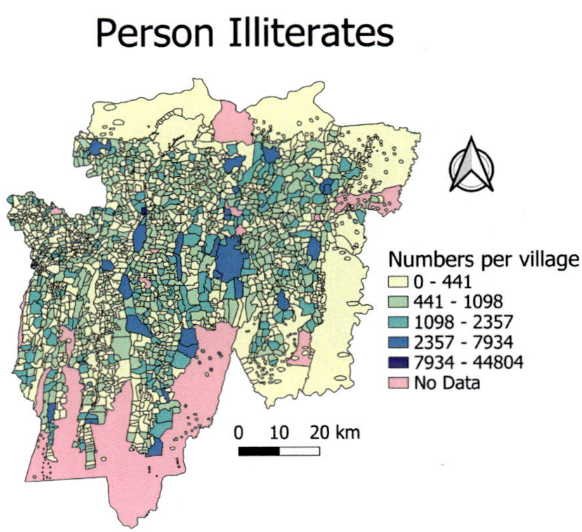

Map 230

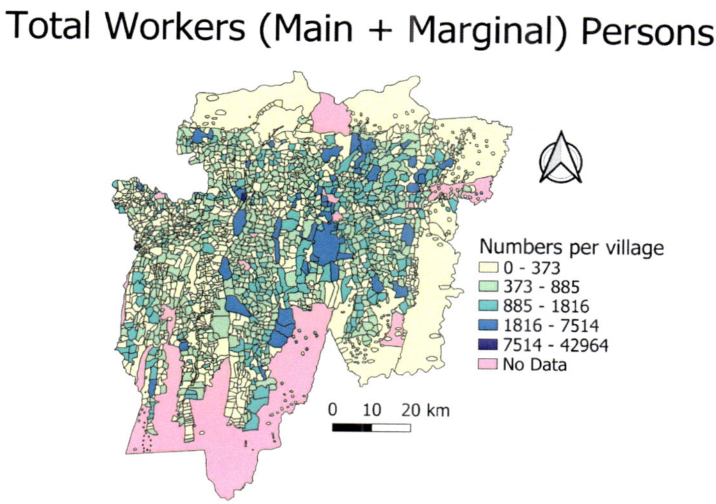

Map 231

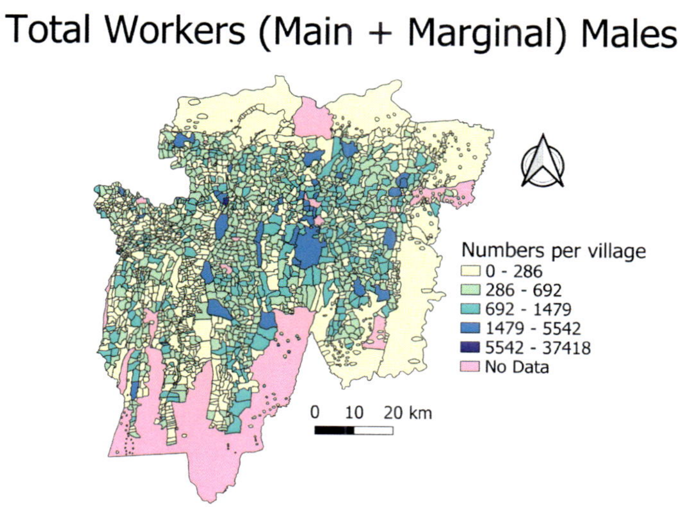

Map 232

Total Workers (Main + Marginal) Females

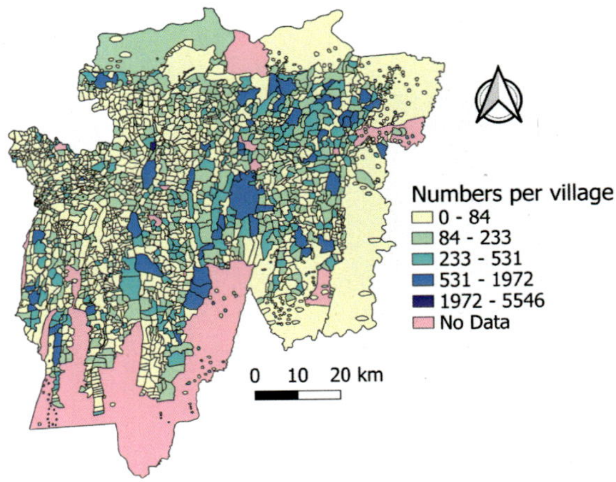

Map 233

Main Workers - Males

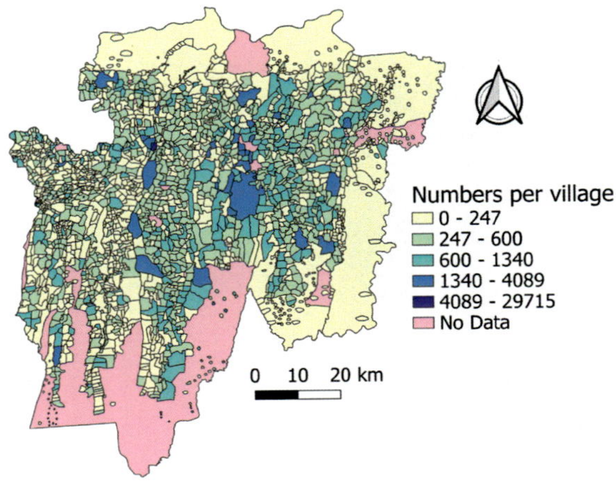

Map 234

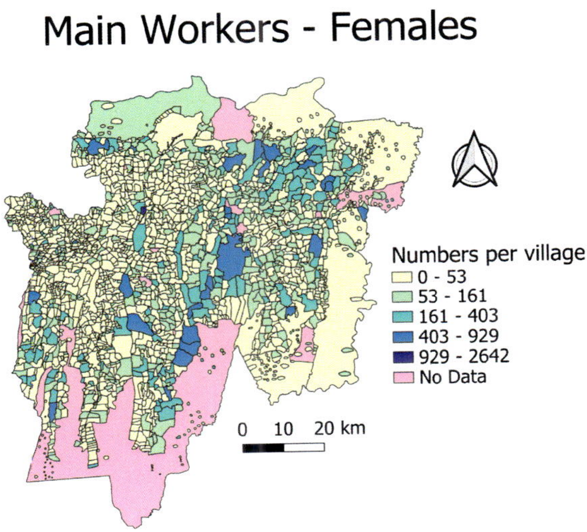

Map 235

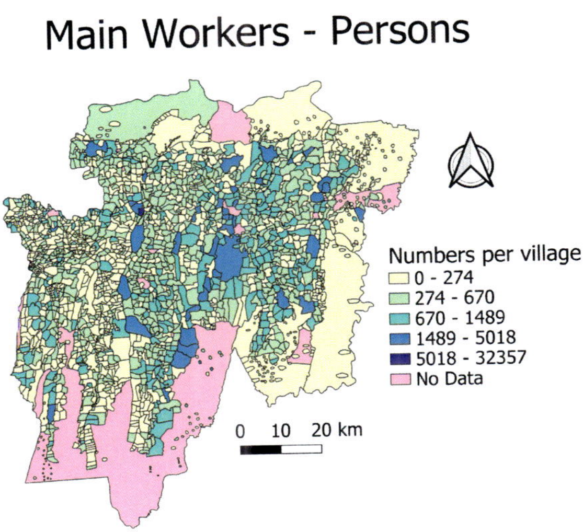

Map 236

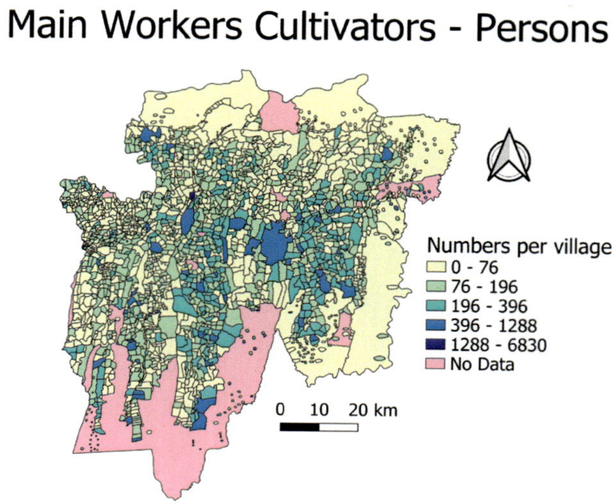

Map 237

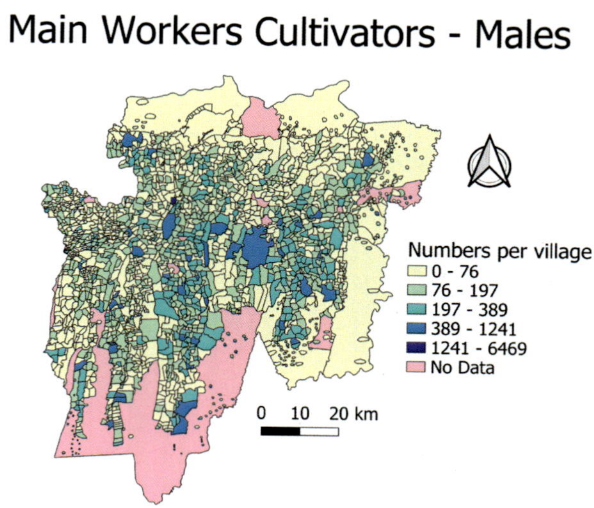

Map 238

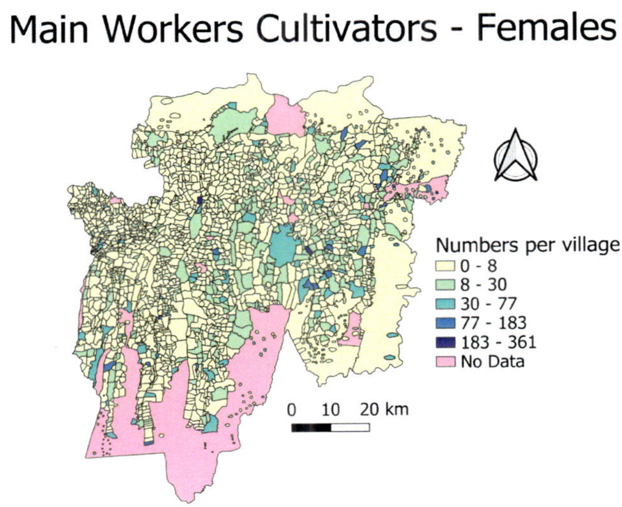

Map 239

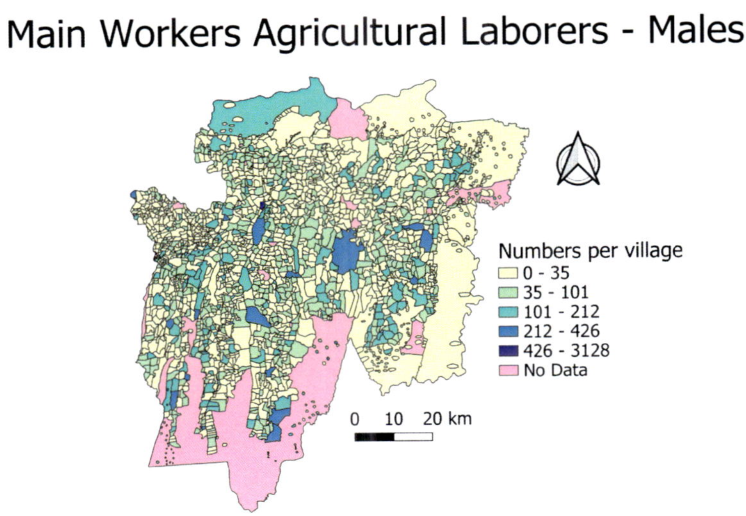

Map 240

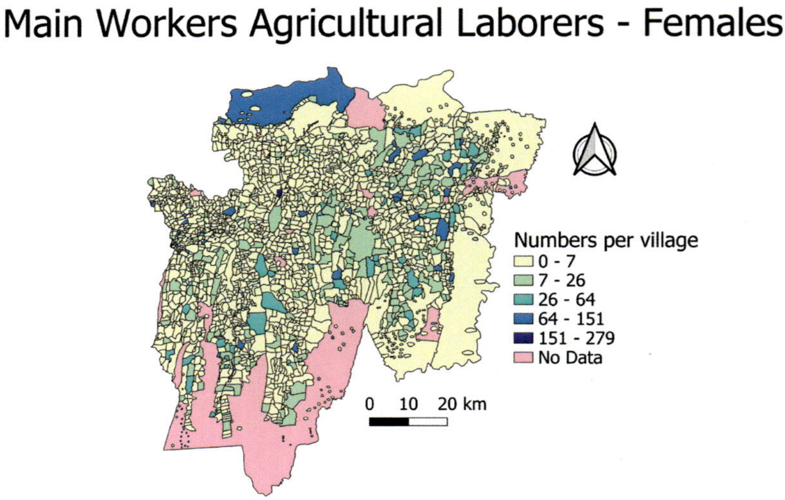

Map 241

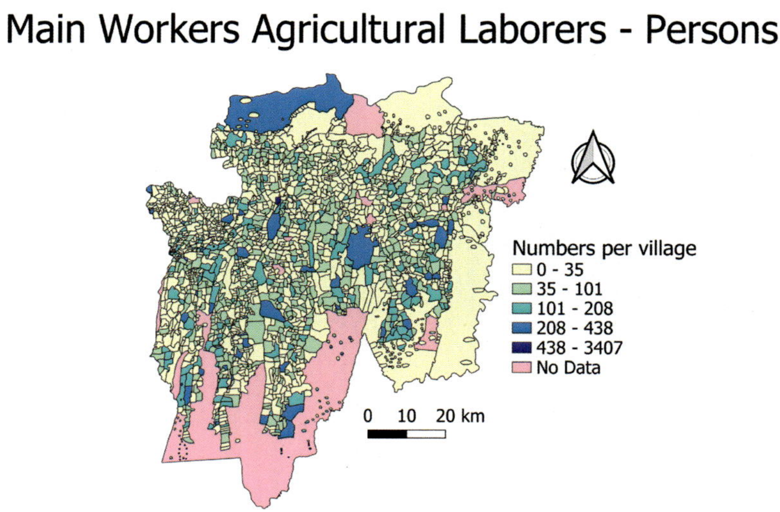

Map 242

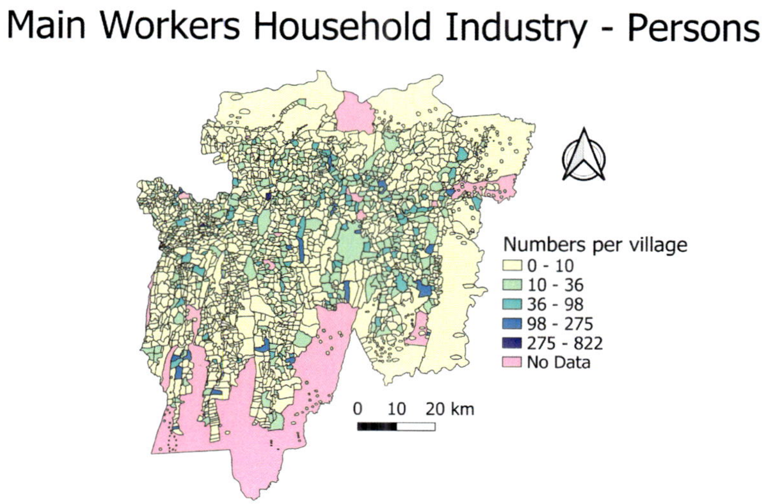

Map 243

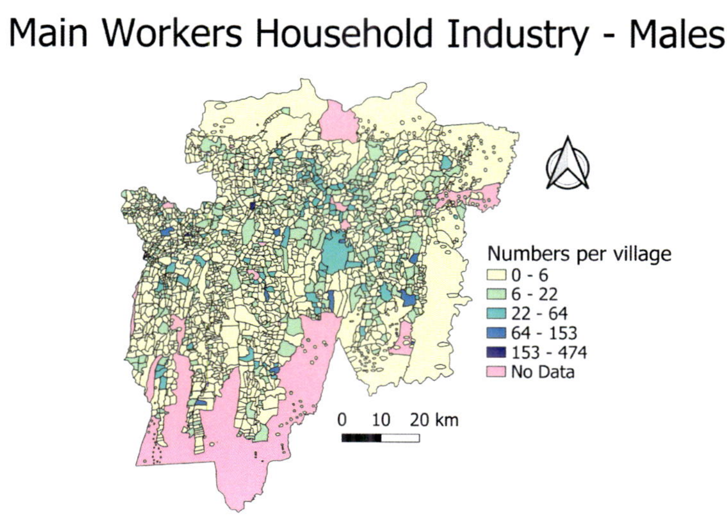

Map 244

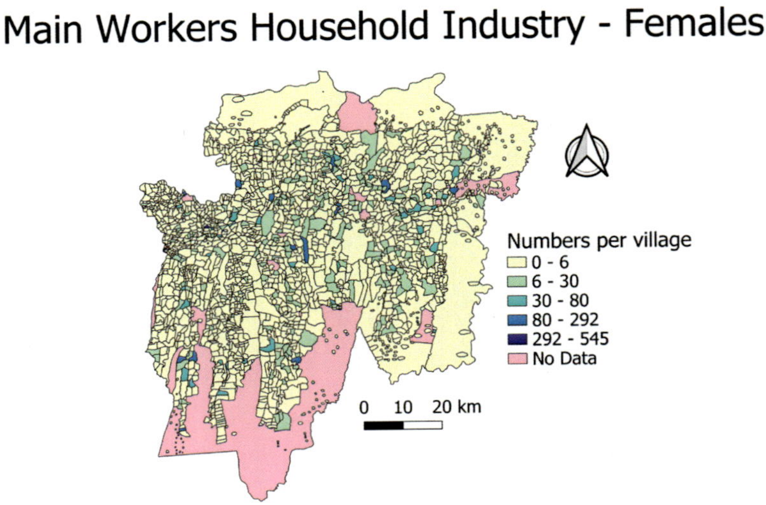

Map 245

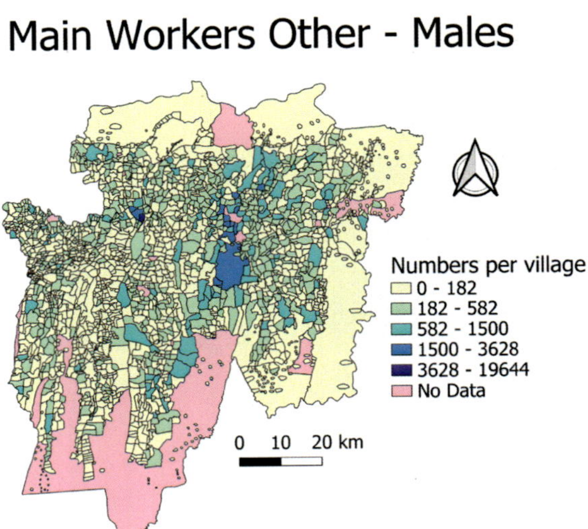

Map 246

Main Workers Other - Females

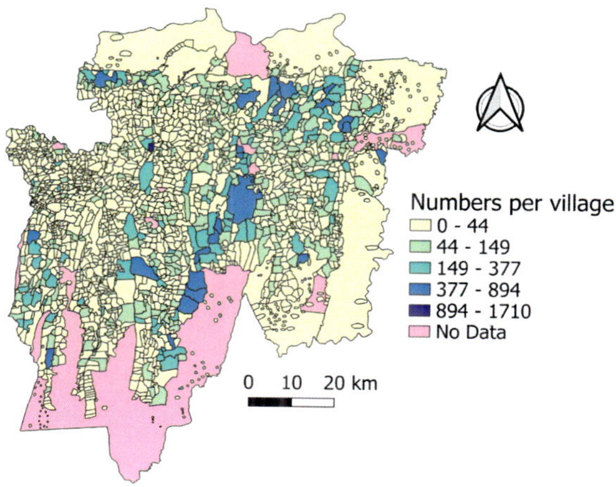

Map 247

Main Workers Other - Persons

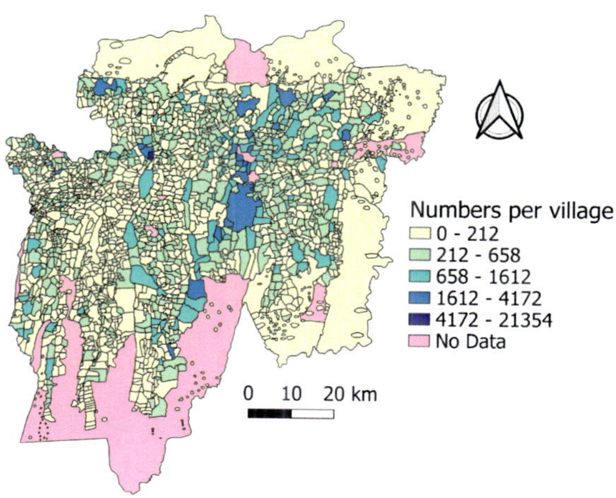

Map 248

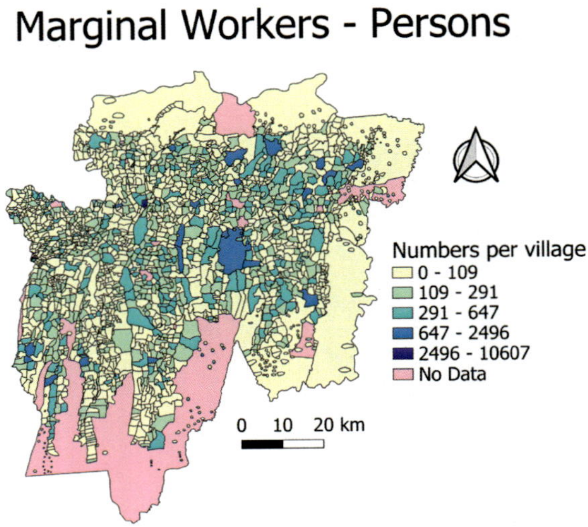

Map 249

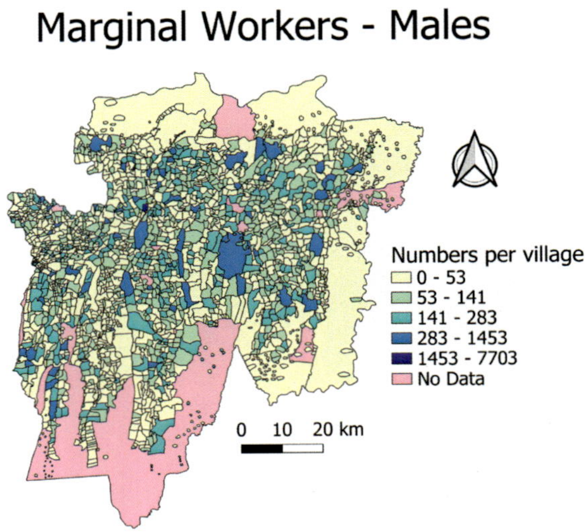

Map 250

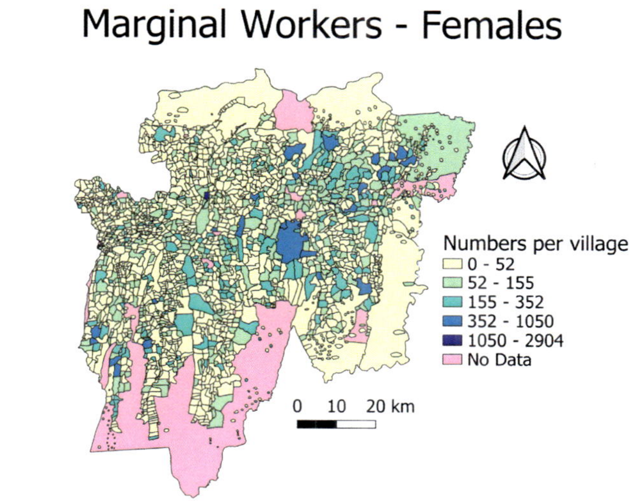

Map 251

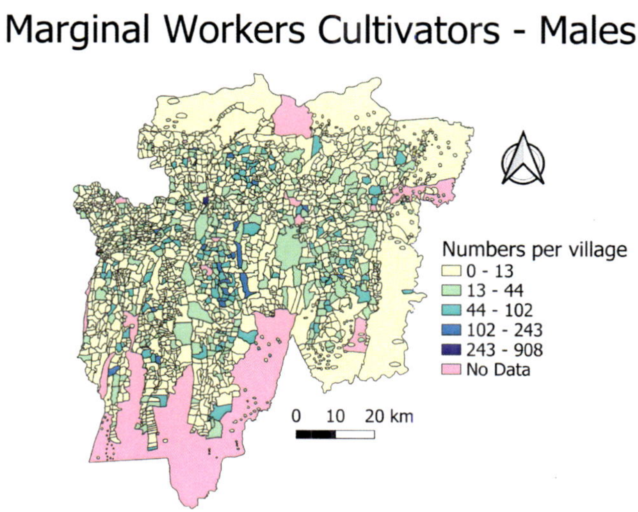

Map 252

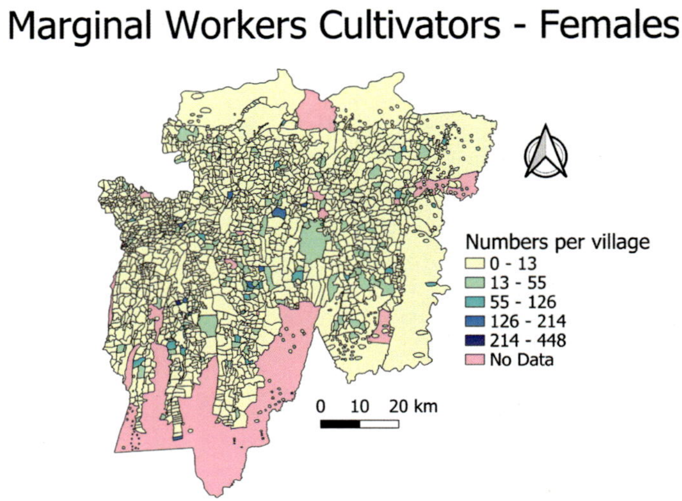

Map 253

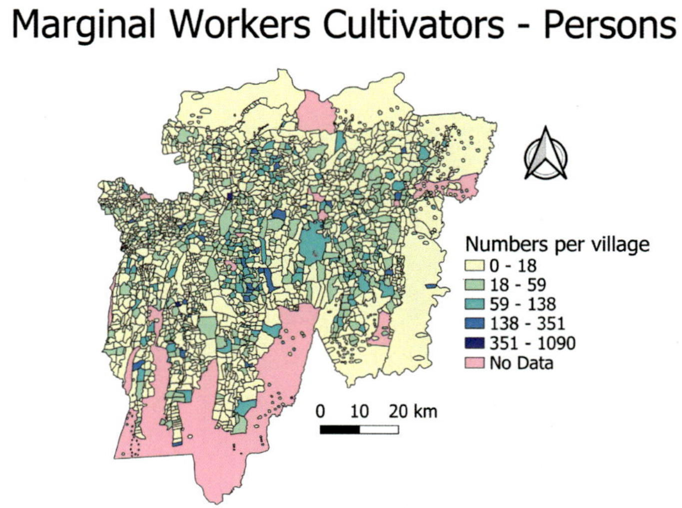

Map 254

Marginal Workers Agri. Laborers - Persons

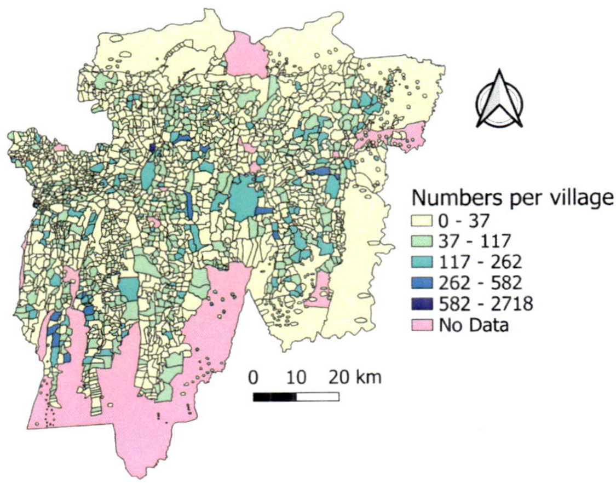

Map 255

Marginal Workers Agri. Laborers - Males

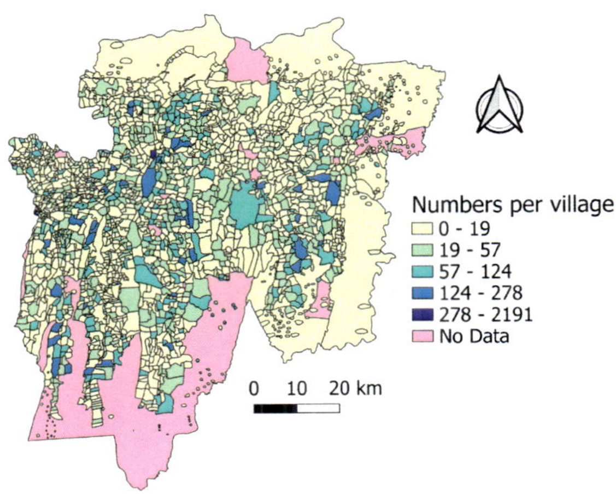

Map 256

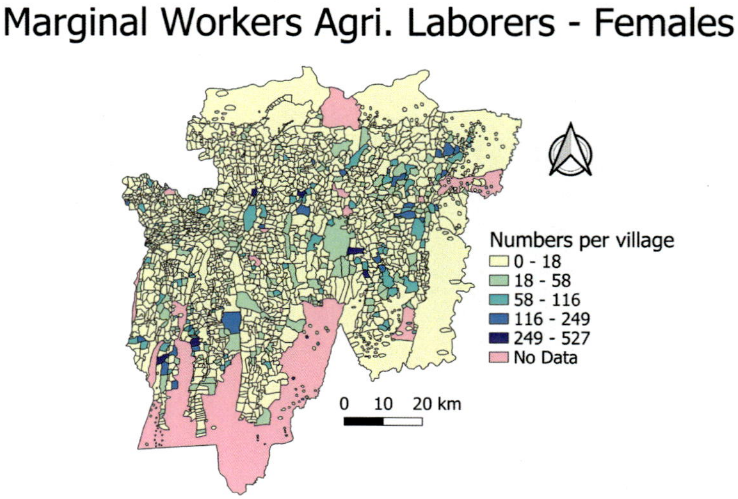

Map 257

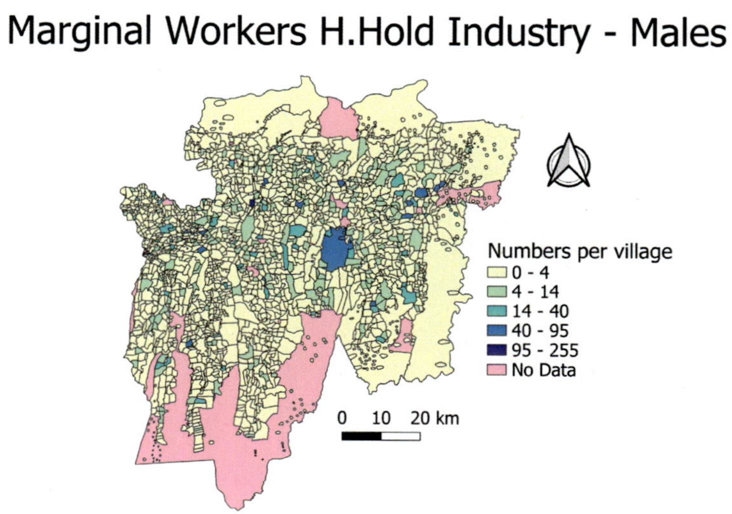

Map 254

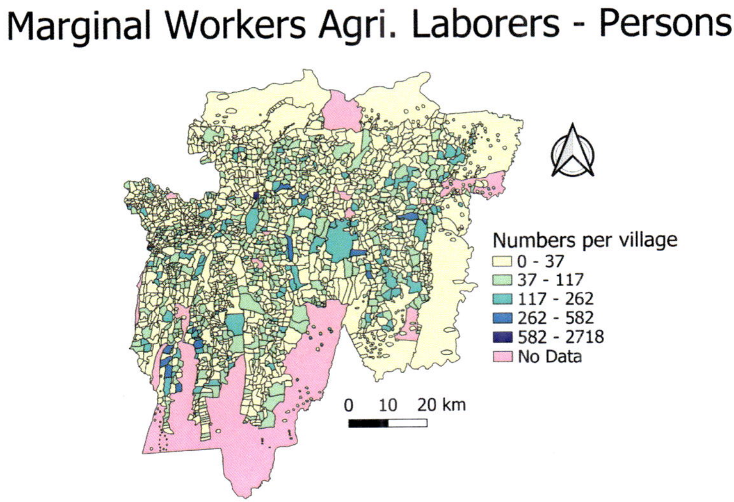

Map 255

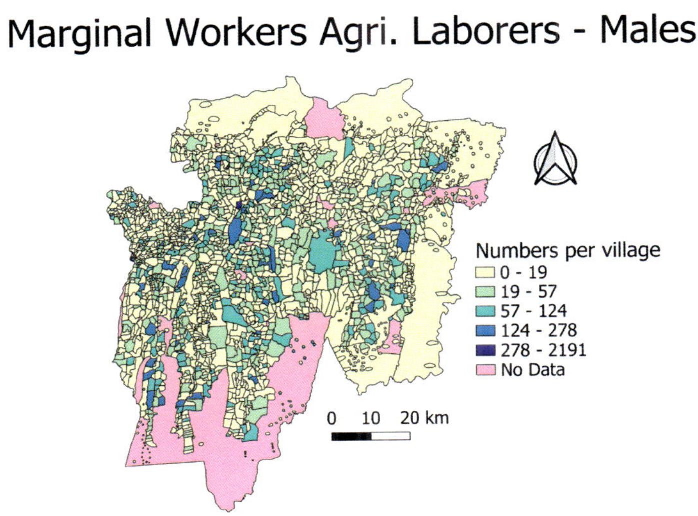

Map 256

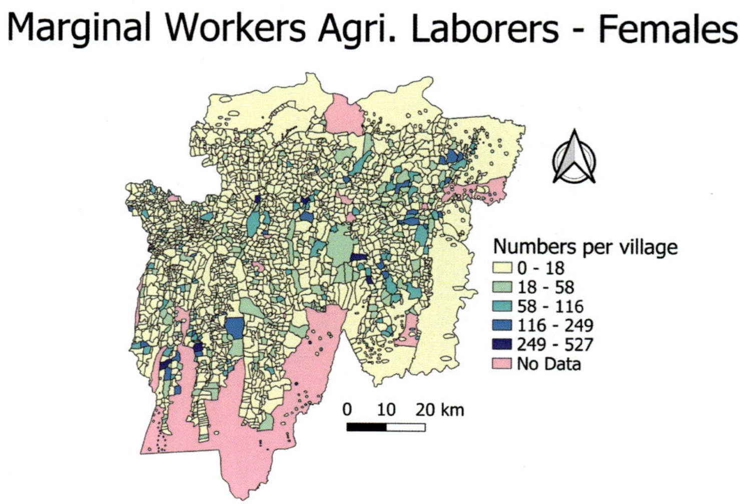

Map 257

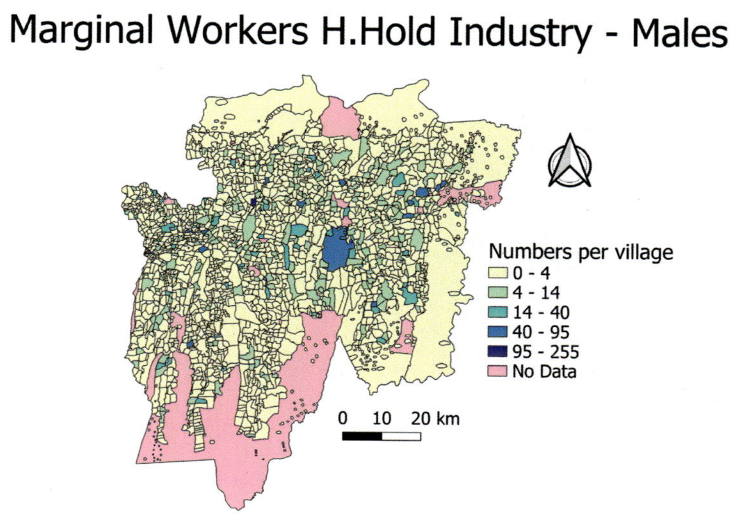

Map 258

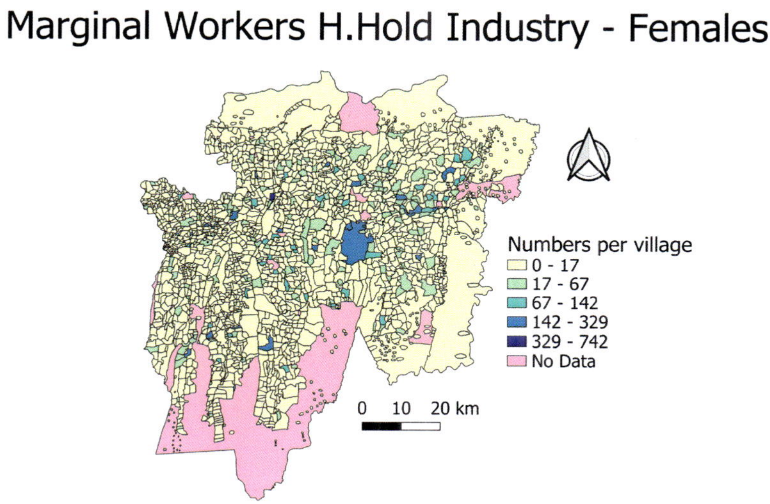

Map 259

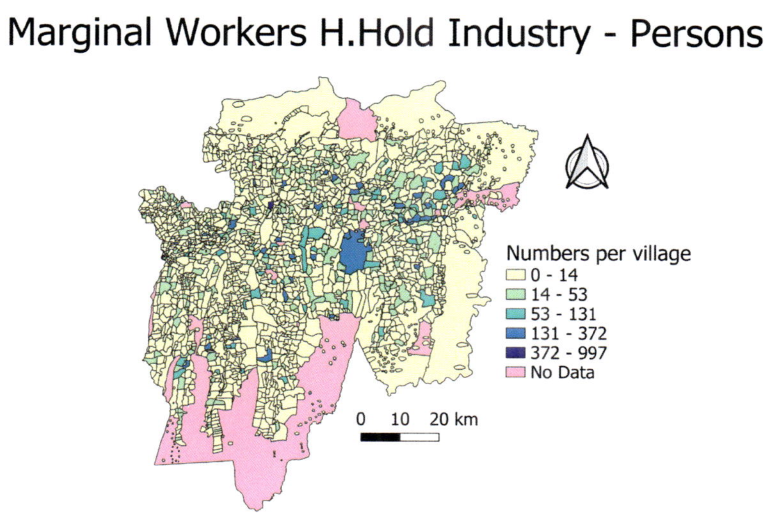

Map 260

Marginal Workers Other - Persons

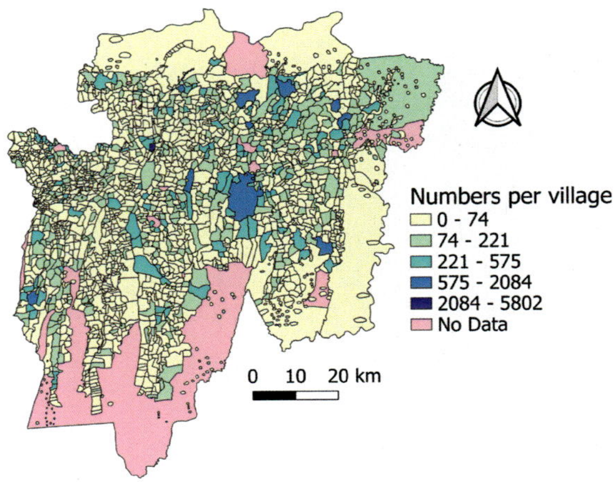

Map 261

Marginal Workers Other - Males

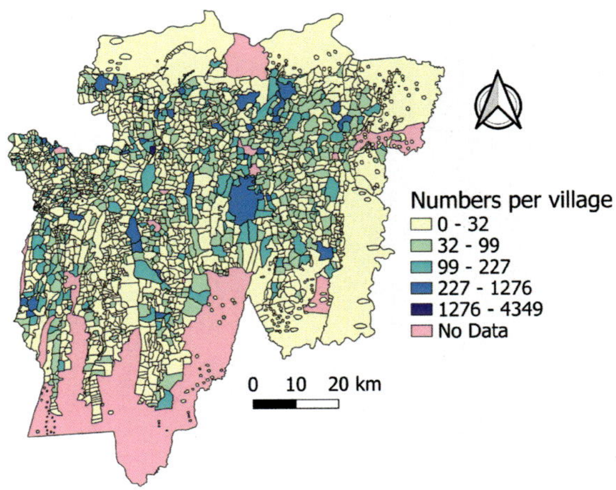

Map 262

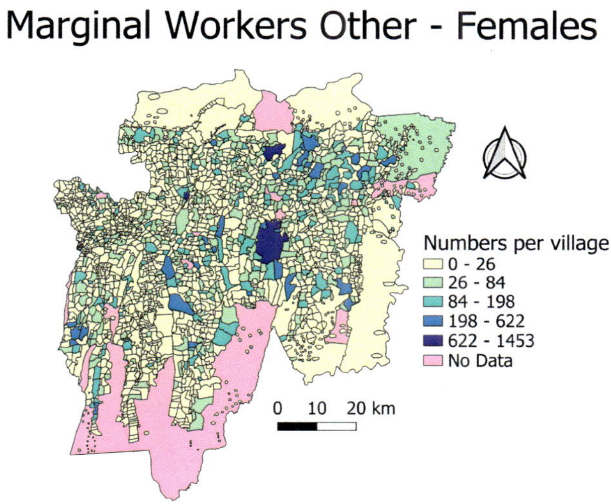

Map 263

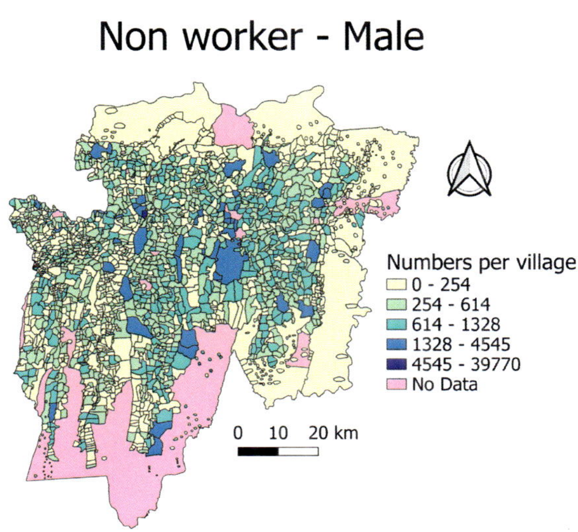

Map 264

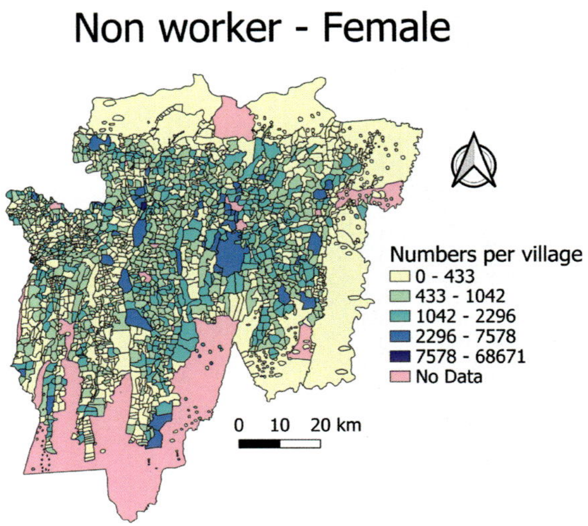

Map 265

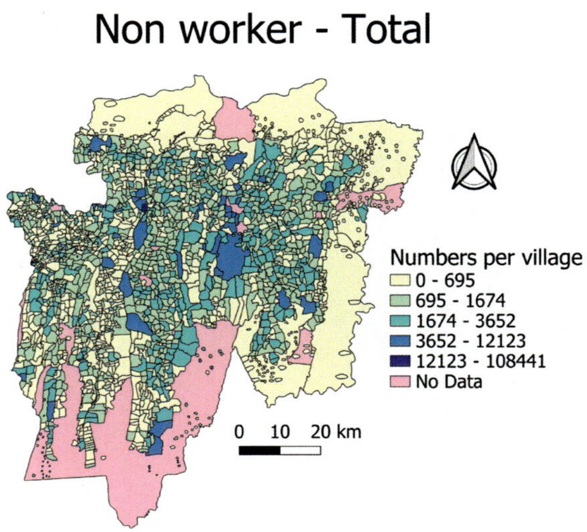

Map 266

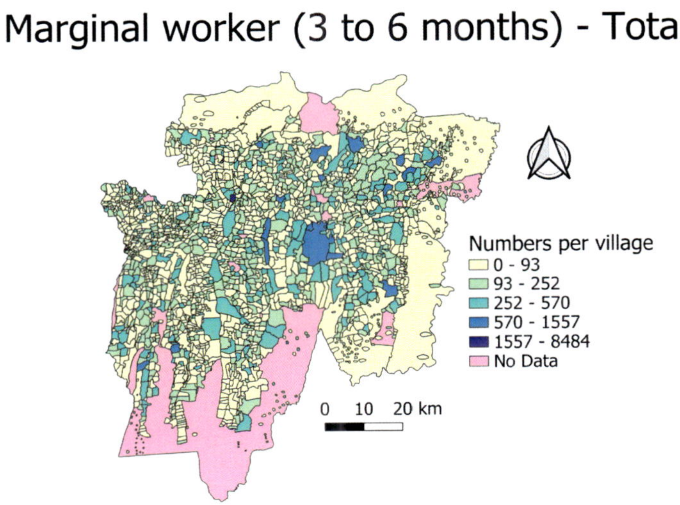

Map 267

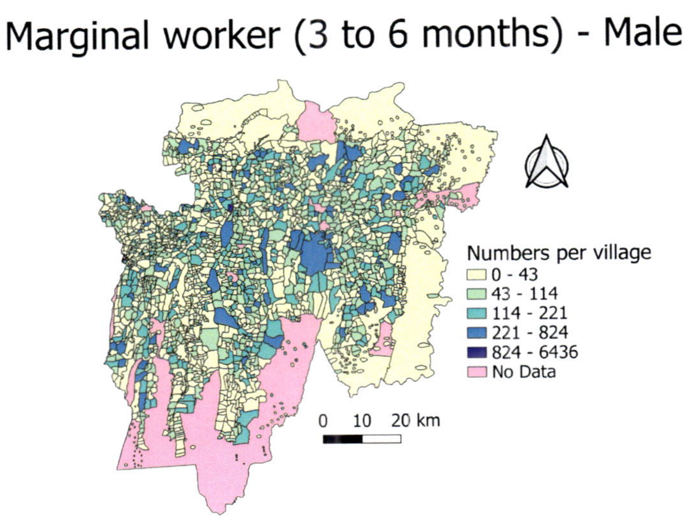

Map 268

Marginal worker (3 to 6 months) - Female

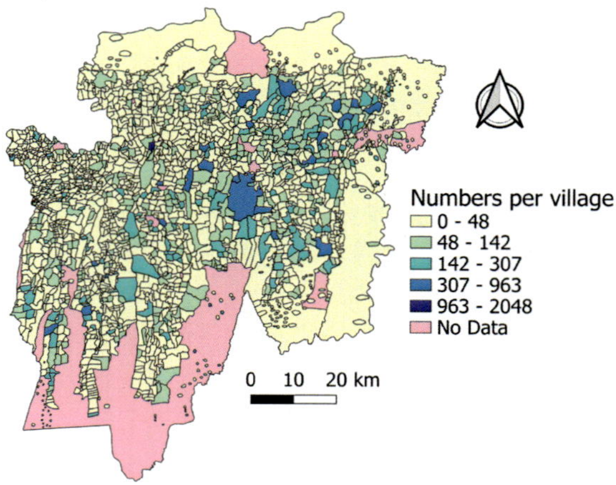

Map 269

Marginal worker (3 to 6 months), cultivator - Male

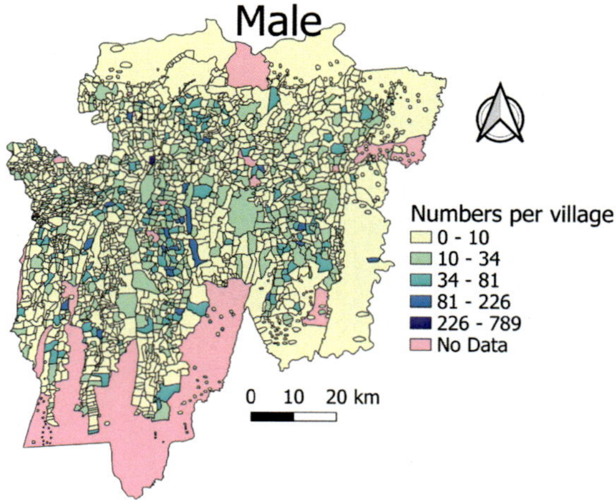

Map 270

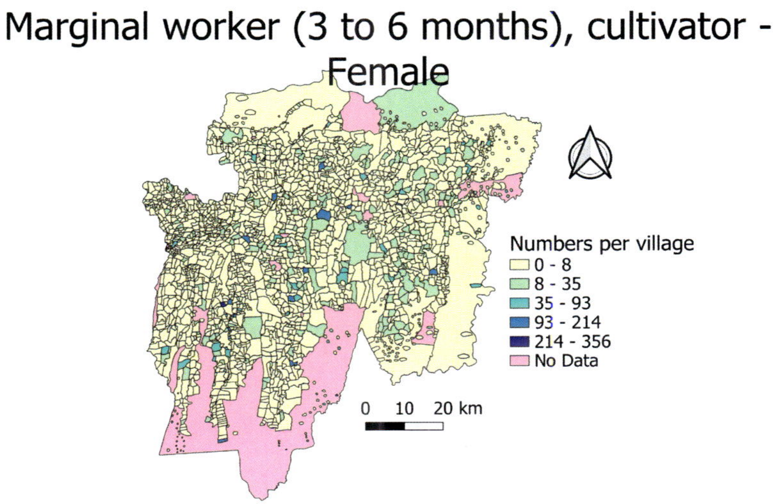

Map 271

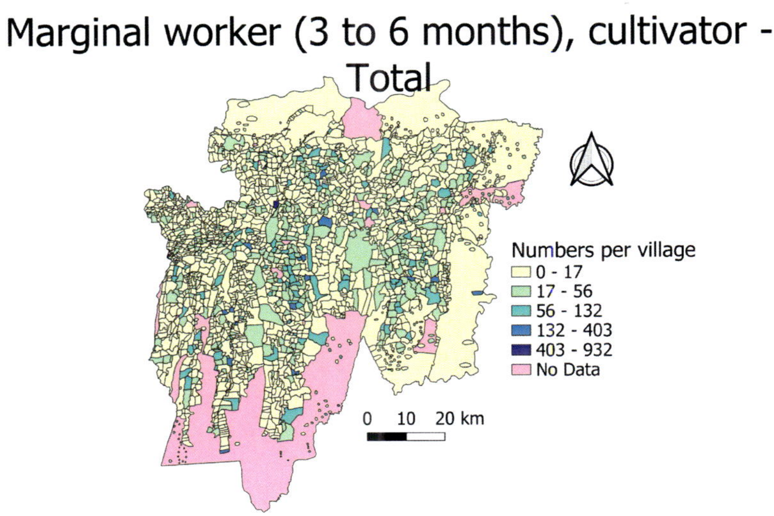

Map 272

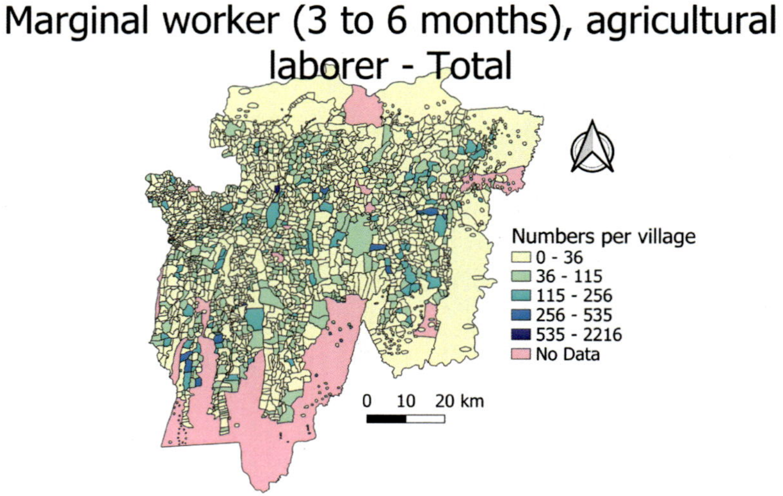

Map 273

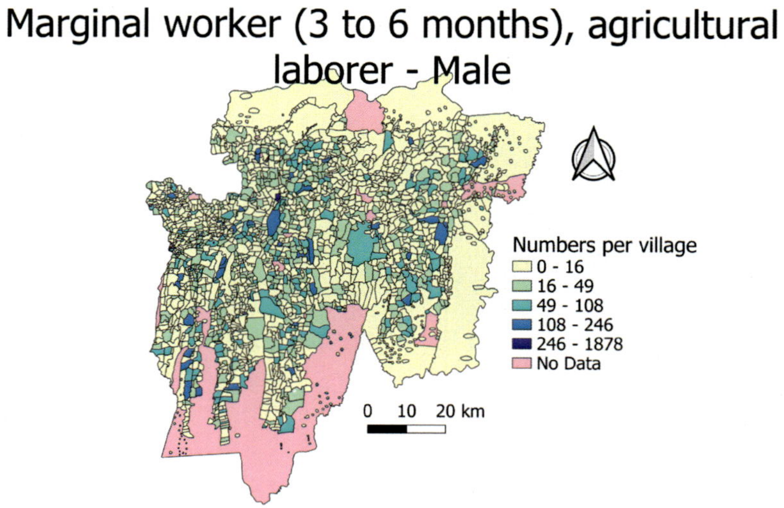

Map 274

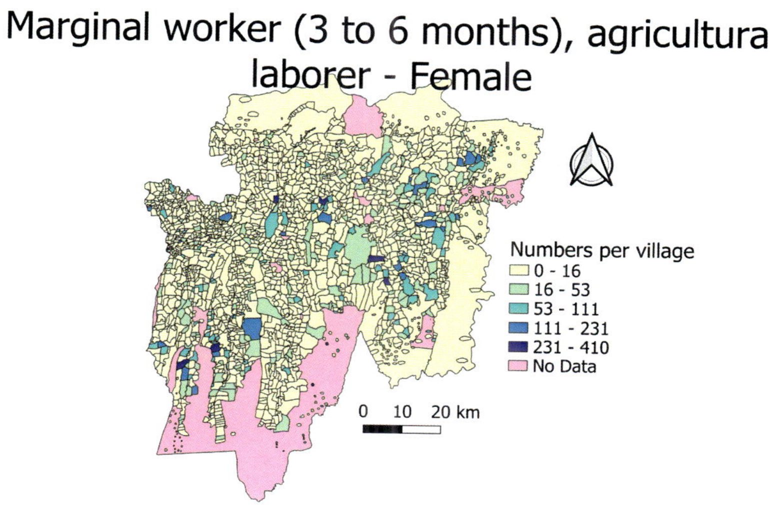

Map 275

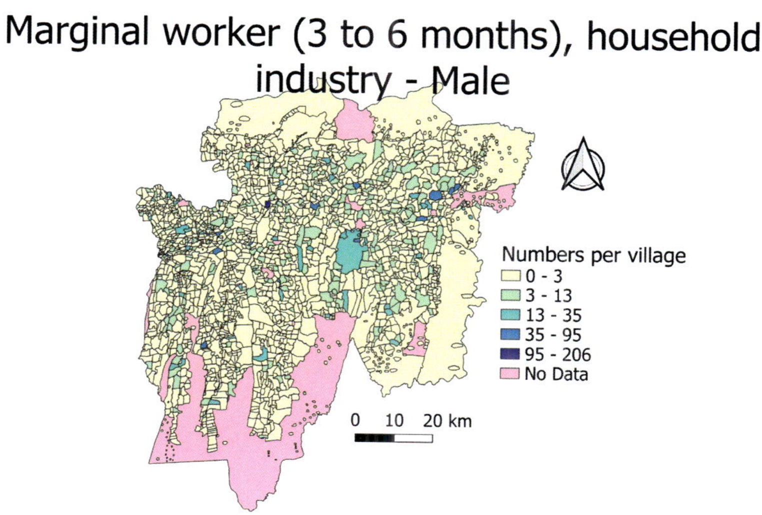

Map 276

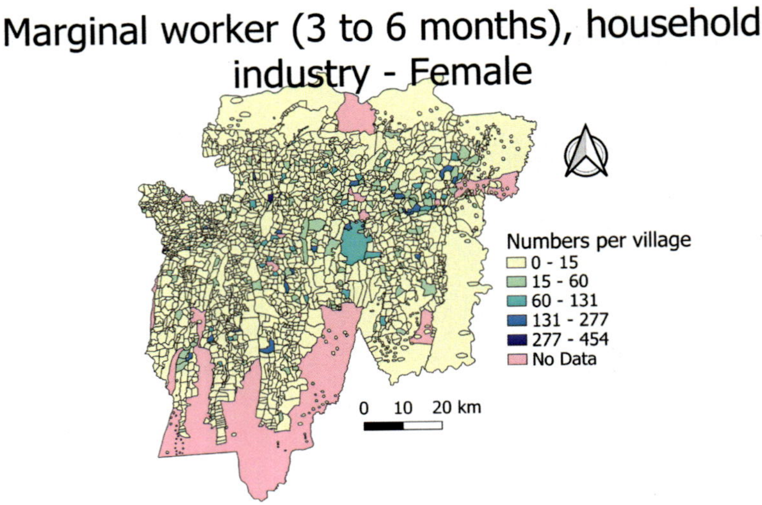

Map 277

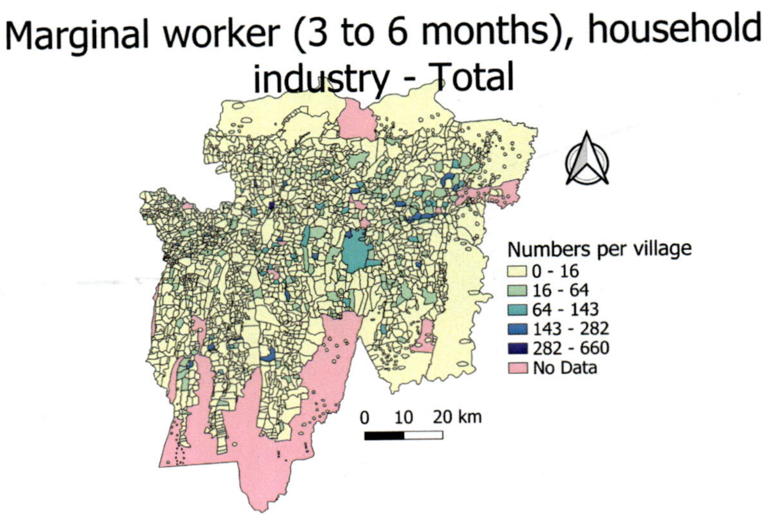

Map 278

Marginal worker (3 to 6 months), other - Total

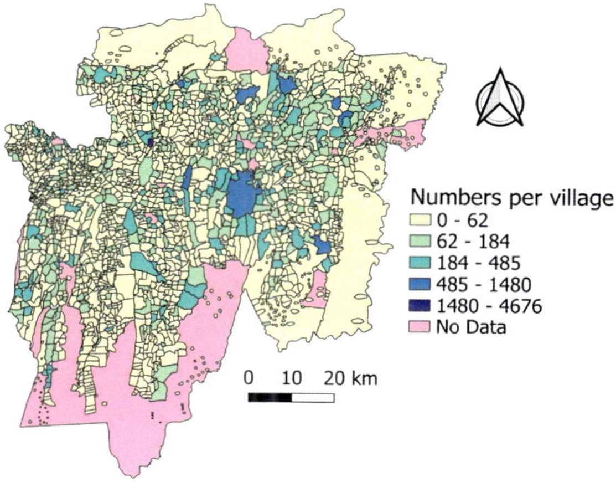

Map 279

Marginal worker (3 to 6 months), other - Male

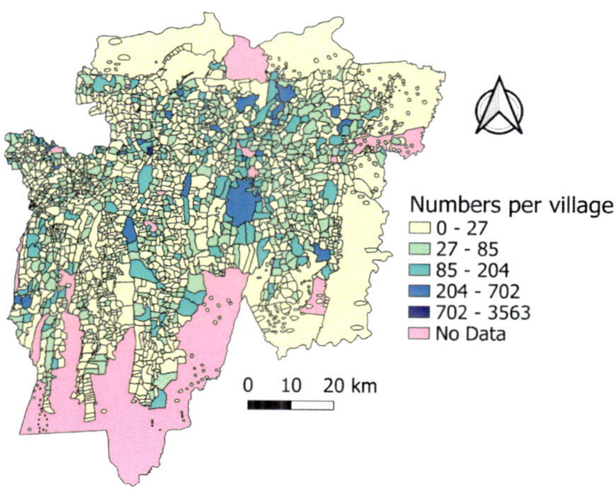

Map 280

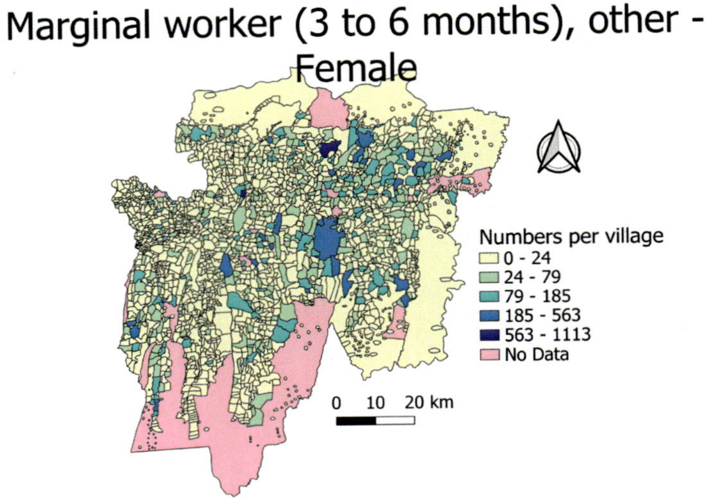

Map 281

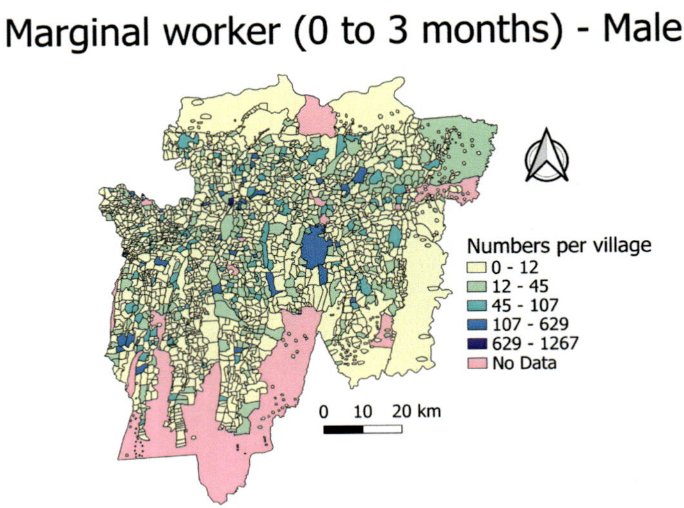

Map 282

Marginal worker (0 to 3 months) - Female

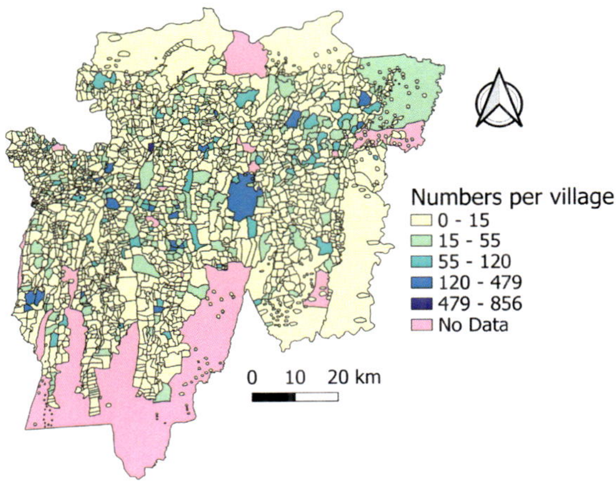

Map 283

Marginal worker (0 to 3 months) - Total

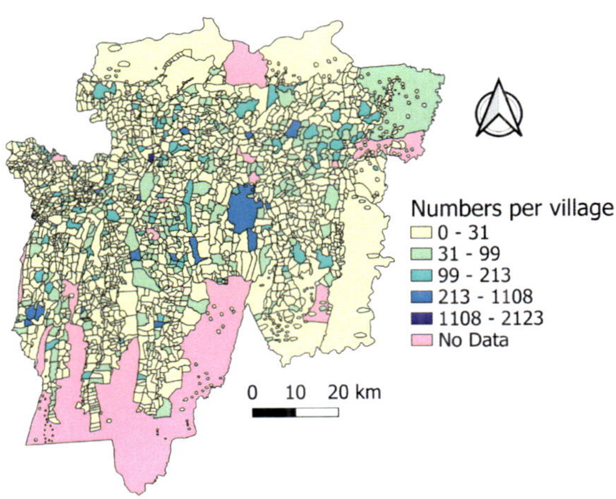

Map 284

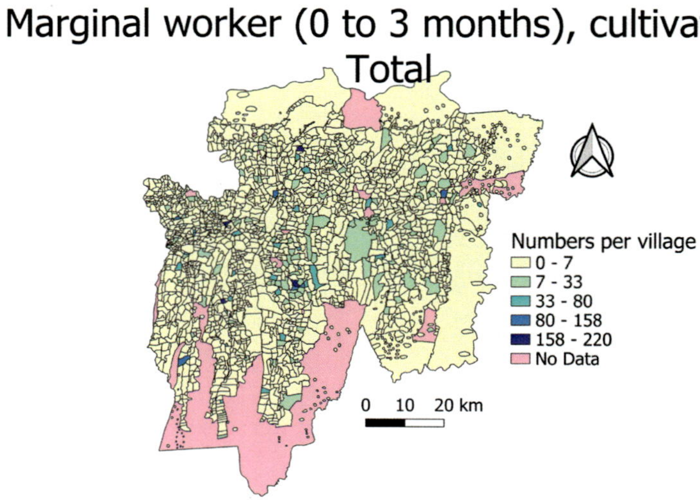

Map 285

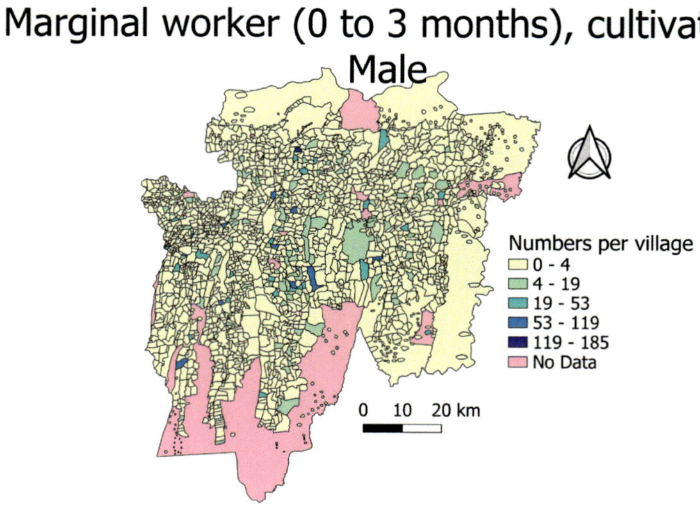

Map 286

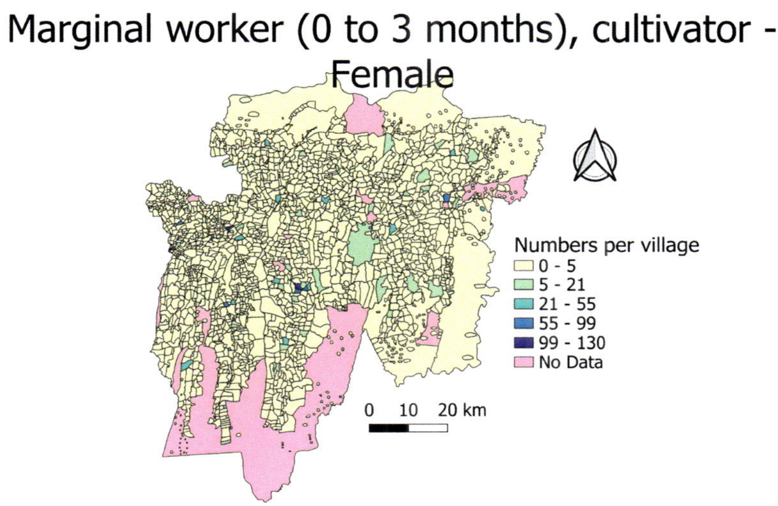

Map 287

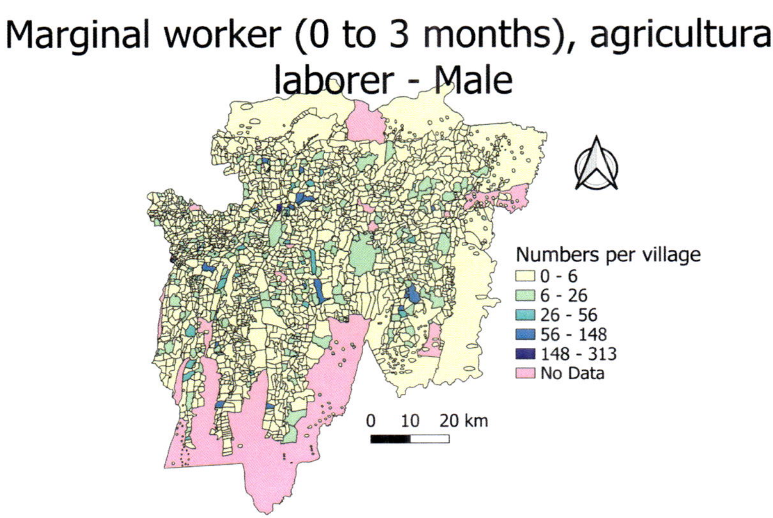

Map 288

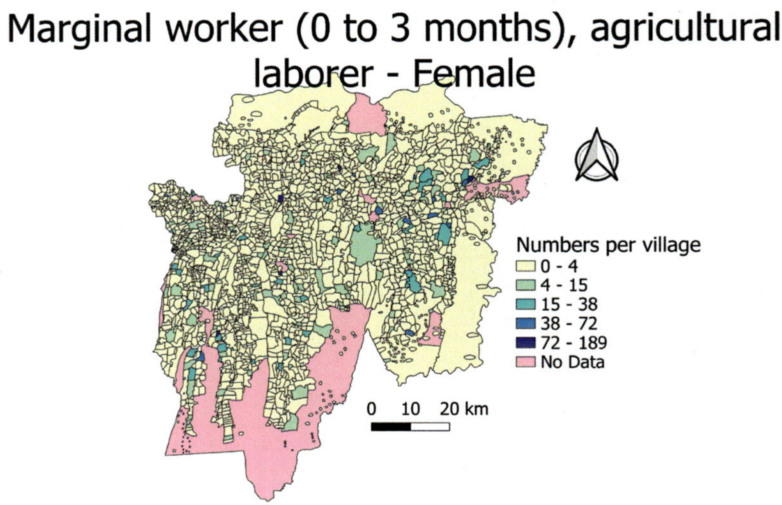

Map 289

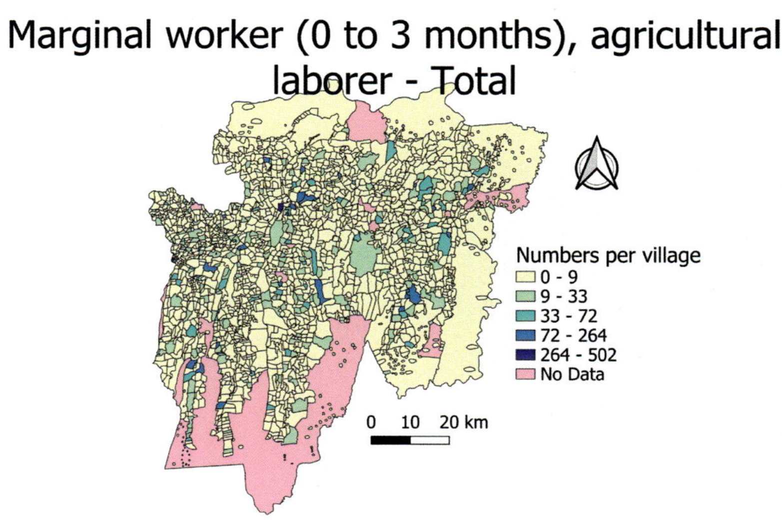

Map 290

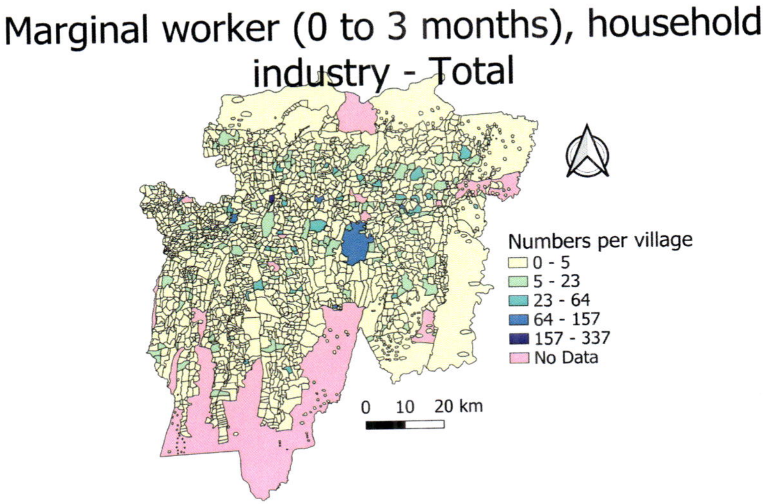

Map 291

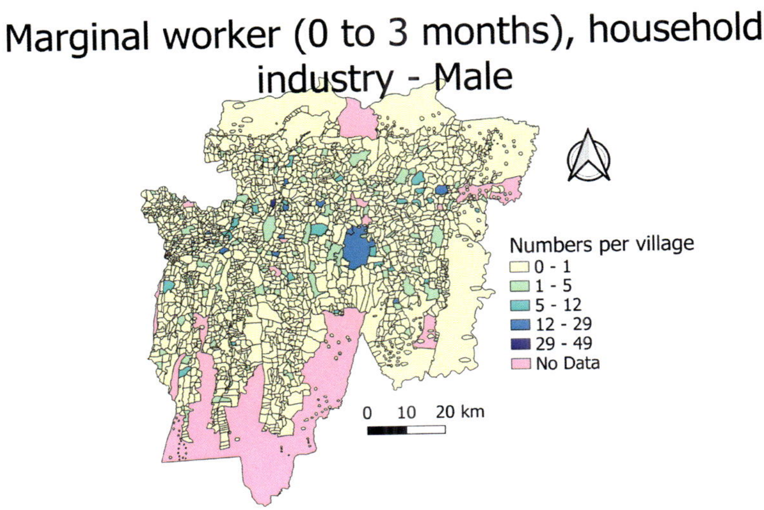

Map 292

Marginal worker (0 to 3 months), household industry - Female

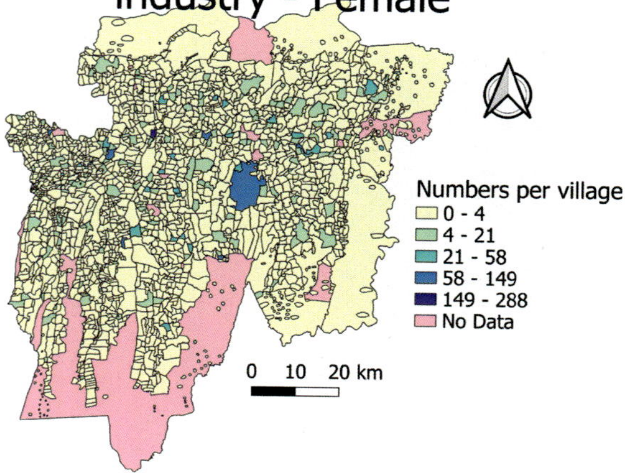

Map 293

Marginal worker (0 to 3 months), other - Male

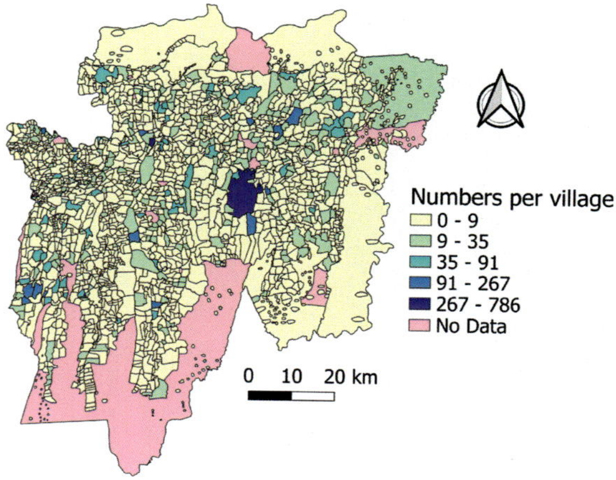

Map 294

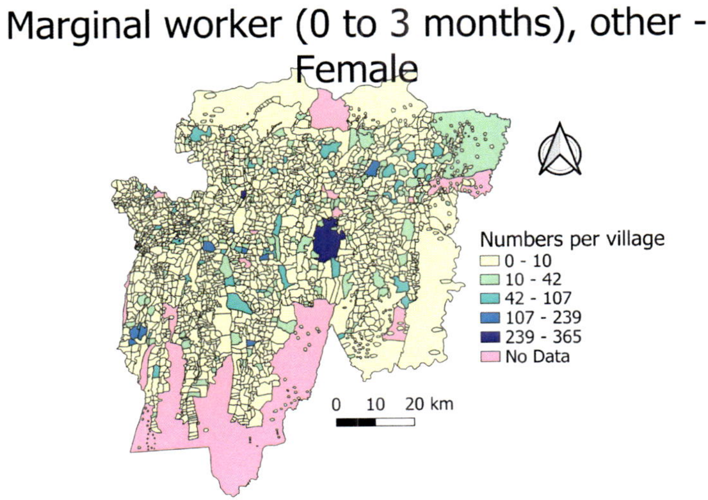

Map 295

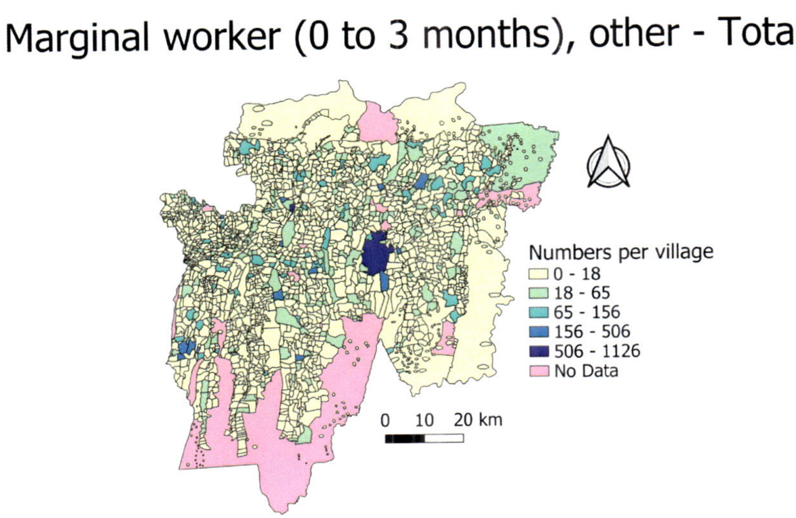

Spatial analysis of socio-economic indicators, 2011

Map 296

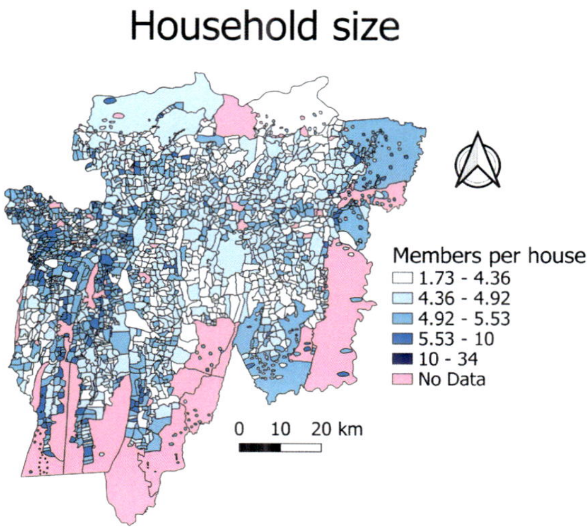

Map 297

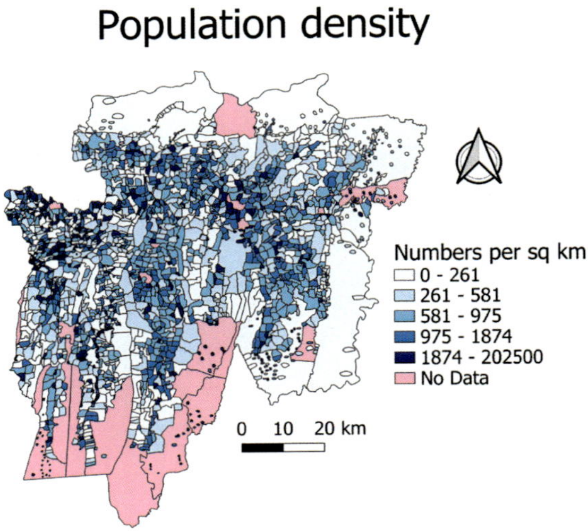

Map 298

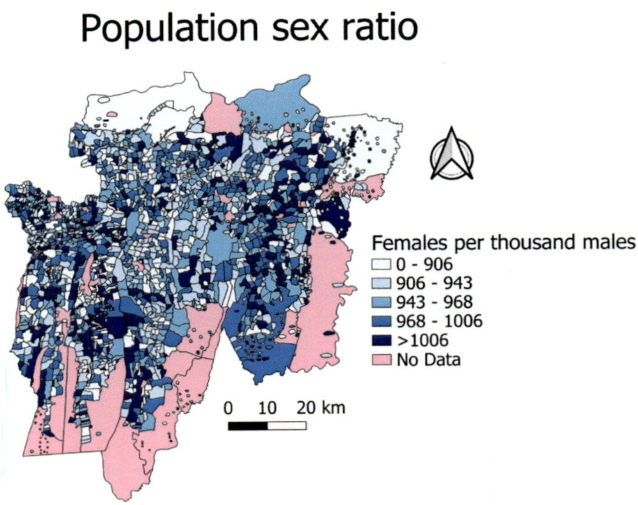

Map 299

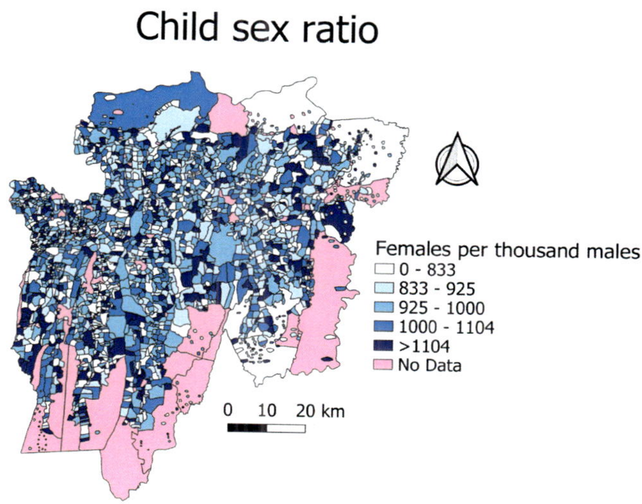

Map 300

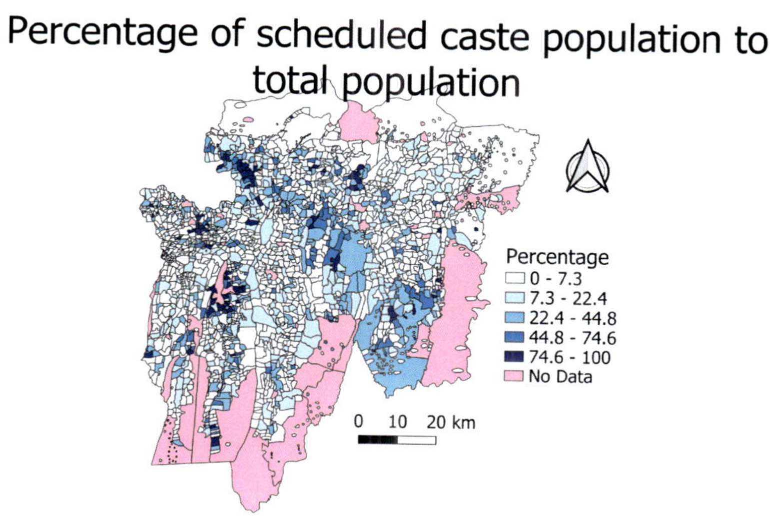

Map 301

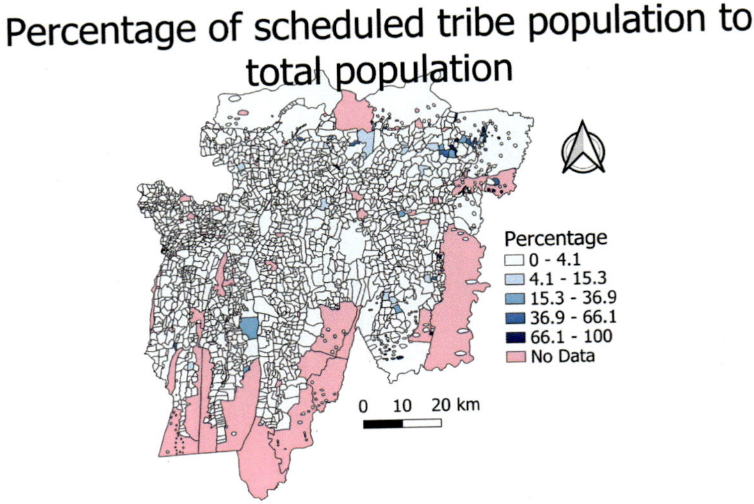

Map 302

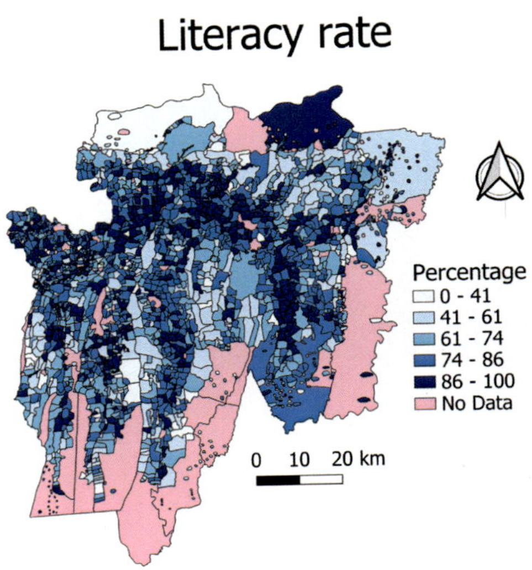

Map 303

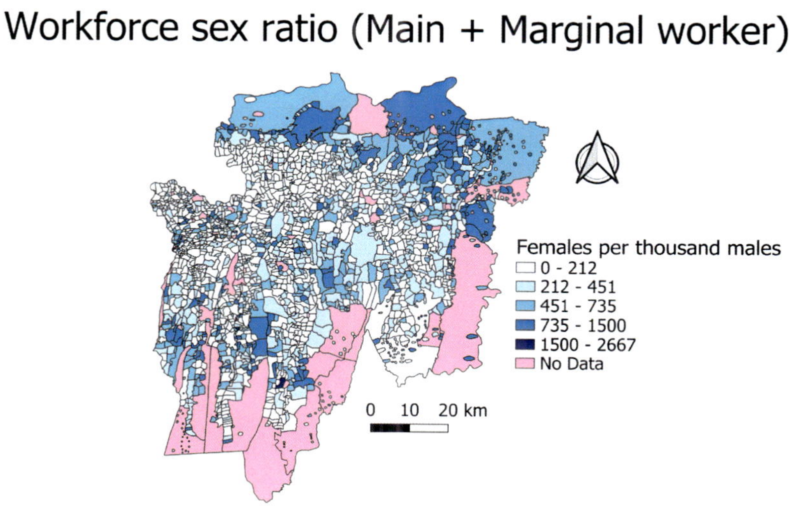

Map 304

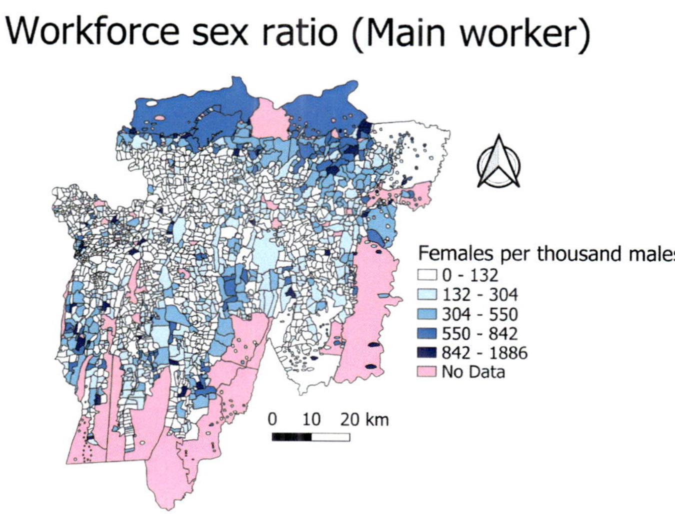

Map 305

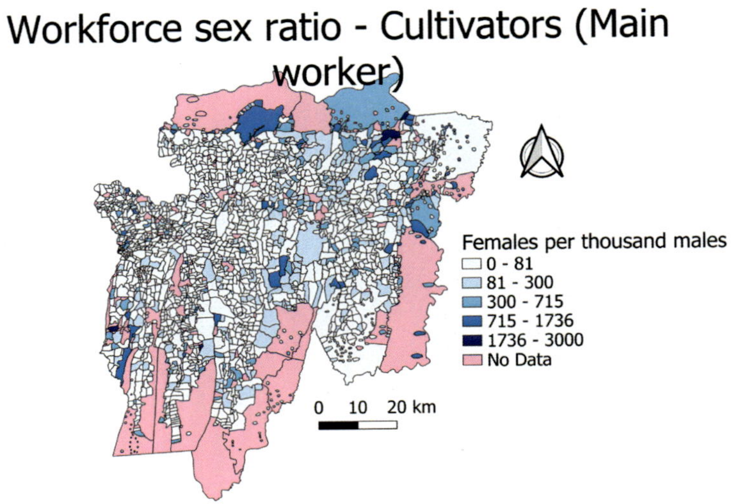

Map 306

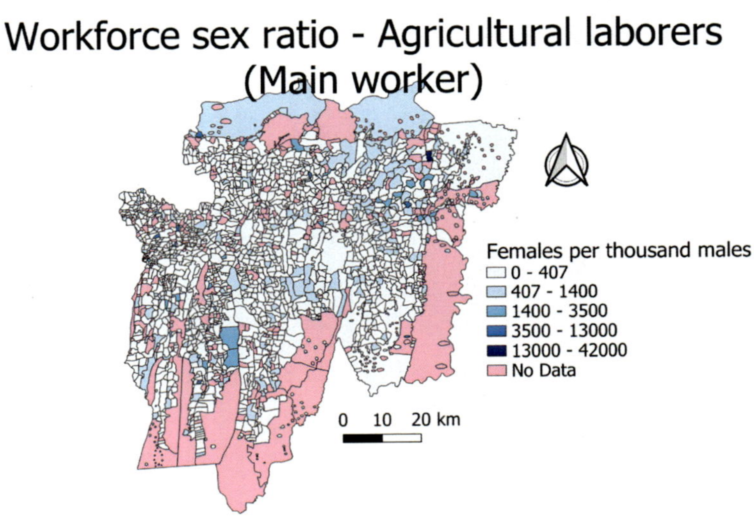

Map 307

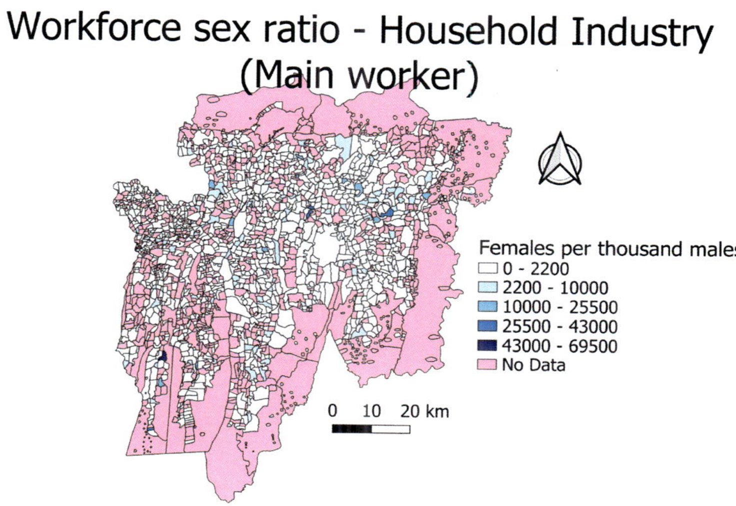

Map 308

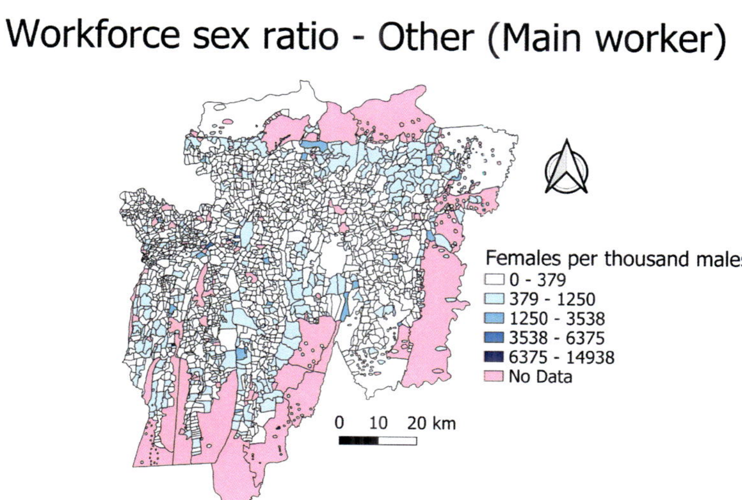

Map 309

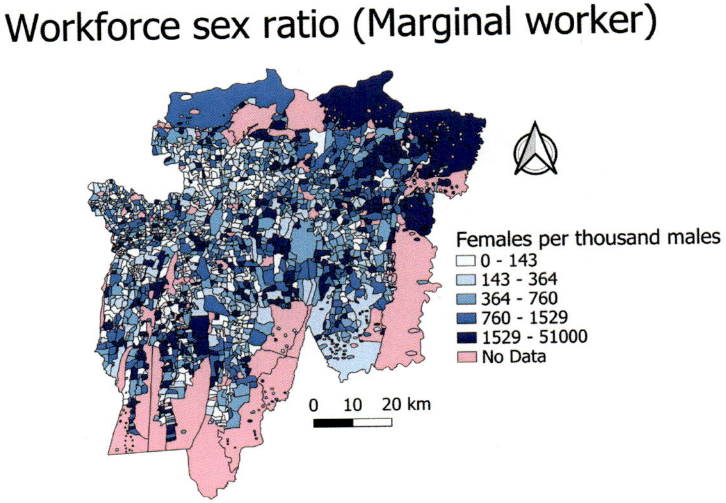

Map 310

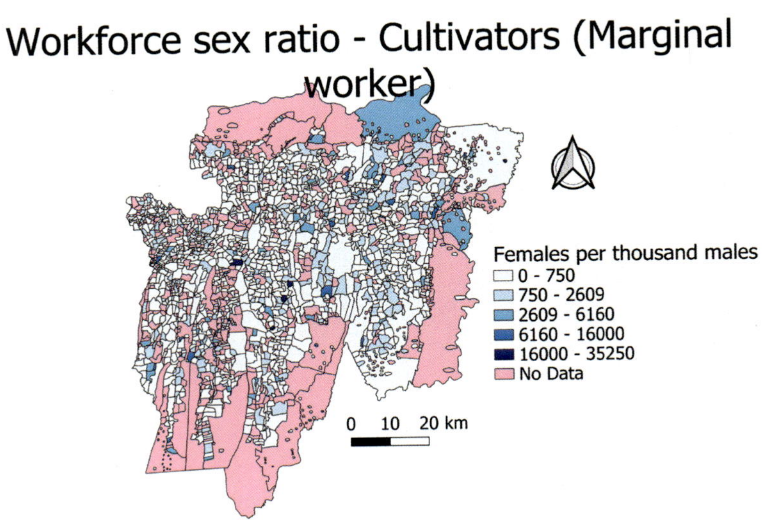

Map 311

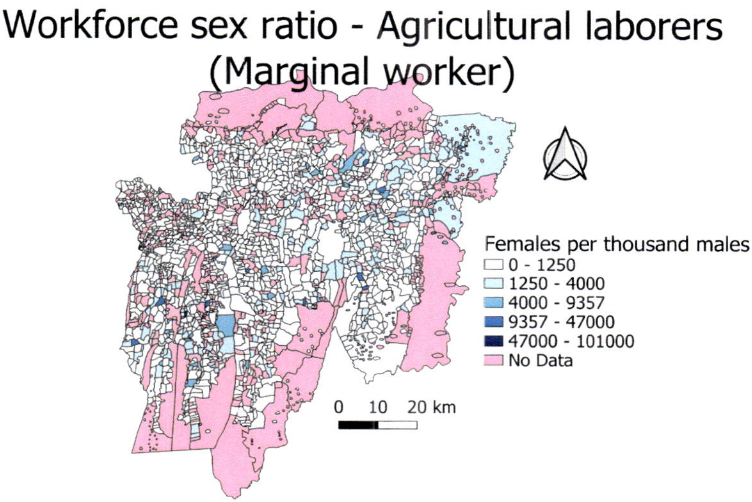

Map 312

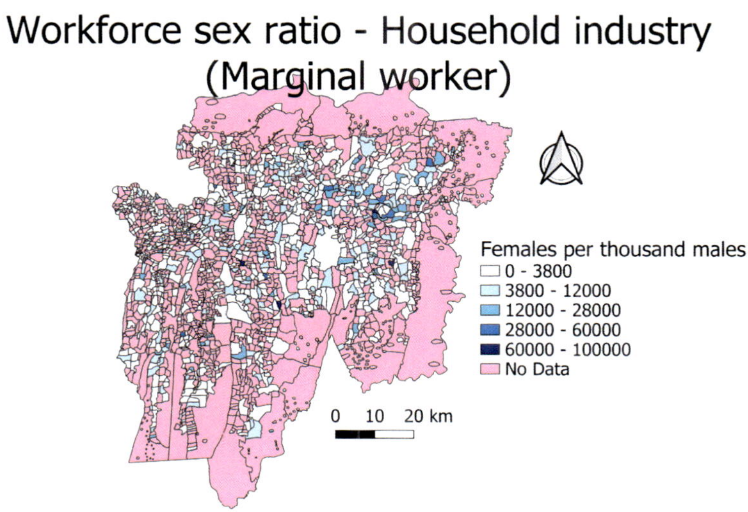

Map 313

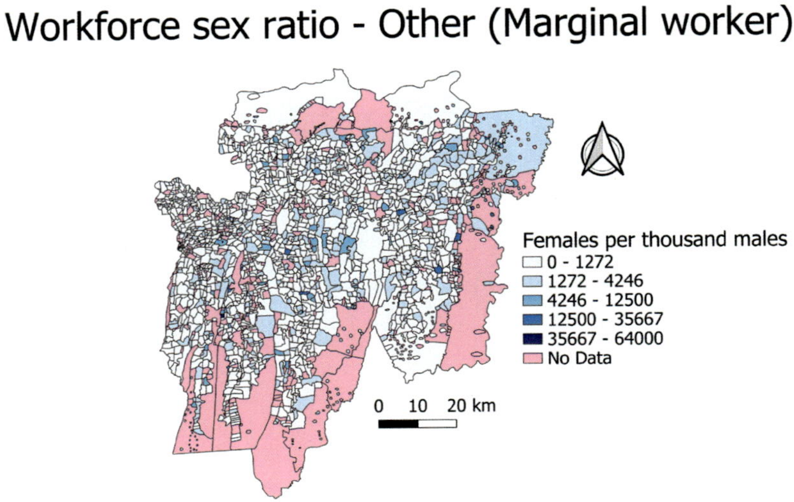

Map 314

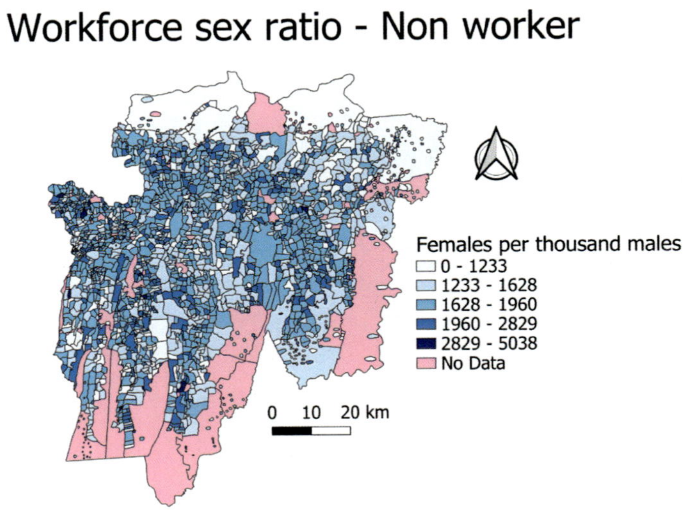

Map 315

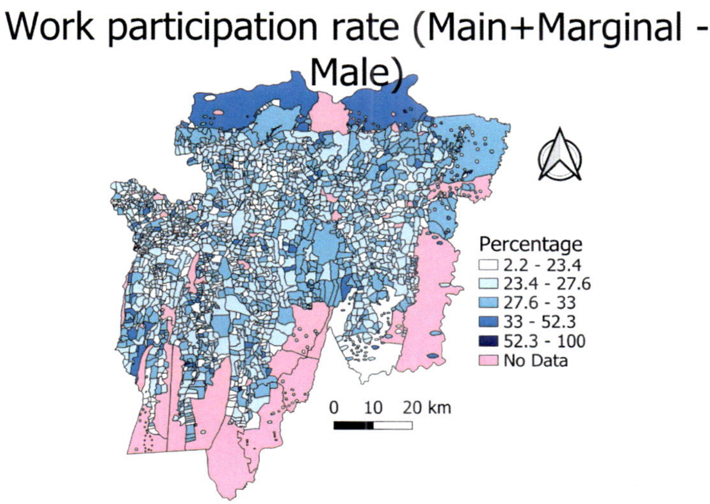

Map 316

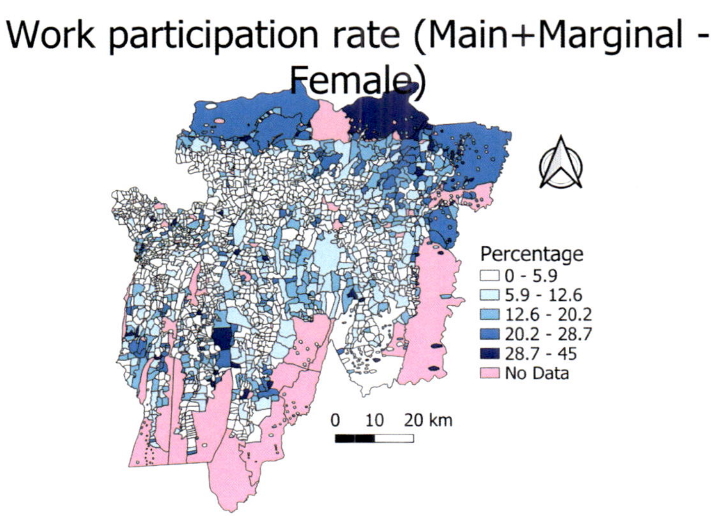

Map 317

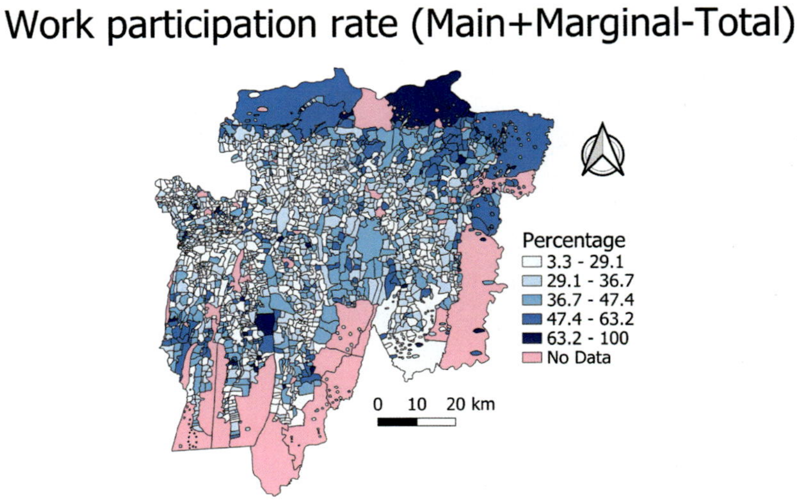

Map 318

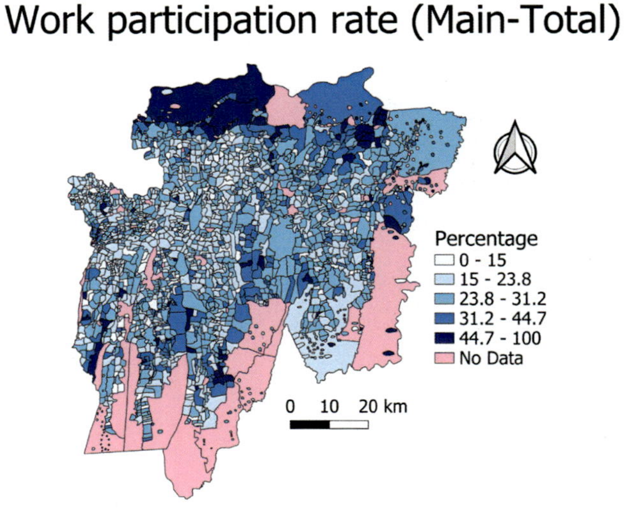

Map 319

Work participation rate (Main - Male)

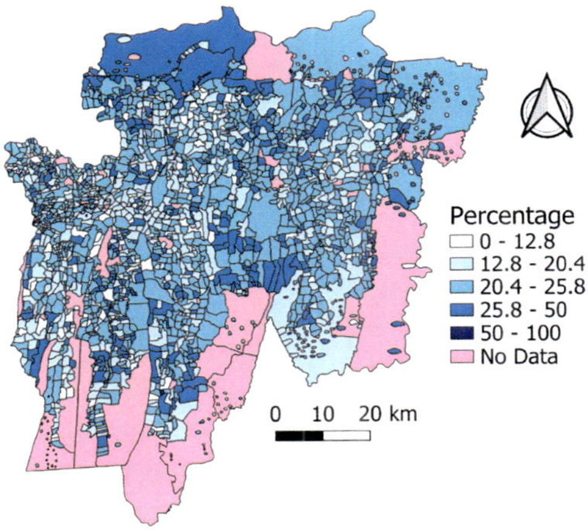

Map 320

Work participation rate (Main - Female)

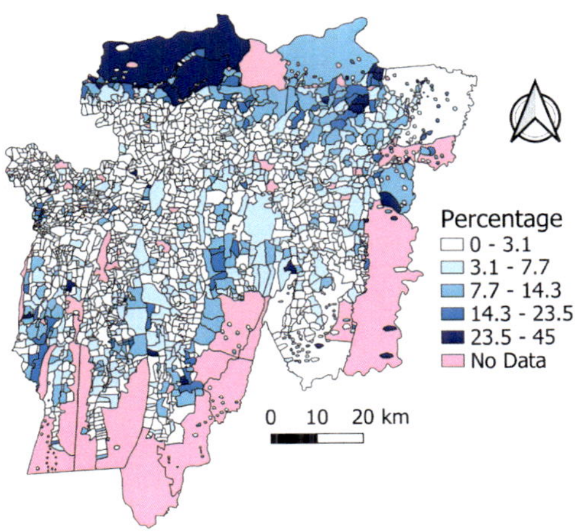

Map 321

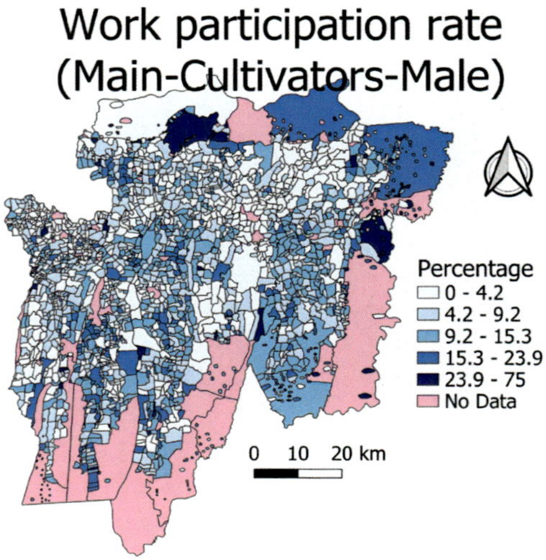

Map 322

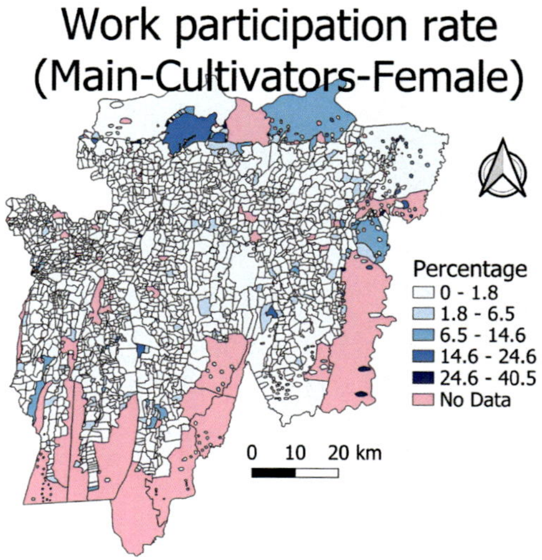

Map 323

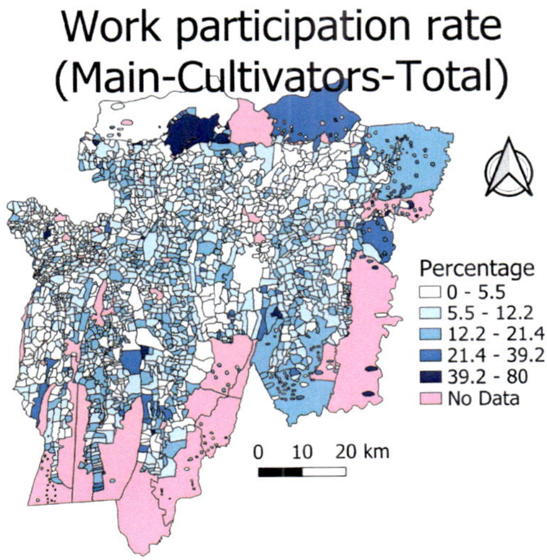

Map 324

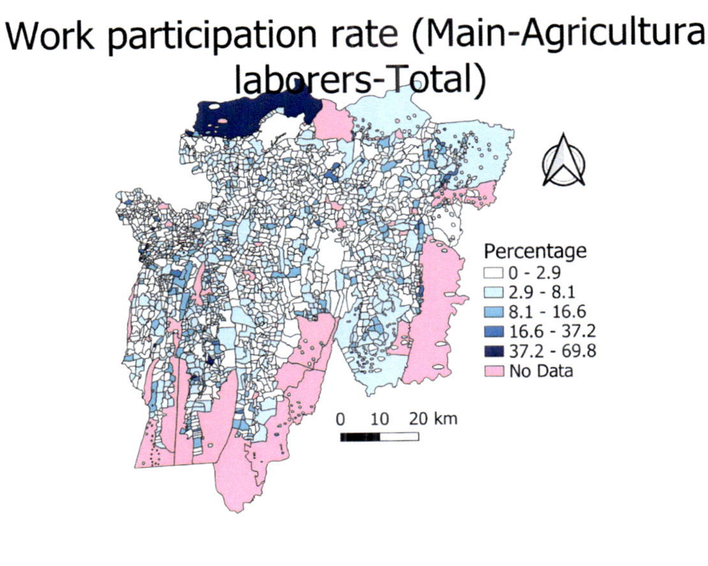

Map 325

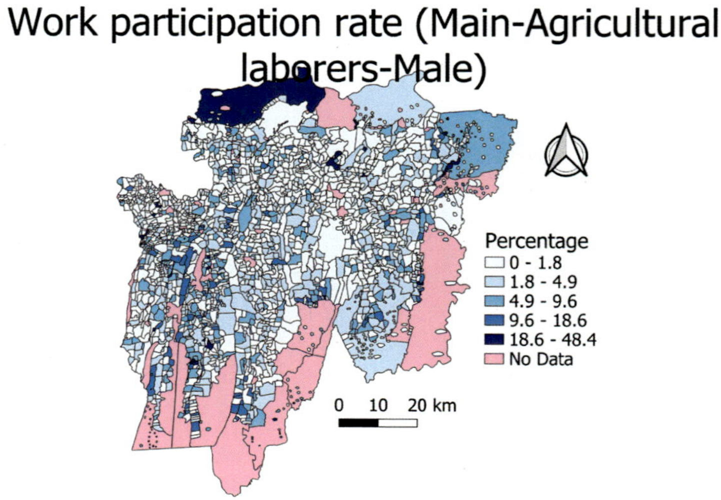

Map 326

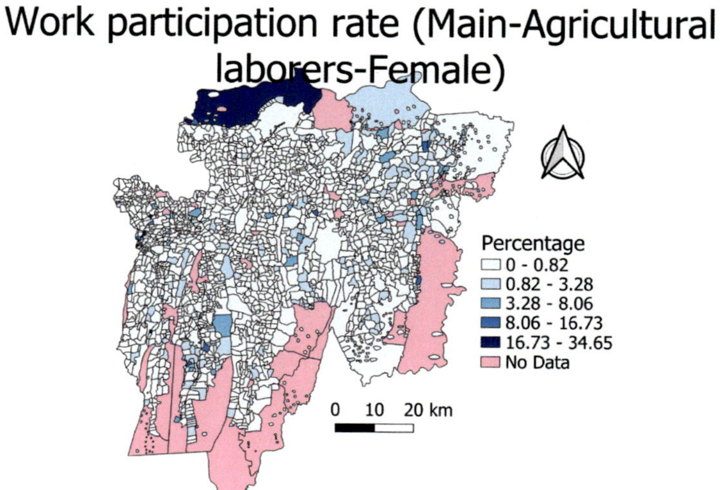

Map 327

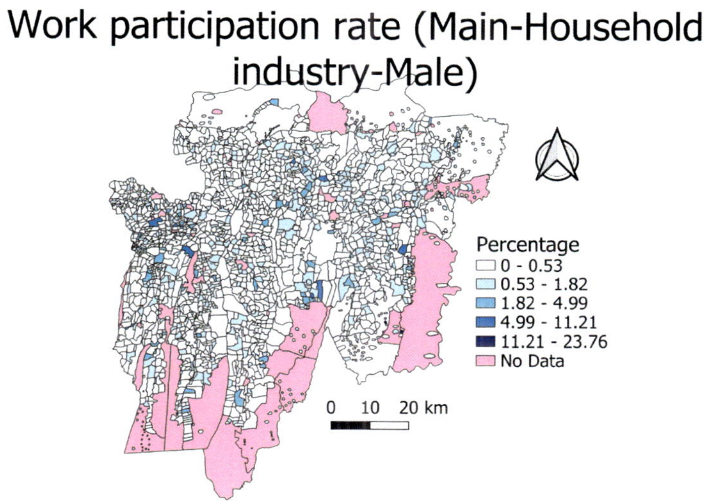

Map 328

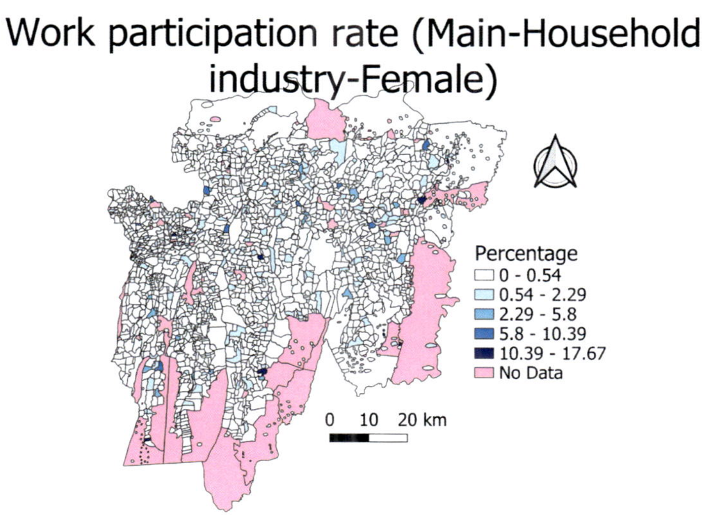

Map 329

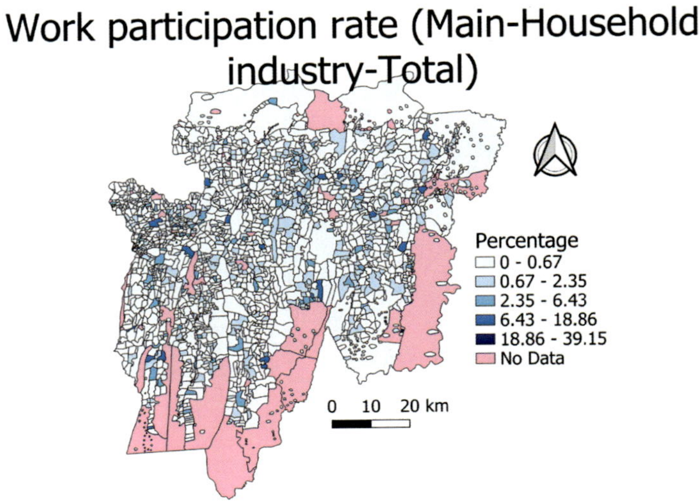

Map 330

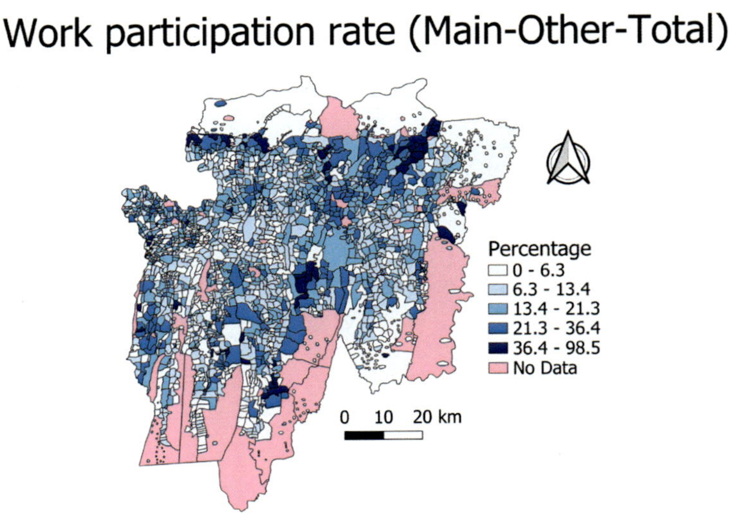

Map 331

Work participation rate (Main-Other-Male)

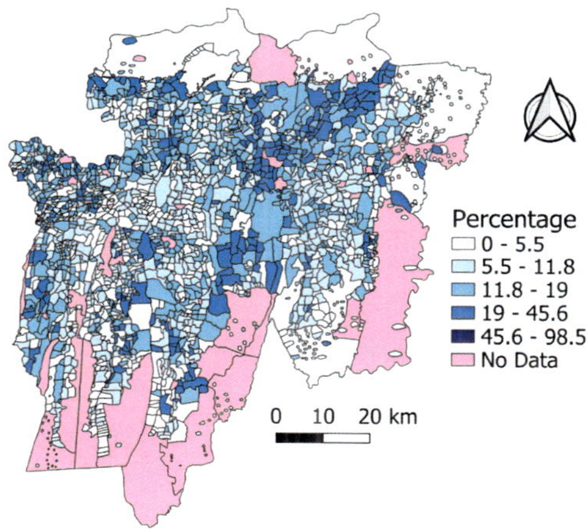

Map 332

Work participation rate (Main-Other-Female)

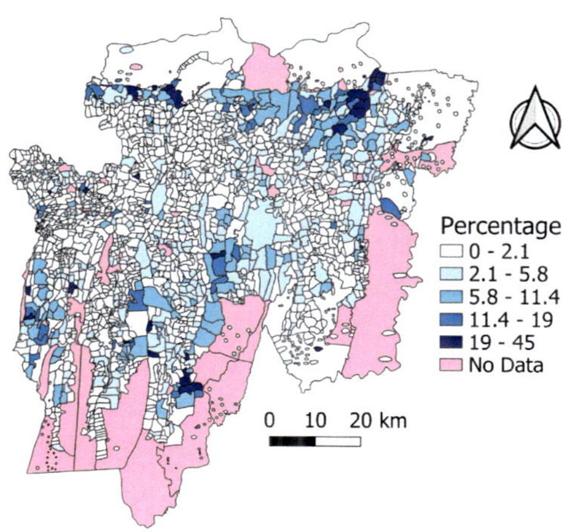

Map 333

Work participation rate (Marginal - Male)

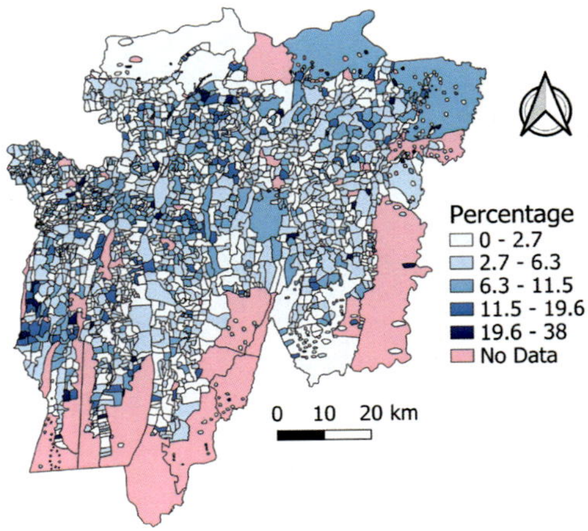

Map 334

Work participation rate (Marginal-Female)

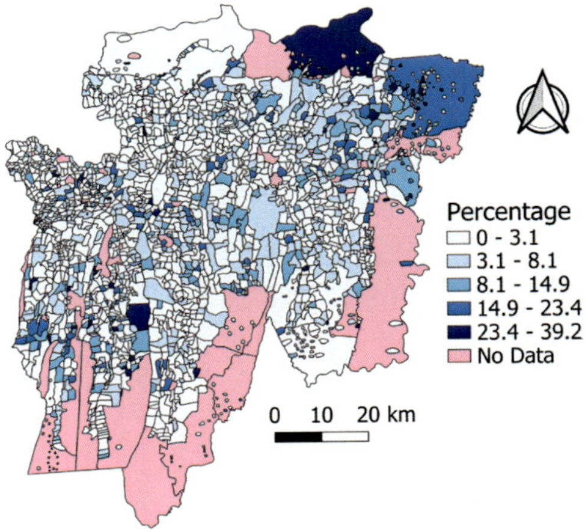

Map 335

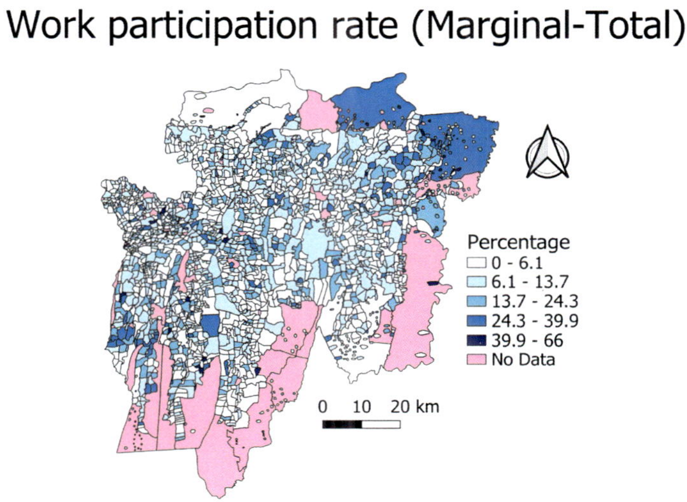

Map 336

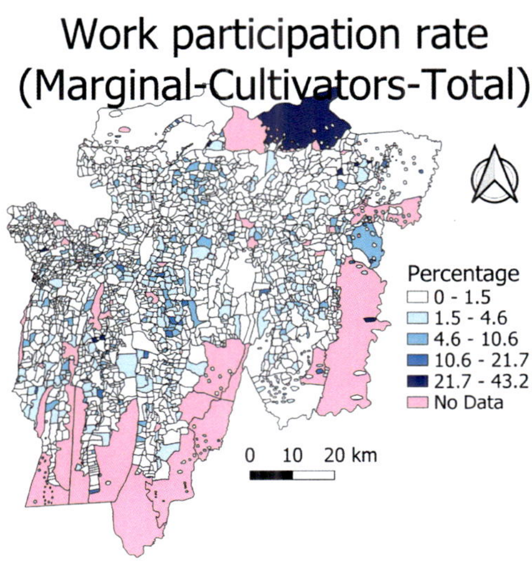

Map 337

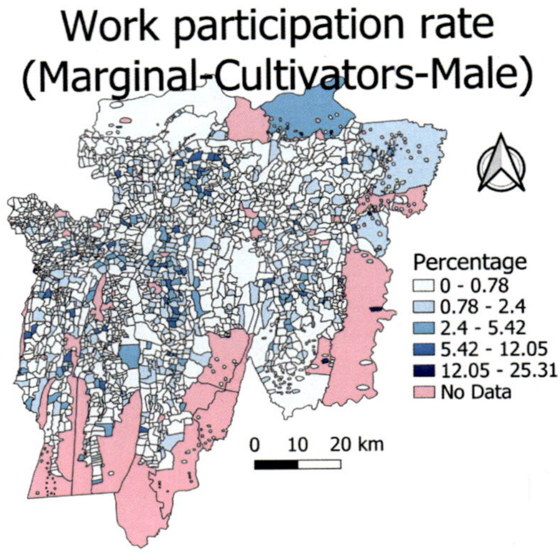

Map 338

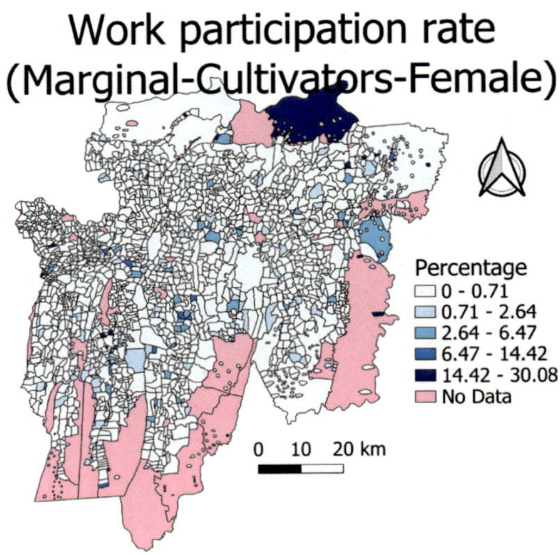

Map 339

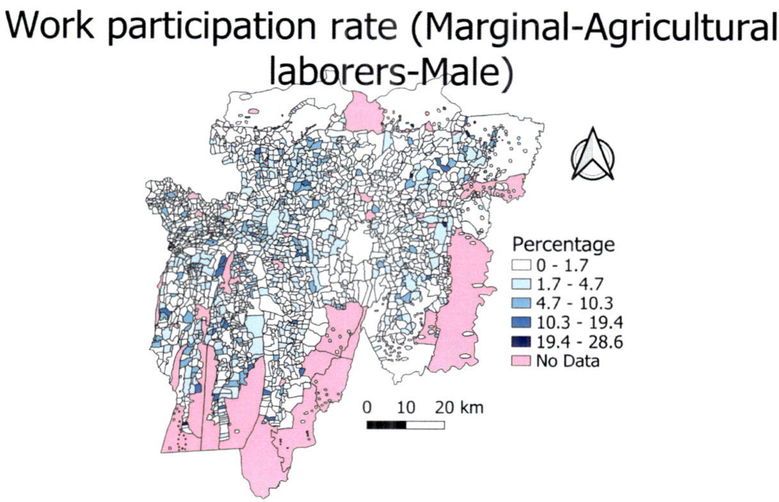

Map 340

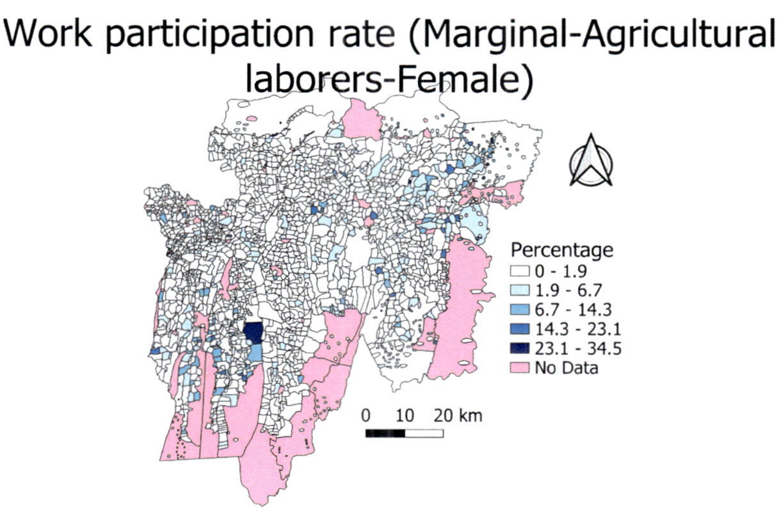

Map 341

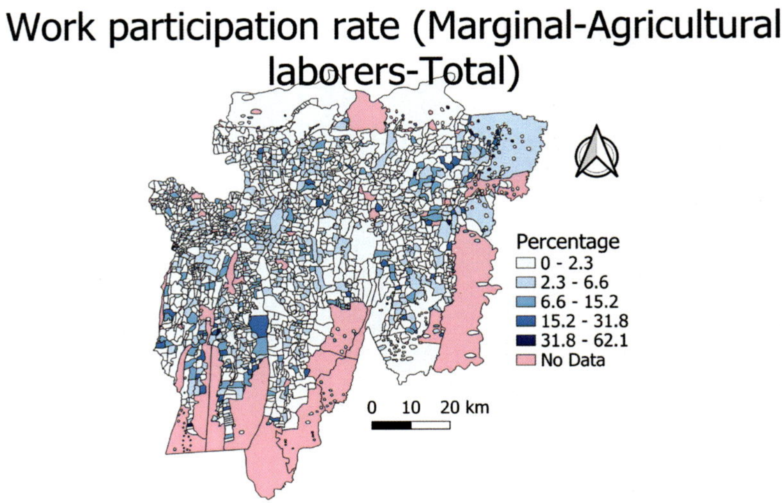

Map 342

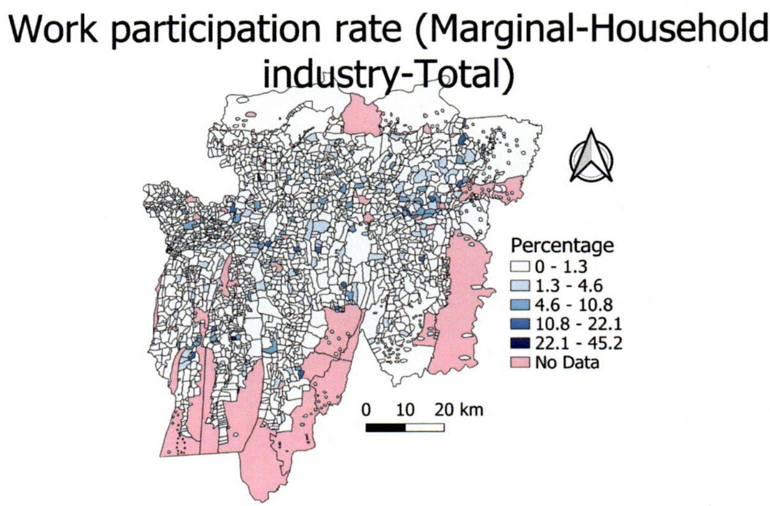

Map 343

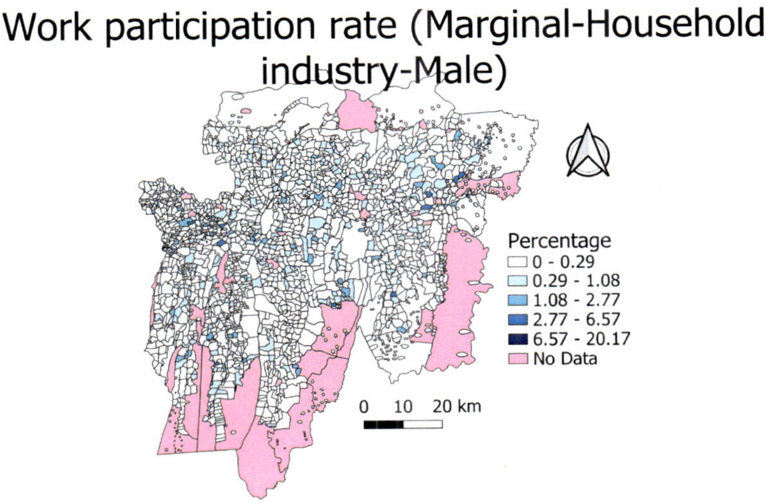

Map 344

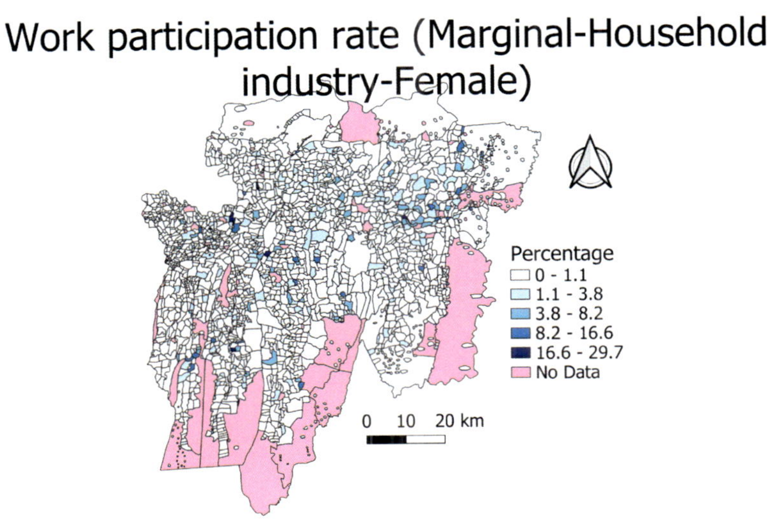

Map 345

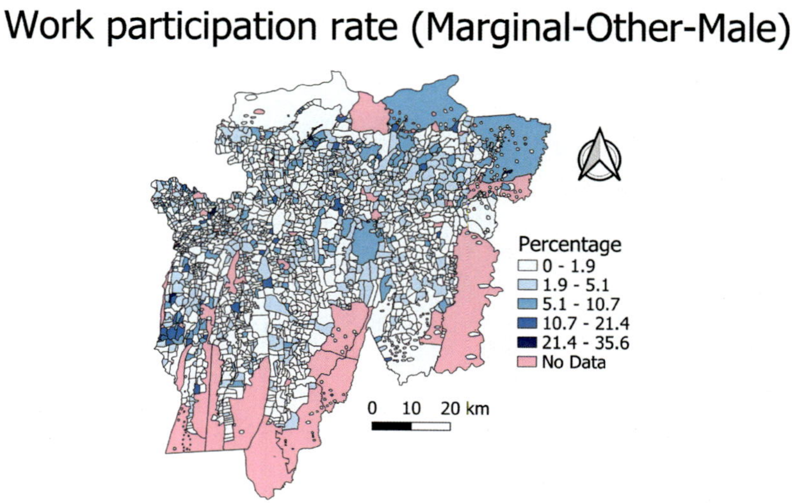

Map 346

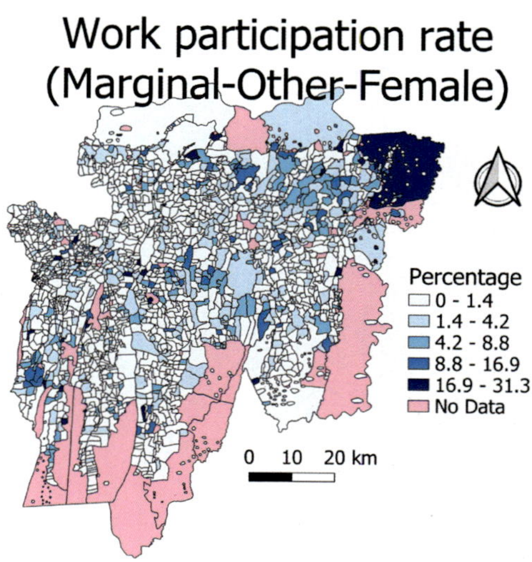

Map 347

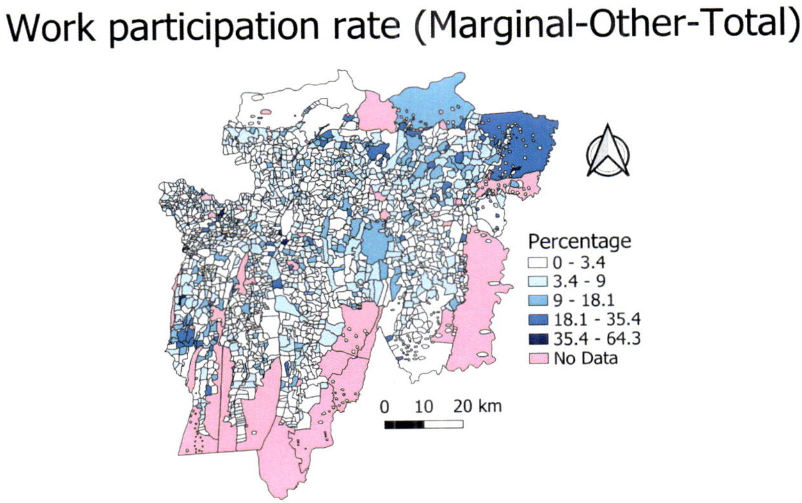

Map 348

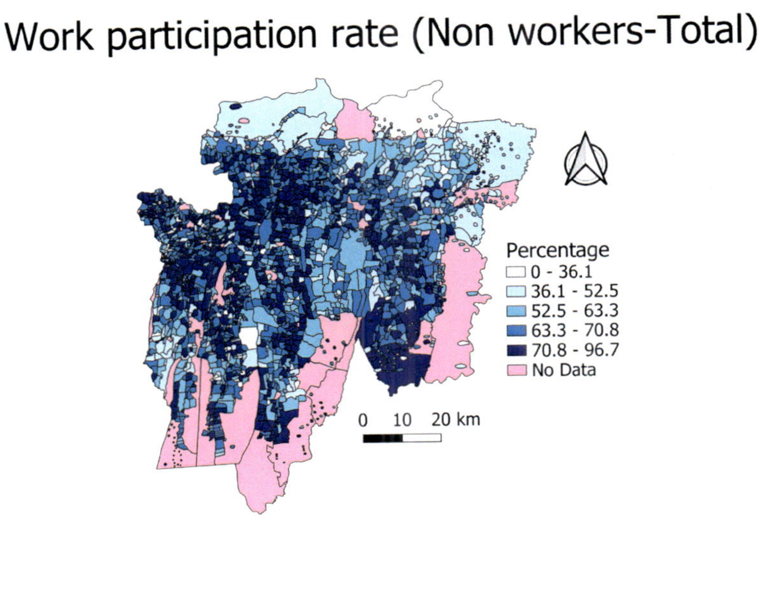

Map 349

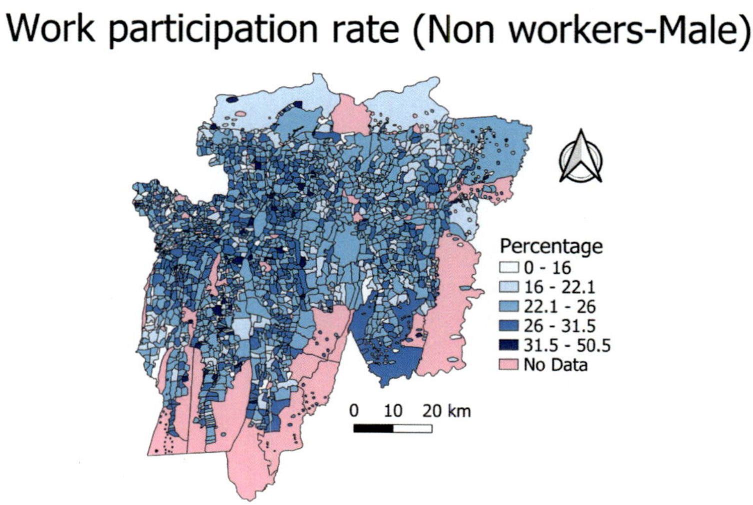

Map 350

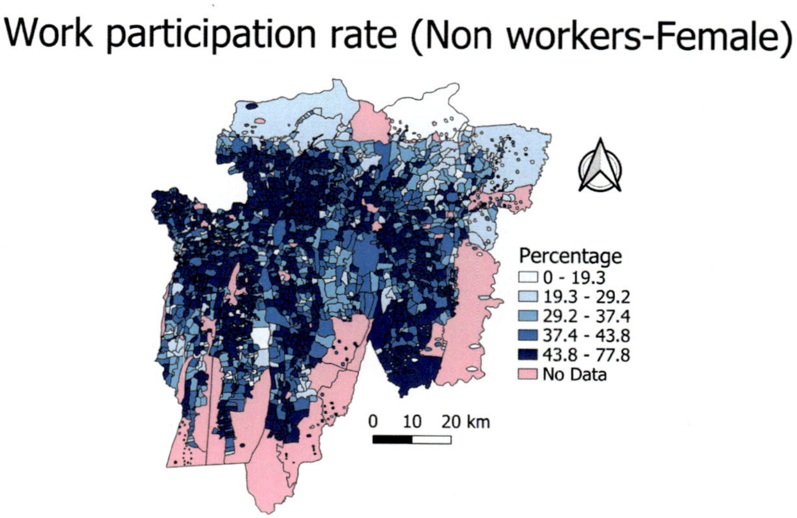

Map 351

Work participation rate (Marginal-3-6-Male)

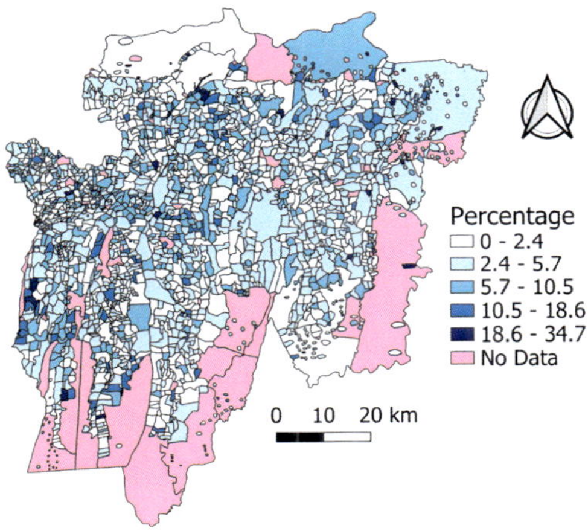

Map 352

Work participation rate (Marginal-3-6-Female)

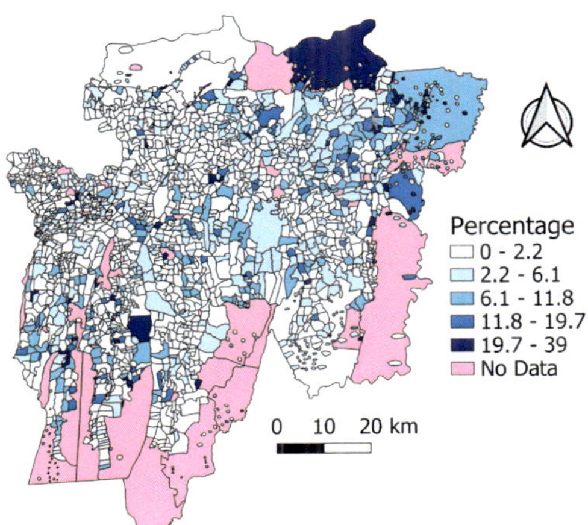

Map 353

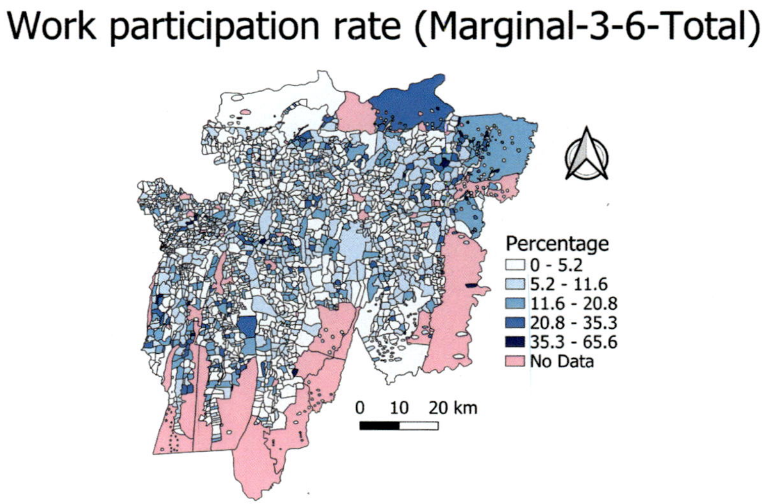

Map 354

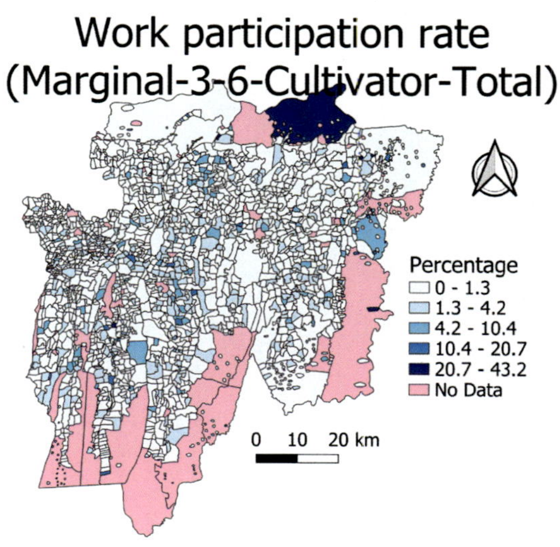

Map 355

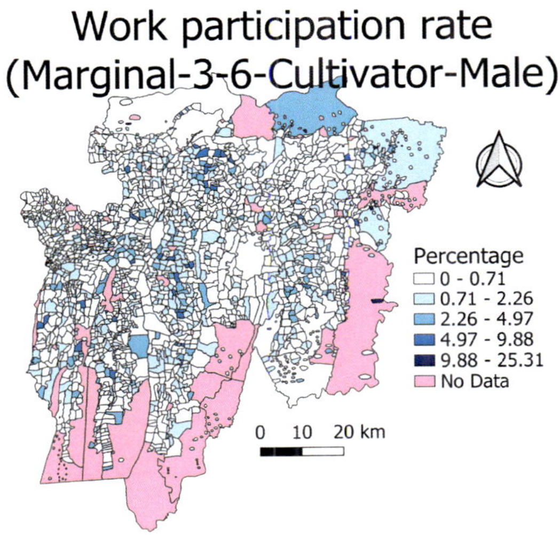

Map 356

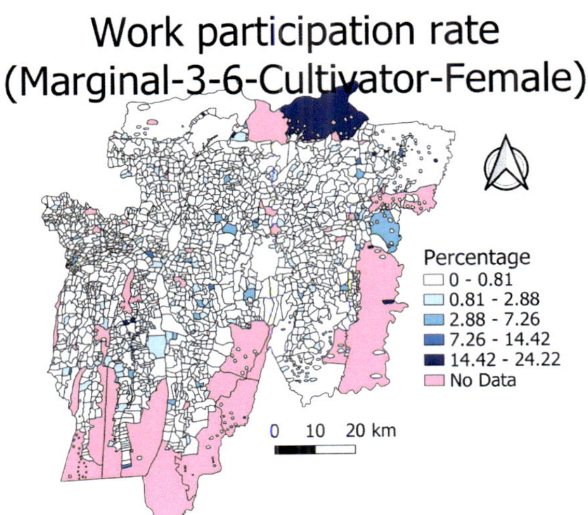

Map 357

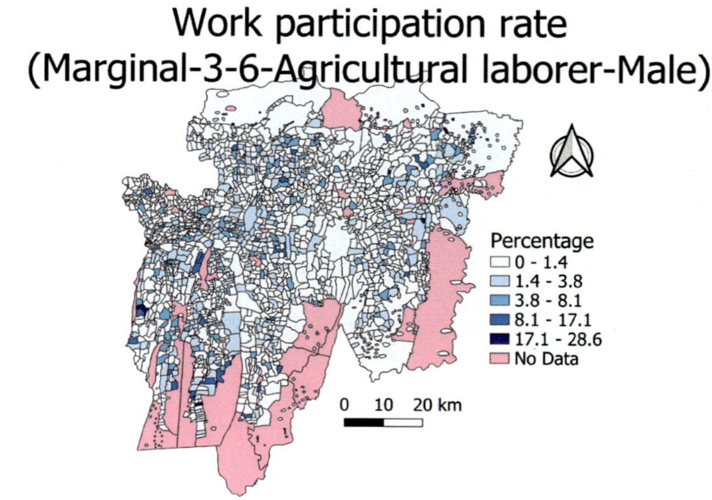

Map 358

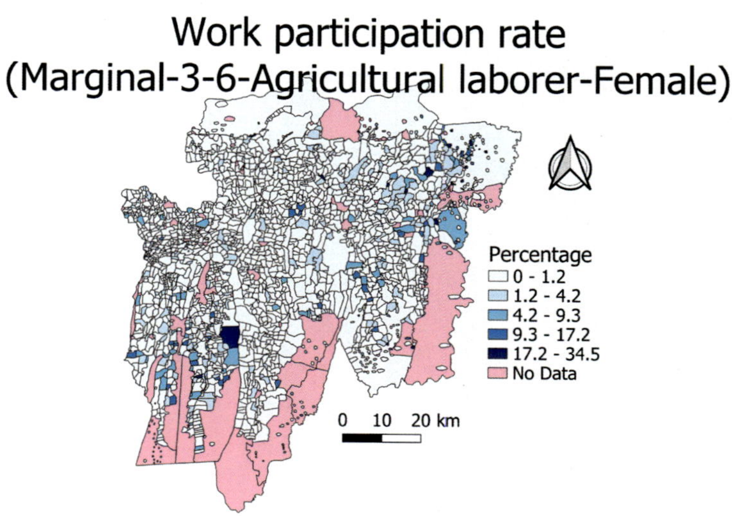

Map 359

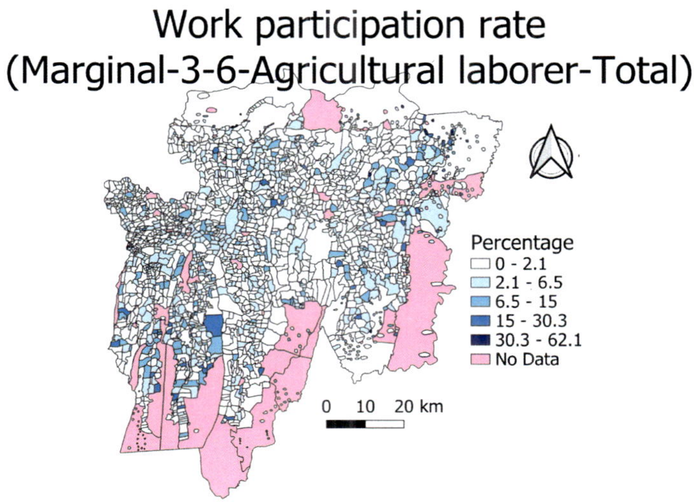

Map 360

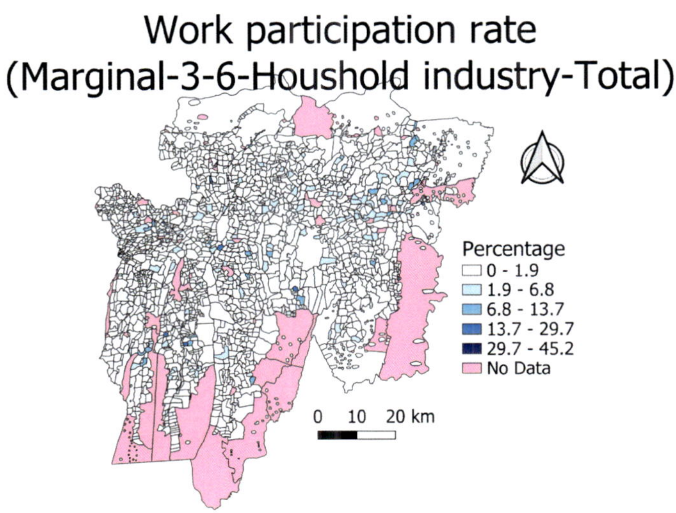

Map 361

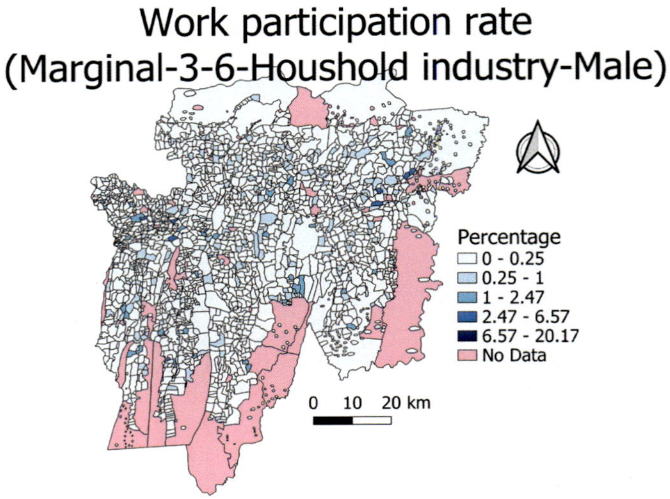

Map 362

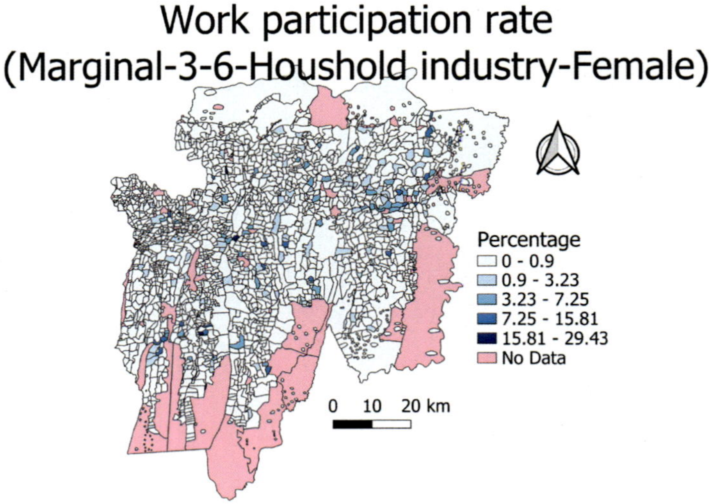

Map 363

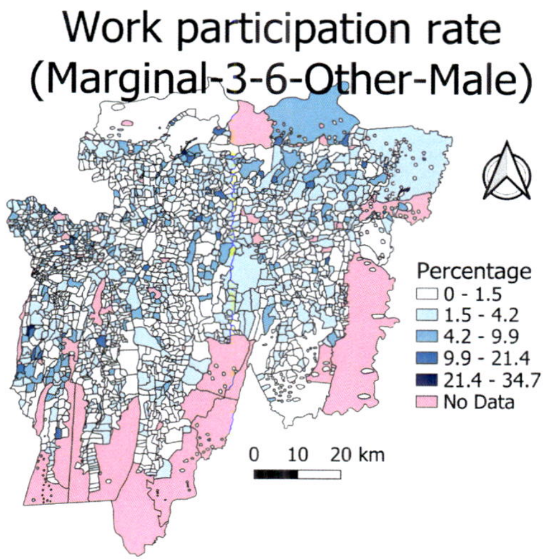

Map 364

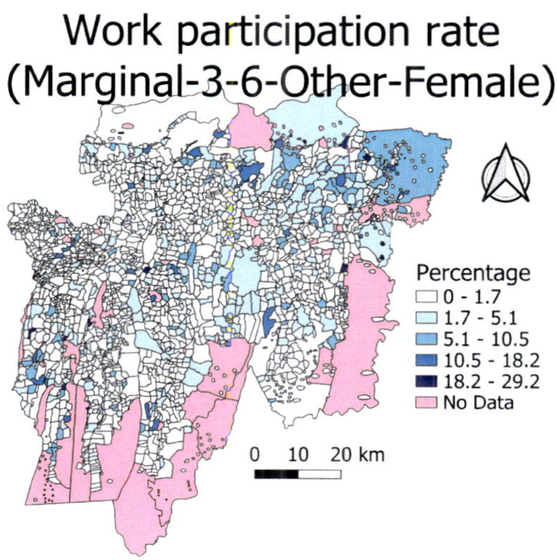

Map 365

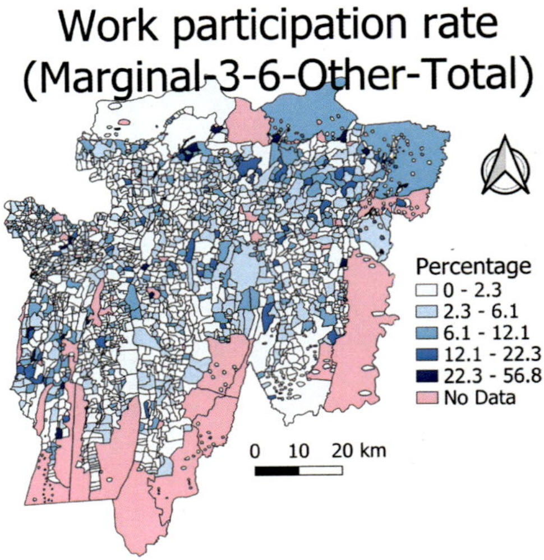

Map 366

Work participation rate (Marginal-0-3-Total)

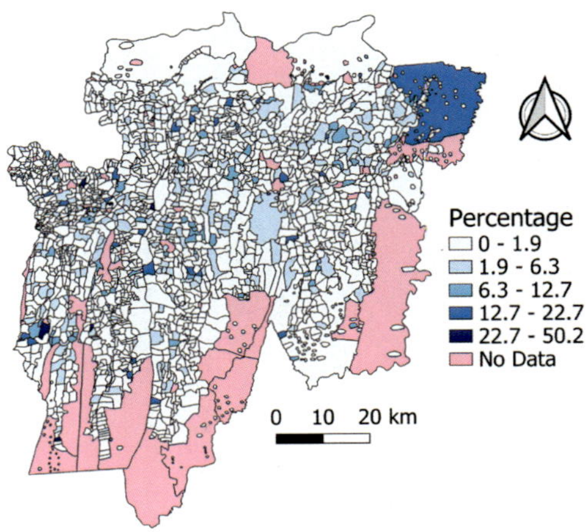

Map 367

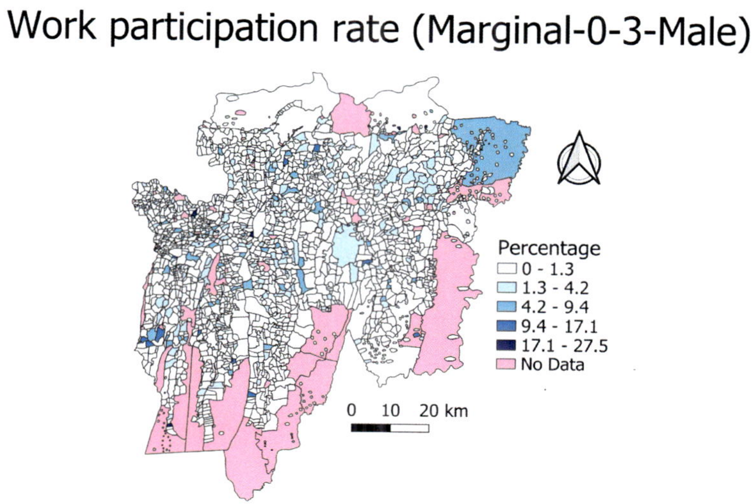

Map 368

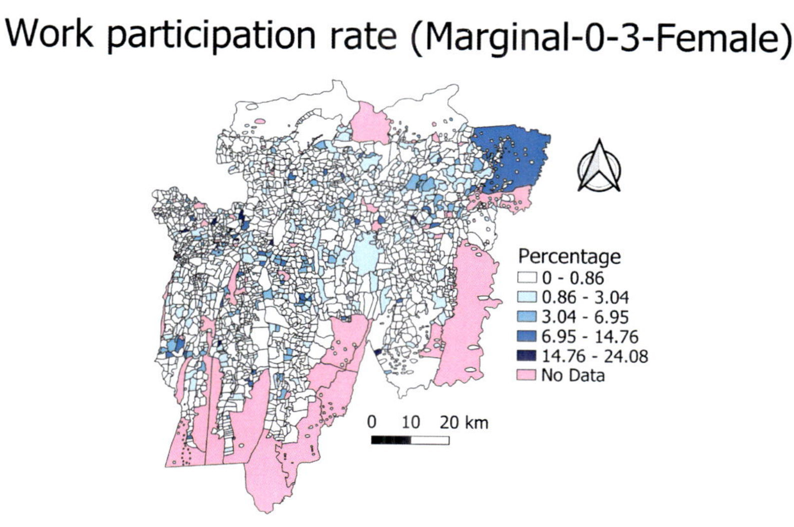

Map 369

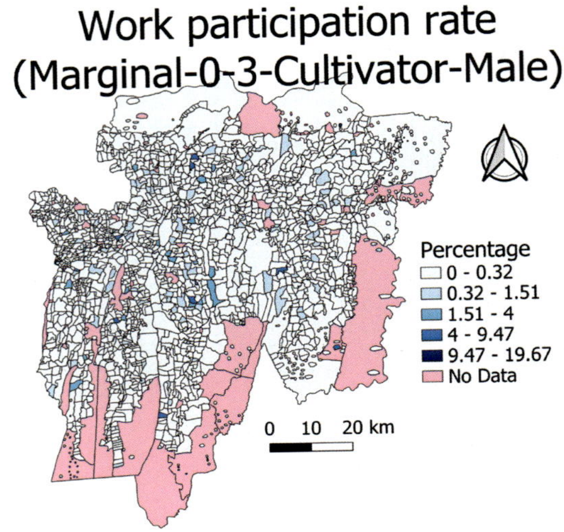

Map 370

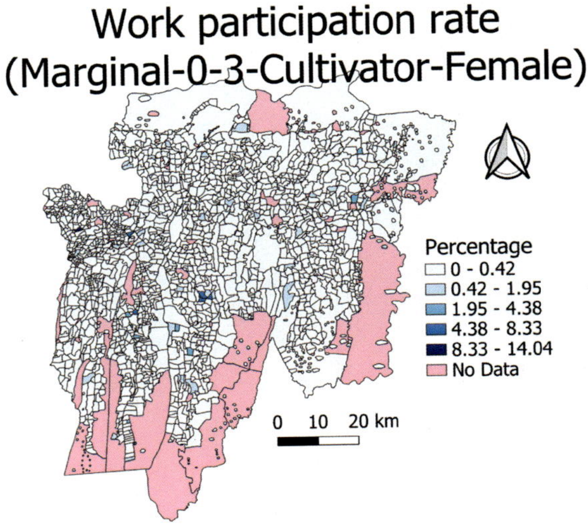

Map 371

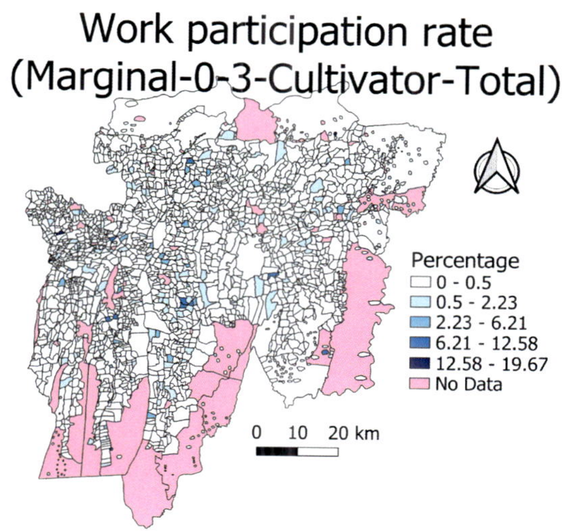

Map 372

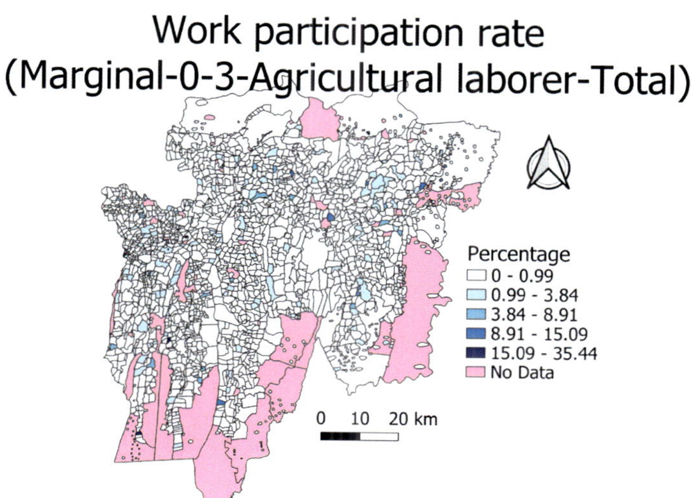

Map 373

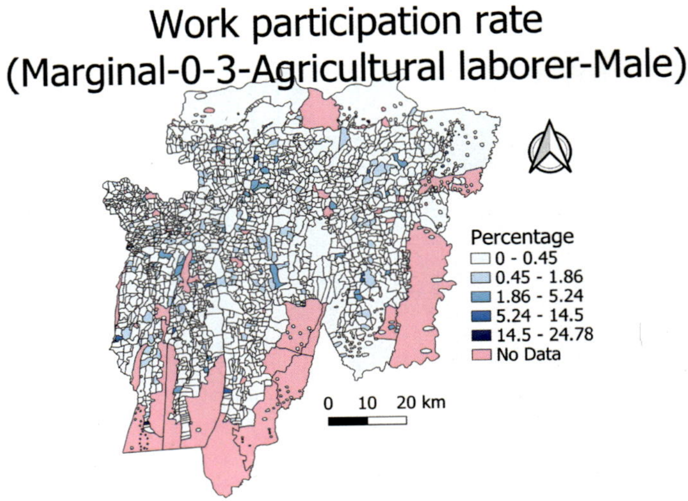

Map 374

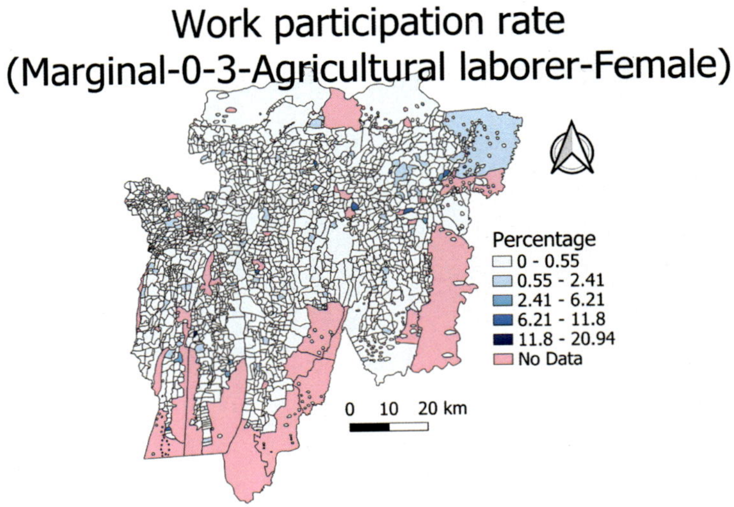

Map 375

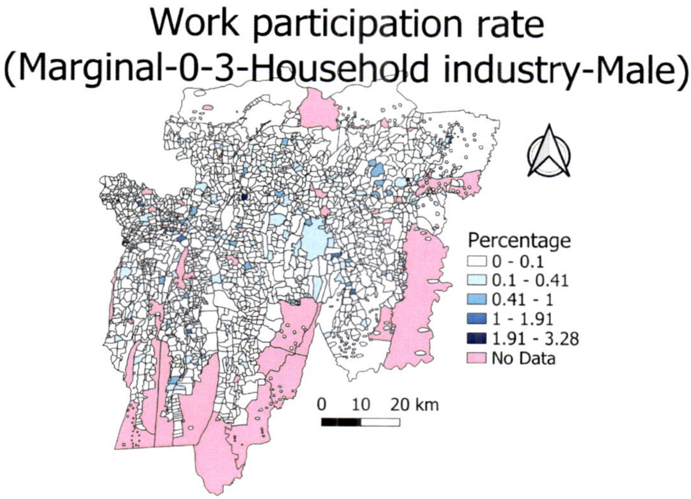

Map 376

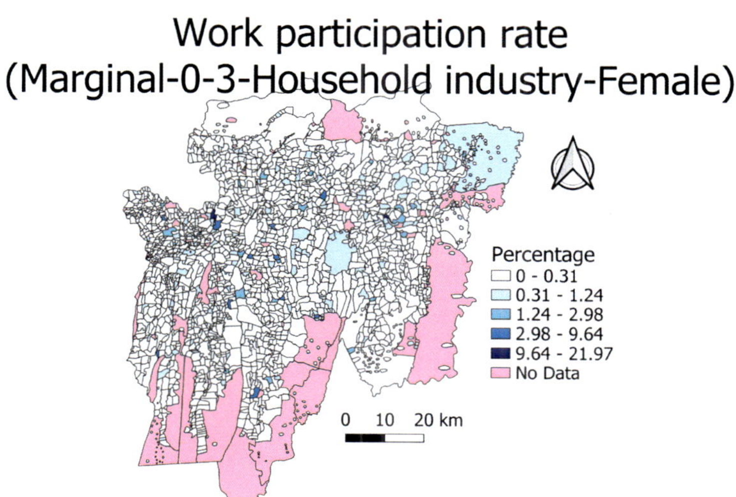

Map 377

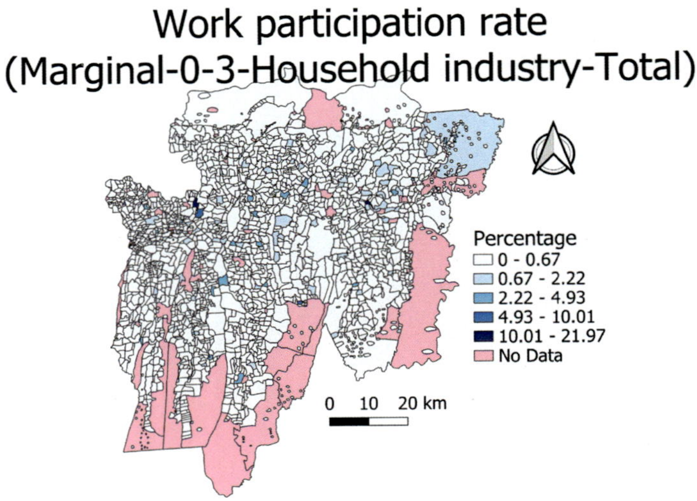

Map 378

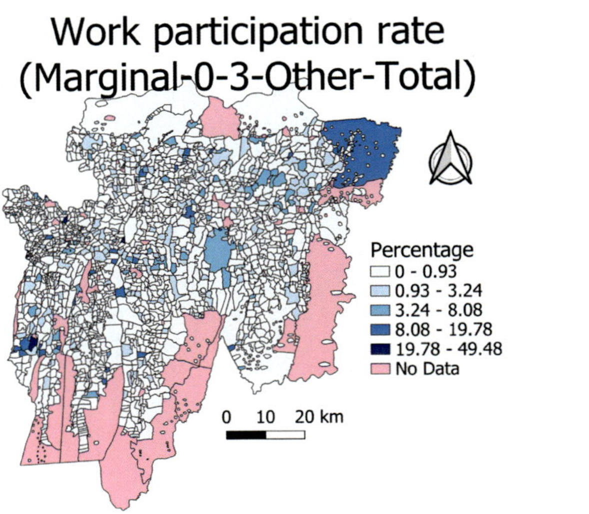

Map 379

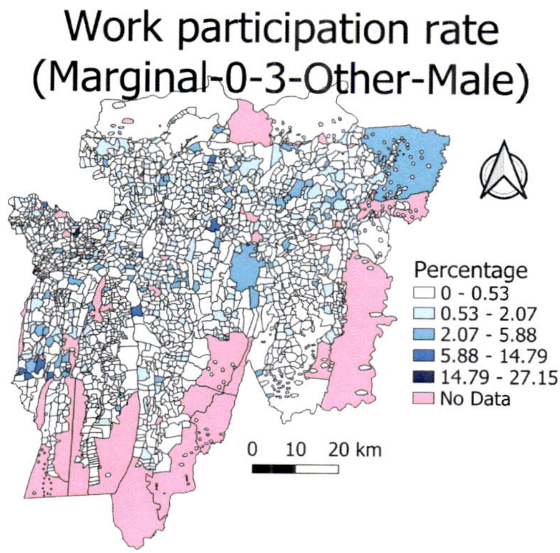

Map 380

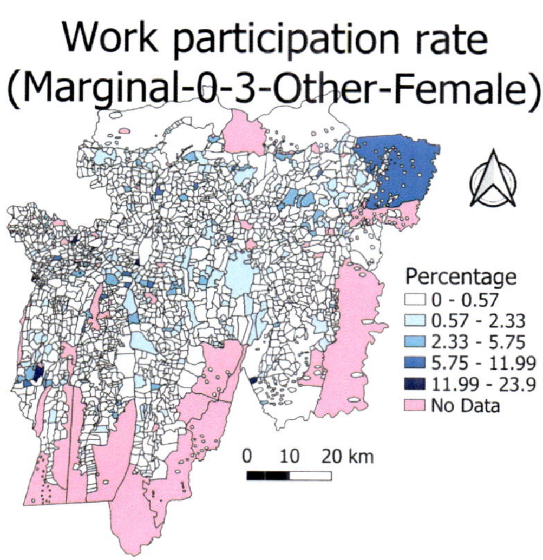

References

Banerjee, S. (2016) Spatial Data Analysis, Annual Review of Public Health 37: 47–60. doi:10.1146/annurev-publhealth-032315-021711

Blum, O., Calvo, R. (2001) Geospatial Data Collection and Analysis as Crucial Process in an Integrated Census, FCSM Paper

Census of India (2011) History of census in India, Drop-in-Article on Census – No.-5. (https://censusindia.gov.in/nada/index.php/catalog/40444/download/44078/DROP_IN_ARTICLE-05.pdf)

Chand, R., Singh, J. (2022) Workforce Changes and Employment, Some Findings from PLFS Data Series, NITI Aayog Discussion Paper 1/2022, NITI Aayog, Government of India, New Delhi

Cromley, R. G., Ebenstein, A. Y., Hanink, D. M. (2009) Estimating components of population change from census data for incongruent spatial/ temporal units and attributes, Journal of Spatial Science, 54:2, 89-99, DOI: 10.1080/14498596.2009.9635180

da Silva, C.F.A., Silva, M.C., dos Santos, A. M., Rudke, A. P., do Bonfim, C. V., Portis, G. T., de Almeida Junior, P. M., de Santana Coutinho, M. B. (2020) Spatial analysis of socio-economic factors and their relationship with the cases of COVID-19 in Pernambuco, Brazil, Trop. Med. Int. Health. 27:397–407

District Census Handbook (DCHB) Cachar (2011) Census of India 2011 Assam, Village and Town wise Primary Census Abstract (PCA), Series 19, Part XII-B, Directorate of Census Operations, Assam, Ministry of Home Affairs, P-492

District Census Handbook (DCHB) Hailakandi (2011) Census of India 2011 Assam, Village and Town wise Primary Census Abstract (PCA), Series 19, Part XII-A, Directorate of Census Operations, Assam, Ministry of Home Affairs, P-240

District Census Handbook (DCHB) Karimganj (2011) Census of India 2011 Assam, Village and Town wise Primary Census Abstract (PCA), Series 19, Part XII-A, Directorate of Census Operations, Assam, Ministry of Home Affairs, P-216

Economic and Social Research Council (ESRC.) (2017) Mapping Census data in QGIS, UK Data Service, University of Essex, University of Manchester

Eichelberger, B., la Rúa, L. D., Bright, P., Le Gall-Queguineur, G. (2022) QGIS for census and survey mapping, 2022 update for QGIS 3.22 Long Term Release: Training manual, Pacific Community, SPC, ISBN: 978-982-00-1469-5, BP D5, 98848, Noumea Cedex, New Caledonia

Federal Communications Commission (FCC). (2021) Finding Census Blocks with QGIS, FCC Form 477

Fisher, O. P. (2022) Geospatial Technology and the Census, International Programs Center, US Census Bureau, US AID

Hanson, B. (2016a) QGIS: Downloading and Preparing U.S. Census Bureau Data, Geospatial Technology Training Program, IOWA State University, Extension and Outreach, PM2082-16q

Hanson, B. (2016b) QGIS: Joining and Mapping U.S. Census Bureau Data, Geospatial Technology Training Program, IOWA State University, Extension and Outreach, PM2082-16r

Jain, A., Kaur, V. (2021) Census Mapping in India and Role of GIS: A Look Ahead at Census 2021. Indian Journal of Public Administration, 67(4), 540-558. https://doi.org/10.1177/00195561211056406

Kasturi, K. (2015) Comparing Census and NSS Data on Employment and Unemployment, Economic and Political Weekly, Vol. 50, No. 22 (MAY 30, 2015), pp. 16-19, Stable URL: https://www.jstor.org/stable/24482484, Accessed: 19-05-2024 06:12 +00:00

la Rúa, L. D., Bright, P. (2020) QGIS for digital cartography in censuses and surveys, edited by Sabrina Juran, United Nations Population Fund (UNFPA) and Pacific Community (SPC), ISBN: 978-982-00-1291-2

Mallapaty, S. (2024) Three-year delay for Indian census frustrates scientists, Nature 631

Meiyappan, P., Roy, P. S., Sharma, Y., Ramachandran, R. M., Joshi, P. K., DeFries, R. S., Jain, A. K. (2017) Dynamics and Determinants of Land Change in India: Integrating Satellite data with Village Socio-economics. Regional Environmental Change 17 (3): 753. https://doi.org/10.1007/s10113-016-1068-2

Meiyappan, P., Roy, P.S., Soliman, A., Li., T., Mondal, P., Wang, S., Jain, A.K. (2018) Documentation for the India Village-Level Geospatial Socio-Economic Data Set: 1991, 2001. Palisades NY: NASA Socio-economic Data and Applications Center (SEDAC). https://doi.org/10.7927/H43776SR. Accessed 16th April 2024

Ministry of Home Affairs (MHA). (2011) Census 2011 – Provisional population totals, Office of the Registrar General and Census Commissioner, India, 31st March 2011

Ministry of Labour and employment (MOL&E). (2022) Labour and employment statistics 2022, Directorate General of Employment, Government of India, New Delhi

Ministry of Labour and employment (MOL&E) (2023) Female labour utilization in India, Employment Statistics in Focus – April 2023, Directorate General of Employment, Government of India, New Delhi

Ministry of Statistics and Programme Implementation (MoSPI). (2012) Manual on labour statistics (I) – 2012, CSO-MLS-(I)-2012, Central Statistics Office, Government of India

Ministry of Statistics and Programme Implementation (MoSPI). (2018) Women and Men in India (A statistical compilation of Gender related Indicators in India), 20th Issue, Social Statistics Division, Central Statistics Office

Ministry of Statistics and Programme Implementation (MoSPI). (2024) Women and Men in India 2023, (A Statistical Compilation of Gender related Indicators of India), Government of India, National Statistical Office, Social Statistics Division

Moose, N., Juergens, C., Redecker, A. P. (2021) Geo-Spatial Analysis of Population Density and Annual Income to Identify Large-Scale Socio-Demographic Disparities, Int. J. Geo-Inf., 10: 432

Moreno, S., Durán, C., Galindo, D., Torres, C., Jácome, J., Montero, A. (2020) Statistical and Spatial Analysis of Census Data for the Study of Family and Industrial Farming in Colombia, Applied Spatial Analysis and Policy (2020) 13:693–713

Motkuri, V., Mishra, R.N., Hansda, L. (2019) Rural Workforce in India: Analysis of Growth and Changing Structure based on Census Data, Gujarat Institute of Development Research, Working Paper No. 254

Motkuri, V., Naik, S. V. (2016) Growth and Structure of Workforce in India: An Analysis of Census Data, The Indian Economic Journal 64(1&2): 57–74, DOI: 10.1177/0019466216652753

NITI Aayog (2023) India, National multidimensional poverty index, A progress review 2023, NITI Aayog, Government of India

Noth, T. (2022) Mapping Census Data in QGIS, Instructional Documentation, Research commons, SFU Library, Simon Fraser University, Canada

Palma, O. (2011) GIS and spatial analysis in the dissemination of census data, Instituto Nacional De Estadistica Y Geografia (INEGI), INEGI-México

QGIS Project (2023) QGIS Desktop 3.22 User Guide, QGIS

Rao, M.V.S. (1976) Socio-economic indicators for development planning. In N. Baster (Ed.) The use of socio-economic indicators in development planning, The UNESCO Press, ISBN 92-3-101329-7, Belgium

Ravichandran, V., Kantamaneni, K., Singh, A., Nair, A., Janakiraman, A., Kumar, S. P., Choudhury, S.D. (2023) Mapping hotspot clustering: An approach to study the spatial pattern of quality of living households in India, Remote Sensing Applications: Society and Environment 31, 101007

Redding, S. J. (2024) Spatial economics, Working Paper 33125, NBER WORKING PAPER SERIES, http://www.nber.org/papers/w33125, NATIONAL BUREAU OF ECONOMIC RESEARCH, 1050 Massachusetts Avenue Cambridge, MA 02138, November 2024

Srija, A. (2023) Potential of India's Future workforce, Productivity 63 (4): 375-388 DOI. https://doi.org/10.32381/PROD.2023.63.04.1

Srinivasan, K. (2011) Training manual on demographic techniques, Office of the Registrar General & Census Commissioner, India, Ministry of Home Affairs, Government of India

Thomas, J. J., Jayesh, M. P. (2016) Changes in India's Rural Labour Market in the 2000s: Evidence from the Census of India and the National Sample Survey, Review of Agrarian Studies 6 (1)

The Economic Times (2024) Economic survey 2024: India has 18.3% unpaid workers, 57.3% of total workforce self-employed, Budget 2024, English edition (https://economictimes.indiatimes.com/budget-2024/economic-survey-2024/economic-survey-2024-57-3-per-cent-of-the-total-workforce-self-employed-18-3-per-cent-working-as-unpaid-workers/articleshow/111920479.cms?from=mdr)

Weeks, J.R. (2001) The Role of Spatial Analysis in Demographic Research, In: Michael F. Goodchild and Donald G. Janelle (eds.), Spatially Integrated Social Science: Examples in Best Practice (New York: Oxford University Press)

Wong, D.W.S. (1990) Spatial Analysis and the Use of Census Data. In: D. Hanink (ed.), Proceedings of the Joint NESTVAL-Middle State AAG Division Meeting, pp.51-56.

Website - https://assam.gov.in/about-us/396, accessed on 16 July 2024

Website - https://cachar.gov.in/portlets/district-profile, accessed on 16 July 2024

Website - https://hailakandi.assam.gov.in/about-district/district-glance, accessed on 16 July 2024

Website - https://karimganj.assam.gov.in/about-district/district-glance, accessed on 16 July 2024

Website - https://knowindia.india.gov.in/states-uts/, accessed on 16 July 2024

Website - https://www.qgis.org/

Website - https://censusindia.gov.in

Website - https://censusindia.gov.in/census.website/CENSUS_ques

Website - https://sedac.ciesin.columbia.edu/